Carl Menger
and the Origins
of Austrian Economics

T0382745

Studies in the History, Methods, and Boundaries of Economics

Series Editors
Axel Leijonhufvud and Donald N. McCloskey

Carl Menger and the Origins of Austrian Economics

Max Alter

Routledge
Taylor & Francis Group

LONDON AND NEW YORK

First published 1990 by Westview Press, Inc.

Published 2018 by Routledge
52 Vanderbilt Avenue, New York, NY 10017
2 Park Square, Milton Park, Abingdon, Oxon OX14 4RN

Routledge is an imprint of the Taylor & Francis Group, an informa business

Copyright © 1990 Taylor & Francis

Library of Congress Cataloging-in-Publication Data
Alter, Max, 1949–
    Carl Menger and the origins of Austrian economics / Max Alter.
        p. cm. — (Studies in the history, methods, and boundaries of economics)
    Includes bibliographical references.
    ISBN 0-8133-0945-X
    1. Menger, Carl, 1840–1921. 2. Austrian school of economists.
3. Neoclassical school of economics. I. Title. II. Series.
HB107.M54A78   1990
330.15'7'092—dc20   89-37661
                                                                                   CIP

ISBN 13: 978-0-367-00366-1 (hbk)
ISBN 13: 978-0-367-15353-3 (pbk)

Contents

Preface

Since the completion of this study, which is a revised and enlarged version of my doctoral dissertation, new life has been breathed into Menger scholarship as Carl Menger's notebooks, personal papers and unpublished manuscripts have been acquired by Duke University. Over a century after the publication of the *Grundsätze der Volkswirthschaftslehre* and the *Untersuchungen über die Methode der Socialwissenschaften, und der Politischen Oekonomie insbesondere*, we may finally have a chance to discover what went into the making of these two books, which have been so influential in the development of economic theory and methodology.

In celebration of the arrival of this material, a conference on Carl Menger and his legacy was held at Duke University in April 1989. Neither the papers presented at the Menger conference nor the material in the Menger Archives at Duke University could be incorporated here (the Menger Archives were not yet publicly accessible when this study was completed). But the discussion at the Menger conference did not persuade me that I had to modify my arguments; indeed, the papers presented there complement and expand on a number of issues dealt with in this study.

The completion of this book has benefited from comments by a number of people whom I want to thank. Professor T. W. Hutchison pointed out some contradictions in an early draft of Essay I, and Dr. J. M. Albala-Bertand discussed with me several sections of Essay III. Bruce Caldwell read the penultimate version of this book; the final improvements owe a great deal to his incisive criticism as well as to Megan Schoeck's admirable copyediting. They are, of course, not responsible for the remaining shortcomings of this book.

There are a few personal debts that I am also very glad to acknowledge: Antonio and Georgina Yunez-Naude were in the right place at the right time on a number of occasions; Lionello Punzo persuaded me to fly with him to Rome instead of meeting him in Pisa; it is no exaggeration to say that this study may never have been finished if it had not been for their interventions. Equally indispensable was Professor Meghnad Desai's encouragement and support, which made me finally sit down and finish this study. This task would have been infinitely more difficult had it not been for the patient support of Stefania Ceccarelli.

Some preliminary results of my work on Menger have been presented on a number of occasions (see Bibliography). Whenever earlier statements contradict the material presented here, the former versions should be discarded as obsolete.

Max Alter

Introduction

Why and how should one study the history of economics? There are many answers to this question, and the one premise they all have in common is the famous dictum, it depends. It depends, above all, on who answers this question. Those who regard the development of economics as continuous progress and refinement of theory will be more inclined to look at it in retrospect or as history of economic analysis. Those who regard it, or at least most of it, as ideology, bourgeois or otherwise, may see very little progress and a great deal of apologetics. Those who are attracted by the concept of paradigm and the methodology of scientific research programmes may take the view that the progress of economics is conditioned by schools of thought fighting each other and that it thus resembles more the drunkard's walk than a straight line.

But it also depends on what one studies in the history of economics. The historian of econometrics will, by the nature of the object of enquiry, have to put a great deal more emphasis on the development of technique than, say, the historian of value theory, who will be more concerned to understand the meaning of the concept of value in different ages. A student of the history of a school of economic thought would, perhaps, want to devote more space to personal relations and to the dynamics or politics of an academic movement than the student of the economics of a great person or innovator. These examples could be multiplied at will, and a perfectly acceptable justification could be found for every single starting point for a journey through the history of mankind's attempt to understand and explain how and why the economy works the way it does.

The view I have taken in this study is that economic theory is a product of the human mind and that this mind does not create *ex nihilo*. It is affected by forces: Cultural, political, socioeconomic and personal factors influence the statement that value is socially necessary labour time as much as the definition of value as the meaning and importance of the satisfaction of a need or want to the valuing individual. What separates and unites these two definitions of value turned out to be one of the themes that surface at various points in this study.

The interaction of the forces shaping the human mind at a specific time and place are the elements through which we can understand a vision of the economic process. Comprehension of the vision allows us to understand the reason why; comprehension of the analytics of a theory allows us to

1

understand the reason how. The difference between the reason why and the reason how is, at bottom, the difference between the *Geisteswissenschaften* and the *Naturwissenschaften*, the humanities and the natural sciences, a distinction that was first drawn very clearly and distinctly by the Italian philosopher Giambattista Vico almost three hundred years ago and that still gives rise to heated debate.

Economics as a social science did not rise above this epistemological and methodological conflict which is the central theme of this study. Students who want to know not only how but also why occasionally face serious difficulties; they may not be able to find anyone to explain to them the reasons why, while everyone seems very keen to explain the reason how, almost as if there was something to hide. There are even universities in which the history of economics is not taught at all—which is certainly one answer to the question of why and how it should be studied.

If, reared on the staple diet which for many generations of students consisted of Hicks's *Value and Capital*, Henderson-Quandt's *Microeconomic Theory* and Arrow and Hahn's *General Competitive Analysis*, one still wanted to know why, there was no alternative but to go back to the words of the fathers. The words of William Jevons and Léon Walras generally do not prove too mysterious, but when one is suddenly confronted with Carl Menger's *Grundsätze der Volkswirthschaftslehre*, preferably in the original, blankness descends on the mind, and there then seem to be only two possible escape routes. One is the flight back to the comforting surroundings of one's *alma mater*; this way invariably leads to what has come to be known as the Walrasian history of economic theory. The other way is more arduous and must eventually lead to the search for meaning: the meaning of concepts belonging to a world of thought that is totally alien to our way of thinking. In the first instance, then, the history of the Austrian school of economics is an exercise in hermeneutics, in *Verstehen*. Only after basic terms and concepts have been understood for what they meant to those who used them can we begin to fit them together until we have re-composed the visions of the first Austrian economists. If, on the other hand, we do not carry this exercise to the end but think we may safely believe the words of an interpreter, and hence stop at a half-way house, we risk understanding neither the original nor the interpreter.

To be slightly more concrete: It is not very easy to find and read Carl Menger's works in the original. If we, therefore, turn to the translations or to the texts, perhaps also translated, of Friedrich von Wieser and Eugen von Böhm-Bawerk, we shall never understand what Menger wrote. But neither shall we be able to understand what Wieser and Böhm-Bawerk have made of him nor what, in the end, some neo-Austrian versions (perversions?) have to do with the original unread and, hence, misunderstood theory.

All of these versions of Menger's theory—Walrasian, Austrian, neo-Austrian and others—create, at best, confusion. In this study I have attempted to bring some order into this confusion. This, it seemed to me, is best done by first explaining the terminology, then the manner in which it was put to use, and discussing the product of its use only at the end. Consequently, I shall first explain the *geisteswissenschaftliche* background, which will allow us to understand the terms and concepts. How these terms and concepts have been put to use, the methodology and epistemology, is discussed next. Only after the ground has been prepared in this way can we proceed to analyse the outcome of their use, the theory itself. This is, in fact, the exact reverse of Menger's order of presentation: Menger first produced a theory, and only after he found himself misunderstood by those to whom the theory was addressed did he decide to clarify the way he had used his terms and concepts. The result was the *Methodenstreit*. Unfortunately, he did not take the last step (my first step) because he thought that everyone knew what he meant; he was, after all, using the same language as his adversaries. Fifty years later, its meaning had been lost.

Each of these steps—background, methodology, theory—is a complex issue not only in itself but also in relation to the others. I have, therefore, chosen to present them in the form of three essays to retain the coherence of each step within itself and to use cross-references to show where the arguments of one essay bear on those of another.

The first essay deals with central elements of the cultural, political and social background of Austrian economic theory in general and Menger's version of it in particular. Personal influences on the Austrians' thought have been left out because this study is an attempt to understand the foundations of Austrian theory; it is not an intellectual biography of its leading exponents.

Menger's at first implicit but in the very end explicit project was to establish economics as a *Geisteswissenschaft* based on sound theoretical foundations. He was, thus, fully a part of the German world of thought of the nineteenth century. The important elements of this world of thought are discussed insofar as they are relevant for our understanding of Menger's, Wieser's and Böhm-Bawerk's theory and methodology. The center of the stage is occupied by Romanticist historicism. This stream of thought, however, can only come into its own if we see it in the context of its opposing movements. Hence, Essay I starts with a discussion of German Romanticism and German Idealist philosophy. This comparison allows us to perceive that the adoption of certain epistemological, methodological and theoretical positions is not at all necessitated by the subject matter itself but involves a large degree of freedom, that is, of choice. Thus, we see Marx and Menger emerging out of this world and making mutually exclusive choices, just as we see Hegel and Schelling sharing the same early intellectual formation but Hegel going the systematic, rational way and Schelling chosing irrationalism. There is, therefore, no inevitability in Menger's adoption of a particular vision of the economic process which is characterised by individualism and subjectivism, introspection and essentialism, just as the adoption of Aristotelianism in nineteenth-century Germany did not necessarily lead to a unified outlook (*viz.*, just to be provocative, Marx and Hegel in comparison to Menger).

The two movements, Romanticism and Idealist philosophy, engendered Historicism, and Menger and Wieser displayed great affinity with its Romantic-Historicist aspects, represented by Grimm and Savigny, rather than with its more Hegelian strands represented by Droysen and the older Dilthey. From here it is but a small step to the Historical school of economics, the dominant school in German economic thought in the second half of the nineteenth century, to which Menger dedicated his economic theory and which he subsequently fought for reasons that can be discerned from his writings only with difficulty. After all, if one develops a theory that others do not understand one does not necessarily have to pour invective over them. Why Menger chose to do so would be the subject of an intellectual biography and hence has no place here.

A discussion of the Historical school of economics concludes the first essay. An interesting by-product of this essay is that we come to be able to see how closely related the roots of the Austrian and Marxist economic theories are. Their differences become revealing only when viewed against this common background, and it is here where the explanation of the Austrians' preoccupation with socialism and Marxism may be found. It was, after all, the Austrians and not Jevons, Marshall and Walras who made it their vocation to fight socialism, be it in Menger's argument with Adam Smith, whom he accuses of a pragmatism which supposedly leads inevitably to socialism; in Böhm-Bawerk's discussion of Marx; or in the planning controversy of the 1930s led by Mises and Hayek.

This general picture of the background in Essay I is followed by the first more detailed analysis in Essay II: methodology. Here, the emphasis is eventually narrowed down from the first generation of Austrian economists to Menger only because there are a large number of issues in Menger's methodology which are still unresolved: the precise character of Menger's methodology and of its component elements; the continuity in his thought throughout his life's work; and, more specifically, his attitude towards Wilhelm Roscher, the head of the older Historical school of economics, to whom he dedicated the *Grundsätze der Volkswirthschaftslehre* in 1871. All of these issues have occasionally been hinted at in the literature on the Austrian school and on Menger, but they have hardly been dealt with in detail.[1]

One of the reasons for this state of affairs seems to be that reading original sources has become unfashionable. It is certainly more convenient to rely on secondary literature, but the result is the propagation of myths which have nothing in common with the subject they purport to be dealing with, as can be seen from the sad characterisations of Menger, Wieser and Böhm-Bawerk published in a number of pamphlets in the late 1970s.[2] One of these myths concerns the role of mathematics in economic theory and says that Austrian economics is non-mathematical as a matter of principle. That this is neither true nor all there is to the matter will be seen in Essay II and in the epilogue of this study where Menger's, Wieser's and Böhm-Bawerk's own words will be decisive, not what they are reported to have said. Another similar issue concerns the origin of Menger's economic theory.

Menger himself wrote in 1871, and Wieser repeated it in 1923, that he had been working within the German tradition of politicial economy. Nowhere in the literature do we find a systematic discussion of Menger's sources, which he quotes in his famous long footnotes in the *Grundsätze*. That the result of such an endeavour can be quite surprising will be seen in the first section of Essay III.

Menger's methodology, its components and their background, compatibility and incompatibility are discussed in detail in Essay II, which draws on Menger's theoretical writings as well as on his explicitly methodological works as source material. Essay II occupies, therefore, a central position in this study since it is through the philosophy of science, that is, methodology and epistemology, that the scientific conception of social reality (the background discussed in Essay I) influences the theory itself and, at times, even shapes the analytics of the argument (the subject of Essay III). There are, indeed, instances when only knowledge of the background allows a full understanding of the methodological concepts.

This is the case, for instance, with Menger's concept of *Bedürfnis*. Needs and wants feature in all the early neo-classical authors but it is, above all, in Menger's theory that they play the central role. Menger inherited this concept from German political economy (see Essay III), but it is only in German thought in general and Hegel's in particular (see Essay I) that we can grasp the extent of its importance. There, *Bedürfnis* and *Bedürfnisbefriedigung* represent the *loci classici* of economic activity and economic development in human life. In Menger's system, too, *Bedürfnis* is the starting point of economic activity and its satisfaction is the goal. The concept of *Bedürfnis*, therefore, is the bearer of Menger's teleological conception of causality in his theory. It also represents his conception of time. In brief, it is the vehicle that carries the characterisation of his vision of the economic process (see Essays II and III).

In the construction of his economic theory, the subject of the third essay, Menger utilised building blocks that he took from nineteenth-century German political economy and systematised their interaction on the basis of one unifying principle—valuation taking place at the margin of *Bedürfnisbefriedigung*. His essentialist, teleological and time-based theory of value organises a world full of ignorance and incomplete information (the world of Romanticism discussed in Essay I) and incorporates in its foundations concepts such as expectations which were to constitute major innovations in other neo-classical approaches. Menger's development of his theory in the *Grundsätze* is traced right to the point where the essentialism of his conception of value becomes self-destructing because it poses a transformation problem from values to prices which remains unsurmountable within his own methodological and theoretical framework. Menger's attempt, therefore, to bridge the dualism between the *Geisteswissenschaften* and the *Naturwissenschaften* by making value "true" and by giving the law of value the same status as the laws of science—indeed, linking it directly to biology—while retaining the Historicist tradition in his theory of prices foundered. This discussion concludes the investigation of the origin and structure of Menger's theory of value and prices.

There is yet another dimension of Menger's economic theory which has never been analysed in detail. Most economists seem to have been quite satisfied, if they displayed any curiosity at all about the origins of neo-classical theory, to accept the story of the founding trinity of Menger, Jevons and Walras and to dip briefly perhaps into Chapter 3 of the *Grundsätze*, which contains Menger's discussion of the marginality principle. But the first and the last chapters are equally important because the former tells us something about the ordering that underlies Menger's choice space while the latter leads us to the transformation problem and Menger's Historicism, which is expressed most clearly in his chapter on money. The question of whether the roots of modern neoclassical theory can be traced back in equal measure to all three members of the founding trinity or whether there exists any significant difference among them is pursued in the second half of Essay III through a comparison of the axiomatic basis of modern neo-classical orthodoxy and the corresponding assumptions in Menger's system. Quite surprisingly for some interpreters, we find that Menger's assumptions do not allow for the standard derivation of well-behaved demand functions because Menger's lexicographic preference ordering prevents the construction of a continuous map of smooth indifference curves, all attempted proofs to the contrary notwithstanding.[3] Only when we come to consider a very specific extension of the neo-classical approach, the much ignored consumer technology developed by Ironmonger in the 1950s which permits an analysis of the demand for new commodities, are we in a position to derive demand functions from Menger's basic assumptions.

This resolution of the problem of demand in Menger's system, however, takes place entirely within the realm of value, not that of prices. It is not a vehicle which allows us to avoid, or even resolve, the transformation problem since this springs, on the one hand, from Menger's conception of the constitution of economic reality, namely, that values are of the essence of economic life while price are only the surface phenomena of economic activity in the market, and, on the other hand, from his philosophy of science, with which it is intimately connected through his Aristotelianism. It is particularly his conception of the nature of "exact" theory (the realm of values), and its truth and certainty by definition, as opposed to that of the nature of refutable realistic-empirical theory (the realm of prices) which constitutes the epistemological basis of the transformation problem. The dividing gulf between Menger's "exact" theory and realistic-empirical theory is unsurmountable. To resolve this transformation problem, one has to jettison Menger's essentialism and the epistemological dichotomy, effectively giving up his conception of "exact" theory. If one wants to travel this road while retaining as much as possible of Menger's original theoretical and methodological structure, one arrives at a theory of price determination based on a marginality principle, although still not in its continuous, indifference-curve-generating form, which relies on introspection as the guarantee of the empirical character of its basic assumptions. But this result, quite obviously, would not be Menger any more but a departure from his original position.

Such a departure reflects, above all in its rejection of essentialism and of the absolute truth and certainty of theories, the scientific mentality of the late nineteenth century rather than that of Menger. It is this road which Friedrich von Wieser and Eugen von Böhm-Bawerk took in their elaboration and extension of Menger's theory. Their departure from Menger is discussed very briefly in the Epilogue; an exhaustive investigation of the issues involved would require a separate study since we are not dealing with minor technical details but with shifts in visions of the economic process and with different conceptions of the scope of economic theory. Böhm-Bawerk was concerned to a very large extent with the role of technology in the discussion of economics: His concepts of production and of capital, his definition of goods and, thus implicitly, his definition of value incorporate an explicit discussion of technology which then becomes an essential part of his economic theory. This is anathema to Menger who was only concerned with economic activity *per se*, activity based on the evaluation of the different options available to the acting subject in his pursuit of the satisfaction of current and future *Bedürfnisse*. Technology, for Menger, belongs in the black box whose contents are of interest to the engineer but utterly irrelevant to the economist. Wieser stuck much more closely to economics as a *Geisteswissenschaft*, but the dilution of Menger's vision and theoretical and methodological framework are equally visible in his work.

What picture of the origin of the Austrian school of economics emerges from this study? In particular, is the picture of Menger that emerges from the three essays in any way different from the one we had before? The logic of the argument requires an answer to the second question first.

Menger emerges as an economist whose theoretical work was immersed in nineteenth-century German political economy, whose intellectual outlook belonged to a particular strand of nineteenth-century German thought and whose philosophy of science was idiosyncratic even by nineteenth-century German standards. His attempt to unite the Romantic-Historicist tradition with rationalist elements, his Aristotelianism and his specifically Austrian conception of individualism combined in the formulation of a methodology which was, at once, ahead of its time and outdated. In Menger's classification of the sciences, realistic-empirical theory is defined as empirically testable in a way that has merit even a century later. His conception of "exact" theory, however, belonged to another era; absolute truth and the certainty of the laws of this type of theory, its introspective recourse to the self as the guarantor of the empirical character of its foundations, had been surpassed by the Kantian critique a century before. The epistemological chasm separating these two types of theory expressed itself as an explosive charge which ultimately blew up the intended structural coherence of Menger's theoretical work.

The traditional characterisation of Menger as a neo-classical economist remains valid even within this re-assessment. If we define neo-classical theory by the following criteria—(1) the marginality principle is all pervasive, (2) value theory is subjective and psychologically based, (3) the individual is at the center of the decision-making process and of the explanation of economic phenomena, and (4) the perspective of the consumer is the perspective of economic analysis—then this study will show that Menger was a neo-classical economist despite the differences which set him off against all the other neo-classical trends.[4] Within this broad classification, however, the foundations of Menger's theory incorporated elements which would be emulated by the other neo-classical strands only a century later. The fundamental roles of real time, uncertainty, incomplete information, expectations and institutions in his theory—manifestations of the Romantic-Historicist background in his theoretical work—still serve as sources of inspiration for neo-classsical economists even today. His hierarchical structure of *Bedürfnisse*, Menger's equivalent of the ordering of preferences, posed problems of formalisation which were only to be resolved after the advent of linear programming. On the other hand, the introspective essentialism of his value theory, which seems as outdated today as it did in 1871, clashed with his realistic-empirical conception of prices and market phenomena to culminate in his epistemologically unsurmountable transformation problem. An acceptance of his theory *toto coelo*—values, prices, epistemology, methodology and all—would land us with a non-operational theory: a highly sophisticated but empirically ungraspable value analysis (unless one is content with unreflected introspection as the source of the empirical dimension) forming the basis of a discussion of empirical phenomena, that is, prices, which it is not able to reach. The question which the modern neoclassical economist has to face, therefore, is which elements of Menger's system ought to be retained and which ones ought to be left behind.

Two possible solutions to this problem were given by Friedrich von Wieser and Eugen von Böhm-Bawerk. They each devised their own modifications to Menger's system, theoretical as well as methodological. They abandoned essentialism and *Verstehen*, let mathematics enter the foundations of pure theory because they gave up Menger's Aristotelian concept of induction, and introduced objective elements into the foundations of what was originally a purely subjective theory of value—modifications which led to Menger's description of Böhm-Bawerk's extension of capital theory as "the greatest error ever committed."

The history of the Austrian school of economics still has to be written. The old myths of the founding generation, of Menger's disciples, of their extension and continuation of his work and of a unified outlook can no longer be believed. In the transition from Menger to Wieser and Böhm-Bawerk, severe transformations of Menger's theory and methodology were implemented; and it was only through these transformations that the foundations of Austrian theory could be fused with the foundations of Walrasian economics (a few minor technical differences are ignored here). In this sense, Menger ought to be regarded not so much as the founder of the Austrian school but as its precursor, as the ceremonial figurehead whose ideas provided the true founders of the school, Wieser and above all Böhm-Bawerk, with the inspiration for their life's work. They may thus claim him as a spiritual ancestor, just as today's neo-classical economists may, but we should no longer believe that Austrian theory developed continuously from 1871 onwards.

In this study I attempt to lay bare the foundations of Menger's thought and to identify the points of Wieser's and Böhm-Bawerk's departure from this thought. The discussion in the three essays and the Epilogue, therefore, contain methodological and substantive pointers which a historian of the Austrian school will have to consider if the obsolete myths about this school are finally to be dispelled. The essays do not present a history of the Austrian school or even of the first generation of Austrian economists. They only clear the ground so that the first step towards such a history may be taken.

Menger in the Literature

Before commencing with the investigation something must be said about the treatment of Menger in the literature. A great deal has been written on the Austrian school: about the Austrian contributions to economic theory and economic methodology, about the Austrians' battles against socialism and planned economies in particular[5] and their conceptions of economic policy in general, about their lives and work in Austria and about their dispersion in the 1930s. In this literature Menger is usually considered to be the founder of the Austrian school and a member of the first generation of Austrian economists, together with Wieser and Böhm-Bawerk. For the most part, the literature does not make too subtle a distinction between Menger's theory and methodology and the theories and methodologies of his successors. A more specialist subset of the literature, however, deals mainly with Menger's work and is more careful in this respect, paying more attention to the specific character of his contributions.

Surveys of the literature on Menger have already been published.[6] Hence, instead of producing yet another I shall confine myself to an overview of the main strands of the discussion of Menger's work in the last few decades and discuss in more detail only those contributions which have a direct bearing on the issues central to this study.

The discussion of Menger and his work has traversed two stages and now entered a third one. The first stage started off with Karl Menger's introduction to the second edition of the *Grundsätze der Volkswirtschaftslehre* and F. X. Weiss's essay on the differences between the 1871 and 1923 editions of the work.[7] It culminated via Hayek, Bloch, Stigler and Knight in Kauder's *A History of Marginal Utility Theory* published in 1965.[8] The literature of this stage brought together diverse strands of information about Menger—biographical, bibliographical, historical, philosophical and theoretical—and attempted a first analysis and interpretation of Menger's work with varying degrees of success.

The second stage built mainly on Hayek and Kauder. Starting with Hansen (1968), though without really following his lead, it lasted approximately a decade, and there were two symposia dedicated to Menger during its course.[9] In this stage, the discussion of Menger and his work proceeded along two, almost separate, lines. Our understanding of Menger's methodology, the *Methodenstreit* and its philosophical underpinnings was deepened by Hansen, Hutchison and Bostaph.[10] Chronologically much later but belonging thematically to this period and to this line of argument are the surveys of the literature on Menger's methodology by Cubeddu and Boos.[11]

Along with this discussion of Menger's methodology, there developed literature on Menger's contributions to economic theory. Streissler began to draw out the specific characteristics of Menger's theoretical work as opposed to the work of Wieser and Böhm-Bawerk and to relate Menger's work to its socio-economic environment.[12] Analyses of Menger's concept of exchange[13] and entrepreneurship[14] not only widened the scope of this theoretical strand but also drew more specific attention to the links of Menger's theory of value and prices with what has come to be called institutionalism. At the end of this period we had at our disposal, on the one hand, a discussion of Menger's economic methodology and its philosophical origins and, on the other hand, a discussion of Menger's economic theory and its environment including some pointers towards institutionalism. What was missing was an in-depth discussion relating these two strands in the literature, namely, one which looked at Menger's theory in the light of his methodology and vice versa.

This was the point of departure of the third stage. Attempts at such a "unified", synthetic analysis and attempts to discuss Menger's theories of value, prices and capital in the light of his methodology and its philosophical origins began to emerge in the 1980s.[15] This study is, in fact, intended as a contribution to this ongoing debate.

In a certain sense, the third stage picked up arguments that Kauder had left unresolved at the end of the first stage. In many ways Kauder had attempted a synthetic interpretation of Menger's theoretical and methodological writings with respect to their philosophical, socio-economic and political background. Above all his paper on Menger's library[16] and his evaluation of Menger's marginal notes[17] in conjunction with his attempts to delineate the intellectual and political roots of Austrian economics[18] put a great deal of material at the disposal of later scholars. Kauder was the first to delve in such a synthetic manner into Menger's work, and it must have been the wealth of material which prevented him from seeing his project through to the end. More often than not he was on the right track, but he simply did not pursue the argument far enough. Let a few examples suffice as illustration of this claim.

Kauder rightly isolates, for instance, Menger's Aristotelianism and essentialism, the specific nature of Menger's conception of "exact" theory, Menger's concern with genetic causality (that is, teleology), his rejection of mathematics and his opposition to Walras. Kauder fails, however, to combine these

elements in order to get to the core of Menger's argument. He points out
that Menger objected to Böhm-Bawerk's terminology of objective value[19]
but does not draw any clear distinction between Menger's work and that
of Böhm-Bawerk in spite of the absence of Menger's Aristotelian concepts
in Böhm-Bawerk's theories and the diametrically opposed attitude of these
two first-generation Austrian economists to the theories of Walras.[20] If Kauder
had pursued this line of thought further, he should have arrived at the
epistemological foundations of Menger's rejection of the use of mathematics
in "exact" theory. Above all, he would not have equated marginal utility
with the final cause[21] (instead of the satisfaction of *Bedürfnisse*), nor would
he have mistaken Böhm-Bawerk's occasional utterances on causality as a
revelation of the latter's Aristotelian philosophy of science.[22] Kauder would,
indeed, not have been baffled by Menger's terminological change from the
first edition of the *Grundsätze* of 1871 to the second edition of 1923 when
he substituted the term "teleology" for the term "causality."[23] He would
have seen that this was, in fact, a mere terminological change and that the
essence of Menger's argument, that is, the application of Menger's conception
of causality in his economic theory, had remained unchanged. Menger had
always understood causality in its fourfold Aristotelian sense as teleology.[24]
Finally, a closer examination of the literature cited by Menger would have
alerted Kauder to the importance of the Romantic-Historicist roots of Menger's
theory, methodology and epistemology which, in any attempt to determine
the *geistesgeschichtliche* roots of Menger's thought, have to be seen as
complementary to the analysis of the Austrian intellectual environment
provided by Kauder.

Hansen's essay of 1968 opened the second stage of the discussion with
an analysis of the *Methodenstreit*, the acrimonious methodological debate
involving a very brief exchange of insults between Menger and Schmoller,
which led to a breakdown in communication between the German historical
school of economics and the emerging Austrian school. Hansen contrasts
Schmoller's post-Kantian conception of methodology and philosophy of
science with Menger's Romantic-Historicist Aristotelianism. Since the analysis
of Menger's methodology and philosophy of science presented in this study
to a very large extent agrees with Hansen's findings, I shall not try to
summarise his contribution here. Instead, I shall try to explain why his
essay had been of no significant influence.

Hansen's essay was first given in December 1966 as a paper at a colloquium
on the development of the nineteenth-century philosophy of science and
summarised the main findings of his doctoral dissertation. Certainly the fact
that it was published in German and the relative obscurity of its place of
publication may explain why it did not catch the attention of a wider
audience.[25] The style of presentation did not help matters, either. Although
the section on Schmoller is explicit, clear and well documented, the section
on Menger is kaleidoscopic, obscure and hardly documented at all—indeed,
deliberately so.[26] It seems that only if one had traversed the same terrain
as Hansen in the investigation of the origins and meaning of Menger's world

of thought could one understand what Hansen had said about Menger.[27] Not even Hayek's and Hutchison's references to Hansen at the conference held to commemorate the centenary of the publication of Menger's *Grundsätze der Volkswirthschaftslehre* made any difference.[28]

Hutchison's paper on Menger's methodology presented at that 1971 conference became a standard reference for most subsequent writings in the field.[29] In it, he deals with a number of issues which are central to the understanding of Menger's approach: Menger's conception of the nature of economic theory and of economic laws, his position in the *Methodenstreit*, and his organicism as the basis of his concept of unintended consequences of human action.

Hutchison raises the problem of the compatibility of Menger's essentialist conception of theory and his methodological individualism and emphasises that methodological individualism is traditionally associated with a nominalist conception of science while essentialism has tended to be affiliated with historicism.[30] Although this problem is correctly perceived, Hutchison does not suggest how it can be resolved. In his discussion of Menger's conception of the nature of scientific laws, Hutchison focusses his attention on Menger's definition of "exact" theory, and hence "exact" laws in contrast to his "empirical" theory, and criticises the untestability of Menger's "exact" laws as scientifically untenable. This narrowness of Menger's approach is then contrasted with Menger's fundamentally progressive vision of an economic process which is based on error, ignorance and uncertainty.[31]

Two aspects remain undeveloped in Hutchison's discussion of Menger's methodology. First, the Romantic-Historicist dimension is not pursued in detail, in spite of occasional allusions to its existence. Second, Hutchison separates Menger's discussion of methodology from his economic theory of 1871.[32] This leads him to underestimate, for instance, the importance of essentialism and teleology for Menger's theory of value and the principles of economic theory derived from it. This dissociation of methodology from theory, however, is consistent with Hutchison's interpretation of the *Methodenstreit* in the last section of his essay. There he points out that although Menger had dedicated the *Grundsätze* to Roscher, the doyen of the historical school, he then proceeded to attack vehemently the historical school's aims and methods in the *Untersuchungen*. As a consequence, "Menger's attitude to the German historical economists, and their concepts and methods" must have undergone a "great transformation between the publication of the *Grundsätze* and that of the *[Untersuchungen]*."[33] An alternative interpretation based on additional evidence is put forward in the Appendix to Essay II of this study. There, it is argued that there was no change in Menger's attitude towards "concepts and methods", that is, no shift in Menger's methodological and epistemological position, between 1871 and 1883 but simply a change of "heart", a change in attitude towards the historical economists themselves.

The synthetic approach to Menger's work would also have permitted Hutchison to develop further his discussion of Menger's principle of unintended consequences of human action.[34] He justly emphasises the link between unintended consequences of human action and methodological individualism in the *Untersuchungen* and traces its specific formulation to Menger's concern with ignorance, error and uncertainty. But he cannot see that, far from being an independent, fundamental methodological principle, the concept of unintended consequences of human action is derivative. It is the composite of teleology and methodological individualism in a world of ignorance and uncertainty. Hutchison could not have seen this because teleology does not feature explicitly in the *Untersuchungen*, although it does play a fundamental and central role in the *Grundsätze*.[35]

In a reworked version of his paper Hutchison incorporated some more recent literature, but his assessment of Menger remained fundamentally unchanged.[36] Since this paper spanned, as it were, almost the entire second stage of the debate on Menger and since it became quite popular, we may safely regard it as representative of the strand of the debate which concentrated on methodology with relatively little regard for the methodology implicit in Menger's economic theory.

Bostaph's paper carried the discussion forward, at least for an Anglo-Saxon audience, by tracing the origin of the *Methodenstreit* back to its epistemological roots.[37] Not only does Bostaph provide a description of the genesis of the *Methodenstreit* and of its reception in the relevant literature, he also demonstrates that it was Menger's Aristotelian epistemology which clashed with Schmoller's nominalism[38] and poses the crucial question to which no definitive answer has been found as yet: Why did Menger squander so much energy over methodological questions?[39]

Bostaph's account of the genesis of the *Methodenstreit* is fairly complete apart from a minor omission relating to the reception of Menger's *Grundsätze* by the German academic world,[40] but it also introduces a certain amount of confusion into the discussion of Menger's methodology and epistemology. One gets the impression that Menger considered his "exact" theories as abstract deductive[41] and that his aim was to clarify the nature of concepts of "exact" theory. As an analysis of Menger's writings shows, the exact opposite was the case. That Menger did not consider his "exact" theory as abstract deductive can easily be seen in his attitude towards mathematics: Why should he have objected to the use of mathematics in "exact" theory if "exact" theory was as abstract deductive as mathematics? It was precisely because "exact" theory was about *Verstehen*, about inductively grasping the essence of economic phenomena, that mathematics was of no help.[42]

Equally serious is the confusion introduced in Bostaph's (correct) assessment that the *Methodenstreit* was at bottom an epistemological debate. In formulating this issue as an argument about the nature of concepts and of causal laws, Menger's position is again inverted. Concepts, for Menger, are not abstract generalisations with universal applicability but *sprachliche Abbilder*, that is, linguistic representations of economic phenomena[43] or, in Bostaph's terminology, "mere labels." But this is how Bostaph characterises Schmoller's position.[44] As is suggested in the Appendix to Essay II, it was precisely because, for Menger, "exact" theory was not about conceptual clarification or analysis but about understanding the essences that he felt compelled to write a critique of Historicist methodology. To characterise Menger as a participant in a debate about the theory of concepts shunts the discussion onto a track which is not helpful at all in understanding Menger's perspective.

Streissler's inaugural lecture and his paper presented at the 1971 conference on the marginal revolution started the discussion, in this second phase, of Menger's theoretical contribution.[45] Streissler characterises the Austrian economists as the structuralists among the neo-classical schools.[46] According to Streissler, it was, above all, the Austrians who disaggregated the elements which made up the world of discourse of the marginal utility theorists,[47] and it was Menger who imparted this structural mode of thinking to his successors. Wants were not simply bundled but hierarchically structured, and goods were ordered by their distance from being immediately consumable in the satisfaction of wants. Menger's main concern was not with some average concept such as market price but with individual price formation, that is, with differences of prices from each other. In other words, not averages but variances were of paramount interest in Austrian economics. And, apparently, nothing serves better to illustrate this than Menger's, and the other Austrians', emphasis on uncertainty in the economic decision-making process and on the role of expectations, that is, on the distribution of probabilities of the outcome of economic action based on incomplete information. Streissler traces this structural approach towards theorising about the economic world from Menger not only through the direct lineage of the Austrian economists but also to the origins of the logical proof in the establishment of a general equilibrium system of prices presented by Wald and von Neumann in Vienna in the 1930s.[48]

In both works, Streissler enriches his argument with reference to the cultural and socio-economic conditions in Austria in the second half of the nineteenth century. But in the 1971 conference paper, in contrast to the earlier work, Streissler emphasises not so much the structuralist element but the influence of change, time, uncertainty and incomplete information in Menger's theory. In particular, Streissler stresses the predominance of monopolistic elements in the discussion of Menger's theory of price formation in contrast to the predominance of perfect competition in Wieser's and Böhm-Bawerk's theories, which served to assimilate the Austrian strand of neo-classical economics into the strands issuing from Jevons and Walras. Streissler also draws attention to Menger's disagreement with Böhm-Bawerk's conception of capital as "the greatest error ever committed" on the basis that Böhm-Bawerk's concept of capital was technical and not economic.[49]

Streissler approaches Menger from the perspective of economic theory and largely neglects the methodological dimension. This prevents him, at least in my mind, from following his discussion of Menger through to the end. Two examples may demonstrate this. Streissler claims that "structural thought and the aversion to full equilibrium models, and not the predilection for marginal utility, are finally the main reasons for the aversion of the Austrians against mathematics. . . . their main objection to mathematics was that economic phenomena are in their essence discontinuous and discrete."[50] Also, "Menger's lack of belief in the appropriateness of equilibrium analysis also explains his lack of belief in the expediency of using mathematics."[51]

This may seem an adequate explanation from the perspective of the theoretician, but when we come to look at Menger's methodology in Essay II, we shall see that Menger objected above all to the use of mathematics in "exact" theory because mathematics as a purely deductive science cannot contribute anything to the problem of *Verstehen*, to the problem of grasping the essence of economic phenomena which, as I shall suggest, is akin to Aristotle's inductive conception of grasping the first principles.

Similarly, one of the main reasons for Menger to take bi-lateral monopoly as the general case and perfect competition as the limiting special case is grounded in Menger's strict adherence to methodological individualism and subjectivism on the basis of his definition of economic activity as the provision for the satisfaction of *Bedürfnisse* under scarcity conditions. Furthermore, Streissler's lack of emphasis on epistemological issues not only leads to the confusion of Menger's concepts of values and prices,[52] it also lets him conclude that "Menger's theory ended in doubt and not in positive theorems" since Menger eschewed deriving concrete results because his was a completely subjective theory.[53] Against this, or perhaps, enlarging on this, I would suggest that Menger's theory ended in doubt because Menger could not resolve his epistemological transformation problem, which required him to transform certain and definitively determined values into probable prices, and not because he eschewed concrete results. After all, not only does the *Grundsätze* contain a large number of very concrete principles of economic theory, Menger also explicitly stated in his *Untersuchungen* that the starting point and the end point of economic activity are strictly determined.[54]

Finally, in a number of footnotes Streissler remarks on the astonishing proximity of Menger to the historical economists and to today's institutionalists. Again, an analysis of Menger's methodology[55] shows the extent to which Menger inhabited the Romantic-Historicist world of the nineteenth century. It can also show how Menger could begin with a few principles of human action and arrive at a Historicist, evolutionary theory of money without leaving his own frame of reference.[56]

Kirzner's discussion of Menger's conception of the entrepreneur takes its lead from Streissler's remark that Schumpeter built on Mengerian foundations.[57] Kirzner regards this position as scarcely tenable in view of the paradox which he uncovers in Menger's theory: Although uncertainty, error and the role of knowledge are all-pervasive, and, hence "Menger's world was one within which we could have expected the entrepreneurial role to have been not only clearly perceived but in fact boldly underlined", Kirzner concludes that there is no recognition of the pivotal role of entrepreneurship in the *Grundsätze*.[58] He arrives at this conclusion through an interpretation of Menger's theory of prices as equilibrium prices established with full information.

This interpretation of Menger's conception of prices is not at all necessary (or sufficient) for an explanation of the appearance of a concept of "full information." It suffices to turn to Menger's methodology and epistemology. Menger's essentialism allows us to interpret—in accordance with his own intentions—values as the essence, *das Wesen*, and prices as the phenomena of economic activity. According to this reading, it is not necessary to take prices to be equilibrium prices with full information. Now the certainty (of subjectively knowing the basis of one's decisions but not necessarily all the forces working on them) is carried by values and not by prices. Values, for Menger, are known beyond doubt because they are the essence of economic activity, and value theory, therefore, constitutes Menger's "exact" theory. It provides, for Menger, the true and certain foundations for any explanation of economic activity. Kirzner is right to focus on a paradox at this particular point in Menger's theoretical edifice, but this paradox, basically, is of an epistemological and not of a theoretical nature.

The same problem area, Menger's theory of prices, was also addressed by Moss at the conference where Kirzner's paper was given.[59] Again, the same tensions beset the argument; for example, in the discussion of Menger's theory of exchange, the methodological and epistemological dimensions of Menger's chapter on price formation are not sufficiently appreciated. Moss somehow misses the importance of Menger's essentialist conception of theory at this point,[60] in spite of the fact that he actually cites the crucial passage where Menger refers to prices as surface phenomena.[61]

The additional dimension provided by a synthetic discussion of Menger's theory and methodology would have allowed Moss to penetrate more deeply into the *Grundsätze* and would have allowed him to highlight the transition which takes place in this crucial chapter. There we witness the transition from the realm of essence to that of surface phenomena, from values to prices, from "exact" theory to empirical-realistic theory, from truth and certainty to probability. It was, after all, Menger who fired the first shot in the *Methodenstreit*. Based on the interpretation of his reasons given in the Appendix to Essay II, it is not entirely unreasonable to investigate Menger's implicit methodology and also to integrate his theory and methodology into a synthetic reading of his work.

Finally, Martin's investigation of Menger's conception of entrepreneurial activity arrives at quite different conclusions.[62] In contrast to Kirzner, she finds quite a comprehensive discussion of entrepreneurship in Menger's *Grundsätze*. Her starting point is the conflicting views of Knight and Schumpeter on this issue. While Knight claims that Menger does not have a concept of entrepreneurship, Schumpeter links Knight to Menger "when he traces the origins of enterprise and entrepreneurship, which have as their basis the uncertain nature of the economic process",[63] and stresses Menger's view that "rewards of entrepreneurship very much depend on the nature of the informational flows within society."[64] After examining Menger's *Grundsätze* and his essay on money of 1892, Martin decides in favour of Schumpeter, though with the proviso that "in contrast to Knight, the Mengerian entrepreneur is not being paid for the bearing of uncertainty. The Mengerian entrepreneur, confronted with uncertainty, gathers information about the economic system, organizes higher-order goods, coordinates and plans production decisions, and seeks to make a good which will have value to some economising individual. This is the basis for the entrepreneur's return."[65]

One major strand of the literature on Menger has not been mentioned yet: the discussion of his theory of money. This stands somewhat apart not only because his theory of money is far less controversial than his theories of value, price formation and capital, but also because his analysis of money as a medium of exchange may even be considered state of the art.[66] Summary accounts and evaluations are readily available in English,[67] and since this topic goes beyond the scope of this study, it is not pursued.

The third, synthetic stage of Mengerian scholarship is only just beginning to take off. First steps included investigating the *Grundsätze* from the perspective of Menger's methodological principle of unintended consequences of human action,[68] emphasising the institutional dimension of Menger's theory of demand[69], analysing his concept of economic rationality[70] and focussing, in an analysis of the axiomatic foundations of his theory, on the reasons for his rejection of mathematics.[71] One long-neglected area of research, Menger's theory of capital, has finally also received attention.[72] It is to be expected that the findings presented in these articles will be developed further on the basis of the as yet unpublished manuscripts at Duke University. Then we may finally arrive, well over a century after its publication, at a full understanding of Menger's economic theory.

Presentation of the Material

A few words must still be said about the method of presentation which I have chosen. I have left all quotations from Menger, Wieser and Böhm-Bawerk in German, and I have retained a number of German terms throughout. The English translation of Menger's *Grundsätze der Volkswirthschaftslehre* is not a reliable tool for serious work. The early publications of the Austrian economists are very difficult to translate into English because of their cumbersome and unnecessarily complicated style, and the translators of the *Grundsätze* had no easy task. They did succeed in making the text far more easily comprehensible than in the original, but unfortunately, they rendered it into Walrasian English which means that the *Principles of Economics* is not the same work as the *Grundsätze der Volkswirthschaftslehre*. There is, in fact, a far greater difference between the *Principles* and the *Grundsätze* than between the first and second editions of the latter work.

The translators acted in good faith when they rendered into less tortuous English what would have been impossible as a direct, literal translation. Unfortunately in the case of the *Grundsätze*, however, the key to an understanding of the theory and the methodology lies in the understanding of nuances, and it is the loss of nuances which is the price paid for expositional clarity. Two instances may illustrate this problem: First, the Aristotelian dimension of Menger's language has been translated away, and second, sense has been made of passages which are contradictory in the original. The most serious of the latter errors concerns Menger's calculation of the value of heterogeneous goods. The original passage is grammatically incomplete and contains a mathematical contradiction.[73] The translated passage is not only grammatically correct but it even corrects, without indication, meaning and the mathematical error by providing an arithmetic example of how to calculate the "value quota."[74]

Menger's language is that of nineteenth-century German Aristotelianism with strong roots in Romanticism. For this reason the translators' licence to render the text into more literary English should have been given up in favour of an absolutely accurate translation which preserves Menger's peculiarities. The accumulation of misrepresentations and shifts of meaning in the only available English translation of the *Grundsätze* eventually amounts to one thing: A significant dimension of Menger's thought has been translated away by forcing his language into that of the twentieth century. The most pertinent example here is Menger's concept of causality. When Menger talks of causality, he has in mind the fourfold Aristotelian notion of cause and not the modern concept in which all but the efficient cause has been dropped. But how can Menger's concept be discerned in the text if the language has been altered so that it becomes almost unrecognisable? How, for example, can the theoretical and methodological insistence on imputation be explained if we are unaware of the existence and importance of the final cause?[75]

Since this study relies to a very large extent on a contextual interpretation of Menger's terminology, I have decided not only to leave all quotations in German rather than to produce another inadequate translation, but to also retain the original spelling because Menger's spelling—frequently outdated by today's rules—is the first visible sign of the difference between his world of thought and ours.[76] This is also the reason for a number of German terms in the text, especially *Bedürfnis*, *Bedürfnisbefriedigung*, *Verstehen*, *Volksgeist*, *Geisteswissenschaften* and *Naturwissenschaften*. They have been retained with the express intention of drawing the reader's attention to the fact that we are dealing with a world of thought which is quite different from the current Anglo-Saxon one and that the scope of these terms is different from the scope of the English terms generally used as equivalents.[77]

To make Menger's work at least somewhat accessible to an Anglo-Saxon readership, I have added references to the extant English translations of the *Grundsätze* and the *Untersuchungen* in the Notes despite the serious reservations mentioned. My argument, however, is based on the relevant German passages; no consideration has been given to implications for meaning raised by the currently available translations.

Notes

1. Exceptions are Hansen(1968) and, to a certain extent, also Bostaph(1978) and Hutchison(1973) and (1981).

2. See, for instance, Littlechild(1978), Shand(1980), Taylor(1980) and White(1977).
3. See, e.g., McCulloch(1977).
4. This characterisation of Menger depends, of course, on the criteria adopted here. For different criteria, which lead to Menger's exclusion from the neoclassical fold, see Mirowski(1984), pp. 370–372.

Menger in the Literature

5. For the most recent contribution see Hayek(1988).
6. See Boos(1986) and Cubeddu(1985).
7. K. Menger(1923); Weiss(1924).
8. Hayek(1934), revised in Hayek(1968); Bloch(1940), but see also Bloch(1937); Stigler(1937); Knight(1950); Kauder(1958), (1959), (1962) and (1965).
9. See the *Zeitschrift für Nationalökonomie*, 32(1972), reprinted in English as Hicks and Weber (eds.) (1973), and the *Atlantic Economic Journal*, 6:3(1978).
10. Hansen(1968); Hutchison(1973) and (1981); Bostaph(1976) and (1978).
11. Cubeddu(1985); Boos(1986).
12. Streissler(1969) and (1972).
13. Moss(1978).
14. Kirzner(1978); Martin(1979).
15. See Alter(1982b) and (1986); Butos(1985); Endres(1984) and (1987).
16. Kauder(1959).
17. Kauder(1962).
18. Kauder(1958).
19. Kauder(1959), p. 63.
20. In his 1958 article Kauder treats Menger, Wieser and Böhm-Bawerk very much as a unity. His discovery of Menger's manuscripts, as he calls them, in 1959 did not lead him to reassess his 1958 position for no such statement can be found in his book on marginal utility of 1965. For a discussion of some of the crucial differences between Menger's, Wieser's and Böhm-Bawerk's theories, see the Epilogue. The difference between Menger's and Böhm-Bawerk's appreciation of Walras's theory is best expressed in their correspondence with Walras (see Walras[1965]).
21. Kauder(1958), p. 417.
22. See Kauder(1958), p. 418.
23. See Kauder(1962), pp. 6–7.
24. On this issue, see Essay II.
25. This may be the reason why it is listed neither in the bibliography of Bostaph's dissertation nor in his 1978 article although both times Bostaph deals with the same topic as Hansen; cf. Bostaph(1976) and (1978).
26. At the time, Hansen feared that a well-documented section on Menger might prejudice the timely completion of his doctoral dissertation thus jeopardising his claim to authorship of a fundamental re-interpretation not only of Menger's methodology and philosophy of science but of the development of the philosophy of social science and, more specifically, of economics. This fear may not have been totally unfounded, but unfortunately for those who were to take up the same issues later on, his dissertation, although completed up to a first final draft, was never submitted and has never been available.
27. Why else did Boos, for instance, in her book on Menger's philosophy of science, ignore what Hansen had said despite the fact that she mentioned him as one of the sources for further information on the *Methodenstreit* (see Boos[1986]). In a survey of literature such an idiosyncratic position should at least deserve a mention if not discussion and attempt at refutation.

28. Cf. Hicks and Weber (eds.) (1973), pp. 4 n.4, 15 n.1, 18 n.6; see also the discussion at this conference, published in *Zeitschrift für Nationalökonomie*, 32(1972), pp. 111–150.
29. Hutchison(1973).
30. Hutchison(1973), pp. 17–18.
31. Hutchison(1973), pp. 19–23.
32. Cf. Hutchison(1973), pp. 15 n.3, 18 n.6, 28, 31.
33. Hutchison(1973), p. 32.
34. Hutchison(1973), pp. 23–27.
35. For a fuller discussion of this issue, see Essay II, esp. p. 111.
36. See Hutchison(1981).
37. Bostaph(1978).
38. Bostaph(1978), pp. 10–12.
39. See Bostaph(1978), p. 8.
40. Schmoller did, in fact, review Menger's *Grundsätze*; see Schmoller(1873).
41. Bostaph(1978), p. 13.
42. On the nature of Menger's "exact" theory, see also p. 105.
43. See Menger(1883), p. 6 n.4 [Menger(1963/1985), p. 37 n.4].
44. Bostaph(1978), p. 8.
45. Streissler(1969) and (1972).
46. Streissler(1969), pp. 248–256.
47. "By a structural analysis, I understand the decomposition of *aggregates in order to increase the explanatory content* which can be derived by viewing the aggregates as undifferentiated wholes. At bottom, structural analysis stresses *an economic contrast, a social tension,* one might even be tempted to say a dialectical process" Streissler(1969), p. 241 (original italics).
48. For a more exhaustive, recent discussion of this issue, see Punzo(1988).
49. For further discussion of some of these issues, see the Epilogue; see also Endres(1987).
50. Streissler(1969), p. 255.
51. Streissler(1972), p. 440.
52. For instance, Streissler(1972), p. 439.
53. Streissler(1972), p. 441.
54. See the title to Appendix VI:"Dass der Ausgangspunkt und der Zielpunkt aller menschlichen Wirthschaft streng determinirt seien" Menger(1883), p. 262 [Menger(1963/1985), p. 216].
55. See, e.g., Hansen(1968).
56. For further discussion of this issue, see Essays I and II. See also Pagano(1985), Chapter 5, and Endres(1984).
57. Kirzner(1978), p. 31.
58. Kirzner(1978), p. 42.
59. Moss(1978).
60. One likely cause for this may very well be the quality of the English translation of Menger's *Grundsätze*; the Aristotelian, essentialist dimension is barely discernable, particularly when compared with the original. On this, see also p. 17.
61. Moss(1978), p. 29.
62. Martin(1979).
63. Martin(1979), pp. 272–273, see also p. 283.
64. Martin(1979), p. 281.
65. Martin(1979), p. 282.

66. See Jones(1976). Clower(1977) actually prefaces his article with a quotation from Menger's "On the Origin of Money"; indeed, "a sample from modern economic textbooks shows that the Mengerian conception is nowadays implicitly accepted" Lagerspetz(1984), p. 3.
67. Streissler(1973), O'Driscoll(1986); see also Hirsch(1928), Roll(1936).
68. Butos(1985).
69. Endres(1984).
70. Alter(1982b).
71. Alter(1986).
72. Endres(1987).

Presentation of the Material

73. Menger(1871), pp. 118–119.
74. Menger(1950/1981), pp. 144–145.
75. It is surprising and lamentable that no effort was made to update the translation for the new edition of the *Principles* published in 1981, particularly in view of the fact that reservations about the quality of the translation were made public as early as 1951 (cf., e.g., Hicks[1951]).
76. The translation of Menger's *Principles* is not the only case in which an English version misrepresents, or re-interprets, to a significant extent the thought of the German original. A famous example with probably much more serious consequences for the English speaking public is the translation of the writings of Sigmund Freud. Its implications for psychoanalysis are discussed in Bettelheim(1985).
77. For a discussion of the problems posed by translating the term *Bedürfnis* as *need*, see Macpherson(1977).

Background

I

The Austrian School
in the History of Ideas

Current tradition has it that the founders of today's mainstream economics were William Stanley Jevons, Carl Menger and Léon Walras. Neo-classical economic theory, with its emphasis on equilibrium exchange based on maximising individuals, is said to have emanated equally from the pens of this triumvirate who independently of each other discovered the unifying principle of utility maximisation subject to a budget constraint, which about sixty years later was given its final form by John Hicks. True, it is usually admitted that Jevons, Menger and Walras did not produce quite identical theories; Menger rejected mathematics and his exposition thus suffered from too much verbiage and occasional imprecisions, and Jevons did not go far enough in the development of the marginal productivity theory of distribution. Walras, however, produced a complete and analytically well-rounded theory which gave clear and superior expression to a body of thought which was common to all three forefathers. As a corollary, it is usually added that the study of Walras's *Elements* therefore suffices if one really wants to go back to one's roots. This, I think, is a fair rendering of the lore of the founding trinity as it is taught at the academies in the Land of the Econ.

The reader who actually ventures into Menger's *Grundsätze* and Jevons's *Theory of Political Economy* and tries to understand these works as expressions of visions of how the economy works rather than just going to look for the analytics of the argument will come up with some surprising discoveries. What has been said above about the three appears to be true for Jevons and Walras while Menger's work seems to have quite a different flavour. Different, in fact, to such an extent that his eschewing mathematics is not just an expression of some bias against (natural) science, or even incompetence, but rather of a difference in vision, although this vision still remains neoclassical. Once this is grasped, the origins of the Austrian school can be clearly delineated and set off against other neoclassical trends.

If one picks up any of the writings of the Austrian school one is struck by how all of them point to the origins of the school—Carl Menger's *Grundsätze der Volkswirtschaftslehre* and *Untersuchungen über die Methode*

der Socialwissenschaften, und der Politischen Oekonomie insbesondere. Various
issues remain unclear in the *Grundsätze*, but looked at in the light of the
Untersuchungen, and also the second (posthumous) edition of the *Grundsätze*,
Menger's thought stands out as being shaped by one all-embracing vision.
For an understanding of the history of the Austrian school, it is therefore
necessary to have a firm grasp of the main thrust and the central elements
of Menger's vision, his methodology and his theory. I shall discuss the
framework of this vision first and then go on to show that what I consider
to be his vision is not merely implicit in his theoretical writings; the influence
of his vision can be discerned in his writings down to the analytics of his
arguments.

Menger's aim was to establish economics, and subsequently also social
science in general, as a *Wissenschaft*, and this aim quite inadvertently took
him towards establishing a *verstehende* economic theory which was quite
similar to Max Weber's conception of a *verstehende* sociology.[1] His interest,
however, was not only in establishing the foundations of a positive economic
theory but also with providing it with theoretical-philosophical foundations.[2]
This essentially "germanic" approach to any kind of scientific endeavour is
usually unappreciated in histories of economic thought written in the Anglo-
Saxon tradition, whose main concern is with how people do the job and
not with the metaphysics of it. Any appraisal of the Austrians, and especially
of Menger, which fails to take account of this "teutonic" strand simply fails
to do justice to this school.

The origins of the Austrian school, therefore, have to be viewed in the
light of the (pre-)history of the concept of *Verstehen*. From this position we
shall be able to dissect the history of the school to give the school its proper
place in the history of economic thought and thus to help rectify the situation
which has arisen out of the excessive pre-occupation of historians of economic
doctrine with economic analysis in particular to the neglect of the treatment
of economic thought as part of the history of ideas. To get an idea of things
to come, let us look at a very concise characterisation of the Austrians
which has been taken from *A History of Economic Ideas*:

> Despite specific disagreements, the Austrian school agreed in its major
> attitudes. The Austrians were anti-historical. As a corollary, they preferred
> abstract analysis. Marshall was full of ethics; the Austrians were full of
> metaphysics. Operating, perhaps, on the premise that important phenomena
> have distinguished origins, they sought the essential, inner meanings of the
> ideas they cherished. Therefore their explanations tended to concentrate upon
> the universal. Cunningham's complaints about Marshall's generalisations of
> economic laws applied much more accurately to Böhm-Bawerk than they did
> to Marshall. In the concept of capital, Böhm-Bawerk discovered an explanation
> of economic behaviour appropriate to all societies. Wieser's natural value
> purported to derive profits, rents, and wages from the most general of all
> economic circumstances, the communist state. The great Austrians were per-
> sistently more abstract, general, and timeless than Marshall ever permitted
> himself to become. Despite obvious differences in aim and manner, the Austrians
> bore strong resemblances to Marx.

It was somewhat paradoxical that these devotees of generality and abstractions avoided the device capable of generating the broadest conclusions, Edgeworth's "sovereign science," mathematics. The fact was that the Austrians condescended to no trace of mathematics, even diagrammatic illustration. These aids to brevity might have considerably mitigated the school's tedious prolixity. An analytical consequence was the failure of Austrian writings to attain the demonstration of interdependence which was the valuable contribution of general-equilibrium theorists.[3]

However many individual truths may be contained in this characterisation, this is precisely what the Austrians were *not* about.

As a preliminary, a justification of the phrase "(pre-)history of the concept of *Verstehen*" seems appropriate in order to prevent some possible confusion and misunderstanding. The concept of *Verstehen* as the methodological and epistemological basis of the *Geisteswissenschaften* and the social sciences is commonly taken to derive from Dilthey, Rickert and Max Weber, to name but a few.[4] To discuss Menger's work in the light of these philosophers, historians and social scientists would be totally erroneous in a historical analysis such as this one. Consequently, no systematic discussion of what I call the "modern" strand of *Verstehen* will be found in this study.[5] The reason for this exclusion is simple and straightforward: When Menger's *Grundsätze* was published in 1871, Max Weber was seven years old; another twenty or so years were to elapse before Rickert published his *Kulturwissenschaft und Naturwissenschaft*, while Dilthey's *Einleitung in die Geisteswissenschaften*—the cornerstone of the modern *Verstehen* doctrine[6]—appeared simultaneously with Menger's *Untersuchungen* (1883). In relation to the modern *Verstehen* doctrine, then, Menger's philosophy of social science can be said to have been one of its precursors,[7] because he based his concept of *Verstehen*, just as Dilthey did, on the thought of Schleiermacher, Humboldt, Ranke and Droysen.[8] Menger, in fact, attempted to do the same for the social sciences as Max Weber was to do a generation later: namely, to fuse what appeared to him to be the most fruitful elements of rationalist, positivist, empiricist methodology and epistemology of the natural sciences with the anti-rationalistic, Idealist-Romantic ones of the *Geisteswissenschaften* to construct a framework for a *sui generis* science of society.[9]

Individuum Est Ineffabile

Verstehen can be variously translated as to understand, comprehend, interpret, see, grasp, know (to avoid misunderstanding I shall use the German word throughout when referring to the concept as the methodological and epistemological basis of the *Geisteswissenschaften*; the term "hermeneutics" will be used synonymously with it).[10] Throughout its history, the concept has acquired various meanings and is still being modified today. There is, nevertheless, a core which is common to all shades of interpretation. *Verstehen*, basically, constitutes a reaction against the introduction of the rationalistic methodology of the natural sciences into the *Geisteswissenschaften*—the humanities and the social sciences—first and foremost, though, into philology and history. The pivot of all *verstehende* argumentation is that the subject matter under investigation in the *Geisteswissenschaften* is characterised by one distinctive feature which is supposed to constitute an unbridgeable difference to the subject matter of the natural sciences: Human beings differ from all other animate and inanimate nature by being endowed with a mind. The implication is that while nature blindly obeys laws and while events in nature can only be observed and explained from the outside— and this holds for man's biological nature, too—in the *geisteswissenschaftliche* sphere the driving forces are not blind causal reactions but motivation, psychological or otherwise. Since this is common to all mankind, past and present, human actions and their results, therefore, become understandable from within.[11]

To illustrate this difference: When one billiard ball hits another the second ball will move in the direction it is pushed while the first one will come to rest. In a crowd, when one person hits another—inadvertently or not— the first one will not necessarily come to rest but may try to run away from the second one because the second one is turning around to retaliate in kind instead of moving away in the direction pushed; then again, this might not happen at all.

This example basically addresses the following problems: First, is the second case merely more complicated than the first one, inasmuch as it requires more information for a satisfactory explanation of the situation, or are these two cases qualitatively different? If the former is the case, then there is no need to develop a different methodology for the humanities and the social sciences as opposed to the physical sciences. Against this position, one might conceivably argue that it is *a priori* impossible to gather all the information necessary to express the world of human activity in the form of causal laws because of the vast complexity of this world. In other words, it is *a priori* impossible to arrive at a *satisfactory* statement of the initial conditions in terms of sense data. Second, although there is certainly no point in searching for a motive (over and above the efficient cause) behind the movements of the billiard balls, intentionality is certainly not a futile premise to base one's investigations into human activity upon. Taking into account, in addition, the impossibility of carrying out controlled historical or large-scale social experiments (the UK monetarist experience of the Thatcher years notwithstanding), one cannot but use the superior access one has to the world of human creation over the physical world (superior because we are on the inside as actors rather than mere observers). Formulated in this way, the problem points to an epistemological difference between the *Geisteswissenschaften* and the *Naturwissenschaften* rather than just a methodological one. Problems relating to logic and consistency are, of course, valid in and appropriate to both the *Geisteswissenschaften* and the *Naturwissenschaften*.

I have chosen this example and this particular formulation of the definition of *Verstehen* to emphasise the psychologistic aspect of this concept. We shall see later that although this is the interpretation usually offered, it does not necessarily have to be understood in this particular way. I shall also attempt to show where this psychologistic tendency originated and, implicitly, why the psychologistic tendency of the *verstehende* tradition was chosen by Menger combining ideological elements and elements which are peculiar to the Austrian *Geistesgeschichte*.

Hermeneutics was originally the art, or skill, of exegesis—of interpreting the Scriptures.[12] Prior to the Reformation this skill was exercised on the firm grounds of Catholic dogma and tradition. With Martin Luther's translation of the Bible from Latin into German, however, a different need for exegesis arose, one that did away with the dogma and tradition of the Roman church and, instead, explained and interpreted the Bible in a way that it could be used as a guide in everyday life. This critical attitude notwithstanding, Protestantism soon began to develop its own dogma. In turn, the Pietist movement sprang up in Germany in the second half of the seventeenth century as a reaction to arid, dogmatic Protestant scholasticism, insisting on a psychological interpretation of the Bible by making its core the "doctrine of deep devotional feelings."[13] Here we find the origins of the psychologistic trend of *Verstehen*, a trend which would eventually move into the center of the doctrine in the wake of German Romanticism, mainly, through the work of Schleiermacher.[14] The connection between Pietism and historiography was prepared by J. Baumgarten in the eighteenth century; influenced by the Enlightenment, he paved the way for a historical hermeneutics by emphasising the importance of the historical situation of the authors who were to be interpreted. In Baumgarten's work, Pietist and rationalistic elements interacted, providing the basis of a historical *Verstehen* which now moved rapidly from theology to history proper to the *Geisteswissenschaften* (the humanities or cultural sciences) in general in the writings of Schleiermacher, Boeckh, Wilhelm von Humboldt, Ranke and Droysen.[15]

The doyen of the great systems of *Verstehen* in Germany was Johann Gottfried Herder (1744–1803), a Protestant clergyman of Pietist background who was the most powerful and influential advocate of the reaction against both the French and the German Enlightenment.[16] His importance, from the point of view of our subject, lay not in the development of a systematic hermeneutic theory—indeed, he never constructed one—but in the stimulation and inspiration he gave to philology and historiography through the stress on the historical, genetic approach which was all-pervasive in his writings.[17] Unlike his teacher Hamann, Herder was neither a mystic nor a diehard opponent of the rationalism of the Enlightenment, but he started off as an adherent of that very movement only to break away from it still rather early in his career. He rejected the belief that timeless, universal laws of nature also apply to the world of human creation. His "relativism" repudiated Eurocentrism and the notion that throughout history one could observe an upward development towards the enlightened age of *les pilosophes*. Reason, for him, did not exist as a separate dominant entity, nor did absolute standards, nor absolute moral truths.[18] Against these central theses of the

Enlightenment he developed his own system of thought which, neither complete nor fully consistent, nevertheless contained a unifying outlook.

Herder was an empiricist, deeply influenced by the development of the natural sciences of his own time, and he tried to apply scientific method, albeit a scientific method *sui generis*, to interpretation in the humanities. He was not a subjectivist but "believed in objective standards of judgement that are derived from understanding the life and purpose of individual societies and are themselves objective historical structures."[19] His position was anti-mechanistic, and he rejected the artificial dissection of man into mutually independent component parts. Man, for him, was indivisible. "Herder's utterances can be reduced to the principle that everything which man undertakes to perform, be it by word or by deed or in any other way, originates from the total united powers of the personality."[20] His world was organic, dynamic, unitary. It could not be analysed by means of some preconceived system of categories. It had to be understood, and to understand the world of man was to understand it historically, genetically. Each period in each place had to be studied according to its own spirit and complex unity. Understanding, or *Verstehen*, for Herder, was to give reason to or justification for activities or events in question. It was almost synonymous with empathy.[21] This kind of understanding was possible "because there are some qualities that are universal in man."[22] He believed in a "universal human essence", but he defined neither this essence nor the universal qualities beyond stating that they are empirical and not occult. Herder also denounced individualism but not *Individualität*. "The individual, for him, is inescapably a member of some group";[23] the "notion of a wholly solitary— as opposed to an artificially self-isolated—man is to him . . . unintelligible."[24]

To finish the summary of Herder's central tenets which are relevant to this study, there is the ideal that is latent in man, towards the achievement of which he continually strives, called *Humanität*. "This is a notoriously vague term, in Herder and the *Aufklärung* generally, connoting harmonious development of all immortal souls towards universally valid goals: reason, freedom, toleration, mutual love and respect between individuals and societies, as well as physical and spiritual health, finer perceptions, dominion over the earth, the harmonious realisation of all that God has implanted in His noblest work and made in His own image. This is a characteristically all-inclusive, general and optimistic formula of Weimar humanism, which Herder does, indeed, adopt, particularly in his later works, but which he does not seem to have used (for it has no precise connotation) as a universal criterion either of explanation or of value."[25]

To investigate the influence Herder exerted, either directly or indirectly, is an almost intractable problem. He inspired German Romanticism and Idealism,[26] and references to his writings are to be found in the works of Schleiermacher, Boeckh, Humboldt, Droysen, Ranke and Savigny. Although he does not feature in the indexes of either Menger's *Grundsätze* or the *Untersuchungen*, all those just mentioned do, and it seems highly improbable that a scholar of such breadth in his reading like Menger should not have been familiar with Herder. However that may be, Menger's thought is so deeply influenced by the *verstehende* (and thus Herderian)[27] tradition that the omission of references to the one particular author can safely be ignored without jeopardising the argument.

Although the German Romantic movement and German Idealist philosophy did not come into their own until about the beginning of the nineteenth century, the tendencies and movements of which they were the culmination had their origins in the beginning of the eighteenth century. For our purposes, German Idealist philosophy will be of interest only inasmuch as the Romantics—amongst whom we find Savigny, the founder of the Historical school and one of the teachers of Roscher, and, in the final analysis, Menger—absorbed certain of its aspects, mainly from the systems of Fichte and Schelling, while rejecting others quite violently, essentially the system of Hegel. I shall return to the differences and similarities of these two movements shortly.

Both the rationalistic Enlightenment and the anti-rationalistic reaction against it took different forms in Britain, France and Germany, although the central themes were very much the same in all three countries. In Britain, the Enlightenment as a *geistige* movement had as its political counterpart the constitutional freedom of the bourgeoisie, the church and the press.[28] In France, it eventually led to the revolution. But in Germany, it went unaccompanied by any real change in the political, economic or social status or rights of the bourgeoisie, who had to rely for any kind of progress on such "enlightened" absolutist monarchs as Frederick the Great of Prussia. Economic and social relations retained their feudal character until well into the nineteenth century,[29] and reforms were introduced from above without any political base in the emerging and developing bourgeoisie. Another salient feature of the German Enlightenment was the virtual absence among its leading figures of atheism which was so typical of the French movement.[30] Apart from its rationalism, the belief that even the most complex things can be explained by appeal to reason, it was also characterised by an optimism, which it took from Leibniz's doctrine of this being the best of all possible worlds, and a cosmopolitanism, which was an attempt to overcome the fragmentation of Germany[31] and to rid oneself of the narrow-minded nationalism that acted as a fetter to free thought.[32]

Long before the German Romantic movement, France and Britain experienced their own anti-rationalistic reaction which, again, was accompanied by concrete political demands to counter the influence of the rationalism of the Enlightenment (*viz.* Rousseau). In Germany, the anti-rationalist movement, from the *Empfindsamkeit* to the *Romantik* and beyond, fulfilled a dual function: on the one hand, it voiced the rejection of the rule of reason to the exclusion of the emotions; on the other hand, it allowed the bourgeoisie to give vent to its opposition to the absolutist regimes. Because of the lack of a power base this opposition expressed itself exclusively, and much more vehemently than in other countries, in literary, artistic and scientific forms.

By the middle of the eighteenth century, while the Enlightenment was still in full swing, the *Empfindsamkeit*[33] provided such an outlet through a sentimental, self-sufficient and self-centered enthusiasm.[34] This psychologistic, introspectionist theme had, of course, Pietistic roots, and in it we can already discern to what extent subjectivism was endemic in German thought in general.[35] We shall see it finally moving to the center of the stage in the wake of Romanticism.

Another point, though, should be mentioned: It is notoriously difficult to separate out elements which pertain to one stream of thought or *Weltanschauung* and not to another. Sometimes contradictory if not mutually exclusive interpretations of one and the same term seem possible, and even people seem to belong simultaneously to two opposing camps. Herder is at times classified as nationalist, even as a precursor of fascism, and at other times as an "enlightened" humanist.[36] Goethe represented the *Sturm und Drang* and the German *Klassik*. Pietism shared its introspection with the *Empfindsamkeit* and its opposition to dogma and authoritarianism with the Enlightenment. The Enlightenment is usually called the philosophy of the emerging class, the bourgeoisie, but because of the socio-political situation in Germany, the same can be said about its anti-thesis, Romanticism.

From the *Empfindsamkeit* emanated the next movement, the *Sturm und Drang* epitomised by Goethe's *Werther*. This movement exalted the creative genius, the extra-ordinarily gifted individual who was considered greater than the reasoning mind. Nature, having been rationalised and demystified by the Enlightenment, was deified: The utopia of a "natural" society for "natural" man, who was placed above the educated, cultured man, gave expression to the frustrations of a politically impotent bourgeoisie condemned to inactivity. The tension between the (emotional) experience of one's finite limits and the feeling for the infinite world of nature formed the Faustian *Lebensgefühl*. Cosmopolitanism was foregone for the sake of nationalism—but a nationalism more akin to that of the nations of the third world in our time than that of the early twentieth century.[37] In the realm of esthetics and culture (conceived of as organic in contrast to civilisation, which was regarded as man-made and rational), the Hellenic ideal was thrown overboard, and the old Nordic and Germanic traditions were re-discovered. This movement was far more radical than the *Empfindsamkeit* and literally swept the nation (immediately after the publication of Goethe's *Werther* a number of suicides modelled on Werther's were reported).[38] But the *Sturm und Drang* was shortlived, and from it emanated the *Klassik*. This movement returned to the Hellenic ideal, restored nature from the chaos it had been thrown into during the *Sturm und Drang* period and returned to reasoning, to more systematic thinking.[39] At this stage, post-Kantian idealism and the Romantic movement were about to unfold.

The very nature of Romantic thought in Germany between 1798 and 1835 makes it well-nigh impossible to characterise it satisfactorily in one sentence. The core of it can be said to be the perennial and never completed struggle to bring the individual soul into harmony with the infinite and endlessly changing world of nature.[40] The Romantics were, of course, building on all the themes discussed above, though they did not simply add their own ingredients to the whole brew but moulded all the elements into a fairly unified outlook.

Romantic thought is lodged in a rift. It thrives on the tension between polar opposites—the finite and the infinite, reason and emotion, the empirical and the spiritual—and it expresses a yearning for death, for the dissolution of the personality. For the Romantics, the polarities of which the world is made up are absolutely necessary. Furthermore, they are conditional upon each other and not conceived of as antinomies as they were in the Enlightenment.[41] Their conception of the world as chaotic[42] and their desire to escape that chaos, to resolve the opposites, resulted in a detached attitude towards reality which expressed itself through irony.[43] Schelling's *Identitäts- philosophie* served the Romantics' purpose very well. Life was conceived of as the "emanation of the absolute spirit in the world"; a spiritual content was discovered in all reality.[44] In the identity of *Natur* and *Geist*, the polarities were to be superseded.[45]

The world, therefore, is ever changing; it is not static, mechanistic but developing, coming into being, an evolving, living organism. Every event is unique in such a world; there is no room for eternal laws of nature; and life, past and present, has to be understood historically. In sharp contrast to the Enlightenment, human nature is not conceived of as being perennially the same but open to change,[46] and history does not progress in a line or serve a purpose. One arrived at an understanding, a *Verstehen*, of history and reality through imagination, intuition and *Phantasie*.[47] The Romantics were epistemological irrationalists, although it might be preferable to speak more broadly of their approach to knowledge than of epistemology since the latter term—at least in current usage—implies too much systematisation and conceptualisation to be compatible with their outlook.[48] This rejection of reason and calculation, of clearly defined concepts and of systematisation, harks back to the chaos and polarities referred to earlier. There is no clear demarcation between art and science, religion and philosophy, irrational and rational elements. Through the postulated identity of the physical with the ideal world "man's imagination becomes pre-condition for Nature to be at all."[49] Since reality is chaotic and infinite, man, being finite, eternally yearns for the perfect, the infinite, yet will never be to reach it.

I have hardly mentioned anything about the Austrian school of economics as yet, and one might wonder how all this and the remainder of this essay will eventually relate to the methodology and the economic theory of the school. The analysis of Menger's methodology and theory and of Wieser's and Böhm-Bawerk's departure from Menger's original position discussed in the later essays must be considered in conjunction with the intellectual background presented here, but to show the direction in which the argument will be moving, let us look very briefly at how Austrian economic theory fits in with what has been said about the Romantic movement so far. The yearning for the infinite and the conception of life as made up of polarities find their equivalent expressions in Austrian theory in the absence of both full information and a general equilibrium system. Individuals attempt to maximise utility subject to their budget constraints, that is, they try to reach their personal equilibrium positions on the basis of incomplete information; their economic life is spent gathering ever more comprehensive information to improve their individual optimisation processes, but the economy as a whole does not move in any predetermined direction (in contrast to the Walrasian economy which permanently strives towards a general equilibrium). The Romantic cult of the individual—that the end of all activity is the perfection of man (but man as an *Individuum*, not mankind in general)—and the notion that "more important than the achievement of a perfect result is the striving for perfection"[50] constitute important aspects of the *weltanschauliche* background of the Austrian system. It is particularly noteworthy, in this context, that the Austrians constructed not an anti-equilibrium system or a dis-equilibrium system but a non-equilibrium system.

The relativism implied by the Romantic position together with the religious component inherent in all German thinking—with the Pietistic strand being of foremost importance—eventually drove the Romantics towards dogmatism and an authoritarian religion, Catholicism, in order to find a direction for or just a foothold in their lives and their thinking. But it also it led to the cult of the individual, the exaltation of the poetic genius, to extreme, often absolute, subjectivity. This individualism, however, must not be confused with the individualism of the Enlightenment which contained currents of universal equality and similar notions.[51] The Romantic individual is unique, different, unequal, complex and, ultimately, undescribable: *Individuum est ineffabile.* Here we are dealing not so much with individualism as with individuality, *Individualität.* True individuality is the indivisible unity, the metaphysical core of a person. It is "not under the rule of time and space" as is the superficial appearance, the personality.[52]

But the individual is even more. The Romantics' idolatry of the individual and their psychologistic, introspective propensity combine with the supposed identity of the spiritual and the physical, mind and world, to form the view that each individual is not only an indispensable part of the organic whole but a microcosm, a perfect image of the macrocosm.[53] Subjectivity is carried even further. Precisely because of the fundamental premise of the identity of *Natur* with *Geist* which, as we have seen, is inextricably tied up with the notion of man's imagination creating the world, there is no need to look outside oneself for evidence. The universe lies within, and exploration of the outside world leads to the same result as exploration of one's own mind, one's inner self.[54]

In this strand of thought, the heritage of the set of ideas developed by Leibniz in the *Monadology* is quite obvious. To take but one example: The monad as the indivisible final element, a microcosm mirroring the macrocosm, has no "windows" and, thus, not being susceptible to outside influences is totally self-contained. If one considers all the central features together—identity and subjectivity, the exaltation of the poetic genius and the relativity of all things, the individual as creator and the indecomposability of the whole (all of these being different facets of the same all-embracing totality)—

the conclusion that "truth is perfect subjectivity" comes as no surprise. In fact, "such notions are an invitation to limitless utterance, for if the poet's language is the language in which Nature conducts all its business, anything the poet happens to say will necessarily correspond to some aspect of natural truth."[55]

The Romantic's pre-occupation with history as a non-linear development, as an organic growth process, led to a search for the origin of that process, the root wherefrom their contemporary world had evolved. In the course of this investigation they came to glorify the Middle Ages as the Golden Age, in part as a reaction to the Enlightenment and what they deemed to have been its natural outcome, the French Revolution. This, in turn, led to the glorification of everything Germanic and medieval as opposed to everything French and Napoleonic.[56] This reverence for everything naturally grown (as opposed to man made) not only found expression in political conservatism but also led to a tendency to withdraw entirely from active political life, to oppose change and to justify and legitimise the existing. Ultimately, it led to the *Restaurationspolitik*.[57] All of this blends with the above-mentioned yearning for the infinite, the unobtainable. It was the expression of nostalgia which was temporarily overcome through irony. In summary, the basic (spiritual and ideological) outlook, the *Weltanschauung*, of the Romantic movement can be characterised as conservative or even as reactionary (although there were some progressive Romantics). Romanticism was something like a spiritual counterrevolution to the Enlightenment.[58]

The fact that the fundamental sensations and emotions of the Romantics were based on polarities and rooted in the desire for the unobtainable did not lead to too much clarity in their expressions or to too much consistency in their thought. But the absence of "clear and distinct ideas" was precisely the point of the whole exercise. Nevertheless, it is worth pointing out some of these apparent paradoxes.

At first glance, the community (*Gemeinschaft*, not *Gemeinde*) appears to be placed above the individual. The latter was part of a "grander totality"; the personality of the individual could only develop and take shape within a community (this tendency prevailed during the later Romantic period; the earlier Romantics were far more individualistic and subjectivistic).[59] In general, though, the community was actually more a *Gemeinde* than a *Gemeinschaft*, a collection of individuals whose main goal of unfettered self-realisation and development of individuality made social co-operation and the development of a social conscience quite impossible.[60]

This also has some important implications for one of the key characteristics of Austrian theory and methodology, for methodological individualism. The environment appropriate to this concept is the rationalism of the Enlightenment with its notion of universal equality of all human beings. This is represented, for instance, in Walrasian theory. Within the Romantic framework, the social, collectivistic aspect is merely superficial; the main emphasis is on the individual. But it would be erroneous to suppose that the application of methodological individualism is compatible with or justifiable in the

Romantic frame of mind. If we agree that, however abstract the analysis, we must not separate essential features, then we have to take into account not only that the individual and the totality are inseparable aspects of the same reality but also that individuality is indivisible. Therefore, we cannot separate the whole into distinct elements and, in order to reconstitute it, simply join the elements together again (which would be required procedure according to the definition of methodological individualism). Analytically— to remain faithful to the Romantic framework—we have to proceed within the hermeneutic circle to reach an ever deeper understanding of whatever we choose to deal with. We may talk of the "dialektische Bezogenheit von Individualitätssinn und Totalitätsbetrachtung"[61]—another of those Romantic polarities—but we must not mechanically divide the whole into its constituent elements. A final point: Although it is perfectly proper, for a Romantic social scientist, to internalise social relations in order to produce a Robinson Crusoe fully equipped to deal with all kinds of unforeseen (social) circumstances, it is highly doubtful whether such an internalisation is correct scientific procedure in the realm of methodological individualism.

Romanticism was essentially a Protestant movement. When its members finally became politically active (during the period of the French occupation and the wars of liberation) and suggested and attempted to implement political programmes, they did so first and foremost in Protestant countries. Romantic individualism was quite the opposite of the hierarchical structure of the Roman Catholic church. Nevertheless, many Romantics showed great sympathy with Catholicism, and quite a few of the leading exponents actually converted, partly because of a need for guidance and authority because of being adrift in a sea of relativism but also because of the glorification of the Middle Ages. Romanticism, after all, was a deeply religious, albeit pantheistic, movement. In the eyes of the Romantics, "religion was the breath of medieval civilisation, and the Church gave the human mind ideals of supreme beauty and truth."[62] The decay of this idealised civilisation apparently had set in with the Reformation and modern rationalism. Their constant preoccupation with death was another factor which drove the Romantics towards Christian dogma. There are implications of this for the Austrian school, too, for Vienna became the center of the (Catholic) late Romantic movement after Adam Müller, Friedrich Schlegel[63] and Friedrich Gentz[64] had gone there "in order to win over the Austrian state in support of their ideas."[65]

In spite of the generally conservative character of the Romantic movement, the initial rejection of Christian dogma, which was quite in keeping with the outright rejection of the natural law doctrine, was a liberating and progressive move since Germany, in contrast to France and Britain, had only experienced the authoritarian version of this doctrine.[66] The Enlightenment with its inherently democratising tendency and with reason as the highest authority, had become the natural *Weltanschauung* of emerging capitalism and of the class which was aspiring to power, the bourgeoisie. This was essentially true in France and Britain. In Germany, though, the bourgeoisie generally did not look towards the future but basically turned inwards and towards the past.

It could be claimed, therefore, that Romanticism, with its retrospective and introspective approach to life was as representative of the outlook of the German bourgeoisie as the world of thought of the Enlightenment. As I have pointed out, this posture coupled with a powerful, authoritarian, absolutist political regime channelled most of the Germans' creative, frustrated energy into the arts, sciences and literary activities. Throughout German history attempts at liberation from such regimes kept failing—in 1815, when the *Deutscher Bund* established under the leadership of Austria's Metternich inaugurated the period of the *Restauration*, when reforms which had been introduced from above anyhow were virtually nullified, if not in the letter then at least in practice; in 1848, when the bourgeois uprising was squashed and all hopes accumulated during thirty years of slowly growing self-confidence and awareness of their importance were blown out and nothing was left but a demoralised, powerless bourgeoisie. Only towards the end of the century, together with the take-off of the German economy, did things eventually start to change. But then it was already too late because the old conflict between aristocracy and bourgeoisie, which had been in the forefront in the first half of the nineteenth century had become an anachronism. The bourgeoisie, without having their own position established firmly, now had to face the rising challenge of the proletariat.

The most influential group of the German bourgeoisie was the civil servants (*Beamte*). Since they were entirely dependent on the state—and, conversely, the state could only rule through them—the most they could possibly attempt was a reform of the worst excesses of the *Obrigkeitsstaat*, but they would never think of replacing it with a radically democratic regime. This intention was expressed in a variety of ways: Freedom of thought was afforded utmost importance; actual political freedom was only secondary. All political demands were subordinated to one overriding goal, the education of the individual. Rousseau had such a formidable influence on the Romantic movement but no effect on its political programme: Although the educational ideals laid down in *Emile* found wide acceptance in Germany, Rousseau's ideals concerning a new, democratic order of society found virtually no acceptance there at all. Even his educational ideals did not penetrate German society fully: The education of the officers' corps—which the bourgeoisie was unable to enter to any significant degree—was the basis of government authority and remained untouched by any of those ideals. Finally, political liberalism in Germany embraced the outlook of the Enlightenment, and thus was naturally oriented towards France, but it still retained conservative elements, elements which were closely associated with Romanticism, and in this respect its political orientation was towards Austria and Russia. This inclination was reinforced by the turn the French Revolution took in 1792–93.[67]

So far, I have discussed only the "emotional" reaction to the Enlightenment which culminated in the vast and all-pervading movement, Romanticism.

This survey is by no means intended to provide a representative or even an adequate picture of that movement. Its purpose is merely to highlight in context certain features which are indispensable for a more comprehensive analysis of the Austrian school. Simultaneous with this reaction was a more systematic and "reasonable" one—German Idealist philosophy.

Romanticism and Idealist Philosophy

In the philosophical field, according to the Romantics, Descartes and his epigones had got it all wrong. Dualism, mechanism, the sterility of "clear and distinct ideas" and a rigid determinism had set modern philosophy off in the wrong direction.[68] Not Kantian transcendental philosophy but Aristotelian self-propelling, immanent teleology and the idealistic development of Kant's critiques furnished the philosophical trimmings of Romantic thought.[69] Of the great Idealist philosophers, Schelling stood closest to the Romantics; Hegel profoundly disagreed with them, and Fichte always resisted their interpretation of his fundamental Idealist concept, the ego. The reason for discussing German Idealism now is not merely for the sake of completeness but also because the Romantics borrowed quite heavily from both Fichte and Schelling. One does, therefore, get a deeper understanding not only of Romanticism but also, by implication, of the concepts which Menger retained in his writings (I shall discuss only the aspects which are pertinent to these). On the other hand, Hegel's (and also Fichte's) criticism of the Romantics puts Menger's concepts into proper perspective since it enables us to follow a kindred thought developing along different lines—in the case of Hegel, along more scientific (in the meaning of the German term *wissenschaftlich*) or "objective" lines. Given this perspective, we shall ultimately be able to see in which ways Menger's theory and methodology are, in fact, expressions of a certain set of value judgements.

The Romantics shared many themes which were central to their thought with the Idealist philosophers. Despite all the differences and disagreements, the ideas behind such notions as dialectics, holism, the infinite and Historicism were common to both strands of thought. These ideas seemed to have been in the air at the time, so to speak (at least in the German air).[70] The dialectic took a rigorous form in (systematic) Idealist philosophy, be it in the reflexive form of Fichte's ego and non-ego or in the logic developed by Hegel—in either, the thesis determined and grew out of its antithesis, this contradiction only being resolved in the next, higher form, the synthesis—the (anti-systematic) Romantic counterpart was the thinking in polarities. Closely related to this mode of thinking about reality is the holism of both movements.[71] The Idealist *Ganzheitsfanatiker*[72] attemped to connect everything in a systematic context in which the individual was inconceivable and incomprehensible in total isolation (if this was to be the final step in an analysis); the Romantics expressed this strand of their thought as a poetic unity or fusion of the finite and the infinite. This "feeling for the infinite" was shared by the Idealist philosophers, too, as in Fichte's "pure ego" or in Hegel's "absolute spirit."[73] Finally, the Idealistic as well as the Romantic world had to be understood historically, dynamically (this in turn goes back to the first similarity pointed out above). The importance of Hegel's Historicism especially will be discussed shortly.

Two notions of Fichte's philosophy—in fact, the central ones—are of immediate concern to us: the ego and the absolute truth and certainty of moral judgement.[74] Fichte thought of himself, and he was by no means alone in doing so, as the immediate successor of Kant. Even more, he was convinced that his version of Kant's system was superior to Kant's own since he had gotten rid of such "extraneous" elements as the thing-in-itself and the synthetic-a-priori by reducing everything to the ultimate founding principle wherefrom everything emanated and could be deduced: the pure ego. This basic principle was "borrowed" by the Romantics and distorted to suit their own purpose. Fichte's subjective Idealism was an attempt to bring to completion the trend of modern philosophy which had started with Descartes's *cogito ergo sum* by putting the *sum*, or more precisely the *ego*, at the center of the stage. But it was not the individual, empirical ego which Fichte was concerned with because this would irresistibly lead to a slide into solipsism. To avoid precisely this danger, he tried to work out the general nature of individuality. The Romantics, however, reduced Fichte's ego to the simple, individual, empirical ego.[75] Furthermore, Fichte's philosophy of the pure ego emphasised its essentially active, creative character. The spiritual and material world did not exist outside and independent of the ego. It was, to paraphrase Haym, nothing but the creative spirit itself in infinite productions and reproductions. And it is in this sense that Fichte's *Wissenschaftslehre* has to be understood: not as theory or philosophy of science but as the philosophical theory of the "consciousness of the spirit itself."[76] In reducing the general to the singular and empirical ego, the Romantics also removed this active, creative element in order to accommodate their meditating, passive, introspective approach to life.

In contrast to Kant, whose first concern it had been to investigate the philosophical and epistemological foundations of Newtonian physics, exploring the relationship between free will and the world of nature only afterwards, in Fichte's system the problems of morality assumed primary importance over the material world. By putting Kant on "ego-centric" feet Fichte inevitably also reformulated the categorical imperative, "So act that you could think of the maxim of your will as a universal (eternal) law for yourself."[77] For this to be valid, Fichte needed an absolute criterion which could be used to judge infallibly between right and wrong. It is obvious that no external authority would have sufficed, and he found the criterion in conscience (*Gewissen*). For Fichte, conscience was the "immediate awareness of a particular obligation. And from this definition it obviously follows that conscience never errs and cannot err", for if it is immediate awareness it cannot be non-awareness.[78] In other words, conscience calls upon itself as the ultimate judge, and according to its definition its own judgement cannot possibly be false. This, nevertheless, did not exclude the possibility of acting wrongly.[79]

Fichte's elaboration of Kantian philosophy not only played a pivotal role as a link between systematic philosophy and Romantic thought in general but also stood at the beginning of Romantic hermeneutics, which was to culminate in Schleiermacher's work.[80] But the importance of Fichte's work for our discussion lies in the fact that it formed the *geistesgeschichtliche* background for Menger's conception of the epistemological status of the truth of his "exact" theory. To see this we simply have to compare the role of conscience in Fichte's philosophy with the Romantics' conclusion that "truth is perfect subjectivity"[81] and with Menger's claim that "exact" laws—which were, ultimately, arrived at by introspection—are infallibly true.[82]

Schelling was first an enthusiastic follower of Fichte's philosophy and of Spinoza's systematisation. He then developed his *Naturphilosophie*, and within a few years that was transformed into the *Identitätsphilosophie*, identifying the systems of nature with the system of the mind, or absolute spirit. Thus he provided the philosophical backing for the Romantics' explorations of nature through soul-searching and meditation. In later years Schelling moved even closer to the Romantic position by abandoning systematic philosophising (because it apparently curtailed the creative potential of the scientist) by adopting more poetic modes of expression and, generally, by switching from science to esthetics.

Fichte's pre-occupation with the moral world led him to "deduce"[83] nature from the ego so as to suit the ego's moral requirements. This deduction was, therefore, teleological, with the absolute ego being the final cause. Schelling objected, not to the teleological character of Fichte's philosophy, but to the fact that the final object of that process lay outside nature itself. His poetic inclination led him to view nature as a living, evolving organism which was an end in itself. He could not, therefore, accept Fichte's approach but placed an independent philosophy of nature, a "speculative physics", next to Fichte's transcendental philosophy. But neither did he want to abandon Fichte's unifying, fundamental principle since there could be only one absolute, unconditional first principle, the ego. In order to be able to maintain the dualism between Fichte's transcendental philosophy and his own independent philosophy of nature, in which he declared that "the system of nature is at the same time the system of our mind (*unseres Geistes*)" and that "nature is visible spirit (*Geist*), spirit is invisible nature",[84] Schelling had to transplant the ego onto nature in a free, imaginative way—using the poet's licence, so to speak. Thus, nature was raised to the status of an "alter ego" and became analogous to the spirit (*Geist*).

This was the situation in 1797–98. Four years later, Schelling's philosophy of identity had been completed, and in it he had developed what Haym called the Romantic world formula. The earlier dualism between transcendental philosophy and the philosophy of nature had been overcome by making the ego the basic principle. In an unconscious state it created nature, and therefore the philosophy of nature, while practical philosophy, which was the philosophy of history, was created by a conscious ego through acts of the will. The identity between the system of nature and the system of spirit (*Geist*) therefore rested in the ego, in the identity between conscious and unconscious activity. The system as a whole was completed by esthetic activity. The keystone of the whole system, then, was the philosophy of art. In the development and completion of this system, Schelling had finally moved from criticism to dogmatism since instead of grounding the subject/object identity in the ego, the ultimate principle,[85] he had started off by simply positing this identity.

Hegel was the system builder par excellence; not only in this respect but in many others he was—in his intentions, at least—the direct opposite of the Romantic movement. There was great affinity in the underlying themes of the writings of both Hegel and the Romantics, and as Hegel did not always manage to live up to his own aspirations, Haym could actually call him a Romantic.[86] Movement, process, the finite and the infinite, the spiritual nature of the world, development, Historicism, the identity between subject and object, the unity of the one and the many, all of these were shared concepts. But in spite of all these affinities, Hegel differed fundamentally from the Romantics: in his insistence on systematic philosophising, on logical rigour and on the determinateness of the (historical) process (but not the single event); in his embracing reason and method and in his rejection of any kind of psychologism, introspection, intuition or mysticism as a basis for the derivation of scientific knowledge; in his derogation of the Middle Ages as the "unhappy consciousness" as opposed to the Romantics' eulogisation of it as the Golden Age. Even if he did not satisfy his own criteria in his completed (and unfinished) work, at least he laid the foundations for a scientific (*wissenschaftliche*) treatment of the central themes of the *Geisteswissenschaften*. And in that respect he, as it were, was the living manifestation of his own method: His work represents the negation—the second step in his dialectical triad—of Romantic thought, the driving force in the "historical spirit" which did not let it come to rest until both, thesis and antithesis (and their differences with respect to many other positions, too), became negated again.[87]

It is precisely Hegel's antithetical role that makes him important for our understanding of Menger. Here I shall briefly deal with two aspects—Hegel's essentialism and Historicism—and try to relate them to Menger without going into too much detail since Menger's methodology is dealt with in depth in Essay II.

"Das Bekannte ist darum, weil es bekannt ist, noch nicht erkannt" is the opening phrase of Hegel's attack on common sense as the basis of scientific knowledge.[88] What appeals to the senses is a necessary, though not at all a sufficient, condition for scientific knowledge. Only after consciousness has travelled the route mapped out in Hegel's *Phänomenologie* will it arrive at absolute knowledge; will the real be identical with the ideal; will the object be taken up by, raised to, encompassed in (*aufgehoben sein in*) the subject.[89] Kant's dictum that the laws of nature are only constructions of the mind—that is, they regulate merely the phenomenal world (because we have no access to the noumena, the "essences")—after it had been taken through its Fichtean, subjectivist stage, has now been transformed into an absolute, objective Idealism. The implication is that "experience and the results of the empirical sciences have to be in agreement with the results of constructive thought. Not epistemological distinction but speculative construction" is thus encouraged.[90] This stance is aptly summarised by the aphorism that if the facts do not agree with the theory, so much the worse for the facts. This essentialist approach, the idea of an objective spirit which exists beyond reality as we see it, the "duplication of reality", entails the danger of deriving pseudoscientific solutions—or better, pseudo-solutions to scientific problems.[91] The growing awareness of this danger led to the rather rapid eclipse of Idealist philosophy and also of Romanticism. Realism became the new spirit of the time, not only because of the spectacular successes of the natural sciences but also because of the changes in the political, social and economic climate.[92] This trend became manifest in not only the sciences but all walks of life, the arts, literature and the *Geisteswissenschaften*.

Menger and the other founders of the Austrian school set out to do precisely the same—to avoid metaphysical speculation in the reconstruction of political economy. Nothing but empirical facts were to be its basis, facts which were immediately available and obvious to anybody who wanted to take the trouble to look for them, and the high-flying Idealist spirit was to be replaced by sound common sense.[93] But Menger and his school were not able to proceed beyond paying lip service to these ideals. Evidence for this can be found in just about all the methodological and theoretical writings of Menger, Wieser and Böhm-Bawerk. Menger's insistence on the superiority of his "exact" laws over empirical reality, his striving for an "exact" determination of the values, the essences underlying the surface phenomena of prices, and the teleological structure of his economic process all make him as much an essentialist as Hegel. (This, of course, is no mere coincidence; at the root of it are the Aristotelian principles which are common to both.) But this does not make Menger a Hegelian. On the contrary, as we shall see in Essay II, his spiritual home is the world of Romanticism and the Historical School. And this makes him by far less scientific (*wissenschaftlich*) than Hegel, for while Hegel at least strove to encompass history and objective empirical evidence—such as law, the state, the economy, art and literature, religious, scientific and philosophical thought, all readily available and accessible to anyone who cared to look for them—in his system, Menger derived his certain and true "exact" laws through introspection.[94] This dogmatic insistence on introspection and on methodological individualism has remained characteristic of Austrian methodology to this day.[95]

Menger conceived of himself as working within the mainstream of German economic thought, and at the time German political economy was historical economics, dominated by Roscher and his school. Menger's complex attitude to Roscher is discussed at length in Essay II, but I would like to note here that he had a deep respect for Roscher throughout his life while he came to feel nothing but loathing for the younger historical economists around

Schmoller, particularly after the *Methodenstreit* had been unleashed. (The *Methodenstreit* is sufficiently documented in the literature, so there is no need to go into it here.)[96] Roscher's historical school of economics was a direct off-shoot of Savigny's historical school of jurisprudence and thus intimately related to the Romantic movement. (Menger was very critical of the way it had developed out of the historical law school. He was far more partial to the latter—despite his protestations to the contrary—and therefore much closer to the Romantic spirit than the historical economists themselves.)[97] A major difference between Roscher's conception of the nature of sound economics and Savigny's conception of the nature of sound jurisprudence was signified by the role attributed to Hegel. The members of the historical school of law were the most important and the most outspoken opponents of Hegel.[98] Roscher, on the other hand, devoted a major part of his chapter "The Immediate Preparatory Work for Historical National Economy" in his *Geschichte der National-Oekonomik in Deutschland* (1874) to Hegel as the philosopher of history par excellence.[99]

We have thus come back to Hegel and his relevance for our interpretation of Menger. Indeed, if we look closely at Menger's *Grundsätze*, we can find this concept of (historical) development almost everywhere, most obviously and convincingly applied in the chapter on money. But it is not this aspect I want to turn to. True, Menger developed his concepts historically, but he also *expressis verbis* denounced all attempts at philosophising about the progress of history.[100] His affinity to Hegel goes deeper than that. Hegel's world is in permanent flux, and the progress of consciousness to absolute knowledge is an entelechial process, a teleological process which is self-propelling, in which the driving force is immanent to the process itself. This contribution, of course, did not originate with Hegel. Entelechy was a characteristic of the systems of all three Idealist philosophers.[101] The history of this concept can be traced back at least to Heraclitus, and it was Aristotle who first brought out the genetic character of the correspondence between essence and appearance. In Hegel's system, this correspondence takes the form of the dialectical development of essence and appearance,[102] and the driving force behind—or better, within—this dialectical development is *Bedürfnis*.[103] The basis for this *Bedürfnis* lies in the awareness of the incompleteness of the finite as opposed to the infinite, a yearning for completeness. The finite thus feels a need, or an urge, to proceed from one step to the next in a dialectical movement. This *Bedürfnis*, or urge, is contained within the notion of the dialectical process of history. It is what makes the process entelechial.

Menger's world resembles Hegel's in a very important aspect: It operates through the same mechanism. To be sure, there is also a fundamental difference: Hegel's world is ultimately one of the spirit[104] while Menger's world is literally much more down to earth. Its substance is material as well as spiritual and requires only that agents *have* spirit. But the driving force in Menger's world is the same entelechial process as in Hegel's: Menger's economic system is driven by *Bedürfnis* and *Bedürfnisbefriedigung* is what makes Menger's economy tick. Menger's concept of *Bedürfnis* has its (meta-physical) roots in the shortcomings of the finite *vis-à-vis* the infinite. Menger's economic process, containing its *telos* and thus being driven by this internal force, is entelechial. Although this is quite clear, to my mind at least, in the first edition of the *Grundsätze*, the second (posthumous) edition of 1923 leaves absolutely no doubt about the validity of these conclusions. A new first chapter deals only with the nature of *Bedürfnis*, and true to the spirit of the Romantic movement and the Historical School, the concept received a biologistic interpretation. But apart from this interpretation of *Bedürfnis*, the likenesses in Menger's and Hegel's conceptual frameworks—if only in their essentialist and historicist aspects—are stunning. Even more revealing are the differences of the two systems in these two aspects.[105]

Historicism

We have come a fair part of the way in the attempt to lay bare the roots of the Austrian school. Most elements of the *geistesgeschichtliche* background which are indispensable for the analysis of the school have been introduced, and the main objective has almost been achieved. The stage has been set, in broad outline at least, and the plot has been hinted at. Before completing the picture let summarise where we are now.

The development of German thought from about 1750 to 1830 and its relation to the socio-political conditions has been traced, and we have an impression of the peculiarities and causes which set German thought off from related movements, for example, in France and Britain. Characteristics of the German Enlightenment and of the reaction to it have been spelled out, and two movements which both took their inspiration from Herder have been discussed. A whole world of thought existed in two guises. On the one hand, there was the "emotional" reaction which culminated in Romanticism—the main strand of thought which we shall have to follow if we want to truly understand Menger. On the other hand, certain aspects of the systematic and "reasonable" reaction to the Enlightenment allow us to view the issues which will be taken up in Essay II in proper perspective. The spiritualisation (*Vergeistigung*) of the world, subjectivism, introspection, Historicism, essentialism and holism have been introduced in their respective contexts. Dealing with the same subject matter as the Idealist philosophers, but in its idiosyncratic way, Romanticism has been aptly described as a "biologistic-emanatistic distortion" of Idealism.[106]

Both Romantic and Idealist thought formed the basis of the new, peculiarly German approach to the moral sciences, Historicism.[107] Two instances of this approach to the *Geisteswissenschaften* are discussed: first, historiography— here, the reaction was against Hegel's speculation and anti-empiricism— personified by Niebuhr, Ranke and Droysen; second, the Historical School, which repudiated, among other things, the absolutist claim of Hegel's objective spirit by means of organicist-biologistic counterarguments. The leaders of this school were Savigny and Grimm. In contrast to the historiographers, they were far more deeply influenced by Romanticism than by Idealist philosophy. From the programmes developed by Savigny, we shall finally arrive at the Austrian position, but to get this position into proper perspective, we shall have to briefly consider the historical school of economics. In this discussion, none of Menger's writings are used as sources of reference or information since the purpose is to obtain an independent (and, one hopes, objective) assessment of the *geistesgeschichtliche* background against which we can judge the Austrian school. To use Menger's writings for this task would be self-defeating.

In spite of the disagreements among the practitioners of Historicism about the need for abstraction or conceptualisation (which, in the opinion of most of them, was a dangerous practise because it was too exposed to the pernicious influence of speculation) or the appropriate extent and scope of Historicist arguments, they still shared a common outlook despite the varying requirements of their respective disciplines. They depicted the world very much as a biological entity and interpreted the spiritualisation of nature in biologistic terms. They thought in terms of organic development, looked for organic laws and principles of life and favoured analogies with the life of plants.[108] This organicist approach displayed two tendencies: Not only were these laws and principles peculiar to individual peoples, countries and ages (this aspect is usually referred to as relativism), but they also operated subconsciously and were not open to external manipulation. This latter aspect contained an inherent tendency towards quietism which, coupled with a demand for respect and reverence of every grown, organic, "natural" life, inescapably led to conservatism.[109] Indeed, even though not all Historicists shared this quietist attitude, they all were conservative.

Barthold Georg Niebuhr (1776–1831), the teacher of Ranke, was the first eminent historian of the German movement. Initially a follower of the Idealist philosophers, he later rejected the speculative approach in favour of a more realistic, critical one, which for him specifically meant going back to the sources, and thus he radically challenged the orthodox "scissors-and-paste" method of historiography.[110] Quite rightly he features before Hegel as the first major pre-cursor of the historical school in Roscher's above mentioned *Geschichte*.[111] Although he was one of the most important Historicist historians, he never systematically laid down his methodology. He exercised his influence through his practical historical work, but not as a methodologist or as a philosopher of history.[112] In tracing the methodological roots of the Austrian school, the easiest way is to trace them to some programmatic expressions by some of the leading Historicists. In this process, Niebuhr could help us only indirectly through the methodology implicit in his work.

Niebuhr's foremost student was Leopold von Ranke (1795–1886).[113] Like Niebuhr he was deeply entrenched in the Romantic world of thought and abhorred speculation. Not only his *Weltanschauung* but also his conception of history, and of the *Geisteswissenschaften* in general, were those of the Historical School. He rejected the idea of progress conceived by "enlightened" historians, but his relativism never became absolute because of his piety and belief in providence. History to him, in all its aspects, was revelation. His aim was "to understand the way it has really been":[114] The ultimate aim of *Verstehen* was the recognition and realisation of the full truth, an aim, however, which he did not think achievable in principle. This *Verstehen* was to be value free, dispassionate, objective. Despite the *a priori* limitations Ranke imposed on a full understanding, he rejected any incorporation, or even recognition, of subjectivity. (In this he differed from both Droysen and Menger.) Nevertheless, the creative act, for Ranke, was not rational but subconscious. He understood empirically, through *Anschauung* (perception, intuition). Theory was *Anschauung*, an attempt to capture "the inner essence of anything living", not the construction of an ideal notion.[115] This essence was dynamic, a perpetual *Werden* (coming into being) in contrast to both Grimm and Savigny who were more interested in the existent being (*das Seiende*).[116] In keeping with the spirit of Romantic thought, this dynamic essence had no forward-looking properties; it was retrospective. Politically, Ranke was conservative, and, indeed, he was regarded as the greatest historian of the *Restauration*. His influence was simply enormous—Wach called him the "incarnation of the historical idea"[117]—but even so, Droysen thought he could not learn anything original from him.

Johann Gustav Droysen (1808–1884) was the last of one of the lineages of *geistesgeschichtliche* ancestors of Menger and the Austrian school. Menger's research programme in his *Grundsätze* was based on a methodology which very closely resembled the one Droysen delineated in his *Grundriss der Historik* of 1858. This issue is dealt with in Essay II, where we shall see that Menger effectively implemented for economics an Aristotelian programme akin to the one Droysen developed for historical research. The availability of a fully formulated version of such a research programme is very fortunate for the purpose of this study. Menger wrote a treatise on economic theory and a critique of (economic) methodology, but he never published a full statement of his own methodology although he quite clearly intended to do so.[118] His own methodology has to be extracted from his treatise and his critique. In Droysen's *Grundriss*, though, we have available an exposition of a *geisteswissenschaftliche* methodology which resembles Menger's approach in so many aspects that we can ill afford to let this opportunity go by unutilised.[119]

In Droysen's work we find the combination, or synthesis, of a speculative mind with a truly historical one.[120] He combined an aptitude for abstract thought (which Ranke did not possess) with an insistence on full empirical investigation of history. Not only do his intellectual origins lead back to Humboldt, Hegel, Schleiermacher and Boeckh (thus constituting an important lineage for the conception of *Verstehen* in this study), but he also took the ideas from the horse's mouth rather than at one remove; that is, he studied Hegel and Boeckh, not the Hegelians and Ranke. From Hegel he accepted the idea of the progress of history, a progress which, of course, was dialectical and not linear as in the conception of history in the thought of the

Enlightenment. Nevertheless, he rejected Hegel's attempt to "reduce" the course of history to a "mere expression" of reason; to Droysen, the meaning of history was a matter of faith and not logically comprehensible.[121] In general, historical experience took precedence over the idea (*Begriff*). He also objected to the biologistic interpretation of history (which he attributed to Hegel). In his conception of history, free will and the unintended consequences of the actions of the creative human spirit were extremely important.[122]

In his methodology, Droysen disagreed with Ranke to quite a significant degree. For him, subjectivity had to be explicitly taken into account. He accused Ranke of being pre-occupied with the technique of historical analysis while he himself regarded interpretation as being of prime importance. The objects of interpretation were the *sittliche Gemeinsamkeiten* (moral partnerships) and the purposes of human behaviour. Despite this insistence on subjectivity, objective criteria and evidence had to be adduced to keep *Verstehen wissenschaftlich*.[123] Ranke's demand for a value-free historiography, then, was countered by Droysen's demand for critical subjectivity. Looked at from a different angle, one can say that Ranke's quietism was confronted with Droysen's ethical activism. In his insistence on his interpretation of *Verstehen*, Droysen was rather dogmatic; he regarded his ideas as final. This attitude contrasts quite sharply with Ranke's low-key approach—he only attempted to move towards the truth but never claimed to be in possession of it. Thus, the essence of the historical method according to Droysen was *forschend zu verstehen* (understanding through—systematic—investigation).[124] Epistemologically he was a strict dualist. For him, the only things we are able to understand are expressions or creations of human nature, that is, of the human mind. Nature itself can only be explained but never understood.

This epistemological dualism is, of course, the backbone of the *Geisteswissenschaften* in the stand against the *Naturwissenschaften*. Throughout a large part of the nineteenth century in Germany, all the sciences dealing with man as a *geistiges Wesen* (a spiritual being), with emanations of the spirit, adopted this position, and they all went through a Historicist phase. Ancient and modern philology, theology, history and the *Staatswissenschaften* (law, economics and politics) all had their historical schools. The most influential of these was the historical school of jurisprudence, and its foundation and dogma, one could almost say, gospel, were laid down in Savigny's famous little book *Vom Beruf unserer Zeit für Gesetzgebung und Rechtswissenschaft*.[125] That book contains the best manifestation of the central themes of the Historicist system, and the following discussion of the Historical School is fundamentally important for the argument of this study.

On such a well-known fact as the intellectual indebtedness of the historical school of economics to that of jurisprudence, Schumpeter, almost half a century after the death of the founder of the former, had the following to say: "Certain nineteenth century economists professed to have derived inspiration for a historical view of the economic process from a school of jurisprudence that called itself the 'historical school' and whose emergence and position must be understood more completely than economists usually do if the elements of truth and error in that view are to be disentangled."[126] If, as is clearly implied in this statement, the final word on this issue has not been said yet and there still appears to be some confusion about the precise nature of the relationship between these two schools, it is even more important to discuss the basics of the Historical School because, as I suggest, the Austrian school, and especially Menger, not only owe much more to Savigny and his school than is usually recognised but also were much closer to him than to the historical economists.

The Menger-Savigny connection has not gone entirely unnoticed in the literature.[127] E. J. Burtt, Jr. recognises the importance of the Burke-Savigny school (as Menger himself calls it) and, in particular, points out that it is not the (Smithian) Edmund Burke of the *Thoughts and Details on Scarcity* who was relevant in this context but the (Romantic) Burke of the *Reflections on the Revolution in France*.[128] Burtt's exposition, however, does not connect Menger's theory sufficiently with his methodology; for instance, Burtt does not draw out the Historicism implicit in Menger's *Grundsätze*, which although most clearly visible in the chapter on money still forms the basis of all of Menger's argument, nor does he trace Menger's four necessary and jointly sufficient conditions for a thing to become a good to their Aristotelian, and Historicist, origins. His discussion of Savigny is somewhat incomplete as well.

In T. W. Hutchison's discussion of Menger's methodology, Menger's evaluation of Savigny is introduced as one of the focal points of the *Methodenstreit*. Hutchison offers an interpretation of this argument, which runs roughly along the following lines: Menger was politically in line with Burke-Savigny, but he entirely rejected that aspect of Savigny's methodology which accepts everything "organically grown" as the final word on institutional matters.[129] This interpretation is based on a passage in the *Untersuchungen*, and repeated in the *Irrthümer des Historismus*, which was written to rebut Schmoller's charges of "mysticism" and "Manchestertum".[130]

The problem with Hutchison's evaluation of this passage is that he accepts Menger's misrepresentation of Savigny and, in addition, does not draw a sharp enough line between Menger's conceptions of "exact" theory and realistic-empirical theory. It is precisely this difference which makes it clear that Menger's rebuttal of Schmoller did, in fact, miss its target and, consequently, that Schmoller's charges of "mysticism" and "Manchestertum" were largely justified. Let us take these arguments in turn.

In the passage under investigation Menger approvingly refers to "fruitful activities along the lines of Burke-Savigny." There is nothing in that passage which accuses Savigny himself of uncritically accepting everything that had developed organically. This charge is raised only in general. The direct accusation comes a little later,[131] but it is instantly mollified in a footnote by reference to some later statements made by Savigny on the issue.[132] There Savigny is, approvingly, quoted as regarding the historical approach as only one—necessary but passing—stage in the development of a truly scientific (*wissenschaftliche*) jurisprudence. According to Menger, this conces-sion was made by Savigny in 1840, but it was actually made much earlier. In 1814, in his above mentioned programme of the historical school of jurisprudence, *Vom Beruf unserer Zeit*, Savigny not only declares that every-thing organic is not unassailable but even malleable, to a certain extent, by human interference but also, and even more importantly, declares such activity to be desirable.[133] To charge Savigny, as Menger does, with having a totally uncritical reverence for every organic development is, therefore, quite a serious misrepresentation of even Savigny's earlier, politically mo-tivated position. Hence, in view of Menger's misrepresentation of Savigny, on the one hand, and in light of his acceptance of organicist arguments, on the other hand, the traditional interpretation of the relationship between the historical school of jurisprudence and Menger clearly needs some revision.

The context for this discussion of Burke-Savigny is the *Methodenstreit* in its full blossom. To analyse in depth why Menger, in fact, never replied to Schmoller in the first place, and why his *Irrthümer des Historismus* went off the mark would require a treatise in itself.[134] To put it briefly, the bone of contention was the divergence in the way Menger and Schmoller defined the term *Wissenschaft*. Menger defined two types of theoretical science, "exact" and realistic-empirical. The results of Menger's "exact" sciences were true and certain by definition; realistic-empirical theories, on the other hand, could only yield probable results. Historical investigations, for Menger, were auxiliary means as far as theory was concerned. They were necessary for serious research, but they could support only the realistic-empirical sciences. In particular, no historical science could ever be "exact." Schmoller, in his review of Menger's *Untersuchungen*,[135] attacked Menger for his dogmatic insistence on and assertion of the truth and certainty of "exact" theory; Schmoller's critical (Kantian) approach did not allow for an uncritical acceptance of untestable theories as final proclamations on whatever the subject matter involved.[136] However, in his review he never made it quite clear that his main target was the status of Menger's "exact" theories; in turn, Menger refused to take a stand on this issue in his reply. He accused Schmoller of attempting to make the impossible come true, that is, to develop an "exact" historical science—which Schmoller, of course, never intended, at least not in the way Menger understood the term "exact." They were, thus, completely at cross-purposes with each other. When Menger talks about the testability of theories in the section quoted by Hutchison,[137] we have to bear in mind that this only can refer to Menger's realistic-empirical theories, not the "exact" ones. Schmoller's criticism was therefore not rebutted by this passage or by any of Menger's other writings.

Closely connected with Menger's conception of "exact" theory is Schmoll-er's accusation of "mysticism" and "Manchestertum" since, to my mind at least, that accusation refers to Menger's essentialism, teleology and intro-spection, on the one hand, and to his methodological individualism, on the other hand. Viewed from this perspective, Schmoller's accusations seem largely justified, and more is said about this and other methodological and epistemological issues in Essay II. At this point, however, I want to return to the outline of the main strands of thought of the Historical School.

As mentioned, the founder and acknowledged leader of the historical school of jurisprudence was Friedrich Carl von Savigny (1779–1861), and his 1814 (methodological) pamphlet, *Vom Beruf unsrer Zeit*, marked the beginning of the victorious march of the historical schools in the *Staatswissenschaften*. Written as the Romantic reaction to the rationalist proposal by A. Thibaut to introduce a common code of civil law for the whole of Germany, made on the occasion of the liberation of Germany from the French occupying forces, the spirit of Savigny's pamphlet was quite nationalistic. The conclusion he reached was that neither the time nor the place was right for the codification of civil law. The arguments he employed to arrive at this conclusion were, of course, not entirely original; they were firmly embedded in the cultural and political climate prevailing at the time.

In his comparison of the existing civil codes he characterised the most important one in operation at the time, the Code Napoleon, as "cancerous", imposed for some "external purpose" and not brought about by "inner necessity." These factors—inner necessity, organic unity and origin of jurisdiction—have to be expressed in any legislation. Law, just like language, stands in organic coherence with the *Volksgeist*, the spirit of a nation, and therefore it is wrong to impose from outside a mechanical concoction (which such a code would be for Germany) upon a body of legal tradition which has developed organically and which expresses a wisdom acquired through the subconscious operation of inner, silent forces to produce the common law (*Gewohnheitsrecht*). The differing legal traditions throughout the German nation, the fact that two legal codes existed (in Austria and Prussia) and the impossibility of creating—within a reasonably short period of time—an organically coherent whole as opposed to a mechanically constructed aggregate of legal prescriptions rendered Germany unfit for a general, uniform code of civil law. Although Savigny was highly critical of both the *Preussische Landrecht* and the *Österreichische Gesetzbuch*, he preferred to keep them rather than abandon them in haste because they already constituted part of the legal tradition. He thought it impossible to change the nature of the legal conditions or the training of the then practising jurists. There existed, thus, an indissoluble connection between all ages and generations, "between whom there was only development, but no absolute beginning or end."[138] The only safeguard against misguided judgement was the study of (legal) history.

Very closely allied with Savigny's historical school was the historical school of philology, and its main exponent, Jakob Grimm (1785–1863), had received his inspiration for a historical investigation of the German language while studying with Savigny. This combination of law and language was not accidental, nor is it of only spurious interest to us. For Savigny, law and language were intimately related to each other (after all, one of the main reasons why Germany did not have a "vocation" for a general code of law lay in the language itself—as opposed to Latin, or even French,

German was far too imprecise for such codification), and he believed that the scientific method proper for investigations into both of these disciplines was the historical one.

For the Austrian economists, jurisprudence was a major influence on their thinking as they had all received their training as lawyers before they turned to economics. As far as the importance of language is concerned, one has only to turn to the first chapter of Wieser's *Ursprung und Hauptgesetze*, where he opens his first treatise on economic theory by discussing the scientific significance of the concepts of language. According to Wieser, the dividing line between *Naturwissenschaften* and *Geisteswissenschaften* is drawn through a discussion of scientific concepts and terminology; while concepts are of only instrumental significance in the former, they are essential to a proper *Verstehen* in the latter.[139]

Of all the Historicists, Jakob Grimm and his brother Wilhelm (1786–1859) became the most widely known throughout the world because of their collection of German fairy tales. This collection of hitherto orally transmitted folklore was not undertaken to frighten little children to sleep but to provide empirical evidence for the historical study of German language and literature. Those fairy tales were considered to be direct manifestations of the *Volksgeist*, the poetic expressions of the spirit of a nation. Jakob Grimm's *Deutsche Grammatik*, the first volume of which he dedicated to Savigny, was written in the retrospective, conservative style which was so characteristic of Historicism, full of "warning of sacrilegious reforms."[140]

This conservatism was an outstanding characteristic of the predecessors of the Historicists as well as of their own position.[141] Edmund Burke (1729–1797), who had such a strong influence on the Romantic movement through his *Reflections on the Revolution in France*, shared not only their Romantic glorification of chivalry and the Middle Ages but also most of their other characteristics.[142] His rejection of the Enlightenment manifested itself in his dislike for speculative argument and in his rejection of a precise (mathematical) formulation of the essence of social and political phenomena. He set social reason against intellectual individualism. He basically saw man as a social animal, as a member of a society in which inequality is inevitable and obedience to the social order—an order which exists prior to the individual—synonymous with reverence for God. As a true Historicist, rules of social behaviour, for him, reflect the "wisdom of the ages", a notion which is extremely close to the Historical School's concept of the *Volksgeist*. Similarly, his use of the term "natural" bears an almost uncanny resemblance to the school's use of the term "organic." As with the German Historicists, Burke's relativism never became absolute: Nature has to fulfill a divine purpose. Hand in hand with these principles went his rejection not only of the social contract but also of any written constitution. He opposed democracy in favour of aristocracy because he believed that the economic stability that class enjoyed because of their landed property was the best guarantee of liberty.

There is no need to discuss at length the other precursor of the Historical School, Justus Möser (1720–1794), because he was so closely aligned with

Burke that I would have to be spelling out more or less the same principles again.[143] The "first great European reactionary", "the forefather of German conservatism and political Romanticism"[144] showed a strong affinity with Anglo-Saxon political thought and with the Pietism of Hamann and Herder. Historicist and anti-democratic, the "Patriarch of Osnabrück" has sometimes been regarded as an even more pertinent ancestor of the Historical School than Burke, although the latter's influence was far more important and immediate.[145]

The world of the Historical School, then, was to a very large extent the world of Romanticism. Its members were concerned with living organisms which developed naturally, whose true origins had to be investigated historico-genetically if they were to be understood in all their diversity and individuality as genuine expressions and manifestations of the *Volksgeist*. In that *Volksgeist* the individual blends in harmoniously with the whole, and the totality is not amenable to a rationalistic, calculating, speculative analysis but only to an empirical, intuitive perception of the processes of life, taking into account the central, pivotal feature which is the wellspring of human freedom—the irrationality inherent in human life.[146]

Given this characterisation of the Historical School, it comes as no surprise that despite all the conceptual affinities, the Historicists were the most ardent opponents of Hegel. The reason for this is obvious: Starting from a common spiritual, intellectual origin and concern about essentially the same problems, they chose to proceed along analytical paths which were incompatible with those chosen by Hegel. If the irrational is preeminent then the science of logic will not help find the driving forces behind the human world. If reason is to rule, then deliberate legislation (*Gesetzgebung*) will have to replace common law (*Gewohnheitsrecht*). This theme also carries over to the discussion of Menger versus Hegel. Menger was, it goes almost without saying, anything but a Hegelian; his conception of life as organic in the sense of the Historical School prevents the construction of any such affinity. But there is another problem: How can Menger's methodological individualism and his abstract-deductive, not to say, speculative, method of his "exact" science be made compatible with his Historicist approach?

Menger himself, of course, did not use these terms to describe his own methodology and epistemology. Indeed, he would most violently object to such a characterisation of his "exact" theories. However, as we shall see in Essay II, although Menger believed he had derived his own "exact" theory of the *Grundsätze* on the basis of an empirically based inductive epistemology, he failed to provide any explanation of how this kind of induction is to be understood. From our perspective today (which is much closer to that of Schmoller than to Menger's own perspective), his "exact" theories can only be described as axiomatic-deductive (or speculative).

The fact that Menger himself did not see any incompatibility between his essentially Romantic (or Historicist) methodology and such rationalistic import as methodological individualism needs no further elaboration. That they are essentially incompatible elements within the *geistesgeschichtliche* framework outlined so far should be apparent. In reconstructing the different intellectual traditions of the first third of the nineteenth century, as I have attempted in this essay, one might be inclined to impute a certain degree of Hegelianism to Menger in order to accommodate somehow the rationalistic ingredients in his methodology since Hegel, of all the Idealists, was probably closest to the rationalism of the Enlightenment. Nevertheless, the picture of Menger as an organicist with a Hegelian inclination or as a Hegelian with organicist tendencies is not only incongruous but unsupported by the evidence. Consideration of another philosopher, however, one who had a major influence on the whole of German thought in the eighteenth and nineteenth centuries will lead to a way out of this dilemma. Not only did Gottfried Wilhelm Leibniz's *Monadology* receive a very peculiar interpretation in Austria, this interpretation formed the basis of educational reforms which became very widespread in Austria by about the middle of the nineteenth century, just in time for Menger to absorb these ideas at the *Gymnasium*.[147] This issue is discussed in Essay II.

Methodologically, Savigny's position can best be described as psychologistic Historicism. Although he required that the jurists be in possession of a "dual sense" (*ein zweyfacher Sinn*) for their work to be *wissenschaftlich*—a systematic sense and a historical one[148]—the historical sense carried the day in the end.[149] Scientific jurisprudence, then, was historical jurisprudence.[150] But to be able to trace the guiding organic principles, to follow the matter to its roots, the Historicists needed *hingebende Einfühlung* (devoted sympathetic understanding or empathy).[151] Only this kind of feeling, intuition, empathy "gives historical jurisprudence its scientific character."[152] That this kind of approach was incompatible, in the eyes of Savigny at least, with what was later to be called methodological individualism is easily seen. He warned of the "undescribable violence which the idea of uniformity" exerts (another reason why there ought to be no common code of civil law for Germany), and he also frequently referred to the *Volksgeist*, which not only enabled the Romans to develop their code of law but also prevented the Germans from obtaining theirs.[153] Underlying this conception of methodology is Savigny's "unshakeable adherence to the dignity of currently effective law."[154] In addition, the proper representation of the results was as important as their correct derivation not only for Savigny but also for Jakob Grimm, whose methodology was virtually congruent with Savigny's.[155] The "harmony of substance and form" was as important as the application of the correct, that is, the historico-genetic, method.[156] Both were basically only different aspects of intrinsically the same thing—of life.[157]

Life was central to Romantic thought, and not surprisingly, it retained its central role in Savigny's methodology in the organicist guise which was so characteristic of German Historicism. History, law, language and all the other disciplines of the *Geisteswissenschaften* represented different aspects of the same living organism whose driving force, that is, its soul, was the *Volksgeist*. They all emanated from it. Life, in its totality, was a teleological process, directed towards an end[158] which was defined either as the all-embracing "divine purpose" of Ranke or more narrowly in historical terms. The purpose of history, then, was to conserve the original, natural forms of life.[159] Since life carries within itself its own driving force which permanently pushes towards its end, the process can also be described as entelechial.

This combination of biology and teleology is explicitly formulated in Menger's new first chapter of the second edition of the *Grundsätze*. There we can see clearly what is only implicit in the first edition of the *Grundsätze*: The biologically conceived concept of *Bedürfnis* acts as the *telos* in the causality underlying Menger's economic theory and also acts as the bridge between the *Naturwissenschaften*, particularly biology, and the *Geisteswissenschaften* in general and economics in particular.

The difficulty one has in coming to terms with the Romantic-biologistic chain of reasoning lies in the ambiguity inherent in its central concepts—life, organism, nature—which arose out of the biologistic interpretation of the originally purely metaphysical term *Volksgeist*. There are two aspects of this term which are of immediate interest: on the one hand, its anti-individualism, which has already been discussed; on the other hand, the implications which arise from this biologistic interpretation.

In the world of the Historical School, the *Volksgeist* was a collective spirit, a subconscious collective force from which the creative community, the nation, drew its inspiration. It was the "real cause of all the separate, merging cultural activities of a nation."[160] To put it differently, it was the idea of a national culture as one unified—but not uniform—activity which was not merely the sum of all individual activities. Individual activities, however much they might differ from one another, contained something that was larger than the personally specific, willed act. There was more to a simple cultural act like talking than just an individual using language because the language itself was something larger than the individual. If it had not been for the *Volksgeist* there would have been no language—or law, literature, art, etc.—unique to a people. This *Volksgeist*, furthermore, could not possibly exist when Robinson Crusoe was on his own on the island; it needed at least a Man Friday, that is, social interaction.[161]

The biological interpretation of this term not only distorted its original meaning but also led to severe repercussions for the concepts which depended on it: life, organism and nature. These originally biological terms, as if in return for services rendered to the spirit, were now given a mystical, spiritualistic twist. The *Volksgeist* itself almost assumed the status of a fact of (nonmystical) nature; its history became a kind of natural history. Through the change in the meaning of the term "nature", the *Volksgeist*, then, became a fact of nature because nature became mystical. On the basis of this shift in the terminology the *Volksgeist* was regarded—unambiguously for the members of the Historical School, confusing for us—as the "principle of life of the organism *Volk*".[162]

From very crude beginnings the concept of organism gradually evolved and became an integral part not only of the vocabulary of the Historical

School but of the *Geisteswissenschaften* in general. Its biological meaning was eventually narrowed down until it had finally moved into the realm of botany: Hugo's "bestial" nature changed into Savigny's analogies with the life of plants. "To get to the roots of an argument" is but one of the phrases which has entered everyday language. Through the dual interpretation of this concept, one burning problem which stood in the foreground of all German thought of the late eighteenth and early nineteenth centuries could finally be solved—for the Romantic movement, at least, in a non-contradictory way: the question of the relationship between necessity and freedom. Biology, or botany, took care of the "blind forces of nature", the realm of necessity, while the spiritual aspect, the realm of mind, divine and human, guaranteed the freedom of the personality, of the will. This realm of mind, it is important to note, was not the bright world of reason but the dark, murky, mystical world of Romantic irrationality. Freedom and necessity were thus not mutually exclusive but only two different facets of one and the same thing, of human life. The proximity of this strand of thought to Schelling and his reformulation of Spinoza's philosophy is obvious.[163]

The concept of life which was an integral part of this *Weltanschauung* of the Historical School was truly conservative. Life was dynamic, and had movement, though this dynamism was not explosive but peculiarly restrained and muted; thus the preference for analogies with the life and growth of plants. It has fittingly been described as "neptunistic with a tendency towards quietism."[164] The cultural development of nations was a slow and gradual process; each age, generation and period left its mark, contributing layer after layer. At any period in time intrinsic, subconscious forces were at work, furthering the evolution of the organism. Any interference had to be avoided, any change had to be slowed down so as not to destroy the beauty of the being of the organism. This was a truly quietist attitude which expressed the spirit of the *Restauration* period extremely well: to sit back in contemplative understanding without interfering. Consistent with this attitude was the *telos*: The purpose of history was to preserve the original, organic forms of life.

At exactly the opposite end of the scale we find the attitude of the Enlightenment: rationalist intervention shaping the world in such a way that it would become as it ought to be according to human will and imagination. The difference was the same as that between liberalism and conservatism in the nineteenth century: The former was concerned only with the final outcome, with what ought to be (*das Sein-Sollende*), and did not waste too much thought and energy on the present state (*das Seiende*); the latter was concerned with what actually existed and how it had evolved, conceiving of the future only as a modification of the past and present and regarding the new order merely as a hidden aspect of the old one but never as a radical transformation.[165] The attitudes of Savigny and Burke were more sophisticated than the simplistic kind of quietism. They believed in interference, albeit of a particular kind, and they attempted to "preserve by changing."[166] Theirs was not an uncritical obedience to the blind forces of nature but a deliberate activity to preserve what they regarded as "good." (Valuation and ontology were inseparable in their frame of reference.) Reforms were necessary because too many rationalists had already interfered with the evolution of the organism. The deformations had to be removed but—and here they remained true to their basic principle—only gradually and slowly so as to minimise the disruption these reforms would cause. What they advocated were piecemeal changes towards the better, which was the good old order.

The most central feature of the Historicist idea of the organism of cultural entities was the internal movement which was conceived of as being inherent in and fundamental to this concept. Organisms were always changing and there was nothing static in them, the conservatism associated with this world of thought notwithstanding. This movement Rothacker regarded as the logical bequest of the Historical School, namely, "the purely theoretical insight that the nature of the mind (*die Natur des Geistes*) can only be understood through its own history."[167] He called this *Emanatismus* "one of the most fundamental categories for the comprehension of historical material."[168] The *Volksgeist* was probably the most important concept in the establishment of this Historicist category because all cultural activities, as we have seen, emanated from the *Volksgeist*.

In Menger's economic theory, *Emanatismus* is equally predominant. All economic activity, the essence of all economic concepts, emanates from the *Bedürfnis* to consume, to satisfy one's needs and wants. *Bedürfnisbefriedigung* is the soul of the economic aspect of the organism as Menger conceived it. And this is also the appropriate background against which Menger's analysis of the concepts of value, prices and money in the *Grundsätze* has to be viewed; not as an additional and illuminating, though basically superfluous, nicety without which his analytic structure would stand unimpaired, but as characteristic of his approach, as an essential, fundamental and indispensable part of his theory without which it would quite seriously be misinterpreted—as has happened in all Walrasian histories of economic analysis.

The Historical Economists

Before finally turning to a more systematic investigation of the foundations of Austrian theory and methodology, we ought to look at the historical school of economics, and—in view of the fact that Menger dedicated his *Grundsätze* to Roscher—particularly at what is commonly called the older school. Primarily we need to establish in which direction and to what extent this school (contrary to Roscher's claim) deviated from the path mapped out by Savigny. By doing so, we shall ultimately be able to assess Menger's critique of historical economics in order to get Menger's own perspective into focus.

Historical economics was practised in Germany for well over a century, from Adam Müller to Max Weber and Werner Sombart, but only during its latter years did it come to be exclusively identified with German academic economics.[169] Although Adam Müller and Friedrich List are considered to be forerunners of the school, the historical school of economics proper was "founded" by Wilhelm Roscher. There is a considerable amount of discussion in the literature on whether one is actually justified in maintaining the distinction between an older and a younger school or whether the older part, indeed, even qualifies for the label "school."[170]

For the purposes of this discussion, these issues are more or less irrelevant, and I therefore retain these labels as a convenient way to refer to Roscher, Hildebrand and Knies, on the one hand, and to Schmoller and the *Verein für Sozialpolitik*, on the other hand. There is, in my opinion, sufficient evidence to justify the distinction between old and young, and for the time being I accept the usual characterisation: that the latter were the real anti-theoreticians and the former objected only to the claim made by classical economics of universal validity without rejecting the theory as such. However, and this a most important proviso, the precise meaning I attach to the term "anti-theoreticians" in this context will become clear in the brief discussion of Schmoller at the end of this section. I also accept the grouping together of Roscher, Hildebrand and Knies as they were united not only in their relativism and rejection of socialism as well as real hardcore laissez faire capitalism but also in their adherence to Historicist concepts like *Volksgeist*, organism, *Emanatismus*, etc., and in their search for laws—which to them meant historical laws—to explain the functioning of different economies. In this section, I shall briefly discuss Adam Müller and Friedrich List and then look at the methodology of the older school. Schmoller and the younger school will be discussed only with reference to their differences from the former, and Max Weber and Werner Sombart, although eminently important in their own right, are ignored since they are too far removed from the main concern of this study.

If we accept that historical economics is, broadly speaking, characterised by its rejection of the claim of classical economics to universal validity, by its opposition to the abstract-deductive method which analysed aspects of the social world in isolation instead of examining them in their full (holistic) context, by its insistence on the historic, genetic nature of all institutions and on the relativity of (social-)scientific analysis, then both Adam Müller and Friedrich List can certainly be considered as forerunners of the historical school of economics.

Adam Müller (1779–1829) is at times regarded as the leading exponent of the Romantic school of economics,[171] but without intending to pursue this issue any further, I am perfectly prepared to accept Schumpeter's view that "it should be frankly admitted that there never was such a thing as a 'romantic school of economics' at all."[172] Müller's career, in a way, displayed quite a few of those features which we have seen were typical for Romanticism. From being an early defender of Adam Smith's liberal economics (against Fichte's *Der geschlossene Handelsstaat*), he later turned against precisely those principles in his writings on economics and politics in order to lend some

philosophical credibility to the reactionary regimes of his time.[173] The son
of a Prussian civil servant and an early convert to Catholicism, he finally
settled in Vienna where he was afforded high recognition, particularly
through Metternich. In his writings, which represented "both the rise and
climax of political and economic thought within the Romantic movement",[174]
he makes use of all the concepts and ideas we have have met with so far:
the state as a living organism embraces the totality of social, cultural, etc.,
life, none of those aspects are comprehensible in isolation. Life is intrinsically
antagonistic (this he attempted to develop in his *Lehre von den Gegensätzen*),
and thus, it is dynamic, having no beginning and no end and flowing along
permanently, mysteriously.[175] Accordingly, there are no "clear and distinct"
concepts in Müller's analysis, only intuitive ideas of, say, institutions and
unique historical events merging into one another in endless sequence.

His analysis, never systematic or constructive, did not leave much of a
mark on German economic theory, which is not really surprising considering
the fact that during that time, classical economics (not undiluted but mixed
with a dose of Cameralism) was about to reach its peak in Germany through
the teachings of Hufeland, Jakob, Kraus, and later Herrmann and Rau.[176] It
was not so much against Adam Smith himself but against his "school" and
the German version of it that Müller turned in his attack on all the liberal,
individualistic ideas which came out of the Enlightenment. (This attitude
was to be adopted by the later writers, too; not only List but also the
historical economists took this stance on Adam Smith *vis-à-vis* his followers.)

Müller rejects a veritable catalogue of arguments which define the central
position of the classical economists. His claim as a precursor of the historical
economists lies precisely here. In picking out for attack a certain set of
principles of economic analysis and presenting another one in its place he
isolates for the first time ideas which are going to be important not only
for the remainder of this essay but also for the rest of this study. One thing,
however, must be kept in mind: I am not interested at this point in whether
Adam Müller (or Friedrich List or the historical economists) was correct or
not in his reading of Adam Smith and the classical economists, only in
how he read them.

As Müller sees it, the sole motive behind classical economic man, an
isolated individual, is self-interest, which sets all individuals in competition
against each other. Their rational, utilitarian calculations merely produce
material gains for individuals, the sum of which represents only national
"riches" not "wealth"; the result is meaningless, purposeless progress. The
only genuine social institution in such a world, the market, is to remain
free of state intervention; the same holds true for all aspects of life, whether
social or private. Furthermore, he regards this kind of life as being dead,
mechanistic, displaying no organic development whatsoever. The analysis
of such an atomistic society is, moreover, static and has been generalised
to such an extent that it now claims universal validity in time and space.

Against this Müller brings to bear the force of the arguments Romanticism
has furnished him with. If we keep in mind that the state is fundamental

and central to his thought on politics and economics and add to this what has been said about Romanticism, then his arguments follow almost logically. The state, a living organism, unites the cultural, political, economic, social life of a nation; in fact, "the state is the Form of Being of society. . . . No spheres exist outside the state."[177] The ideal state is the medieval, feudal one; man not only has a firm place in society but is defined only through it, is inconceivable without it. It is to this state that Müller wants to return. Although the state evolves and develops, taking its purpose from religion and containing it entirely within itself, it never dies. Through this evolutionary process, which is its essence, it becomes the "mysterious and blissful alliance of past and present generations."[178] Thus, the economic process, far from being antagonistic competition, is reciprocal and harmonious; the economy is a totality, not just the sum of its individuals, and thus the wealth of a nation is more than the mere sum of individually accumulated material fortunes. It also comprises the moral and spiritual wealth. It is obvious that on the basis of such an "ethic-organic" structure no systematic, rational analysis of the economic process is possible. All terminology is laden with metaphysics and mysticism, and of his central concept, the state, Müller says that there can be no (clearly defined) concept, only an idea.[179]

There is no need to go into the details of Müller's economic analysis, but I would like to emphasise one aspect here: his discussion of the factors of production. For Müller, the "factors of production are not land, labour and capital, but nature, man and the past. The last includes all the capital, physical and spiritual, which has been built up in the course of time and is now available to help man in production."[180] This idea, apart from involving what has come to be called the concept of "human capital", is found again in Knies (though not Roscher or Hildebrand) in slightly modified form and, finally, as the basis of Böhm-Bawerk's theory of capital.[181] Müller, however, uses the past not only as a vehicle to introduce dynamics into the economic process but also as the pivot for his apologetics of reactionary politics. Such a conception of economic and state life clearly has very little in common with Adam Smith and his followers, and, as was to be expected, the demand for historical relativity of theory and policy is made with particular reference to the actual differences in the sociopolitical and economic conditions in Germany and Britain.

All of the arguments which were eventually to be brought forward by the historical economists are found in Adam Müller's writings, and most of the historical economists were quite aware of this fact. His *Weltanschauung*, his motivation, his scientific conception of social reality and his methodology were, of course, pronouncedly Romanticist and thus quite different from those of the historical school of economics whose main motive, at least that of the older school, was the introduction of Historicist methodology into economics. But all this notwithstanding, the arguments are certainly there.

If Adam Müller was the first to produce the arguments, albeit in the spirit of the Romantic movement, Friedrich List (1789–1846) was both in time and in spirit much closer to the main concerns of the historical economists.[182] His *National System of Political Economy* of 1840, however, was not the work of a theoretician attempting to put theory onto "proper" foundations for its own sake, but that of a politician systematising and unifying all his previous thought on the subject. The theoretical underpinnings of practical policy conclusions, goal-oriented towards the future but applicable there and then to a specific set of circumstances, were his explicit concern. The necessary methodological and theoretical postulates, consistent with his relativism, were almost entirely subsidiary to this purpose. List, unlike Müller, was a fervent liberal and "a champion of industrial capitalism."[183] His practical experience in the New and the Old Worlds had shaped his outlook and culminated in his infant-industry argument while his being German explains not only his emphasis on the importance of "nationality" and of "productive forces" as central concepts in economic analysis but also the specific brand of liberalism which he represented.[184]

Despite the congruence in their terminology, the worlds of Müller and List were widely different. The point at which they met was in the rejection of Adam Smith and the classics.[185] List, too, saw their theory as materialistic and mechanistic, as static, as individualistic and cosmopolitan, advocating laissez faire and free trade on the basis of an English experience which made not only their economic policy conclusions but also their theoretical foundations inapplicable to the Germany of the early nineteenth century. This thinking and his method of historical comparison of actual economies— his comparative economic history as the inductive basis for economic theory— are the elements which made List a forerunner of the historical school of economics. Like Müller, he advocated a dynamic analysis which displayed the interdependence of all branches of the life of a nation as indispensable for economic analysis. But the similarity stops here, at an overly general classification of his vision of the economic process. As soon as we look at details, the way in which he differs with Adam Müller becomes obvious.

True to his fundamentally liberal *Weltanschauung*, List was concerned with coming into being (*das Werdende*) rather than with being (*das Seiende*); the present was not to be preserved, it was merely a transitory stage in the development of a nation from the past to the future. The ultimate goal was the realisation of a nation's productive potential, the full development of the "productive forces" which contained not only physical but also human capital in the widest meaning of the word. Only a nation which had reached this stage, the "agricultural-manufacturing-commercial" one, could be called "normal." Britain, in his day, was the one nation which came closest to being "normal"; France followed next, and Germany was thoroughly under-developed. Of all the productive forces of a nation, manufacture was the one which had most potential since "manufactures develop the moral forces of a nation to a superlative degree."[186] The government, then, was under an obligation to assist in the establishment of manufacture even if this meant implementing policies which resulted in foregoing current consumption in order to develop productive forces to maximise future consumption— nowadays a fairly commonplace argument. The best way to promote manufacturing was to exclude competition from the more advanced industrialised countries. The means to achieve this aim was the *Industrieerziehungszoll* (educative, protective customs tariff for industry). As soon as the infant was able to stand on its own feet, however, protection was to be abandoned so that it could thrive in competition; then free trade was desirable because then every nation could benefit from it. Accordingly, List defined political economy as "the science which teaches in which way each individual nation can be raised to that stage of development where the union with other equally developed nations and, thus, free trade would be both possible and beneficial."[187]

In economic policy, as in economic theory, List and Müller stood in opposing camps: While List was instrumental in the shaping of the German customs union (*Zollverein*), the "embryo of German national unity",[188] Müller, having gone in 1815 to Leipzig as the Austrian consul general, was recalled to Vienna in 1825 at the insistence of the Prussian government because of his opposition to its *Zollunionspolitik* (policy of the costums union). In economic theory, List, unlike Müller, did not reject the classical economists *toto coelo* but regarded their theory—as Roscher and the others were to do later on—as incomplete, as a premature generalisation from an isolated special case. In introducing the concept of nationality, as opposed to the individualism and cosmopolitanism of the classics, and in developing a theory of "productive forces", as opposed to their exclusive concern with exchange value, he attempted on the basis of empirical data drawn from historical comparisons to produce a theory appropriate for a different special case—the budding industry of the Germany of his day (a theory he most likely would have been happy to abandon once history had moved on so that a different set of policy recommendations was required for a different set of circumstances).

In 1843, with the publication of Roscher's *Grundriss*, the historical school of economics in Germany was officially ushered in, and during the decade 1843–1853, the relevant writings by Roscher, Hildebrand and Knies were published.[189] In spite of the disagreement among the three on the precise nature of the methodological postulate on which a rejuvenated economic science was to be built, there was still enough common ground among them to justify not only the label "school" but also the division into older and younger.[190] The task ahead was, according to Roscher, to do for economics on the basis of Savigny's method what this method had done for jurisprudence.[191] That this was not what he then went on to do will not only become obvious shortly but was pointed by Menger in 1883.[192] Hildebrand's model was not Savigny but the historical school of language, a difference which cannot be considered very significant.[193] Knies, the most radical of the triumvirate, did not have a particular school in mind which he wanted to imitate but took the writings of Roscher and Hildebrand, both of whom he attacked, as a starting point for his approach to historical economics. They all, though, agreed on the fundamentals in their criticism of the classical economists: economic laws are different from the laws of physics; they are, therefore, not universally valid. People act, even only in the economic sphere, as the result of a variety of motives; thus, to isolate egoism as the sole motive and to apply it within the framework of a mechanistic psychology to economic behaviour is not sufficient as a basis for economic analysis. Finally, and closely related to the previous point, economic laws cannot possibly be deduced from one simple, and even erroneous, principle. They can only be arrived at inductively through careful observation of (historical) reality.[194]

The aim of the older historical economists was to introduce historical technique as the sole method for economic investigation and analysis. The task of political economy, then, was the derivation of the laws of development of economies in their full concrete reality. The specific tool was to be the "method of analogy" advocated especially by Roscher and Knies. The result was a relativism in regard to economic policy and, to a certain extent, also to economic theory, which led to an apologia of past and present policy decisions since due to the absence of higher, more general rules every case had to be judged entirely on its own merits.[195] Politically, they all agreed in their rejection of Manchesterism as well as socialism. This programme for research into economics, though, was never realised in the writings of the older school. They singularly failed to actually carry out what they felt to be imperative if the science was to progress at all. No historical economic theory was ever developed; whenever they had to take recourse to theory, they adhered to the canons of the classical economists.

In the 1860s and the 1870s, the younger school of historical economists under the leadership of Schmoller[196] set out to succeed where the older generation had wanted to but failed. But they differed from the latter in two important aspects. First, rejecting all theory, which meant classical theory, they began to investigate all aspects of economic life, past and present, in a series of monographs to establish the inductive basis for a "proper" economic theory. The result was a phenomenal expansion of the literature on economic history. Second, all attempts at philosophising about history, the idea of the derivation of (historical) laws of economic development, were entirely abandoned. This period included also the *Methodenstreit* between Menger and Schmoller, a polemical exchange on the method appropriate to economics which, at the time, led absolutely nowhere. The *Methodenstreit* did not introduce any new dimension into the economic discourse since, as we have seen in the course of the last few pages, the reaction against the classical economists was essentially nothing else but a more or less heated argument about the "correct" method. The Menger-Schmoller exchange was only one more step along the path being discussed in this essay.

Wilhelm Roscher (1817–1894) defined economics as the science of the natural laws of economic development which were to be discovered by comparing all available economic histories.[197] The crucial concepts in this definition are, of course, "natural" and "law", and, given Roscher's background, we shall not be surprised to find a conflation of speculative and empiricist tendencies in these concepts. Roscher was a historian and philologist by training; the major influences on his intellectual outlook were Gervinus and Dahlmann, two historians of the Göttinger school, and, according to his own testimony, Ranke.[198] He assimilated Romanticist concepts such as "organism" and *Volksgeist*, the latter, though, in a form more akin to Hegel's interpretation of it than that of the Historical School, despite of his assertions to the contrary. His empiricism, in line with the tendency away from speculation which had been gathering momentum in Germany towards the middle of the nineteenth century, never got the upper hand over his religiosity, which was the unifying element that was fundamental to all his thinking.[199] These strands combined to form an epistemology and Historicist methodology which was truly *sui generis*, though neither consistent nor very original.[200] With the help of analogies he intended to discover similarities, typically occurring over and again in different economies. Discarding accidental deviations from these supposedly generally present characteristics, laws of development could be arrived at. In this respect, "the work of the historian and that of the natural scientist resembled each other."[201] The ultimate aim was to discover laws that were "objective, unquestionable, and thus removing any dispute."[202]

Epistemologically, Roscher was a monist; he did not subscribe to the view that there was an essential division between the sciences and the humanities. Any difference in method, then, arose out of the subject matter of inquiry, but this difference could not be established *a priori* by assigning a particular field of inquiry to either of these categories. Since he was not a materialist, his conception of nature contained elements of both the spiritual and the material spheres. The central concept here is the "organism." Through this biological analogy, he built a bridge between an individual and a nation: Both are spiritual and physiological "totalities"; nations have life cycles just like individuals; the historical method, then, becomes the "physiological method" designed to produce an "anatomy and physiology of the economy";[203] economic policy, accordingly, becomes the "therapy" of an ailing economy. Through the biological analogy, he also amalgamated historical regularity to the regularity of the natural sciences,[204] contradicting his own fundamental distinction between historical and philosophical perceptions of reality: It is the task of the former to give a full description of reality while the latter is a conceptual characterisation based on "generalising abstraction under the elimination of essentials."[205] In this way, the empirical and the concrete are collapsed into an "ideal" and an abstract in order to make possible the discovery of "natural laws of history."

As Max Weber has shown, this operation becomes meaningful only within the framework of Hegel's conceptualisation, in which the idea encompasses individual concrete instances as its realisation and the concepts are metaphysical counterparts of reality, necessarily generating those instances.[206] In spite of Roscher's rejection of Hegel (reflecting the influence of Ranke and the Göttinger school) there is no other way to make sense of his identification of conceptual (philosophical) and concrete (historical) cognition—as well as that of causality and regularity (*Gesetzlichkeit*) and of his use of the concept of *Volksgeist*—but to view it through Hegel's *Emanatismus*. The final acceptance of Hegel's conceptual apparatus, though, is forestalled by Roscher's belief in God. His religiosity imposes a boundary beyond which only irrational, transcendental powers prevail, beyond which scientific knowledge is not obtainable. The notion that the life cycle of nations emanates from both natural and divine forces imposes a limit not only on the realm of the idea and reason but also on the empirical investigation of those forces. Complete knowledge of reality is impossible in principle. The only result which persistent research can hope to achieve is to push this transcendental horizon as far back as possible.[207]

When it finally came to re-writing economic theory along historical lines, Roscher undertook nothing like the reconstruction which he had demanded but produced a historically embroidered version of classical theory which left room for digressions into the specifically German condition and for the introduction of some Cameralistic elements to act as guidelines for decision making in the public sector.[208] Roscher's turn of mind was not that of a theoretician; his work was very much in the tradition of the Göttinger school of historiography which fused cultural, economic and political history on the basis of its "comparative" methodology. He was, as Schmoller put it, the "universally educated cultural historian among economists."[209]

Bruno Hildebrand (1812–1878), like Roscher, was essentially a historian emphasising the relativity of all (applied and theoretical) systems of economics, and he shared the latter's approach to a large extent. His rejection of classical theory, however, was much more radical than Roscher's: He did not believe in the existence of "natural" laws regulating the economy and therefore also rejected Roscher's attempt to discover natural laws of development. Hildebrand's aim, nevertheless, was to discover "laws of development not only of individual nations but of humanity as a whole."[210] Humanity, to him, a politically active liberal, progressed towards ever-higher levels of perfection, an idea firmly embedded in the tradition of the Enlightenment and based on Lessing's conception of the "education of mankind."[211] Far from actually expounding an economic theory which would have had to be encompassed within the totality of the social sciences, the undivided *Staatswissenschaften*, according to the new "whole" view of social reality, he never went beyond postulating the new methodology. The ideas which he produced were quite often confused or even contradictory, but in addition (as in the case of his theory of stages) instead of having been dictated by the logic of the argument or suggested by the actual historical material, they were politically motivated, a desperate attempt to preserve the achievements of bourgeois society while trying to curb its worst excesses in order to stem the swelling tide of socialism.[212] The result of this could only have been the emphasis on *Sozialpolitik*, an undogmatic, totally relativistic social policy, and, indeed, if there is any continuity between the older and the younger historical school of economics, then it is in the person of Bruno Hildebrand. He was not only among the founders of the *Verein für Sozialpolitik*, but he also, in 1863, established the *Jahrbücher für Nationalökonomie und Statistik*, a journal devoted to statistical investigation of the economy which emphasised the importance of detailed historical research.

The most thorough methodologist of the older school was Karl Knies (1821–1898), who also rejected the classical doctrine most consistently but also disagreed with Roscher and Hildebrand on some fundamental issues. In his eyes theirs were but incomplete versions of the true methodology of historical economics. He did not advocate the introduction of Historicist methodology into economics because he was a historian (he was not, in contrast to Roscher and Hildebrand) but because he deemed no other methodology appropriate on epistemological grounds.[213] The inconsistency of his approach is analysed by Max Weber in his famous article, but it had already been pointed out by Schmoller[214] on the occasion of the publication of the second edition of Knies's *Politische Ökonomie*. Indeed, Knies had himself implicitly admitted this inconsistency when he changed the title of his book for the second edition.[215]

My statement that the aim of the historical economists was to derive laws of economic development ought to be interpreted quite carefully since it is on the definition of "economic laws" where Roscher, Hildebrand and Knies part company. If Roscher was looking for "natural" laws, Hildebrand was interested in "laws" only, and Knies admitted only "laws of analogy." Knies's rejection of the applicability of natural laws to economics was grounded in his epistemological dualism. Although Roscher concedes that man is endowed with reason (*ein Vernunftwesen*) and that natural laws of the economy are somewhat different than laws of physics, he nevertheless regards them as laws and does not see any essential (or logical) difference between them.[216] Knies, on the other hand, draws an unsurmountable line between nature, the realm of necessity and *ratio*, and *Geist* (spirit), the realm of freedom and irrationality. The former can be explained by laws because of the regularity prevailing in the material world; the latter encompasses only individual phenomena which are devoid of any constantly recurring elements. In between these two spheres (the *Naturwissenschaften* and the *Geisteswissenschaften*) are the historical sciences in which both rational and irrational elements interact in such a way that the only means of explanation is through "analogies."

Economics, according to Knies, is a science of human action in which the blind forces of nature are given their direction through the influence of the free will. Regularities are precluded *a priori*, and the laws of economics are, therefore, "laws of analogy."[217] According to Knies's definition, then, Roscher's historical laws of economics do not exist; the accidental variations which Roscher discards as irrelevant are of the essence of historical events since they represent the irrational element. The direction in which the economy moves, through the interference of the human will in the determinate and necessary outcome of the operation of the forces of nature, is that of progress towards an ever-higher ethical development of humanity in which each nation, just as each person, has its unique, individual role to play.

Ethics was central to the thought of all the older historical economists.[218] Although Roscher lacked Knies's concept of linear progress, he still judged any kind of progress by its consequences for the "spiritual and ethical side of life."[219] Development and progress were two different things for him. The former recurs over and over again throughout history, every nation going through the same stages analogous to the human life cycle, and the latter is a theistically interpreted remnant of the "enlightened" idea of progress of humanity handed down to him through the tradition of the Göttinger school.

Knies, on the other hand, identified progress and development. Absorbing some of the ideas of the Historical School, his idea of development was that of an "organic" process: The organism is the *Volk* and the driving force is the *Volksgeist* which, analogous to the soul of an individual, is the ultimate, indivisible substance, the real cause of all events in the cultural sphere.[220] It is here that we find Knies's psychology clashing with Roscher's (and Hildebrand's). Roscher had been postulating, on Herbartian lines, the existence of drives (*Triebe*), but Knies's holistic conception, not only of the *Volksgeist* but also of the individual personality, would not allow for such an isolation of different aspects of the totality even as a heuristic fiction.[221] There is a curious blend in Knies's work, perhaps even more so than in Roscher's or Hildebrand's, of empiricism, Historicism and ideas of the Enlightenment as handed down by the epigones of Hegel. The reception of Hegelian ideas, despite protestations to the contrary (a feature which all three shared), is to be found not only in Knies's conception of progress and *Emanatismus*— which was thus inconsistent in itself since he had also identified it with the Romantic (Savigny's) conception of organic development and conflation of *Volk* and state—but also in his identification of regularity and causality and, most important, of empirical contents and conceptual extension.[222] Although Schmoller rated Knies very highly indeed as a historical econo- mist,[223] apart from an (inconsistent) Historicist methodology, no further contribution towards a construction of historical economics came forth from his pen.

Roscher, Hildebrand and Knies, then, called for a revision and recon- struction of political economy along Historicist lines, but all they were able to offer were incomplete methodologies and no positive alternatives to the body of classical doctrine. The implication of their position was relativism in economic theory and policy which ultimately, and quite consistently, led to a *Sozialpolitik* based on a theoretical agnosticism, with each individual case judged entirely on its own merits.[224] In their political aims, broadly defined, they agreed in their opposition to capitalism (in any case to its extreme form) and to socialism.[225] Roscher was a moderate conservative without political ambitions, while Hildebrand and Knies were both politically active liberals, but given the nature of liberalism in Germany and the outcome of the 1848 revolution, this difference really amounted to very little.

The members of the younger historical school of economics under the leadership of Gustav von Schmoller (1838–1917) followed their elders in their criticism of classical economics but went their own way when it came to positive, constructive work. Their avowed aim was to establish an empirical basis for economic theory, rejecting the classical method as inappropriate and classical theory as premature generalisation—though not rejecting the concept of economic law and theory *a priori* as they are sometimes said to have done. Their anti-theoretical bias was meant to last only until economic reality had been sufficiently well investigated to warrant "sound" generalisation.[226] The laws they did reject as being totally unfeasible were the laws of historical development, and thus they really reformulated the programme of the older school to a large extent.[227] Schmoller's programme, in particular, was to introduce the methods of the natural sciences by utilising Whewell's inductive schema within a neo-Kantian framework.[228]

Meanwhile, as the detailed historical investigations went on, something had to be done about the real world. To promote their views and to support the young German empire against the threat posed by socialism,[229] the *Verein für Sozialpolitik* (Association for Social Policy) was founded in 1873, and it expounded a policy of social reforms, which led to the nickname *Kathedersozialisten* (socialists of the chair). Public, and also academic, opinion focussed mainly on the historical economists' political activities, as expressed by the *Verein*, to the neglect of their aims and achievements in their work on (or better, towards) economic theory. They did not, in the end, produce an alternative to the classical system. By the time they began to concede that their exclusive pre-occupation with the empirical basis had been somewhat excessive, the neo-classical revolution had already established a powerful alternative to classical economic theory. In the field of value, price and capital theory, the Austrian school of economics had become the leading school, not least because of the efforts of Friedrich von Wieser and Eugen von Böhm-Bawerk, who had eclipsed Menger's original contribution.

Notes

The Austrian School in the History of Ideas

1. For a very general description of Max Weber's notion of *Verstehen*, see, e.g., Prewo(1979), p. 202.

2. In this sense, Menger's project was the same as Dilthey's. The latter attempted to give the *Geisteswissenschaften* in general a philosophical basis by carrying on Kant's critique of pure and practical reason to a critique of historical reason. On this, cf., e.g., Gadamer and Boehm (eds.)(1976), p. 35.

3. Lekachman(1959), pp. 276–277.

4. Cf., e.g., Apel(1955); Outhwaite(1975); Stegmüller(1969); Rickman(1967).

5. Such a discussion would, of course, be necessary if one intended to investigate the influence and the success or failure of the Idealist-Romantic reaction in the social sciences on the intrusion of rationalist methodological and epistemological precepts from the natural sciences in general. This study, of course, deals with this problem situation, but only with reference to one particular instance: the foundations of Austrian economic thought laid by Menger in his *Grundsätze* of 1871 and their development through Wieser and Böhm-Bawerk in the 1880s.

6. Cf. also Rothacker(1930), pp. 4–5.

7. With the benefit of hindsight, one has to admit that Menger's attempt misfired. For an interesting comparison of Menger's *Untersuchungen* and Dilthey's *Einleitung*, see Schmoller(1883), which, in fact, was Schmoller's opening shot in the *Methodenstreit*.

8. Dilthey's biography of Schleiermacher was published in 1870 when Menger's basic ideas were already fixed in the form of marginal notes to Rau's *Grundsätze der Volkwirthschaftslehre*; cf. Kauder(1965), p. 62 n.18.

9. But unlike Weber, Menger did anything but try to remove all vestiges of Romanticism; cf. Antoni(1962), the chapter on Max Weber.

Individuum Est Ineffabile

10. Cf. Diemer(1977), p. 13; Pöggeler(1972), p. 11. For a summary of the various meanings of *Verstehen*, see Apel(1955); Diemer(1977), pp. 17–29.

11. Cf. Stegmüller(1969), pp. 361–362.

12. The history of this concept is discussed in Apel(1955); Bauman(1978); Diemer(1977); Gadamer and Boehm (eds.) (1976), introduction; Wach, especially (1926) and (1933).

13. This is the *Lehre von den Affekten*: "War es nicht ein Dogma, sondern ein Seelenzustand, was man aus der Schrift gewinnen sollte: so mußte der Interpret vor allem sich dem Seelenzustand, der sich in den Heiligen Schriften ausspricht, hingeben" W. Dilthey, quoted from Gadamer and Boehm (eds.) (1976), p. 20.

14. See Diemer(1977), p. 55.

15. I dwell somewhat on the development of the *Verstehen* doctrine not only because there is very little to be found on it in the literature on the history of economic thought, but also because the writings of the neo-Austrians in the United States and elsewhere have created nothing but confusion in the field; cf., e.g., Lachmann(1973), who actually elevates *Verstehen* to being the retrospective aspect of methodological individualism, and the papers collected in Dolan (ed.) (1976). It is, in fact, one of the purposes of the arguments developed in Essays I and II in this study to show that the connection established by the Austrian school between methodological individualism and *Verstehen* does not spring at all naturally from the subject matter but that these two concepts are historically incompatible if not mutually exclusive. On this, see below, pp. 99–102.

16. Cf. the essay on Herder in Berlin(1976) and Coplestone(1964), pp. 157–171 and 198–206. The influence of the British Enlightenment was, of course, also felt, but it did not have as immediate an impact as the German and French movements; the latter's importance was due mainly to the fact that French was the accepted language of the ruling class and the intelligentsia in Germany, especially in Prussia.

17. Herder's influence, of course, reached much further (for a discussion and survey, see Berlin[1976]). Herder's Historicism, and the Historicism of the nineteenth century in general—which was defined by Meinecke as: "Historismus ist eben zunächst nichts anderes als die Anwendung der in der großen deutschen Bewegung von Leibniz bis zu Goethes Tode gewonnen neuen Lebensprinzipien auf das geschichtliche Leben. . . . Der Kern des Historismus besteht in der Ersetzung einer generalisierenden Betrachtung geschichtlich-menschlicher Kräfte durch eine individualisierende Betrachtung" (Meinecke[1959], p. 2) and which found its expression in the *dicta* of Ranke that "das Ziel sei zu verstehen, wie es gewesen ist" and "jede Epoche sei unmittelbar zu Gott"—are not to be confused with the historicism attacked by Popper and Hayek (as, for instance, in Popper[1974] and Hayek[1955]). Nothing could have been further from the minds of Herder and the nineteenth-century

Historicists than the construction of large-scale, universal laws of historical development. This theme is further developed in this essay.

18. Cf. Berlin(1976), pp. 145, 167, 186–194 and *passim*; Coplestone(1964), Chapter 7.

19. Berlin(1976), p. 211.

20. Coplestone(1964), p. 159.

21. Cf. Berlin(1976), p. 187; Diemer(1977), p. 28; Meinecke(1959), p. 378; Wach(1926), p. 72. "Meist muß man den Gehalt des Verstehensbegriffes bei Herder geradezu unter dem Stichwort 'Fühlen' aufsuchen" Apel(1955), p. 163.

22. Berlin(1976), p. 192.

23. Berlin(1976), p. 201.

24. Berlin(1976), p. 168.

25. Berlin(1976), p. 193; cf. also Coplestone(1964), p. 201.

26. Cf. Benz(1960), p. 202; Holborn(1965), pp. 346, 349; Haym(1920), *passim*.

27. Cf. Hansen(1968), p. 169.

28. Cf. Frenzel and Frenzel(1966), vol. 1, p. 130.

29. See Holborn(1952), p. 364, and also Adamov-Autrusseau(1974), pp. 111–113.

30. "Schopenhauer was the first German of name who displayed an outright hostile attitude towards Christian religion" Holborn(1965), p. 345; cf. also Holborn(1952), p. 369.

31. Germany did not exist as a political entity then but had developed slowly from some 300 independent states after the Thirty Years War to 39 states in 1815.

32. Cf. Frenzel and Frenzel(1966), vol. 1, p. 131; Eisermann(1956), p. 60.

33. This term should be translated as "sentimentalism" since the German movement took its name from Lessing's translation of the title of Laurence Sterne's *Sentimental Journey*, rendering it as *Empfindsame Reise* (see Benz[1960], p. 198).

34. "Selbstgenügsame Empfindungsseligkeit und Schwärmerei" Frenzel and Frenzel(1966), vol. 1, p. 159.

35. Cf. Rintelen(1977), pp. 2–3.

36. Adamov-Autrusseau(1974), p. 113. Cf. also Berlin(1976), p. 146 and *passim*.

37. That is to say, German nationalism during the *Sturm und Drang* and, above all, the *Romantik* bore the features of an independence movement—directed at first against the domination by French thought and finally against physical domination, against the Napoleonic conquest of Europe. To be sure, this nationalism was the historical origin of later events, above all of the Second World War, but at the time it had nothing in common with the militant and expansionist European nationalism which led to the First World War. On this, see Benz(1960), pp. 216–217; Holborn(1965), p. 351.

38. Cf. Frenzel and Frenzel(1966), vol. 1, pp. 169–171; also Adamov-Autrusseau(1974).

39. Cf. Frenzel and Frenzel(1966), vol 1, pp. 193–194; Holborn(1965), p. 346.

40. Cf. Cardinal(1975), pp. 30, 43; Frenzel and Frenzel(1966), vol. 1, p. 250; Holborn(1965), p. 347.

41. Cardinal(1975), pp. 28, 30; Kluckhohn(1966), p. 22.

42. "The Romantic faces a reality which is chaotic, fragmented, without meaning. He cannot accept the explanations of rationalism, for they seem to censor authenticity and amputate feeling, reducing man and the world to a mechanism" Cardinal(1975), p. 28.

43. Holborn(1965), p. 347; Kluckhohn(1966), pp. 19–21.

44. Holborn(1965), pp. 346, 347.

45. Kluckhohn(1966), p. 17.

46. Kluckhohn(1966), p. 108.
47. Kluckhohn(1966), p. 57. See also Cardinal(1975), pp. 36–37 and p. 12: "Poetic rather than scientific explanation of the real world gained increased currency."
48. See also Eisermann(1956), p. 18.
49. Cardinal(1975), p. 35.
50. Cf. Frenzel and Frenzel(1966), vol. 1, p. 253.
51. This confusion, in fact, is at the root of the inconsistency of Austrian methodology; on this, see the discussion of the interpretation of Leibniz's *Monadology* in Austria below, pp. 100–102.
52. Kluckhohn(1966), pp. 55–57.
53. Kluckhohn(1966), pp. 36–37; Cardinal(1975), pp. 35–36. The simile of Robinson Crusoe which features so predominantly in Austrian theory and which provides the starting point for all Austrian theoretical discourse is, of course, a representation of this congruence between microcosm and macrocosm.
54. "In this way, the Romantic scientist posits the ideal conditions under which Nature should be investigated; he rejects the damaging one-sidedness of empirical analysis, which to him is no more than a classification of dead bits of Nature showing no respect for its living spirit. The Romantic scientist is a practitioner of Nature Philosophy, which means that at the same time as he studies things, he studies mind. His techniques of speculation combine with meditation, awareness of outer with awareness of inner processes" Cardinal(1975), p. 36. Compare this with the following section from Böhm-Bawerk's preface to his *Positive Theorie*: "Man wird in diesem Buch überwiegend eine Darstellungsweise angewendet finden, die man—oft nicht ohne einen gewissen aburteilenden Beigeschmack—als 'abstrakt' zu bezeichnen pflegt. Dennoch, behaupte ich, enthält meine Lehre nicht einen einzigen Zug, der nicht von echter empirischer Grundlage abgenommen wäre. Man kann eben in verschiedener Art Empirie treiben. Man kann Erfahrungstatsachen, auf die man sich stützt, entweder aus der Wirtschaftsgeschichte schöpfen, oder man kann sie durch die Statistik sich vorführen lassen, *oder man kann sie dem gemeinen täglichen Leben, so wie es jedem von uns sich darbietet, durch schlichte und formlose Beobachtung unmittelbar abzulauschen suchen.* Keine dieser drei Weisen hat ein Monopol, sondern jede von ihnen hat ihren besonderen, eigenartigen Wirkungskreis. Es liegt in der Natur der Sache, daß die historische und statistische Forschung uns das Erfahrungsmaterial in viel größerem Stil und aus viel umfangreicheren Beobachtungsgebieten erschließen; dafür vermögen sie überall nur die gröberen und mehr äußerlichen Tatsachen zu erfassen: sie sieben gleichsam die wirtschaftlichen Ereignisse mit einem groben Siebe, durch welches eine Menge von zarten, unscheinbaren und zumal mehr innerlichen Zügen des Wirtschaftslebens unerfasst hindurchschlüpft. *Will man nun auch diese zu Forschungszwecken heranziehen—und man kann für sehr viele wissenschaftliche Aufgaben ihrer Kenntnisse durchaus nicht entraten—so erübrigt nichts, als zu der verhälnismäßig engen, aber eindringlichen persönlichen Lebensbeobachtung seine Zuflucht zu nehmen"* Böhm-Bawerk(1961b), pp. xvii–xviii (emphasis added).
55. Cardinal(1975), p. 38. This, in addition to the Aristotelian strands in Menger's thought, is also part of the background for his dogmatic stand on the truth and certainty of the results of "exact" research. This issue will be discussed in detail in Essay II.
56. Cf. Beck(1967), p. 302; Benz(1960), pp. 216–217; Eisermann(1956), pp. 13, 18; Holborn(1965), p. 351; Kluckhohn(1966), p. 187.
57. Cf. Eisermann(1956), pp. 23–39; Frenzel and Frenzel(1966), vol. 1, p. 250.
58. Cf. Eisermann(1956), p. 16.
59. Cf. Kluckhohn(1966), p. 61; Eisermann(1956), p. 18.

60. "Die Weltanschauung führt zu einer pluralistischen Individualethik, aber zu keiner wirklichen Sozialethik." "Die Kirche blieb auch für Schleiermacher ein Verein von Einzelnen, die dadurch zu einer Gemeinschaft wurden, daß sie sich zu Füßen desselben Pfarrers setzten" Holborn(1952), p. 379; see also Russell(1975), pp. 656–659.

61. Eisermann(1956), p. 19.

62. Holborn(1965), pp. 350, 351; cf. also Holborn(1952), pp. 373–375; Benz(1960), pp. 195–196; Briefs(1941), p. 288; Russell(1975), p. 654.

63. Both were converts to Catholicism, the former the first Romantic political scientist, the latter one of the founders and one of the most influential exponents of the Romantic movement and co-translator of the classic German language edition of Shakespeare's works. On Adam Müller, see also pp. 55–57.

64. He was the translator of Burke's *Reflections on the Revolution in France* and one of the most important influences on Metternich's politics.

65. Holborn(1965), p. 351; see also Kluckhohn(1966), p. 9, and Eisermann(1956), pp. 21–24, on Austria's reactionary influence on the *Deutschen Bund*. One further remark on the relevance of all this seems to be necessary here: Kauder discusses exactly the same topic as this essay in Kauder(1958), yet no discussion of Romanticism is to be found there. Instead, he refers to Dilthey and Simmel (p. 416) and, among others, Grillparzer, Stifter and Anzengruber. (Aristotle will be discussed in Essay II; on this issue, I am more or less in agreement with Kauder.) On Dilthey, I have already commented above (cf. p. 25). In the same vein, Georg Simmel (1858–1918) began to publish only in the 1890s. Grillparzer and Stifter are generally known as representatives of the *Biedermeier*, a literary movement in Germany and Austria from about 1820 to 1850. The *Biedermeier* displayed all those intellectual properties which we shall find in the Historical School, too: quietism, passivism in political life, subordination; its undercurrent was *Lebensangst*. This movement was a continuation of the stream of thought which had issued from Romanticism. In addition, it took account of the changing political climate (*Restaurationsperiode*), the rejection of speculation and the increasing importance attributed to facts in life, or realism, in the *Geisteswissenschaften* (cf. Rothacker[1930], Chapter 4). The connections which Kauder establishes between Wieser and Stifter sound highly probable, and Kauder may well be right. But why base one's case on tentative and as yet unverifiable conjectures if one can take the direct route via the discussion of Romanticism and Historicism, above all, if this route is directly indicated by Menger and Wieser themselves in their classification of economics among the *Geisteswissenschaften*? (This will be dealt with in detail in Essay II.) On Anzengruber, not much needs to be said. He was a Naturalist (along with Gerhart Hauptmann), his first play was performed in 1870 and the majority of his writings were published in the 1870s and 1880s, hardly early enough to have exerted an important influence on Menger.

66. As a curious aside, it might be worth pointing out the later attempts, in the wake of the wars of liberation and the creation of the *Deutschen Bund*, to establish a "national religion", particularly in view of the ridicule poured over the earlier French counterpart, the "religion of reason" (cf. Holborn[1952], pp. 375 ff.).

67. Eisermann(1956), Chapter 1; Holborn(1952).

Romanticism and Idealist Philosophy

68. "In the whole theory of the material world, Cartesianism was rigidly deterministic. Living organisms, just as much as dead matter, were governed by the laws of physics; there was no longer need, as in the Aristotelian philosophy, of an entelechy

or soul to explain the growth of organisms and the movement of animals" Russell(1975), p. 551.

69. On Hegel and Aristotle, see Haym(1857), pp. 226–228.

70. Both movements flourished roughly at the same time. Romanticism is usually dated from 1798 to 1835 (cf. Frenzel and Frenzel[1966], vol. 1, p. 249). Fichte's *Grundlagen der gesamten Wissenschaftslehre*, the cornerstone of post-Kantian idealism, was published in 1794. The young Schelling published his most important and influential writings between 1795, *Vom Ich als Prinzip der Philosophie*, and 1801, *Darstellung meines Systems der Philosophie*. With the rise of Hegel, whose *Phänomenologie des Geistes* appeared in 1807, Schelling's fame began to sink and did not rise again even after the former's death in 1831, although Schelling was to outlive Hegel by more than twenty years.

71. Cf. Diemer(1976), pp. 15–17.

72. Beck(1967), p. 301.

73. Cf. Coplestone(1965), p. 35.

74. This discussion of Fichte is largely based on Coplestone(1965); Haym(1920); Jergius(1976); Kluckhohn(1966); Rosenkranz(1870).

75. "Wenn man folgenden Satz ausspricht: Das Subjekt der Romantik ist das transzendentale Ich, welches Fleisch und Blut geworden ist—so hat man in wenigen Worten das Wesen der Romantik umgriffen. Zwei Hauptdinge werden damit genannt, welche die beiden Pfeiler sind, auf dene jene Geistesart beruht. . . . Das erste ist, daß das Subjekt der Romantik ebenfalls das transzendentale Ich ist, und das zweite besagt, daß dieses transzendentale Ich zur in die Wirklichkeit der Zeit hineingestellten Person geworden ist, zur konkreten und leiblichen Realität. Durch die erste Kennzeichnung allein ist die Romantik noch nicht völlig charakterisiert, weil dieselbe Kennzeichnung auch für die Philosophie des Idealismus gilt. Mit der zweiten aber wird die Eigentümlichkeit dessen, was romantisch oder Romatik heißt, vollständig klar; sie präzisiert die Romantik als eine vitalistische Richtung, als eine zeitlich-weltliche Verwirklichung gegenüber der bloßen Theorie. Der Idealismus als philosophische Tendenz steht außerhalb jeder Zeitlichkeit, die Romantik dagegen steht innerhalb der Zeit. Diese innere Stellung zur Außerzeitlichkeit oder zur Zeitlichkeit ist der einzige wichtige Unterschied, welcher zwischen diesen beiden wesentlichen Kundgebungen des deutschen Geistes besteht.

Wir können auch sagen: Wenn man das transzendentale Ich betrachtet und auf die Welt bezieht, dann erhält man die Romantik. Diese ist durchaus keine komplizierte Geistesart, sobald man sie in ihrem Lebenszentrum zu packen versteht. Ja, sie erscheint sogar so einförmig wie ihre Meisterwerke, welche zuerst unübersehbar und unbestimmbar dünken mögen und dann, wenn man sie näher betrachtet, sich als endlose Variationen über ein und dasselbe und immer gleichbleibende Motiv herausstellen" Pensa(1948), pp. 292–293.

This erroneous Romantic interpretation of Fichte was also adopted by K. Rosenkranz, Hegel's biographer: "Die Einleitung der Wissenschaftslehre war sehr geeignet, ihr einen großen Kreis zu gewinnen, denn sie was leicht faßlich, weil sie die abstracten Bestimmungen sofort an dem Ich verdeutlichte. Jedermann konnte an seinem eigenen Ich sogleich die Probe machen, ihm das Nicht-Ich entgegengesetzt finden, es als identisch mit sich, als sich selbst setzend, als Ursache u.s.w. erkennen. Das Ich, aus welchem die abstracten Bestimmungen abgeleitet wurden, blieb zugleich das Beispiel für sie" Rosenkranz(1870), p. 27.

76. Cf. Jergius(1976), p. 87.

77. Jergius(1976), p. 80 (my translation).

78. Coplestone(1965), p. 88.

79. Coplestone(1965), p. 90.

80. "An der Spitze der romantischen Epoche der Hermeneutik steht Fichte. Er war der wahre Held und anerkannte Vorläufer der idealistischen Philosophie in den Jahren der Formation der romantischen Bewegung, die schließlich in Scheiermachers theoretischer Arbeit, aber auch in seiner epochemachenden hermeneutischen Praxis, seiner Platonübersetzung, ihre Krönung fand. Auf die Grundlage der *Gesamten Wissenschaftslehre* von 1794 bezogen sich wie selbstverständlich Schiller und Schlegel, Novalis, Jean Paul, Hölderlin und Kleist, Schelling und Schleiermacher. Dies wurde das Grundbuch des Idealismus. Zwar erkannte jeder die epochemachende Bedeutung von Kants *Kritik der reinen Vernunft* an, aber in Fichtes systematischem Hauptwerk sah man allgemein die Vollendung und konsequente Durchführung des kritischen Gedankens der Transzendentalphilosophie" Gadamer and Boehm (eds.) (1976), p. 31.

81. See above, pp. 32–33.

82. This is discussed in detail in Essay II. Suffice it to say here that although Menger never used the term "introspection" himself, introspection is the only logically consistent way in which he could have justified the empirical character of his inductive process, which he had modelled on Aristotle's epistemology.

83. On the meaning of this kind of deduction, see Haym(1920), p. 659.

84. Quoted from Haym(1920), p. 646 (my translation).

85. Cf. also Coplestone(1965), pp. 18–19.

86. Haym(1857), p. 230.

87. Cf. E. Bloch(1972); Coplestone(1965); Rothacker(1930).

88. Hegel—*Phänomenologie des Geistes*, quoted from E. Bloch(1972), p. 79.

89. It is important to distinguish this identity of subject and object from Schelling's: the former is the result and the end of the process, it is what makes the process teleological; it exists only once the spirit has arrived, so to speak (cf. E. Bloch[1972], pp. 98–99). When Eisermann(1956), p. 77 (my translation) says, "An essential characteristic of Hegelian philosophy . . . is . . . the identity between thought and being which it postulates", then "postulate" must be understood to refer to the Idealist system as such, not to identity as a first principle on which the system is built. This contrasts sharply from Schelling's system in which identity is postulated as a first principle. Another way of looking at this difference is to say that Hegel's system is historical throughout while Schelling's is not.

90. Eisermann(1956), p. 77 (my translation).

91. Cf. Eisermann(1956), p. 78, and also Hansen(1968), p. 169.

92. Cf. Rothacker(1930), Chapter 4, and also n.65 above.

93. See, for instance, the quotation from Böhm-Bawerk in n.54 above.

94. In this context, I fully agree with Theodore Abel's "The Operation Called *Verstehen*" if (and only if) every time Abel writes *Verstehen* one substitutes *introspection*. This is not at all to say that I consider these two concepts equivalent in general.

95. For the modern perversion of these concepts, see Lachmann(1973) and some of the papers collected in Dolan (ed.)(1976). Not even Hayek escaped this affliction. Nowhere in his *Counter-Revolution of Science* does he adduce any reason or justification of—philosophical or otherwise—why economics is necessarily subjective and why introspection and methodological individualism constitute the only legitimate basis for economic theorising.

96. See, for instance, Bostaph(1978); Hansen(1968).

97. See Menger(1883) and especially the fifteenth letter in Menger(1884).

98. See Rothacker(1930), p. 41. Savigny even prevented Hegel's admission to the Berlin Academy of Sciences (ibid., p. 62).

99. "Die unmittelbare Vorbereitung der geschichtlichen Nationaloekonomik", Roscher(1874), Chapter 33, pp. 912–948; on Hegel, Section 188, pp. 925–930. Roscher was by no means the only one to return to Hegel. This trend is quite readily exemplified by the father of the modern *Verstehen* doctrine, Wilhelm Dilthey: "Dilthey's work can conveniently be divided into two periods: an early one in which the emphasis is individualistic and psychologistic, and a later period, under the influence of Hegel, in which the concept of objective mind or spirit (*objektiver Geist*) supplants the earlier individualism. The emphasis shifts from the empathetic penetration or reconstruction of other people's mental processes to the hermeneutic interpretation of cultural products and conceptual structures" Outhwaite(1975), p. 26.

100. Menger(1883), pp. 128–129 n.44 [Menger(1963/1985), p. 121 n.44]. This, however, did not prevent Menger from developing a very primitive philosophy of history in the *Grundsätze* (mainly in his footnotes) which seems to owe more to the Enlightenment than to the Romantic movement.

101. "Das absolute Ich ist immanente Kausalität" Haym(1920), p. 625, on Fichte; and "Die Zweckmäßigkeit . . . [sei] . . . der eigenste Charakter des Geistes und der Geist daher eine sich selbst organisierende Natur" ibid., p. 645, on Schelling.

102. Cf. E. Bloch(1972), p. 168.

103. E. Bloch(1972), pp. 137–140.

104. Cf. Rothacker(1930), p. 9.

105. A detailed analysis of these issues in Menger's work is presented in Essay II.

Historicism

106. Eisermann(1956), pp. 84, 86. Cf. also n.75, above.

107. Cf. Rothacker(1930), e.g., pp. 107–108. A definition of Historicism is given in n.17, above.

108. Cf., e.g., Rothacker(1930), p. 136 n.1.

109. Cf. Eisermann(1956), pp. 82, 84; Kluckhohn(1966), pp. 111–112. See also pp. 53–54.

110. Cf. Rothacker(1930), pp. 43, 153.

111. Roscher(1874), Section 187 (pp. 916–924) is devoted to Niehbur.

112. Cf. Wach(1933), p. 55.

113. On Ranke, see Eisermann(1956), pp. 91–93; Rothacker(1930), pp. 153–162; Wach(1933), pp. 89–133.

114. Cf. n.17, above.

115. Cf. Rothacker(1930), pp. 156, 162.

116. Cf. Wach(1933), pp. 105–107.

117. Wach(1933), p. 89.

118. For details on this issue, see Essay II.

119. On Droysen, cf. Burger(1978); Leyh(1977); Rothacker(1930), pp. 169–179; Wach(1933), pp. 134–189.

120. Cf. Rothacker(1930), p. 169; Wach(1933), pp. 135–139.

121. Rothacker(1930), p. 174.

122. Cf. Wach(1933), pp. 147–149, and also Burger(1978), p. 9.

123. Cf. Wach(1933), pp. 185–186.

124. Droysen(1977), p. 423 (para. 8).

125. It was first published in 1814; references are to the 1892 reprint of the third edition of 1840. On the importance of this book, see, e.g., Eisermann(1956), p. 84, and Schumpeter(1954), p. 423.

126. Schumpeter(1954), p. 26 n.2.

127. Cf. Burtt(1972); Cubeddu(1985); Hansen(1968); Hutchison(1973) and (1981). The absence of discussion of this connection in the literature, however, is simply astounding. In the Anglo-Saxon literature, Blaug(1973), Bostaph(1978), Hunt(1979), Rogin(1956), Roll(1973), Schumpeter(1954) and Seligman(1971) ignore this theme completely; so do Gide and Rist(1948) whose originally French book has been translated into English as well as into German. In the German literature, Salin(1967), Schneider(1970) and Stavenhagen(1969) fall into the same category.

128. Burtt(1972), pp. 197–198; but see also Roll(1973), p. 215.

129. Hutchison (1973), pp. 26–27, and (1981), pp. 186–187.

130. Menger(1883), pp. 207–208 [Menger(1963/1985), pp. 176–177], and (1884), pp. 93–94.

131. Menger(1883), p. 214 [Menger(1963/1985), pp. 181–182].

132. Menger(1883), p. 214 n.103 [Menger(1963/1985), p. 181 n.103]; this note carries over to p. 215 where the relevant passage is to be found.

133. "Betrachten wir nämlich unsern Zustand, wie er in der That ist, so finden wir uns mitten in einer Masse juristischer Begriffe und Ansichten, die sich von Geschlecht zu Geschlecht fortgeerbt und angehäuft haben. Wie die Sache jetzt steht, besitzen und beherrschen wir diesen Stoff nicht, sondern wir werden von ihm bestimmt und getrieben nicht wie wir wollen." "Dieser überwiegende Einfluss des bestehenden Stoffes also ist auf keine Weise vermeidlich: aber *er wird uns verderblich seyn, solange wir ihm bewusstlos dienen, wohltätig, wenn wir ihm eine lebendig bildende Kraft entgegensetzen, durch historische Ergründung ihn uns unterwerfen*, und so ganz den Reichthum der vergangenen Geschlechter uns aneignen. Wir haben also nur die Wahl, ob wir wollen, nach Baco's Ausdruck, sermocinari tamquam e vinculis, oder ob eine gründliche Rechtswissenschaft uns lehren soll, *diesen historischen Stoff frey als unser Werkzeug zu gebrauchen*: ein drittes gibt es nicht" Savigny(1892), pp. 68, 69 (emphasis added).

134. Some of the issues are, of course, dealt with in Essay II. For more detailed discussions of the *Methodenstreit*, see Bostaph(1978) and Hansen(1968).

135. Schmoller(1883).

136. For a detailed discussion of Schmoller's position, see Hansen(1968).

137. Hutchison(1973), p. 27, and (1981), p. 187.

138. "Denn es ist unmöglich, die Ansicht und Bildung der jetztlebenden Rechtsgelehrten zu vernichten; unmöglich, die Natur der bestehenden Rechtsverhältnisse umzuwandeln; und auf diese doppelte Unmöglichkeit gründet sich der unauflösliche organische Zusammenhang der Geschlechter und Zeitalter, zwischen welchen nur Entwicklung aber nicht absolutes Ende und absoluter Anfang gedacht werden kann" Savigny(1892), p. 68. Another point which ought to be emphasised here is the affinity of this idea to Leibniz's conception of change and development in his *Monadology* (cf., e.g., paras. 6, 10, 73 of the *Monadology*).

139. "Die wissenschaftliche Bedeutung der Sprachbegriffe" Wieser(1884), pp. 1–10.

140. Cf. Eisermann(1956), p. 86.

141. Savigny himself refers to Hugo and Möser as predecessors (Savigny[1892], p. 9). On Gustav Hugo see also ibid., pp. 73, 117 (for a review of Hugo's textbook on natural law, see Marx[1970]). On Justus Möser see also Savigny(1892), p. 78.

142. Cf. Eisermann(1956), p. 6; Meinecke(1959), p. 278. "To this imposing but romantic philosophical edifice, which reached completion in the Idealism of Hegel and with which the nineteenth century proposed to replace the system of natural law, Burke made an important contribution" Sabine(1941), p. 607. The section on

Burke is based on Auerbach(1968); Canavan(1963); Meinecke(1959), pp. 267–281; Sabine(1941), Chapter 29.

143. Cf. Heer(1953), pp. 577–579.

144. Heer(1953), p. 577.

145. Cf., e.g., Roscher(1874), p. 753.

146. Cf. Rothacker(1930), pp. 47–48, 72–73.

147. Cf. Mülher(1948).

148. Savigny(1892), p. 29.

149. Savigny(1892), e.g., pp. 90, 91.

150. Savigny(1892), pp. 71, 72.

151. Kluckhohn(1966), pp. 111–112.

152. Savigny(1892), p. 14.

153. Cf. Savigny(1892), p. 25. Methodological individualism without at least a certain degree of uniformity would be a contradiction in terms, or—in the language of economics—an insurmountable aggregation problem.

154. Rothacker(1930), p. 53.

155. "Worauf es dabey ankommt, ist nicht schwer zu sagen: das vorhandene, was nicht geändert, sondern beybehalten werden soll, muss gründlich erkannt und richtig ausgesprochen werden. Jenes betrifft den Stoff, dieses die Form" Savigny(1892), p. 13.

156. Cf. Rothacker(1930), p. 72.

157. "Leben . . . heißt teils Gehalt und Formung neu in Einklang bringen, teils rückwärts gewendet in ihrer ursprünglichen Identität erfassen" Rothacker(1930), p. 73.

158. This conception of goal-directedness or purposiveness, must not be confused with determinateness.

159. Rothacker(1930), p. 70.

160. Eisermann(1956), p. 84; cf. also Kluckhohn(1966), pp. 112–113.

161. "Die Charakteristik des 'Volks' als eines 'Aggregates der Privaten', vulgus not populus, kommt zur Anwendung auf Savigny's Volksgeist gar nicht in Frage" Rothacker(1930), p. 101. The index of Rothacker's book is also interesting from this point of view: under "collectivism" the entry reads: "Kollektivismus s. Volksgeist" ibid., p. 286.

162. Kluckhohn(1966), p. 112.

163. "Aber welcher philosophischer Gedanke konnte ihr gemäßer sein als der einer gegenständlich und ästhetisch aufgefaßten Entfaltung der geistigen Welt als eines göttlichen Organismus, der ihr die Möglichkeit gab, das Ineinander von Sinn und Notwendigkeit, das jede geistige Entwicklung zeigt, wissenschaftlich gerechtfertigt zu wissen und schließlich in der Unbestimmtheit des Absoluten, die Hegel zu einem seiner berühmten Sarkasmen veranlaßte, Ellenbogenfreiheit für die Empirie zu haben? Die metaphysisch-ästhetisch-organische Weltbetrachtung der Identitätsphilosophie so als Rahmen, in welchem—ohne spekulative Ansprüche, aber ganz der Anschauung der Sache hingegeben,—der Lebensbegriff der Historischen Schule Gestalt gewann" Rothacker(1930), pp. 68–69.

164. Rothacker(1930), p. 69.

165. Cf. Rothacker(1930), pp. 118–120.

166. Sabine(1941), p. 614.

167. Rothacker(1930), p. 115 (my translation).

168. "Eine umfassende Untersuchung aber gerade der in der Jahrhundertmitte weit über Hegel und die Romantik hinaus noch mächtigen Volksgeistvorstellungen müßte in dieser emanatistischen Denkgewohnheit und ihren Nachwirkungen eine

der wesentlichsten Kategorien überhaupt entdecken, die es uns ermöglichen, den historischen Stoff geistig zu umfassen, und mittels derer unser historisches Weltbild sich logisch überhaupt konstituiert." "Daß es sich hier um eine ganz fundamentale Denkkategorie handelt, ein unentbehrliches Mittel jeder geistigen 'Charakteristik', könnte nur in einer umfassenden Erörterung des 'Verstehens', einer wahren 'Kritik der historischen Vernunft' gezeigt werden" Rothacker(1930), pp. 116, 117; cf. also Salin(1967), p. 93.

The Historical Economists

169. Cf., e.g., Schumpeter(1954), p. 804. This section is based on Briefs(1941); Eisermann(1956); Hansen(1968); Hüter(1928); Schumpeter(1926); and Weber(1973). In addition I have consulted Friedrichs(1913); Gide and Rist(1948); Hutchison(1953); Mitchell(1967) and (1969); Nicholson(1966); Recktenwald (ed.) (1971); Roll(1973); Schmoller(1888); Schneider(1970); Schumacher(1931); Schumpeter(1924); Stavenhagen(1969); and Suranyi-Unger(1968).

170. Cf., e.g., Schumacher(1931); Schumpeter(1954), pp. 507, 808; Schumpeter(1924), pp. 100–101.

171. Cf. Roscher(1874), pp. 751–790; Stavenhagen(1969), p. 191.

172. Schumpeter(1954), p. 421; on the concept of "school", see n.190 below.

173. Cf. Briefs(1941), p. 297; Eisermann(1956), p. 103.

174. Briefs(1941), p. 279.

175. His main works are *Elemente der Staatskunst* (1809); *Versuch einer Theorie des Geldes mit besonderer Berücksichtigung auf Grossbritannien* (1816); *Von der Notwendigkeit einer theologischen Grundlage der gesamten Staatswissenschaften* (1819).

176. Cf. Briefs(1941), p. 281; Eisermann(1956), p. 104; Schumpeter(1954), p. 421.

177. Briefs(1941), p. 281.

178. Briefs(1941), p. 282.

179. Cf. Roll(1973), p. 221.

180. Roll(1973), p. 224; cf. also Briefs(1941), p. 287.

181. On Knies, see also Hüter(1928), pp. 66, 69–70. Cf. also below, p. 157.

182. Closer, that is, to what they actually did, not to what they professed to be doing.

183. Roll(1973), p. 231.

184. Cf., e.g., Gide and Rist(1948), p. 286.

185. Cf. Eisermann(1956), p. 220 and *passim*.

186. Gide and Rist(1948), p. 282.

187. Eisermann(1956), p. 14; cf. also Gide and Rist(1948), p. 279.

188. Schumpeter(1954), p. 504.

189. Wilhelm Roscher, *Grundriss zu Vorlesungen über die Staatswissenschaft nach geschichtlicher Methode* (1843); Bruno Hildebrand, *Die Nationalökonomie der Gegenwart und Zukunft* (1848); Karl Knies, *Die politische Ökonomie vom Standpunkt der geschichtlichen Methode* (1853; the second, revised edition was published in 1883 with the title: *Die politische Ökonomie vom geschichtlichen Standpunkt*).

190. The term "school", here, refers to a group of scientists who share a common aim, a common method, a common attitude on the relevant issues, and the awareness that they are consciously and deliberately working on the same programme. This is a fairly wide definition of the term, but if one were to adopt, for example, Schumpeter's definition of "one master, one doctrine, personal coherence; . . . a core; . . . zones of influence; . . . fringe ends" (Schumpeter[1954], p. 45), doubts about whether even the Austrians constituted a school could not be dispersed very easily.

191. "Diese Methode will für die Staatswirthschaft etwas Ähnliches erreichen, was die SAVIGNY-EICHHORNsche Methode für die Jurisprudenz erreicht hat" Roscher (1843), quoted from Schneider(1970), p. 284 n.2.

192. Menger(1883), p. 222 [Menger(1963/1985), pp. 186–187].

193. "Sie [i.e., his book] bezweckt eine ähnliche Reform für die Erkenntnis der wirtschaftlichen Seite des Volkslebens, wie sie in diesem Jahrhundert die Sprachwissenschaft erlebt hat" Hildebrand (1848), quoted from Schneider(1970), p. 288.

194. This characterisation of (post-Ricardian) economic theory reached its climax in the statement by Schmoller: "Es trat die geistige Schwindsucht eines von der Empirie gänzlich losgelösten Rationalismus ein" Schmoller(1888), p. 149. On the classification of the older historical economists' objections to the classical school, see also Gide and Rist(1948), pp. 393 ff.; Schumpeter(1924), pp. 110–112; Stavenhagen(1969), p. 197.

195. See, e.g., Eisermann(1956), p. 215.

196. The label "school" was now applicable even according to Schumpeter's definition (cf. n.190 above).

197. Cf. Eisermann(1956), p. 133; Schmoller(1888), pp. 153, 168; Weber(1973), pp. 8–9.

198. Cf. Eisermann(1956), p. 127.

199. Cf. Eisermann(1956), pp. 120–122.

200. "Bei Licht betrachtet, ist es die kritiklose übertragung historischer Arbeit auf das theoretische Gebiet der Nationalökonomie, ohne jedes tiefere Durchdenken der Voraussetzungen oder Möglichkeiten eines solchen Vorgehens." "Der Historismus Roschers bildet deshalb ein aus lutherisch-protestantischer Religiosität, romantisch-organologischer Metaphysik, aufklärerisch-liberalen Progressvorstellungen, historischer Dialektik Hegelscher Provenienz und humanistischen Bildungselementen uneinheitlich und unzureichend verschmolzenes, werder logisch noch erkenntnistheoretisch geklärtes Ganzes sui generis, dessen Wirksamkeit bei so viel offenkundiger Unzulänglichkeit nur verstanden werden kann, wenn man sie einfügt und im Zusammenhang mit der historisch-soziologischen Gesamtkonstellation sieht, in die Roschers Lebensgang eingespannt war" Eisermann(1956), pp. 130, 157; see also Weber(1973), p. 41. It would take a detailed study of Roscher's writings to settle the dispute which Hüter (1928, p. 83 n.3) raised against Weber's interpretation as to whether Roscher was an empiricist, a clandestine positivist who became side-tracked by speculative argument, or, as Weber sees it, an organicist, which is to say, a speculatively inclined historian, whose religiosity kept the speculative element from overrunning the entire argument and who became side-tracked by positivist strands of thought through his liking for the natural sciences. This is certainly not the place to settle this dispute; what remains beyond doubt, however, is that Roscher did mix (up) arguments and modes of thinking from both the *Naturwissenschaften* and the *Geisteswissenschaften*, as they were to be called later.

201. See Eisermann(1956), pp. 130–133.

202. Eisermann(1956), p. 133.

203. Cf. Schmoller(1888), p. 169.

204. Cf. Weber(1973), p. 11.

205. Weber(1973), p. 3.

206. Weber(1973), pp. 15–20, 41–42.

207. See also Eisermann(1956), pp. 120–123, 141–144.

208. Cf. Schmoller(1888), p. 145.

209. Schmoller(1888), p. 152.

210. Cf., e.g., Eisermann(1956), p. 172.

211. Eisermann(1956), p. 173.

212. Cf. Eisermann(1956), pp. 168–169, 173–174. The publication of Hildebrand's book (1848) was triggered off, according to Eisermann, by Friedrich Engel's book on the English working class (*Die Lage der arbeitenden Klasse in England* [1845]).

213. That is to say, while theirs were empirical reasons, wanting to introduce this methodology because it had worked in another field of inquiry, his were logical reasons for declaring economics a historical science. Cf. also Schmoller(1888), p. 206.

214. Schmoller(1888), p. 209; Weber's article—"Roscher und Knies und die logischen Probleme der historischen Nationalökonomie"—was originally published in *Schmollers Jahrbuch* (1903–1906) and is reprinted in Weber(1973), pp. 1–145.

215. Cf. Eisermann(1956), p. 211, and also n.189 above.

216. Eisermann(1956), p. 133.

217. Cf. Eisermann(1956), pp. 208–210; Hüter(1928), pp. 48, 91; Weber(1973), pp. 44–45.

218. This group is, at times, also referred to as the "ethical school of economics" (on this, cf. also Schumpeter[1954], p. 812).

219. Schmoller(1888), p. 171.

220. See, e.g., Weber(1973), p. 142.

221. This ultimate substance, soul or *Volksgeist*, plays the same role in Knies's epistemology as the religiosity does in Roscher's: Being asserted dogmatically, it constitutes the barrier beyond which rationalistic explanation cannot advance. The difference is that Roscher's theistic limit marks the end of any explanation—beyond it lies only belief—while Knies's Idealist limits marks the starting point for a qualitatively different type of explanation.

222. Weber(1973), pp. 144–145.

223. Not only did he compare him very favourably with Friedrich List—"he is in the theoretical field, what Friedrich List was in the practical"—but he also called him the "theoretical founder of historico-psychological modern German economics", that is, of Schmoller's economics (Schmoller[1888], p. 207).

224. Cf. Eisermann(1956), pp. 212–215.

225. Knies objected to economic liberalism particularly because, according to him, it leads to socialism: "In völliger übereinstimmung mit Karl Marx, . . . ist Karl Knies der überzeugung, daß die Theorie der klassischen Schule, mit innerer Logik und Notwendigkeit fortentwickelt, auf eine wissenschaftliche Rechtfertigung des Sozialismus hinauslaufen müßte—vor dessen praktischer Herbeiführung er Deutschland . . . unter allen Umständen bewahrt sehen möchte" Eisermann(1956), pp. 202–203. In this instance, Knies and Menger are in complete agreement (cf. Menger[1883], p. 208 [Menger(1963/1985), p. 177]).

226. Schmoller's programme was summarised by Schumpeter as follows: "Mit einer Minimalbelastung an Apriori an das Material herantreten, damit Zusammenhänge zu erfassen suchen, dabei das Apriori für die Zukunft vermehren und neue Auffassungsweisen erarbeiten, die weiterem Material gegenüber als (provisorisch) vorhandenes Rüstzeug dienen und so weiter in steter Wechselwirkung zwischen Material und gedanklicher Verarbeitung" Schumpeter(1926), pp. 381–382. This definition is, of course, only a modified statement of the hermeneutic circle.

227. On the reasons for rejecting philosophy of history, see Schumpeter(1926), p. 384 n.1.

228. For a detailed discussion of Schmoller's programme and background, see Hansen(1968), pp. 140–160.

229. Schumacher(1931), p. 372.

II

Methodology

On Menger's Methodology

The launching pad both for Austrian economic theory and for the methodology associated with it was Menger's writings; to be more precise, his *Grundsätze* of 1871 and the *Untersuchungen* of 1883. The only problem with this statement, or statements of a similar kind, is that this interpretation of Austrian economics as a historical event has no factual basis. The "founding" of the Austrian school is a convenient myth, an *ex post facto* rationalisation, which provides historians of economic thought with a point of origin for an allegedly unified system of thought. Menger, unlike his compatriot Freud a generation later, did not set out to "found" a school. Rather, he intended to make some fruitful contributions to an already existing school of economic thought—the historical economists around Roscher.[1] It was only after his *Grundsätze* had come to the attention of two young Austrian economists, namely, Friedrich von Wieser and Eugen von Böhm-Bawerk; after it had acted as the basis for their own ideas on economic theory; and only after they had begun to develop and publish their ideas, which in turn occurred only after the *Methodenstreit* between Menger and Schmoller had taken place, that the talk of an Austrian school gradually began to make the rounds, aided, no doubt, by Böhm-Bawerk's powerful capacity for propaganda. The tale that Menger initially refused to accept these two as "disciples" has been told too often to have to be repeated here.[2] In fact, what came to be known as the Austrian theory of value and price was not so much Menger's own words and thoughts but Wieser's and Böhm-Bawerk's versions of them. In reproduction, though, the original Menger was lost, and— certainly for an international readership but also to a certain extent for the German-speaking audience—the voice of Böhm-Bawerk substituted for it. What has become known as Menger's theory was, therefore, mostly the elaborations of this theory by Wieser and Böhm-Bawerk, and only their references to Menger as their spiritual ancestor created the impression that everything was a smooth line from Menger onwards.

Menger's economic theory is discussed in Essay III; in this essay, I take a closer look at his methodology. Although the Austrian economists' main contribution was in the field of pure theory, they were, nevertheless, pre-occupied with methodological issues for a significant part of the time because they wanted to clear the ground for pure theory within German academic economics, which was dominated in the second half of the nineteenth century by the historical economists.[3] Böhm-Bawerk proved to be the most prolific writer, purporting to follow the path mapped out by Menger. As it turns out, he was the least philosophically minded of the three older Austrians, hardly able to raise himself above the level of mere propaganda. Wieser, on the other hand, wrote very little on methodology.[4] He kept out of polemics, and apart from the first chapter of his first book[5] (which soon went out of print and proved far less influential than his *Der natürliche Wert* of 1889 which contained no systematic discussion of methodology whatsoever), he expressed his methodological views in writing only twice more. Least known is his review of Schumpeter's then widely acclaimed first work, *Das Wesen und der Hauptinhalt der theoretischen Nationalökonomie*, in which he effectively expelled Schumpeter from the Austrian fold, at least on methodological grounds.[6] Thirty years after his first discussion of the *Sprachbegriffe* he returned to the issue very much along the same lines in the introductory chapter of his *Theorie der gesellschaftlichen Wirtschaft*.[7]

The quite dramatic contrasts in the quantity of output and style are not the only differences between Böhm-Bawerk and Wieser as methodologists. The most fundamental difference is their characterisation of economics as *Naturwissenschaft* and *Geisteswissenschaft*, respectively. While Wieser quite unequivocally claims economics for the *Geisteswissenschaften*, Böhm-Bawerk, despite his verbalisations to the contrary, treats economics as a natural science; he does not offer a single substantive argument which demonstrates that economics should not be treated like one of the *Naturwissenschaften*.[8] The most interesting aspect of this situation, however, is that both claimed descent from Menger and rightly so. Elements of both conceptions are to be found in Menger's work, in the *Untersuchungen* as well as in the *Grundsätze*. Thus it becomes all the more important to start this investigation of the history of the Austrian school of economics with a discussion of Menger's methodology which is based on his expressly methodological writings as well as on the methodology implicit in his economic theory.

Theory and methodology are, of course, not separable. Methodology without theory ultimately remains idle talk, and theory without methodology does not exist. That is to say, to write theoretical treatises one has to use certain (intellectual) tools; the way these tools are used constitutes the realm of methodology. In certain instances, theoretical positions can be clarified by analysing their underlying methodology, and similarly, methodologies can be elucidated by investigating their application in the construction of theories and in the derivation of results from these theories. Both these approaches are used in this discussion. But this is only a necessary not a sufficient step towards a reasonably satisfactory characterisation of the positions taken by the older Austrian economists. For this we shall have to refer to the epistemological background as that provides the basis upon which they constructed their theories, or—to put it differently—it provides the justification for, or the validity of, constructing theories in a certain way.

Menger quite clearly refers to the need for a methodology resting on epistemologically sound foundations[9]—that is, on a "correct" explication of the nature and validity of economic knowledge—as well as insisting on clarifying the methodological basis for research in economics. Wieser expresses the same concern,[10] and even Böhm-Bawerk refers to the philosophical foundation of his conception of methodology.[11] Although the importance of the discussion of methodological issues varies greatly for Menger, Wieser and Böhm-Bawerk, it nevertheless remains an aspect which cannot be ignored if only because it was an area of great concern for Menger. Before embarking on a discussion of Menger, however, I shall have to specify the perspective from which I intend to look at his theory and methodology and why I have chosen this particular approach.

The perspective from which Menger will be viewed is that of the nineteenth century controversy of explanation versus understanding, (*Erklären* versus *Verstehen*), the confrontation of the Galilean tradition with a revived Aristotelianism. What, though, justifies the adoption of such an approach? To my mind, the most suitable path towards uncovering Menger's intellectual position is to look at his Aristotelianism in relation to the role of the revival of interest in Aristotle in nineteenth-century German thought. Revived by Hegel, Aristotle was to play an important role in the reaction of the *Geisteswissenschaften* against the positivist monism of the *Naturwissenschaften*,[12] in particular in the programme of a Historicist methodology developed by Droysen.[13] But Aristotle was also used in the attempt to combat Hegelian Idealism without having to return to the Kantian separation of subject and object.[14] This strand of thought took its inspiration from Trendelenburg (originally a collaborator on the Hegelian *Jahrbücher für wissenschaftliche Kritik*). In his studies Trendelenburg was strongly influenced by Boeckh and Schleiermacher, and thus he constitutes for this discussion, a not insignificant link with the pre-Dilthey *Verstehen* doctrine.[15]

The three philosophers who provide the points of reference for the philosophical framework of the theories and methodologies of Menger, Wieser and Böhm-Bawerk are Friedrich Ueberweg, Franz Brentano and Friedrich Paulsen, respectively. They were all Aristotelians of one kind or another; they were all influenced by Trendelenburg; and particularly in the cases of Ueberweg and Brentano, they were interested in establishing the basis for immediately evident, and thus true and objective, knowledge of real entities (material and immaterial, such as psychological, phenomena). Knowledge, for them, should be objective, constituted by the entities of the real world, and not subjective, constituted by the human mind as in Kantian epistemology. Most important, theoretical discourse for them was able to go beyond the merely formal and logical and offer true knowledge of the real world. These aims were to be achieved through a union of the real with the ideal without any loss, however, of the characteristic features of either realm. The labels chosen by Ueberweg and Paulsen for their systems—

Real-Idealismus and *Idealistischer Monismus,* respectively—exemplify these objectives very clearly.

Let me compare this perspective with a few salient features of Menger's own approach: the essentialism of his economic theory, his insistence on the objectivity and truth of theoretical explanation of experiential phenomena in his "exact" theory, his characterisation of the task of economic theory as the explication of the nature (essence) and origin of economic phenomena (and, in this connection, his rejection of mathematics), and his final turn towards classifying theoretical economics among the *Geisteswissenschaften.* On the basis of this *prima facie* evidence, at least, the perspective indicated above appears to promise to be more fruitful for an investigation into Menger's thought and the development of Austrian economics than, for instance, the interpretation of Menger as a Kantian.[16]

Menger's Publications

Menger's known publications span almost half a century (or more if we include the second edition of the *Grundsätze*). The most important of them have been gathered by Hayek in his edition of Menger's writings which also contains a bibliography.[17] This (hitherto) standard edition of Menger's works serves as the basis for this discussion, but I have also drawn on other items listed in Hayek's bibliography and, in addition, on the second edition of the *Grundsätze* and the two volumes of marginal comments edited by Emil Kauder.[18] Menger's correspondence has not been published to any significant extent; consequently, only those few letters which have appeared in print could be consulted.[19]

Menger's first known publication is also his most important one: the *Grundsätze der Volkswirthschaftslehre* of 1871. It was originally planned as the first part, dealing with the general foundations, of a treatise on economics comprising four volumes;[20] but the full plan was never carried to completion.[21] His second academic publication followed twelve years later, in 1883: the *Untersuchungen über die Methode der Socialwissenschaften, und der Politischen Oekonomie insbesondere.* The intervening period saw only book reviews which appeared in the *Wiener Zeitung* and the *Wiener Abendpost.* For the next thirty years Menger continued to write for various newspapers and magazines, mainly reviews and short commemorative pieces within the area broadly defined by the *Grundsätze* and the *Untersuchungen.* On the academic front, the 1880s appear to have been devoted to some further theoretical and methodological work, and most of his publications on money appeared in the 1890s. After the turn of the century he did not publish anything new. The second edition of the *Grundsätze*, almost twice as long as the first edition, was published posthumously by his son Karl Menger from a manuscript which had to be edited to a certain extent from notes and disconnected fragments.[22]

Not all of the 110 items which comprise Menger's bibliography[23] are, of course, relevant for this study, the main concern of which is with the substantive content of Menger's theory and methodology and not with his intellectual biography (mainly because the sources available are as yet quite inadequate for such a task to be carried out satisfactorily). I will, therefore, not discuss all the items exhaustively and in chronological order but rather draw on them as required by the argument. However, since a large number of these items are not readily available in English translation (nor are they easily accessible in the German original), I provide a brief chronological description of those which are relevant for this study. I organise this description and the discussion of Menger's methodology around three fixed points—the *Grundsätze* of 1871, the *Untersuchungen* of 1883 and the *Grundsätze* of 1923—and I treat them as different facets of the same argument, not as presenting different arguments.

In adopting this approach, two important problems arise which must be pointed out. First, is it admissible to use the second edition of the *Grundsätze* in the same way as all the other writings which were seen through the press by Menger himself? Second, can we plausibly assume that Menger's position regarding theory and methodology remained more or less the same from 1871 to 1921? In particular, if we assume this how do we explain the apparent transformation between 1871 and 1883 in his attitude towards the concepts and methods of the historical economists? My answer to the first question is that we can use the second edition; regarding the second question, there was no transformation in Menger's attitude regarding theory and methodology, and thus towards the concepts and methods of the historical economists. Instead, the explanation of the positions taken in 1871 and 1883 lies in the change in his attitude towards the historical economists themselves. The reasons for these answers will be given in a moment.

The *Grundsätze der Volkswirthschaftslehre* is concerned with developing the foundations of what would nowadays be called pure theory. Beyond some brief remarks in the preface and in the text, the work does not contain any explicit treatment of methodological issues. Rather, it presents Menger's application of his own methodology to the theoretical foundations of economic theory, and thus it represents the closest approximation to a positive statement of his methodology by Menger himself. This is precisely what constitutes the importance of this work for this part of the study. The impressions one does *not* get from reading the *Grundsätze* are one of hostility towards the historical economists or of pre-occupation with establishing "the correct methodology" for economic theorising. Indeed, the volume is dedicated to Wilhelm Roscher, and German economists are credited with having established the basis upon which Menger's theory is built.[24] This impression is borne out by the reviews and *feuilletons* written between 1871 and the end of 1874.

From 1875 onwards, however, the situation changed, and Menger now missed no opportunity to point his finger at the dogmatism and the methodological imperialism of the historical economists, whose domination of German academic economics was allegedly so detrimental to the development of economic science. This turning point, or transformation, from respectful and friendly criticism to outright refusal to recognise the historical economists' right to pronounce on matters methodological seems to have been prompted by a remark Roscher made about Menger's *Grundsätze* in the former's monumental *Geschichte der National-Oekonomik in Deutschland* (1874). It must have been this friendly and—from Roscher's point of view, certainly—favourable remark which incensed Menger because it showed quite clearly that Roscher had not grasped at all what Menger was up to. Menger's attitude is quite clearly expressed in his review of Roscher's *Geschichte* in January 1875.[25] This "psychological revolution" of 1875 was to result in the publication of the *Untersuchungen* in 1883, Schmoller's devastating review of that work in the same year,[26] Menger's retort in *Die Irrthümer des Historismus* (1884), and complete breakdown in communication between German historical economists and the Austrian economic theorists.

The *Untersuchungen über die Methode der Socialwissenschaften, und der Politischen Oekonomie insbesondere* is chiefly devoted to a clarification of the proper place for the historical approach in political economy. It is an essentially "negative" book: It attempts to point out the shortcomings of Historicist methodology and its improper use when applied to theoretical economics. Although this critique of Historicist methodology is inevitably interspersed with "positive" statements, i.e., with direct formulations of Menger's conception of the methodology which constitutes the basis of his, and all "correct", economic theorising, the remarks are still insufficient to reconstruct with certainty their precise meaning since we have no explicit formulation of Menger's epistemological framework at our disposal. This meaning has to be extricated from Menger's theoretical work, and thus the problem of a transformation—in his attitude rather than in his thinking—between 1871 and 1883 becomes very important since the operation of his most fundamental concepts, such as essentialism, causality and subjectivism (*Verstehen*), can only be observed in the *Grundsätze*. There is still hope, however, that one day we might find out "what Menger really meant" if publication of his hitherto unpublished manuscripts should finally be made possible. It does not seem unlikely that such manuscripts exist since even in 1883 Menger had planned to publish his thoughts on methodology and epistemology.[27]

No fundamentally new methodological or epistemological arguments were to appear in Menger's subsequent writings. The introduction of another principal category, that of "morphology of economics", in the "Grundzüge einer Klassifikation der Wirtschaftswissenschaften" in 1889 merely broadened the spectrum somewhat within which the different branches of political economy were to be classified.[28] It did not change the scope, nor the thrust, of Menger's argument. Several of his publications on this issue notwithstanding, in Menger's opinion one of the most important tasks was still to establish the epistemological foundations for a methodology of the social sciences.[29] *Die Irrthümer des Historismus in der deutschen Nationalökonomie* of 1884, written in the form of sixteen letters to an anonymous friend, was at any rate not much more than a repeat of the arguments of the *Unter-*

suchungen, the main difference being that in 1884 he not only criticised historical economics in general but also attacked Schmoller directly.

The breakdown of all communication between the Austrian theorists and the German Historicists seems almost to have been a natural outcome of this exchange in view of the fact that, fundamentally, both Menger and Schmoller were absolutely at crosspurposes.[30] In the years to follow, the main vehicle for the propagation of Menger's own views and for his criticism of Historicist positions were to be reviews of economic literature. These reviews were full of jibes, especially at the expense of the younger historical economists, and a climax was reached when he railed against the "theoretical nihilism" of German economics and especially of the "neo-historical" economists.[31] To be fair, however, one ought to point out that Menger was not vindictive at all costs, as can be seen in his argument with Roscher. From 1875 onwards, Menger could never resist pointing his finger at Roscher; this, however, ceased with the latter's death in 1894. *De mortuis nihil nisi bene:* Not only was Menger's obituary of Roscher eminently fair,[32] he also dropped a reference to Roscher's disparaging remarks on Austrian academic life he had made when reviewing the first edition of the *Handwörterbuch der Staatswissenschaften* in 1890 from his review of the second edition of the same work in 1901.[33]

Shortly after the completion of *Die Irrthümer des Historismus* Menger wrote his famous letter to Walras[34] in which he emphasised the fundamental difference between their respective systems despite their formal similarities. Published for the first time by Antonelli in 1953, this letter became generally accessible only in 1965 with the publication of Walras's correspondence, but Menger's views on the applicability of the mathematical method to economics were made public beyond doubt in 1889 in his review of Auspitz and Lieben's *Untersuchungen über die Theorie des Preises*.[35] He rejects their mathematical approach because it is hypothetical and not resoluta-compositive and because they make use of the *graphische Methode* (this is perhaps best translated as "geometric method") not only for purposes of diagrammatical representation but also as a tool in theoretical research.[36]

With the exception of the "Grundzüge einer Klassifikation the Wirtschaftswissenschaften" in 1889, Menger did not address methodological issues again directly for their own sake. Further discussion of individual aspects of his methodology has to be derived from his remaining theoretical writings. Confirmation of the methodological position taken in 1871 and 1883 can be found in his 1888 essay on capital theory, "Zur Theorie des Kapitals"[37] (his only theoretical contribution, outside monetary theory, which went significantly further along the lines of the *Grundsätze*), and in his 1892 article on money in the *Handwörterbuch der Staatswissenschaften*.[38] In the essay on capital theory he applies and elaborates his organicist conception of economic theory; his article on money is an elaboration of the final chapter of the *Grundsätze*, making his proximity to the historical economists quite clear, his protestations to the contrary notwithstanding. This latter essay underwent some considerable changes for the second edition of the

Handwörterbuch—most of his methodological remarks were omitted—but its substance, as far as this study is concerned, remained unchanged.[39]

A close reading of Menger's writings from January 1875 onwards reveals undisputable continuity in the argument and a unity of the underlying conceptual structure. The only problem which arises in extending this description to all of Menger's writings, ironically, concerns his *magnum opus* which, as it were, brackets his life's work as an economist. How does the *Grundsätze* fit in with the rest of his writings? It seems we are faced with a dilemma: The second edition was not prepared for publication by Menger himself, and between the publication of the first edition and the *Untersuchungen* a fundamental reorientation in his thought is alleged to have taken place. Even more, some changes were introduced in the second edition which cast considerable doubt on the conceptual identity of the two editions.[40] Two examples will make this problem obvious. First, in the preface to the first edition Menger argues against the dualism of *Geisteswissenschaften* and *Naturwissenschaften* on the basis of a pluralist conception of science, but this dualism is fully accepted in the new first chapter of the second edition. Indeed, the purpose of the insertion of this new chapter is precisely to attempt to overcome this dualism while at the same time accepting its existence. (Ironically, since Menger did not live to put the second edition together for publication, no new preface was available, and the editor decided to reprint the old preface of the first edition. The preface and the new first chapter therefore allow the reader the choice between two mutually exclusive philosophies of science.) Second, as one commentator has pointed out,[41] *causal* connections between goods, in the first edition, have been replaced by *teleological* connections in the second edition. As if these apparently fundamental conceptual differences were not sufficient to set the second edition in opposition to the first edition, Menger also proceeds to distinguish the former from the *Untersuchungen* by classifying economics now firmly among the *Geisteswissenschaften* (as does Wieser). Previously he had called it a social science, thus apparently transcending the above-mentioned dualism.

What are we to make of these differences? The answer, in brief, is, nothing, because they are mere conceptual differences. In this particular instance, I am using Menger's definition of concept (*Begriff*) as a "linguistic representation" of real phenomena.[42] The concepts changed from the first to the second edition, but the substance of his argument remained the same. Indeed, I believe that we can justifiably argue that in 1923 the conceptual apparatus was finally adapted to Menger's theoretical practise of 1871. The implicit argument of the first edition became explicit in the second edition.

This is certainly not an orthodox interpretation of Menger, and furthermore, it seems to depend on the acceptability of the 1923 edition of the *Grundsätze* as authoritative. In fact, the interpretation does not depend on that acceptance at all. There is sufficient evidence in the writings seen through the press by Menger himself to warrant the interpretation of his theory and methodology put forward here. The second edition of the *Grundsätze* may therefore be viewed as a confirmation of my interpretation but not as its cornerstone. I also believe that we should give the editor of the second edition the benefit of the doubt and believe that he attempted to edit the material which was finally included in the spirit of the author. It seems highly unlikely that he would have deliberately tried to falsify it so as to fit the argument presented here. At any rate, if Menger's unpublished manuscripts—and perhaps also his correspondence—become available at some point, the interpretation put forward in this study will then have to stand the test of that material. On the basis of the currently available evidence, however, I cannot see any other interpretation which is more convincing.

These are the main reasons for my affirmative answer to the first question posed above.[43] As will have become obvious, this answer does depend on an equally affirmative answer to the second question, for if there was no continuity between 1871 and 1883 in Menger's attitude towards the concepts and methods of the historical economists, and thus by implication in his own methodology, the methodology implicit in the theory of the first edition of the *Grundsätze* could bear no relation to the critique of the methodology developed in the *Untersuchungen*. Both editions of the *Grundsätze* would therefore have to be considered as disconnected from Menger's writings published between 1875 and 1921, at least as far as methodology is concerned. *Prima facie* this appears to be highly unlikely. But is there any substantive evidence for a rejection of this argument? Can we demonstrate what I said earlier, that there was merely a change of heart not a change of mind concerning the historical economists?

The case for a transformation in Menger's attitude usually rests on the facts that, on the one hand, the *Grundsätze* is dedicated to Roscher and Menger attributes the basis on which his reform of economic theory is constructed to the achievements of the then recent developments in German economics.[44] On the other hand, the *Untersuchungen* in its entirety is a very sharp criticism of the historical economists' pretentions that they are reforming economic theory. This change in Menger's attitude has been interpreted as a change in his "attitude to the German historical economists, *and their concepts and methods*",[45] i.e., to their methodology and epistemology. Implicit in this argument is that the direction of the change was from acceptance of their concepts and methods to rejection. To remain consistent one then ought to argue that Menger's attitude to his own concepts and methods changed, too.

The most immediately persuasive argument against such an interpretation is provided by Menger himself in his correspondence with Walras when he emphasises, after the completion of *Die Irrthümer des Historismus*, the fundamental unity of his scientific enterprise.[46] If we look at some more substantive arguments, especially his attacks on Roscher, we find that in 1875 he charges Roscher with methodological imperialism, that is, with subsuming everything "good" under the label of historical economics irrespective of whether the work in question does lend itself to such a characterisation or not. In 1883, to substantiate this charge, he picks on the description and characterisation of the *Grundsätze* in Roscher's *Geschichte der National-Oekonomik* to demonstrate the historical economists' lack of understanding of the fundamentally different aims of theoretical and historical research. To be able to do this, Menger develops his classification of the sciences which, according to Menger, applies to all scientific enquiry and according to which each specific field of enquiry is divided into subsections which differ according to the different aims pursued. Menger distinguishes between historical (and statistical), practical (or applied) and theoretical enquiry. The last subsection is itself divided into realistic-empirical theory and "exact" theory.[47] Menger claims that in the *Grundsätze*, he has undertaken to derive the most fundamental and general laws of economics; that is, the *Grundsätze*, in his view, constitutes the "exact" theory on which all research in political economy has to be based.[48] His aims, therefore, have been totally different from the aims of historical enquiry, and it is nothing but complete misunderstanding, or ignorance, of the epistemological and methodological differences between these fields of research when the historical economists apply their criteria in judging theoretical work.

So far we have seen nothing that either contradicts Menger's version of the story or requires the assumption of a transformation in attitude towards "concepts" and "methods." The explanation of a change of heart, i.e., of a change of attitude towards the historical economists themselves—rather than towards the position they represent—seems to be quite sufficient, for who could blame a young economist with an original mind for turning his wrath on those to whom he had dedicated his work but who did not seem to have understood the fundamental changes brought about by it; indeed, who simply refused to acknowledge its importance and thus obstructed the path towards progress in economic science.[49] One of the reasons why they had failed him appears to have been their faulty methodology, and, unfortunately, they did not share his conception of the classification of the sciences.[50] The critique of methodology in the *Untersuchungen* was to prepare the way for the acceptance of genuine theory in Germany. The reception of the book, however, made it quite clear that the historical economists still refused to see Menger's point. The most important thing that therefore remained to be done to bring about the desired change was to establish the epistemological and methodological foundations for political economy. But this is precisely what Menger said in 1889,[51] and we seem to have arrived at an explanation of Menger's reasoning without any need for the assumption of a radical transformation in his thought. On the contrary, the reconstruction of the development of the argument presented here seems to have the advantage over rival reconstructions of being able to incorporate Menger's own account of the sequence of events without being faced with contradictions.

On the other hand, one might conceivably argue that there are still certain conceptual differences between the *Untersuchungen* and at least the second edition of the *Grundsätze*, if not both editions, and that mere historical arguments are not really adequate to remove conceptual contradictions. Indeed, if one were to argue along these lines, one would be open to precisely the same charge which Menger brought against the historical economists. Instead, what will be argued in this essay is that the historical account can very well incorporate the conceptual structure and its underlying epistemology and methodology without irresolvable contradictions, because Menger's argument in the first edition of the *Grundsätze* runs on two levels. Both the *Untersuchungen* and the second edition of the *Grundsätze* correspond directly to the first edition but each to a different level. To be able to show this, however, we shall first have to turn to a more detailed discussion of Menger's methodology.

Menger on Methodology

The *Untersuchungen über die Methode der Socialwissenschaften, und der Politischen Oekonomie insbesondere* is Menger's best known work. Although less influential than his *Grundsätze der Volkswirthschaftslehre* as far as the development of economics is concerned, the *Untersuchungen* was far more controversial at the time. More people have commented on the issues raised by Menger's critique of the historical economists than have commented on, or actually seem to have read, his development of value theory. Economists concerned with the methodology of their science, historians of economic thought, philosophers of science and sociologists have all attempted during the last 100 years to interpret the *Untersuchungen* either within the context defined by the *Grundsätze* or on its own. The *Untersuchungen* became the reference point for all discussion of Austrian methodology, at least until the rise to fame of Hayek and Mises in the middle of the twentieth century. The work contains all the central methodological arguments which Menger was to put forward in his subsequent publications, including *Die Irrthümer des Historismus*, the "Grundzüge einer Klassifikation der Wirtschaftswissenschaften" or his newspaper and review articles.[52]

Currently, the most generally informative summaries of Menger's methodology are those by T. W. Hutchison;[53] specific investigations of the *Methodenstreit* have been undertaken by R. Hansen and S. Bostaph,[54] and R. Cubeddu has compiled a very detailed commentary of the German, French, Italian and English literature concerned with the *Untersuchungen*.[55] Given the general availability of summaries of and comments on Menger's methodology, I shall not enter into an extensive presentation of the arguments put forward in the *Untersuchungen*. Instead, I shall first look at the methodology implicit in the *Grundsätze* of 1871 and then use the information thus obtained as the basis for the discussion of the *Untersuchungen*.

It is, of course, not possible, or it would at the very least be intellectually dishonest, to claim that one can jump into such an analysis without any preconceived ideas or that one will find "the truth" in such a way. Hence, I had better "own up" to my own scientific prejudices. In my analysis of Austrian theory and methodology, I have taken the hermeneutic road, which focusses on meaning and intention. The search for the meaning of some of Böhm-Bawerk's concepts and phrases led me to Menger and from Menger to the background mapped out in Essay I. This allowed me to fill the words which Menger, Wieser and Böhm-Bawerk used with their appropriate meaning and also allowed me to discover that their scientific intentions did not always agree with the meaning of the terminology they employed. This, in turn, led to the unravelling of differences not only among the theories and methodologies developed by Menger, Wieser and Böhm-Bawerk but also within each of their systems. On the basis of this work, I decided not only to discuss Austrian theory and methodology in terms of the nineteenth-century *Erklären* versus *Verstehen* controversy (that is, within the framework provided by those who claimed the existence of an epistemological dualism between the *Geisteswissenschaften* and the *Naturwissenschaften*) but also to abstain from any attempt to present Austrian theory and methodology in the form of the Lakatosian methodology of scientific research programmes simply because neither the theory nor the methodology of the Austrian school has as yet been analysed in sufficient detail to warrant such a step. Even today, we do not really know what the terms "Austrian theory" and "Austrian school" actually mean. To unravel the meaning of these terms, I started with Menger in an effort to find some markings against which the development of Austrian theory and methodology could be measured. This study is therefore only a first step towards a history of the Austrian school, and Wieser's and Böhm-Bawerk's systems are included only insofar as they represent a significant departure from Menger's path. Hence, the hermeneutic approach will, in the first place, be directed at Menger's methodology, then at his theory and only at the end, in summary form, at the work of Wieser and Böhm-Bawerk.

Analysing Menger's intention and meaning is the only way to establish Menger's methodology since he never published a full statement of it. For instance, in the preface to the *Grundsätze*, he stated his intention to overcome the epistemological dualism of the *Geisteswissenschaften* and the *Naturwissenschaften*, on the one hand, and the one-sided rationalism or positivism, on the other hand. He intended to achieve this by allowing for pluralism in method based on monism in epistemology.[56] What he meant by methodology, however, is revealed only by its use in the development of his economic theory: He chose Aristotelianism as the vehicle to overcome the dualism and rationalism at the same time; thus he chose the *geisteswissenschaftliche* tradition over the *naturwissenschaftliche*, Galilean tradition. This is exemplified by his choice of the fourfold Aristotelian conception of causality over the modern conception of efficient causality. Hence, the *Geisteswissenschaften* are given priority over the *Naturwissenschaften* in the *Grundsätze* of 1871 and again in the *Untersuchungen*. In spite of his original intention, analysis of the meaning of his methodology reveals that he actually chose to associate with those who claimed at least different if not superior epistemological status for the humanities over the natural sciences. Only in 1923 can we see the convergence of intention and meaning when he not only replaces the term "causality" used in 1871 and 1883 with the more appropriate one of "teleology" but also relocates economics from the

Socialwissenschaften to the *Geisteswissenschaften*, thus publicly embracing the epistemological dualism.[57]

Methodology in the Grundsätze

In the preface to the *Grundsätze*, Menger sets out the epistemological and methodological basis of his economic theory. Economics is an empirical science, just like the natural sciences, but pursues knowledge through a method *sui generis*. As in other empirical sciences, complex phenomena are analysed by reducing them to their simplest constituent elements and subsequently recomposing them in such a way that the complex phenomena are reconstituted by these constituent elements and their laws of development. The specificity of economics, like that of all the other empirical sciences, lies in the operation of the laws of development on the constituent elements; it is determined by their nature and finds its expression in the measure appropriate to the elements. In other words, the way in which the elements are measured cannot be determined from the outside, by a method imported from a different branch of knowledge, but must be determined from the inside. The measure is an essential, an organic part of the constituent elements.[58] To take one not entirely remote example: The emulation of physical methods in economics imposes among other things differentiability of the underlying object space. Should the measure of the constituent elements of this space not permit the requisite type of differentiability, then, according to Menger, differentiability must be rejected, but according to others, the necessary properties simply have to be assumed.[59] This analytic method is the basis of all "exact" theoretical research and is not invalidated by the existence of human free will.[60]

This is the core of Menger's methodology and epistemology. Although at first sight it appears to be rather straightforward and simple common sense, it nevertheless contains a very complex network of interconnections among its constituent elements, the meaning of which can be clarified only by reference to his economic theory. At the center of this network is Menger's analytic method, which Menger himself called variously analytic, analytic-synthetic, analytic-compositive and, finally, "exact"[61] and which today is known by the name given it by Hayek, the resoluta-compositive method. This method is, of course, not Menger's invention but goes back to Aristotle,[62] and it appeared in a number of different methodological guises in the nineteenth century, such as Marx's "Aufsteigen vom Abstrakten zum Konkreten" and the famous hermeneutic circle. The comparison with the hermeneutic circle is particularly interesting because according to this approach knowledge is acquired by going continuously round the circle to deepen one's understanding in the light of previously acquired knowledge and new evidence and thus climbing to ever-higher levels of knowledge and understanding. Menger's resoluta-compositive method, however, represents only one round of the hermeneutic circle. The question which this poses is, How can he arrive at "exact" knowledge in this way? Menger does not tell us directly, but there are quite a few clues in the *Grundsätze* and the *Untersuchungen* which allow us to deduce Menger's solution to this problem.

It is important to note that this is not just a methodological question and that it addresses the very foundations of Menger's epistemology. In the *Untersuchungen* Menger goes a little further in his description of "exact" knowledge, although he still does not provide us with a fully developed epistemological argument. There he tells us that "exact" theory is true by definition, that it is not amenable to verification or falsification against empirical reality. He postulates this for the "exact" theories of the *Naturwissenschaften* as well as for economic theory.[63] The only further qualification he provides is that the truth of "exact" theory is epistemologically necessary because it is epistemologically impossible for it to be otherwise.[64] The full explanation of this method and of its epistemological foundations was supposed to be provided in a separate treatise which was never written.[65]

What are we to make of these statements? Without further explanation they appear to characterise an extreme epistemological dogmatism. "Exact" theory is true because that is the way we know. However, if we look at these statements in the context of Menger's life's work as a whole, and especially with reference to the *Grundsätze*, his position can be interpreted more charitably. The perspective which his work suggests, and which serves as the basis for the interpretation of his methodology, is that of nineteenth-century Austrian Aristotelianism. I shall have more to say about Menger's Aristotelianism later on,[66] and we shall also encounter Aristotle's concept of induction as the basis for the apprehension of "first principles." It is the epistemological basis which generates the simplest constituent elements in Aristotle's sciences that are grasped through inspection of simple facts. What we apprehend as first principles are, furthermore, true statements because scientific results are deduced from them. Since science is necessary knowledge of the true, the premises of the syllogism, the first principles, must also be true. Viewed in this light, Menger's insistence on the truth *per definitionem* of "exact" theories looks less dogmatic and more amenable to epistemological analysis. It also explains why he never published his "positive" philosophy of science.

This argument, in turn, raises two closely related questions: What is the basis for reading Aristotelianism into the *Grundsätze*? And what is the basis for reading induction into the foundations of Menger's epistemology? My argument for induction rests on three elements, the first of which is the general Aristotelianism of the *Grundsätze* (I shall discuss this point last because it goes much further into Menger's methodology). Second, it rests on numerous passages throughout the *Grundsätze* in which Menger refers to simple everyday experience from which he derives his fundamental statements and on which he then bases the development of his principles of economics.[67] But this is precisely how Aristotelian induction would work. Third, my argument for induction rests on Menger's reference to his planned treatment of the philosophy of science in which he specifically mentions speculation and a critique of Bacon's concept of induction.[68] I interpret this, in conjunction with the first two elements, as an indication of the importance of the concept of induction for his epistemology.

The last two elements cited as evidence for considering that Aristotelian induction is fundamental to Menger's epistemology rely on the *Untersuchungen* at least as much as on the *Grundsätze*. However, the *Untersuchungen* can be understood in the way I propose in this study only if we accept the reading of Menger as an Aristotelian in his development of economic theory in the *Grundsätze*. In other words, only the methodology and epistemology which Menger uses in his theoretical work allow us to understand more fully his critique of methodology developed in the *Untersuchungen*. The *Grundsätze* is, in a way, almost more important for Menger's methodology of economics than the *Untersuchungen*.

There are a large number of strands in the *Grundsätze* which testify to its Aristotelian character: the conception that knowledge is by causes, the teleological character of Menger's causality, his essentialism, the notion that each branch of knowledge is *sui generis* rather than being classified among either the *Geisteswissenschaften* or the *Naturwissenschaften* (as was the tradition in the German speaking academic world in the nineteenth century), and his resoluta-compositive method. All of these methodological elements of Menger's economic theory taken together testify to his fundamental Aristotelianism; each taken by itself may also be located in other *geisteswissenschaftliche* traditions. The problem of the precise character of Menger's Aristotelianism will be discussed later,[69] but first I want to look at the Aristotelian strands in the *Grundsätze* in more detail.

Aristotle's notion that knowledge is by causes is the starting point of the *Grundsätze*: "Alle Dinge stehen unter dem Gesetz von Ursache und Wirkung"[70] (all things are subject to the law of cause and effect) is the first sentence of Menger's first book. He intends to present the development of the causal relationships from the most basic elements, human *Bedürfnisse* and things, through the intermediate stage of valuation, to the determination of surface phenomena such as prices, commodities and, finally, money, the ultimate commodity.[71] Passages in the *Grundsätze* in which Menger uses the terms *Causal-Zusammenhang, Causalnexus, Ursache* and *ursächlich* are too numerous to be mentioned separately. Although Menger's emphasis on the lawlike behaviour of economic phenomena, which is guaranteed by the operation of the causal relationships on the elements of his "exact" economic theory, is certainly inspired by the natural sciences,[72] his conception of causality in the *Grundsätze* is teleological, modelled on the fourfold Aristotelian conception of causality which was so popular in the Romantic inspired thought of the *Geisteswissenschaften* and the historical schools and which was turned into a programme for historical research by Droysen.[73] In fact, a closer look at Menger's discussion of the most basic constituent elements of his economic theory, the relationship between *Bedürfnisse* and things and the conditions which turn things into goods (and which in conjunction with scarcity define the economic world), allows us to observe the operation of this fourfold conception of causality in the formulation of the four conditions on which Menger's theory rests:

Damit ein Ding ein Gut werde, . . . ist demnach das Zusammentreffen folgender
vier Voraussetzungen erforderlich:
1. Ein menschliches Bedürfniss.
2. Solche Eigenschaften des Dinges, welche es tauglich machen, in ursächlichen
   Zusammenhang mit der Befriedigung dieses Bedürfnisses gesetzt zu werden.
3. Die Erkenntnis dieses Causal-Zusammenhanges Seitens der Menschen.
4. Die Verfügung über dieses Ding, so zwar, dass es zur Befriedigung jenes
   Bedürfnisses thatsächlich herangezogen werden kann.
Nur wo diese Voraussetzungen zusammentreffen, kann ein Ding zum Gute
werden, wo immer aber auch nur eine derselben mangelt, kann kein Ding die
Güterqualität erlangen; besässe es aber bereits dieselbe, so müsste sie doch
sofort verloren gehen, wenn auch nur eine jener vier Voraussetzungen entfallen
würde.[74]

These four conditions can easily be seen to correspond to the material,
efficient, final and formal cause, respectively. Throughout the *Grundsätze*,
the satisfaction of *Bedürfnisse* is taken to be the purpose of human economic
activity. But it is not simply conceived of as purposive in a general sense
but teleological in the most authentic meaning of the term: It is directed
towards a goal, and this goal is present at the very beginning of every
economic act. This is why it must also be contained in the statement of
the most basic constituent elements. There are a number of passages in the
Grundsätze according to which teleology can be the only meaningful interpretation of Menger's concept of causality.[75] Furthermore, the identification
of causality with teleology is confirmed twice by the author himself: In the
first edition of the *Grundsätze*, Menger equates "Bedürfnisse befriedigen"
with "Zwecke verwirklichen",[76] i.e., the satisfaction of *Bedürfnisse* equals
the attainment of a goal; in the second edition of the *Grundsätze* he replaces
the word "cause" (*Grund*, *Ursache*) with "purpose" (*Zweck*) without making
the slightest impact on the substance of his economic theory.[77]

Menger's concept of cause is a veritable node in his methodology. In it
he unites influences from rationalist thought (through the references to the
natural sciences) and Romantic-Historicist thought (through his Aristotelianism). The Romantic-Historicist dimension becomes even more pronounced
through another aspect of his concept of cause which also takes it beyond
its purely Aristotelian bounds. Menger identifies causality with time;[78] on
the one hand, he thus incorporates the Aristotelian notion that time is
merely the number of change,[79] and, on the other hand, he goes beyond
that by locating the process of change in Romantic-Historicist thought
through its identification with *Werden* and *Entstehen* (coming into being).
Time is of the essence of the economic process, it is real, an element of
the ontological basis of his economic theory, and it is fundamentally irreversible just as the teleological process is uni-directional and real.[80]

There is yet another Romanticist element in the four conditions quoted
above: the notion of uncertainty and incompleteness of information. This
element becomes equally enshrined in the ontological basis of Menger's
theory, precluding any attempt to assimilate the rationalist notion of complete
information to Austrian economics, or at least to Menger's version of it.

The four conditions which are necessary and sufficient for a thing to become a good are the true premises of Menger's economic theory. All of his results can be deduced from them, the specific form of each result depending on the specific (empirical) context within which these premises are located. Here we can also discern the epistemological roots of the *Methodenstreit* in the *Grundsätze* as the difference in opinion between Menger and Schmoller is founded in their respective interpretations of the status of the starting points of a theory. For the Aristotelian Menger they are fully empirical, immediately known, true and not amenable to testing. For the Kantian Schmoller, such starting points are inevitably hypothetical and abstract, and the theory is therefore hypothetico-deductive without any foundations in empirical (that is, for Schmoller, historically investigated) reality.

Another node at which Romantic-Historicist and Aristotelian thought meet is Menger's conception of the aim of "exact" theory. This is most clearly stated in a letter to Walras in which Menger says that pure economic theory investigates not only quantitative relationships but also the essence of economic phenomena.[81] One offshoot of this conception is Menger's evaluation of the role of mathematics in economic theory: At best, mathematics is able to serve in the demonstration or representation of economic results, that is, it can at the most be an auxiliary science for economics. But it will never be able to be the tool *par excellence* in "exact" economic theory since mathematics is epistemologically unable to discover essences. Economics, therefore, can never be a mathematical science.[82]

Menger's essentialism is the basis of the investigation of the real nature of phenomena which underlies their appearances on the surface, at the level of the perceivable, and it constitutes the epistemological foundation of Menger's economic theory. It penetrates his analysis to such an extent that he ends up with a formidable transformation problem of values into prices which he is unable to resolve because of his epistemological determination of values as essences and prices as appearances on the surface.[83] An epistemological resolution of Menger's transformation problem would imply, among other things, that his position in the *Methodenstreit* was untenable and that Schmoller had been right all along.

Essentialist terminology permeates the *Grundsätze* from the beginning to end. *Wesen, Natur, Erscheinung* and *Oberfläche der Erscheinungen* characterise all his fundamental analytical concepts. It is, however, not only the investigation of essences but also the characteristically Historicist pre-occupation with the *Ursprung* (the origin) of concepts and categories which occupies Menger in the *Grundsätze*. We must recall that, for Menger, a concept is a linguistic representation of reality, of essences; the discussion of the concept of, say, value is therefore the discussion of the essence of economic activity and not merely the discussion of a verbal construct. Menger's ontological realism is revealed in two passages in the *Grundsätze*. In one, he rejects the concept of *Gattungswerth* because it is not real, because it does not exist;[84] in the other, in defining value as a relationship, he states that the only objectively existing entities are things or, rather, their quantities.[85] This, in fact, was the basis of his argument against Roscher in 1875 and the beginning of the road towards the *Methodenstreit*.[86]

The essence and origin of goods, of human economic activity, of the value of goods, of economic exchange and, finally, of money is the thread which runs through his "exact" economic theory. This conjunction of *Wesen* and *Ursprung* which enters through his definition of the aims of economic theory opens up another aspect of his methodology: How does one investigate *Wesen* and *Ursprung*? In his methodological writings, Menger answers that essences have to be understood (as opposed to explained). Hence, his idiosyncratic formulation of the essentialism of his economic theory locates already the first edition of the *Grundsätze* among the *Geisteswissenschaften*, the protestations in his preface notwithstanding. But we do not have to wait until we get to the *Untersuchungen* to be able to discern the *geisteswissenschaftliche*, the *verstehende* dimension in his methodology. It is already an integral part of the *Grundsätze* since his definition of value incorporates both a quantitative and an interpretative, that is, a *verstehende*, dimension.

Menger defines value as the *Bedeutung* of the satisfaction of *Bedürfnisse* for our life and well being.[87] In English the term *Bedeutung* may be rendered as both "meaning" and "importance"; in Menger's definition of value, it carries both connotations. Its intuitive, non-quantifiable strand, "meaning", conveys the interpretative, *verstehende* dimension.[88] Its quantifiable strand, "importance", expresses the quantitative dimension, the measure of value as expressed by the degree of the satisfaction of a *Bedürfnis*.[89] What is important for us here are the ramifications of the non-quantitative strand of Menger's measure of value for his methodology and epistemology. The cognitive aspect of this strand, the *Erkenntnis der Bedeutung*, is emphasised in Essay III; here, I stress the interpretative, *verstehende* connotations of *Bedeutung*.

In Essay I we saw that Menger really belongs to the period immediately preceding the birth of the modern *Verstehen* doctrine, which received its philosophical foundations with Wilhelm Dilthey's "critique of historical reason" and remained a pre-occupation of especially the German speaking academic world well into the second half of this century. In fact, Menger's *Untersuchungen* and Dilthey's *Einleitung in die Geisteswissenschaften* were both published in 1883, by the same publishing house, and they were both reviewed in the same famous article by Schmoller.[90] One of Dilthey's predecessors was Droysen, who designed a *verstehende* programme for historical research and who certainly also influenced Menger.[91] In a way, we can regard the *Untersuchungen* as Menger's preliminary (because negatively formulated, as a critique) formulation of a *verstehende* programme for research in economics and the social sciences in which he attempted a reconciliation of the controversy of the *Geisteswissenschaften* versus the *Naturwissenschaften* from a position within the *Geisteswissenschaften*. (An explicit confirmation of this interpretation is provided by Menger himself in his new first chapter of the second edition of the *Grundsätze*.)[92] The economic theory of the

Grundsätze, or to be more precise, its first formulation of 1871, is Menger's realisation of his programme for economic research.

This is the background necessary for an understanding of the significance of the concept of a *verstehende* methodology for the *Grundsätze*. When Menger says in the *Untersuchungen* that *Verstehen* is *Erfassung des Wesens* (understanding as the grasping of the essence),[93] he is merely spelling out the methodological precept underlying his subjective moment of value. We, as human beings, can understand human action in a way we cannot understand nature. We can understand (economic) value, not because the meaning of the satisfaction of a *Bedürfnis* is based on an objective, external property of the good consumed or the biological foundations of this act, but because the satisfaction of the *Bedürfnis* has meaning for us, the economic agents. The observing economist can understand the action of an economic agent because the economist *is* an economic agent. This idea is not explicitly stated in these words by Menger but, it is the inescapable starting point for a *verstehende* methodology. Without it, Menger's insistence on the subjective moment of value would not make sense.

The problem raised by this issue is, What kind of *Verstehen* is implied by Menger's position? (It can only be implied because Menger never published his "positive" philosophy of science.) A first indication is given by Menger's conception of value: Value, that is, the *Bedeutung* of the satisfaction of *Bedürfnisse*, is *for us*. It is the meaning of the satisfaction of *Bedürfnisse* for the economic agent, the acting subject's private experience; value is subjective. Hence, the subjectivism of his value theory is primarily founded, not on an atomistic vision of society and the requirements imposed by an analytical form, as was the case with Walras's development of marginal utility theory (which really is an individualistic rather than a properly subjectivistic theory of value), but on the methodological precept of *Verstehen* in its empathic form as we find it in, say, Savigny and Droysen, and in the explicitly subjective form given it by Droysen.[94] The subjectivism of Menger's value theory is enshrined in his definition of value and in his principles of value formation;[95] it informs the perspective from which value is viewed and the development of its analysis and ultimately makes even Menger's quantitative moment of value, the measure of value, subjective.

Nevertheless, one does not have to accept the subjectivist conception of *Verstehen* as necessary if one wants to adopt a *verstehende* methodology. It is merely a historically relative position, as is attested by the *geisteswissen-schaftliche* approach developed by the Italian philosopher Giambattista Vico at the beginning of the eighteenth century. Vico developed a *verstehende* methodology and epistemology which did not rely on empathy, subjectivism or even introspection but on the *verum-factum* principle: I can truly only know what I have made myself. Hence, we can know history in a much superior way than we shall ever be able to know nature. Vico developed, to my mind, a methodology and epistemology that was far superior to Menger's. Be that as it may, Vico's theory highlights the fact that Menger's philosophy of science is historically relative, very much an organic part of certain strands of the German *geisteswissenschaftliche* tradition (even though he was pursuing his own rather idiosyncratic way to disaster, as we shall see in a short while). The first step in this direction is not the acceptance of a *verstehende* position as such, as one might be led to believe from an analysis such as Theodore Abel's,[96] but the introduction of psychologism into a subjectivist conception of *Verstehen*.

Friedrich von Wieser is commonly credited for introducing psychology into subjective value theory, not Menger. One highly likely explanation for this attribution is that, as with so many other issues, Menger's *Grundsätze* was not available or at any rate not read, during the decades of the Austrian school's hegemony in value theory. As a result, only Wieser's and Böhm-Bawerk's elaborations of value theory have been taken as the reference works for the discussion of Austrian theory from Menger onwards so that the first author who appears to define marginal utility theory as applied psychology is Wieser. It is, however, not really difficult to see that Menger's theory of value was as overtly psychological as Wieser's.

In his discussion of the interpretative moment of value, Menger develops his famous numerical table to demonstrate that the *Bedeutung* of the satisfaction of *Bedürfnisse* varies greatly.[97] The importance of this section of the *Grundsätze* for his economic analysis lies in his development of the lexicographic (or hierarchical) ordering of *Bedürfnisse*.[98] For the interpretation of his methodology, the importance lies in his identification of the argument developed there with an "as yet unexplored area of psychology."[99] In his discussion of the quantitative moment of value, Menger designates the process of identifying the *Bedeutung* of the satisfaction of a *Bedürfnis* (its value) with the satisfying capacity of a specific good (the value of the good) as transference (*Übertragung*), quite in keeping with the modern psychological meaning of the term,[100] and codifies this psychological process in his first principle of the explanation of value.[101]

If, on the basis of the passages cited here, psychologism, the reduction of the explanation of value to psychology, is given such a central position in the *Grundsätze* of 1871, then this interpretation is confirmed by Menger himself in two passages written in 1889, one published and the other one unpublished at the time. In his methodological essay of 1889, Menger defines the task of exact theory as the analysis of complex economic phenomena by means of the resoluta-compositive method, that is, by reducing them to their ultimate constituent elements and, above all, to their psychological causes.[102] In the same year, Menger drafted an introduction for the planned new edition of the *Grundsätze* in which he repeated this definition of economic theory as being based on psychology.[103] Thus, in the same year that Wieser published his *Der natürliche Wert*, Menger restated publicly a fundamental methodological precept which he had applied and also identified as such eighteen years previously.

But this is not the end of the matter, for Menger not only makes a methodological claim for the fundamental role which psychology has to play in economic theory, he also postulates that psychology is a fundamental epistemological element. *Erkenntnis*, that is, achieving conceptual knowledge of the world around us, is nothing else but becoming aware of the effects which things have on ourselves.

Wie eine tiefer gehende Untersuchung der seelischen Vorgänge uns die Erkenntnis der Aussendinge lediglich als die zu unserem Bewusstsein gelangte Einwirkung der Dinge auf uns selbst, das ist in letzter Reihe als die Erkenntnis eines Zustandes unserer eigenen Person erscheinen lässt, so ist auch alle Bedeutung, welche welche wir den Dingen der Aussenwelt beimessen, in letzter Reihe nur ein Ausfluss jener Bedeutung, welche die Aufrechthaltung unserer Natur in ihrem Wesen und ihrer Entwickelung, das ist unser Leben und unsere Wohlfahrt für uns haben.[104]

This is a very dangerous epistemological position. It echoes the Romantic conception of the unity of the microcosm with the macrocosm and moves perilously close to introspection as an epistemological postulate. Retracing Menger's conception of *Verstehen* implicit in the *Grundsätze*, we discover a conceptual and substantive affinity not only with the subjectivistic strand of the *Verstehen* doctrine which relies on empathy, but also with its more narrowly defined psychologistic tradition. This latter position had initially also been adopted by Dilthey, but he had become aware of its inherent dangers and had abandoned it later in favour of a return to the Hegelian tradition. Thus, certainly at the time of the publication of the *Untersuchungen*, Menger can be seen to be part of a stream of thought which takes the understanding of the self as the basis for scientific work in chosen disciplines. But he then goes further than anyone else by narrowing this self to the specific individual human being.

Hermeneutics and *Verstehen* have traditionally been associated with a holistic conception of reality. Menger breaks with this tradition and imposes methodological individualism on his psychologistic conception of *Verstehen*, thus creating an explosive mixture of *Verstehen*, subjectivism, psychologism and individualism. This forms a specific kind of understanding which allows only private experience as the basis of factual knowledge and thus this kind of understanding is restricted to psychological facts and acts of individual persons only. In other words, if I want to know something essential about the social world, I have to look into myself. Menger's methodological and epistemological practise in the *Grundsätze* imposes introspection as the only logically admissible epistemology on the researcher who wants to follow the path mapped out in Menger's economic theory. Menger himself never put it in these terms, but neither did he ever publish a final, positive statement of his methodology and epistemology, nor did he himself complete the second edition of the *Grundsätze*. An epistemology which ultimately admits only of introspection as the path to the discovery of knowledge is highly unsatisfactory, not to say a dead end, unless applied to a wholly solipsistic universe. However, Menger's interest in the analysis—that is, in the explanation and understanding—of complex social phenomena and his ontological realism are incompatible with the conception of a solipsistic world. But before proceeding to a summary assessment of his methodology and epistemology, I must first specify a few more methodological strands in the *Grundsätze*.

Menger's methodological individualism is not stated explicitly in the *Grundsätze* as a separate methodological postulate. It is, nevertheless, another characteristic element of his economic analysis. Apart from being an important part of his resoluta-compositive method, this principle goes beyond the postulate that complex social phenomena have to be reconstituted from their most basic constituent elements. It imposes on the resoluta-compositive method the stipulations that the ultimate constituent elements must not be wholes but individuals and that complex phenomena must not be anything more than the sums of their constituent parts. The Romantic-Historicist concept of *Volksgeist* and the Aristotelian conception of human nature, being defined as truly human only if conceived as *zoon politikon*, are therefore inadmissible on Menger's methodological grounds.

There is ample evidence of the application of this principle in the *Grundsätze*. Not only does Menger start his analysis of value with the isolated individual, his extension of this analysis to groups and societies treats these groups and societies merely as sums of individuals.[105] Value is conceived of as independent of any social structure.[106] There are instances where this concept seems to run amok in the *Grundsätze*, for instance, when Menger mistakes free primary education and free drinking water provided by the state with free economic goods because individuals make no direct payments for these services.[107] In general, though, methodological individualism is adhered to strictly and consistently. All analytical results derived in the *Grundsätze* are based on individual instances, and all complex phenomena are nothing but the sums of their individual elements which, in the case of the economic theory of the *Grundsätze*, are usually individual motivations acting in a social context.

We must recall that, for Menger, all these concepts are not just elements of his methodology but also have an ontological standing. Methodological individualism is, therefore, not just a useful working hypothesis for the analysis of complex social and economic phenomena, it is a faithful reflection of the real structure of society and economy. In this sense, Menger stands in direct opposition to the *verstehende*, Historicist tradition. Individualism, or social atomism, as a methodological concept is traditionally associated with rationalism and the philosophy of the Enlightenment. Its central position in Menger's thought is certainly a puzzle given his own characterisation of economic theory as a *verstehende* discipline and his extensive knowledge of Romantic-Historicist tradition. Ideological motivation is definitely a part of the explanation, as his remarks on Adam Smith in the *Untersuchungen* show, but there are also other factors which may play at least as important a part.[108]

The precise origins of Menger's *Zusammenschau*, his conceptual integration of *Verstehen* and methodological individualism, would be the subject of an intellectual biography. They remain untraceable on the basis of the sources cited in his writings and hence will have to remain an unresolved problem for the purposes of this study. But there are some particular facets of Austrian cultural history which may help put this puzzle at least into a general context. I am referring here to the specifically Austrian interpretation of Leibniz's *Monadology*.

In the nineteenth century, Austrian thought was characterised by a vehement reaction against Romanticism and the German Idealist philosophy.[109] Central to this reaction was the philosophy of Leibniz, especially his *Monadology*, as transmitted and interpreted by Johann Friedrich Herbart and his students. In their interpretation the *Monadology* was turned into a qualitative atomism, and thus it provided the pluralistic counterpart to Spinoza's monism as represented in German Idealist philosophy. Through these channels, Leibniz's system furnished the Austrian mind with an ontological basis and with the optimism of the Austrian *Weltbild*, with the conception of a harmoniously ordered universe in which the elements are monads. What is important is this Austrian identification of the monad with an atom since the Leibnizian conception of the monad makes it anything but an atom. True, the monad is the ultimate constituent element of Leibniz's universe, just as the atom is the ultimate constituent element of matter, but while an atom is always the same, static and additive so that the whole is always the sum of its parts, an element pertaining to the mechanistic conception of the universe, the monad is an entirely different entity. It is different in the sense that no two monads are the same; it is dynamic and windowless, hence not additive, and it is organic.[110] It is, in fact, the original Leibnizian interpretation which defines the affinity of the *Monadology* with, and its relevance for Romanticism and Idealism.[111]

According to the argument developed by Mülher, Austrian thought blended atomism and monadology in such a way that through the integration of these two mutually exclusive conceptions of the ultimate building blocks of reality, an atomistic (or individualistic) conception became endowed with the ontological basis of an organicist philosophy.[112] That is to say, if one interprets the monad as an atom, though without shedding its other characteristic features, and if one does not conceive of this as a conceptual contradiction, then one presumably feels equally free to marry methodological individualism with the essentially holistic elements of the Romantic-Historicist world of thought. It is this rather idiosyncratic interpretation of Leibniz which, I believe, lies at the root of Menger's conviction that there is no contradiction between *Verstehen* and methodological individualism.

Furthermore, we are also told that this interpretation of Leibniz's *Monadology* was very widespread indeed in Austria, penetrating secondary education from 1848 onwards and even being echoed in popular trivial literature,[113] so Menger could have been able to absorb this philosophy at a very early, highly impressionable stage of his intellectual formation without necessarily being aware of it.[114] Whatever the real origin or the actual sources of Menger's conceptual identification of methodological individualism and *Verstehen* might have been—and here, again, we shall be the wiser only after we have access to the documents which were held by his son—the story provided by Mülher's analysis of ontology and monadology in Austrian thought provides us at least for the time being with a plausible scenario for a discussion of this dimension of Menger's methodology and epistemology.

But now I return to Menger's definition of value as *Bedeutung* because the methodological import of this term has not yet been exhausted. It offers yet another indication of the links between Menger's thought and the Romantic-Historicist tradition through the concepts which signify the object of the satisfaction of *Bedürfnisse*. *Leben* and *Wohlfahrt* are the central terms in this context, and they appear everywhere in the *Grundsätze*. The maintenance of human life and of human well being is the *telos* of economic activity. This *telos* is expressed by Menger in characteristically Romanticist language: "Bedürfnisse befriedigen aber heisst *leben* und *gedeihen*" (to satisfy one's *Bedürfnisse* is to live and to thrive), and inadequate satisfaction of *Bedürfnisse* leads to a withering away (*verkümmern*),[115] to *Störung des Organismus* (disturbances of the organism).[116] The final cause of human economic activity is part and parcel of human nature.[117] This human nature is biologically conceived, and the language used by Menger abounds with analogies from the life of plants and animals. In short, value is a *Lebenserscheinung* (a manifestation or phenomenon of life).[118]

This biologistic language links Menger firmly with the Romantic-Historicist world of thought and also blends in effortlessly with his Aristotelianism.[119] Menger himself confirms the former in the introduction to the new first chapter of the second edition of the *Grundsätze* when he defines the theory of *Bedürfnisse* as the basis of economic theory and as the bridge which links the *Naturwissenschaften*, especially biology, to the *Geisteswissenschaften* in general and economics in particular.[120] However, the *naturwissenschaftliche* element is not fully subdued by the Romantic-Historicist framework as human nature itself is conceived statically. The emphasis on growth and development does not prevent Menger from defining human nature as universally and eternally the same.[121] The implication is, of course, that his economic theory is universally applicable. But this could not be otherwise or else his claim of the truth and certainty of his "exact" theory could not be upheld.

It should be quite obvious by now that the *Grundsätze* of 1871 is based on a methodology and an epistemology which draw on both the rationalist and the Romantic-Historicist traditions, though not quite in equal measure. The integration of Menger into the founding trinity of neo-classical economic theory, which has been a long-standing tradition in the historiography of economic theory, means among other things that Menger has been identified with the mechanistic paradigm of general equilibrium analysis. To what extent this position can be upheld on theoretical or analytical grounds will be investigated in Essay III. So far we have seen that there is no basis for such an interpretation on methodological grounds. For an assessment of Menger, the mechanistic paradigm has to be replaced by a biological, organicist paradigm as far as the impact of natural-science thinking on Menger's thought is concerned, his methodological individualism notwithstanding. But this paradigm is embedded in the Romantic-Historicist framework which itself dominates the rationalist or natural science elements so that we may very well ask whether the concept of paradigm should be applied to the latter at all.

Strictly speaking, Menger derives from the rationalist tradition only his methodological individualism and his static conception of human nature. His emphasis on regularity and law-like behaviour of economic phenomena is equally at home in the rationalist and in the Aristotelian traditions, and hence, through the latter, it does not appear (to Menger at least) to contradict the Romantic-Historicist framework. The Romantic-Historicist elements of this *geisteswissenschaftliche* framework comprise his Aristotelianism, his essentialism and ontology, his teleological conception of causality, his search for the origin, his emphasis on organic growth and development, the subjectivism and psychologism of his conception of *Verstehen* and, ultimately, his rejection of mathematics.

The methodology and epistemology implicit in the economic theory of the *Grundsätze* are part and parcel of the programme of the *Geisteswissenschaften* in the second half of the nineteenth century. This programme, spurred on by the rejection of rationalism and positivism and by the evident success of the *Naturwissenschaften*, was an attempt to establish the humanities as equally worthy of the epithet *Wissenschaft*. Within this *geisteswissenschaftliche* and especially Historicist tradition, Menger adopted the Aristotelian conception of the science of man, the humanities, as part of the *Ethics* and the *Politics*. The world, historically understood, was ethically founded. This was, above all, also Droysen's programme. At the same time, however, Menger remained with Aristotle's conception of knowledge and science developed in the first philosophy, attempting in this way an integration of Aristotle's practical and first (or speculative) philosophy. Menger thus claimed to have arrived at a methodology and epistemology which can serve theoretical investigation of all empirical disciplines and to have transcended the dualism of the *Geisteswissenschaften* and the *Naturwissenschaften*.

In this project, however, Menger was caught by the primacy his system afforded the *Geisteswissenschaften* and by his admiration for the success of the *Naturwissenschaften*. He was thus forced to attempt the integration of the *Naturwissenschaften* into his conception of the *Geisteswissenschaften* if he wanted to arrive at a uniform basis for theoretical research in all empirical sciences. The result, as we have seen, was a collapse of his methodological and epistemological strategy, at least as far as the *Grundsätze* is concerned, since his conception of induction, the postulate necessary for the immediate perception of the starting points of theoretical investigation, turned out to be introspection, the logical conclusion to be drawn from his psychologistic conception of *Verstehen* in liaison with his individualism and subjectivism. To what extent this assessment is confirmed by his critique of Historicist methodology is investigated in the next section.

The Untersuchungen

Menger's *Untersuchungen über die Methode der Socialwissenschaften, und der Politischen Oekonomie insbesondere* was published in 1883 to counter the historical economists' claim to hegemony in economic research. The work is a critique of Historicist methodology and at the same time a defence of pure theory. But it is not a dispassionate analysis of competing research programmes in an effort to establish an objectively acceptable basis for economic research, as would be becoming of dignified academic discourse. It is, above all, a polemic[122] which issues from a very specific scientific conception of social reality (that already encountered in the discussion of the methodology in the *Grundsätze*) and claims, just as the historical economists did, to present the key to the solution of it all. However reasonable Menger's position throughout most of the *Untersuchungen* may seem, his insistence on the undisputable truth of exact theory is as intransigent as the historical economists' insistence that only they follow the righteous path to knowledge. Why Menger took this stance is a biographical question and hence beyond the scope of this study. That it was not because of youthful enthusiasm may be taken for granted since Menger was forty three when the book was published.

In this discussion, I try and stay clear of Menger's polemics as much as possible and concentrate on his substantive statements. There are two problem areas which I want to pursue in particular, that of Book 1 of the *Untersuchungen*, where Menger explains his conception of science, and that of Book 3, where he discusses the organicist conception of social life.

In Book 1 Menger sets out his philosophy of science. Sciences or, rather, *Wissenschaften*—the German *Wissenschaft* has a much wider scope than the English "science", as it encompasses systematic and publicly accessible knowledge of any subject, not just that of what has come to be known as the hard, or natural, sciences—are demarcated from each other according to the nature of the phenomena they investigate. There are three major demarcation lines. History and statistics investigate concrete individual phenomena and their relations while theory investigates the general forms, or *types*, and their relations, or *laws*, underlying these phenomena. The third type, the practical sciences—or arts—of the field of enquiry in question, does not investigate what is or the underlying *Wesen und Gesetze* (nature and laws) but how to achieve a certain end. In the field of economics, the practical sciences are economic policy and public finance. The theoretical and practical sciences constitute political economy as such.[123] This is the fundamental methodological or, as Menger says, formal criterion on which he builds his critique.

Menger insists on the strictest observation of the threefold division—historical, theoretical, practical—of all scientific work if methodological confusion is to be avoided. The aim of all scientific research is *Erkennen* (to become cognisant of) and *Verstehen* (to understand) the phenomena.[124] *Erkennen*, for Menger, is to grasp the concept, the mental image or linguistic representation, of a phenomenon.[125] Understanding a phenomenon is to grasp its essence, the reason for its being and its being-in-a-certain-way. There is a definite distinction between *Erkennen* and *Verstehen*. They are not just two different ways of obtaining scientific knowledge but are also related through an epistemological hierarchy, and *Verstehen* is epistemologically prior to *Erkennen*.[126] This is clear from the use of these two concepts throughout the *Untersuchungen*, and Menger confirms this distinction in the new first chapter of the second edition of the *Grundsätze* through his references to the *Geisteswissenschaften* and the *Naturwissenschaften*.

In the *Untersuchungen*, however, Menger gets himself into a conceptual muddle because he reduces *Verstehen* to *Erkennen* so that, not *Verstehen* (understanding the essence), but *Erkennen* (grasping the concepts) becomes fundamental:

> Wir verstehen eine concrete Erscheinung in *theoretischer* Weise (auf der Grundlage der entsprechenden theoretischen Wissenschaften), indem wir dieselbe als einen speziellen Fall einer gewissen Regelmässigkeit (Gesetzmässigkeit) in der Aufeinanderfolge, oder in der Coexistence der Erscheinungen erkennen, oder mit anderen Worten: wir gelangen zum Bewusstsein des Grundes der Existenz und der Besonderheit des Wesens einer concreten Erscheinung, indem wir in ihr lediglich die Exemplification einer Gesetzmässigkeit der Erscheinungen überhaupt erkennen lernen.[127]

What he, in fact, says is that *Verstehen* is to grasp the mental image or the linguistic representation of the reason for the being and being-in-a-certain-way of a phenomenon. But as we have seen in the discussion of Menger's argument with Roscher, it is not concepts but an understanding of the essences that he is after.[128] This confusion is caused, and perpetuated throughout the *Untersuchungen*, by his rather loose usage of the words *erkennen* and *Erkenntnis* which at times refer to "grasping concepts" and at other times to *Verstehen* of essences. What this confusion highlights are the difficulties inherent in any attempt to use the *Untersuchungen* as the *locus classicus* for Menger's own philosophy of science and to attribute an unambiguous formulation of his methodology and epistemology to his critique of Historicist methodology.

Just as there are several historical and practical sciences, there is also more than one branch of theoretical research. Menger distinguishes between theory which produces certain results and does not admit exceptions and theory which generates only probable results and does allow for exceptions.[129] Realistic-empirical theory concerns itself with the empirical investigation of types and laws (i.e., typical relations). Empirical reality, however, does not admit derivation of strict laws; hence, an exhaustive theoretical explanation of full empirical reality is not achievable using this type of theory. At best, we can obtain probable results or, in other words, results which are empirically refutable.[130] "Exact" theory, on the other hand, is certain and hence true. No exceptions are possible. This truth is, according to Menger, epistemologically guaranteed and pertains to the essence of the phenomena as well as to their measure.[131] The path to knowledge on the basis of "exact" theory is described by the resoluta-compositive method, which is the essence of "exact" theory and the necessary basis and pre-condition for establishing ideal types and ideal-typical relations ("exact" laws) which are necessarily true.[132] Furthermore, "exact" theory is not empirically testable.[133]

This is a very strange brew, indeed, and the least we can ask for is some clarification of the epistemological foundations of such bold statements. These foundations were, of course, to be provided in the never-completed "positive" philosophy of science, an absolutely indispensable step since the whole of Menger's critique of the historical economists is founded on his classification of the sciences in general and his conception of "exact" theory in particular. In the *Untersuchungen*, however, we are left in limbo since he refers to the *Denkgesetze* (laws of thought) in his description of "exact" theory. These laws guarantee the truth and certainty of this type of theory, but he does not state what they are. Having completed the description of "exact" theory, he then refers to the "above-stated rule for the derivation of knowledge" (*die obige Erkenntnisregel*) without, in fact, having stated one.[134]

In dubito pro reo. Let us assume that Menger was not deliberately cheating but that the laws of thought and the *Erkenntnisregel* were so obvious to him that it simply did not occur to him that they needed to be stated. There is, nevertheless, still some hope because if we look at the discussion of the methodology implicit in the *Grundsätze* within the context of his Aristotelianism, we are in a reasonably good position for some educated guessing.[135] We can interpret Menger's *Denkgesetze* as references to a kind of Aristotelian syllogism in which "exact" theory furnishes the inductively derived premises or starting points from which the "exact" laws would be deduced. Since, for Aristotle, scientific knowledge is knowledge of the true, the premises of the Aristotelian syllogism have to be true if the result is to be true. Thus, Menger's insistence on the truth and certainty of "exact" theory would blend in effortlessly if this Aristotelian connection could be substantiated. Unfortunately, on the basis of Menger's extant publications, we cannot go any further if we do not want to engage in wild and *unwissenschaftliche* speculation.

Menger himself, however, provides yet another clue to support at least this small step which we have taken. Early in his discussion of theoretical research, he gives a threefold definition of the aim or purpose of theoretical research:

Der Zweck der theoretischen Wissenschaften ist das *Verständniss*, die über die unmittelbare Erfahrung hinausreichende *Erkenntniss* und die *Beherrschung* der realen Welt. Wir verstehen die Erscheinungen durch Theorien, indem dieselben in jedem concreten Falle lediglich als Exemplification einer allgemeinen Regelmässigkeit *vor unser Bewusstsein treten*, wir erlangen eine *über die unmittelbare Erfahrung hinausreichende* Erkenntniss der Erscheinungen, indem wir im concreten Falle, auf Grundlage der Gesetze der Coexistence und der Erscheinungsfolge, aus gewissen beobachteten Thatsachen auf andere, unmittelbar nicht wahrgenommene *schliessen*; wir beherrschen die reale Welt, indem wir, auf der Grundlage unserer theoretischen Erkenntnisse, die in unserer Gewalt befindlichen Bedingungen einer Erscheinung setzen und solcherart diese letztere selbst herbeizuführen vermögen.[136]

The theoretical sciences aim at *Verständnis, Erkenntnis* and *Beherrschung*—understanding, cognition and control. The second step, cognition, is defined as deduction. The first step, understanding, is, on the one hand, deliberately worded differently from the second one and, on the other hand, formulated vaguely as "vor unser Bewusstsein treten" (stepping into our consciousness). This formulation, in combination with the description of the second step as "über die unmittelbare Erfahrung hinaus" (beyond immediate, that is, *unmediated* experience), suggests the interpretation of the first step as induction. This interpretation of *Verständnis* fits in perfectly with the Aristotelian conception of induction as the method of grasping the starting points of science.[137] Translation of *Verständnis, Erkenntnis* and *Beherrschung* in the light of this epistemological context would yield the methodological description of Menger's threefold aim of theoretical research as induction, deduction and application. That description bears an almost uncanny resemblance to the Aristotelian syllogism, but it also goes even further. It shows to what extent Menger has altered Aristotle's conception of the classification of sciences which covers the fields of inquiry of the first philosophy, ethics and poetics. These three different domains with their own epistemological and methodological foundations and their individual aims—knowledge for its own sake, knowledge for the sake of control and knowledge for the acquisition of skill, respectively—have been collapsed in Menger's system into the domain of theory only, a shift which is paralleled by his transposition of economics from the epistemological and methodological realm of Aristotle's ethics to that of the first philosophy.[138]

This passage also lends support to another element of my interpretation of Menger. The ranking of *Verstehen* as epistemologically prior to *Erkennen* (induction being the precondition without which there could not be any deduction in the sciences dealing with the real world) introduces the by now well-known controversy of the *Geisteswissenschaften* versus the *Naturwissenschaften* into Menger's own conception of method. Although Menger talks in terms of the unity of method and the plurality of sciences (the trinity formula of historical, practical and theoretical applying to the classification of all *Wissenschaften* while the *Wissenschaften* themselves differ according to the nature of their objects of inquiry),[139] he still retains the Romantic-Historicist terminology to describe his philosophy of science and ultimately affords the *Geisteswissenschaften* priority over the *Naturwissenschaften* by giving the concept of *Verstehen* priority over that of *Erkennen*. The anti-rationalist world of understanding is epistemologically prior to the rationalist world of deduction. This position is explicitly formulated in the second edition of the *Grundsätze*, but it can be discerned in the *Untersuchungen* of 1883 just as in the first edition of the *Grundsätze* of 1871. But just as the Romantic-Historicist element did not entirely subdue the rationalist element in the *Grundsätze*, in the *Untersuchungen* we find an expression of the *naturwissenschaftliche* optimism which was so typical of the nineteenth and early twentieth centuries. Unhampered by his Historicist heritage, Menger believes that the combination of "exact" and realistic-empirical theories of all the sciences of man will eventually allow for an exhaustive scientific explanation of full empirical reality.[140]

One theme becomes overwhelmingly clear in the first book of the *Untersuchungen*. The main thrust of Menger's attack on the historical economists is to reduce everything to their alleged confusion of "exact" theory and research with realistic-empirical and even purely historical work and to their "errors" committed by testing "exact" statements against full empirical reality. This argument, mostly couched in fairly polemical terms, appears over and over again in the *Untersuchungen*. In addition to the repetitiveness of Menger's approach, it was a tactically rather unfortunate step not to provide any epistemological foundations for his own position so that neither his opponents nor anyone else was in a position to assess the validity of his argument.

The same criticism applies to Menger's defence of the use of methodological individualism in pure, or "exact", theory.[141] His criticism of the Historicists' attack on atomism is based on the argument that they are guilty of not understanding "the true nature of the national economy in its relation to the individual economies" of which it is composed.[142] Atomism is, to all intents and purposes, congruent with methodological individualism; at least here we do not have a problem understanding the meaning of Menger's concept. Methodological individualism and the resoluta-compositive method are considered as complementary; hence, we can deduce that, according to Menger's characterisation of the resoluta-compositive method, methodological individualism must also be of the essence of "exact" theory. But he never offers a single argument why this must be so.

Menger's polemic against the historical economists' attack on atomism rounds off his discussion of the concept of theory in general and "exact" theory in particular. Nothing serves better as a summary assessment of Menger's own position than a passage from Book 1 of the *Untersuchungen*:

> Den Prüfstein für die Bürgschaft der exacten Gesetze der Volkswirthschaft in ihrer Congruenz mit den empirischen Gesetzen der letzteren suchen zu wollen, bedeutet die Verkennung der elementarsten Grundsätze wissenschaftlicher Methodik. Ein solcher Vorgang wäre jenem eines Naturforschers vergleichbar, welcher *an den empirischen Gesetzen der Naturerscheinungen die Gesetze der Physik*, der Chemie und der Mechanik, oder etwa gar an den in ihrer Art jedenfalls höchst nützlichen Bauernregeln, wie man sie in den für das Landvolk bestimmten Schriften findet—desshalb, weil sie zumeist auf sehr alter Erfahrung begründet sind,—*die Ergebnisse der exacten Forschung eines Newton*, Lavoisier oder Helmholtz *prüfen und berichtigen wollte!*[143]

In this passage, Menger unwittingly casts his own judgement. Unfortunately, his comments on the relevance of the empirical verification of Einstein's theory for the Newtonian universe seem to have been lost for posterity. His own "positive" philosophy of science is equally still awaiting publication.

In the remainder of the *Untersuchungen*, Menger continues to point out a large number of methodological errors and flaws in the historical economists' writings on economic theory. One does indeed get the impression that he cherishes every opportunity which allows him to point an accusing finger at a misplaced empirical argument within an "exact" framework. Needless to say, the missing epistemological foundations remain elusive while the themes of the theoretical versus the historical and the realistic-empirical *versus* the "exact" surface in a number of different guises. Still, a few issues emerge in the course of his excursions into Historicist failures which are of immediate relevance for our discussion of the methodological argument of the *Grundsätze*.

In the course of the discussion of the role of the historical perspective in economic research, Menger emphasises the importance of the concept of development which must be part and parcel of economic theory because the phenomena of the real world are characterised by development.[144] Everything in the real world changes in the course of time; time is of the essence of the real world. This is a clear and unequivocal confirmation of his position of 1871.[145] Time is an element of the ontological basis of all scientific work and must be reflected in the theory of the object under investigation.[146] However, he then moves on to specify that this methodological maxim regarding the concept of development holds for realistic-empirical work but not for "exact" theory because ideal types and ideal-typical relations are ideal, that is, free of contingency and individuality.[147]

Menger's conception of development is thoroughly Historicist. This is of course no mere accident; in light of the discussion in Essay I we should not expect anything else. His concept of development has nothing in common with the linear and continuously rising version of the Enlightenment conception of progress; his concept is organic and is characterised by birth, rise, fall and decay.[148] He actually regards this genetic concept as an inseparable element of theoretical science.[149]

The concept of organism and the place of the organic analogy in social science is scrutinised in Book 3 of the *Untersuchungen*. In this context, Menger juxtaposes the biological paradigm of the organism to the mechanical paradigm. Social life and social phenomena are organic. The constituent elements of an organism define their function and their essence through their place in the organism as a whole and through the other constituent elements (organs), but the same is not the case for the elements of a mechanism. In addition, organisms are the results of "natural" processes, unplanned, while mechanisms are the results of human calculation.[150]

At first sight, this position may seem to contradict Menger's insistence on the fundamental role of methodological individualism in theoretical work since an organism is quite clearly more than the sum of its parts. Menger, however, resolves this problem quite elegantly by pursuing two arguments which issue from his conception of organism. On the one hand, he discusses natural organisms in contrast to social ones, and, on the other hand, returning to his favourite theme, he differentiates between the role of the organic analogy in realistic-empirical theory and its role in "exact" theory.

The holistic concept of the organism is admitted only in realistic-empirical theory, in the realm of the probable where general types and general relations come under the influence of the contingent and the individual. In "exact" theory, however, organisms are ruled out of order; the atomistic, or mechanistic,[151] conception of complex phenomena is the only admissible paradigm.[152] This holds for complex phenomena in both the social and the natural sciences and seems to constitute a strong confirmation of Menger's fundamental conception of the unity of method (i.e., his tri-partite methodological demarcation criterion) within the plurality of the sciences. Nevertheless, in his next step, the distinction between natural and social organisms, Menger affords explicitly epistemological superiority to the *Geisteswissenschaften* and the associated *verstehende* approach, thus effectively cancelling his previous merely methodological classification.

Organisms, just as mechanisms, are composed of elements which are characterised by *Zweckrationalität*, by a rational orientation towards a final purpose.[153] Natural organisms, though, are the result of purely causal, mechanical processes driven by mechanical forces; hence they have to be explained by efficient causality. Social organisms, on the other hand, are the result of human effort, of the human will and of purposive human action. It follows logically that social phenomena require teleological explanation.[154] But Menger does not rest here; in his juxtaposition of the "ethical" (human) world to the "organic" (natural) world,[155] social organisms, the result of the *Gemeinwillen* (collective will), are derived from "thinking, feeling, acting" human beings.[156] This, however, is nothing but the *verstehende* Romantic-Historicist conceptualisation which serves to underpin Menger's epistemological priority of the *Geisteswissenschaften* over the *Naturwissenschaften*:

> [In den exacten Socialwissenschaften] sind die menschlichen Individuen und ihre Bestrebungen, die letzten Elemente unserer Analyse, empirischer Natur und die exacten theoretischen Socialwissenschaften somit in grossem Vortheil gegenüber den exacten Naturwissenschaften. Die "Grenzen des Naturerkennens" und die hieraus für das theoretische Verständniss der Naturphänomene sich ergebenden Schwierigkeiten bestehen in Wahrheit nicht für die exacte Forschung auf dem Gebiete der Socialerscheinungen.[157]

The subject matter of the social sciences in general and economics in particular is epistemologically accessible in a way the subject matter of the natural sciences can never even aspire to. "Exact" investigation of social phenomena can therefore be more profound than "exact" investigation of natural phenomena. But this is nothing but the traditional argument, advanced from Vico onwards, for the superior intelligibility to us, as human beings, of the human world over the natural world. Thus already in 1883, Menger explicitly confirms his position expressed in 1923, in the new first chapter of the second edition of the *Grundsätze*, that economics is part of the *Geisteswissenschaften*. It is his acknowledgement in 1883 that, at bottom, the epistemological dualism between the *Geisteswissenschaften* and the *Naturwissenschaften* is the terrain on which his theory and methodology have to be located. None of this contradicts, either from Menger's point of view or from the perspective of this study, the economic theory and the implicit methodology of the *Grundsätze* of 1871.

The last of Menger's themes in the *Untersuchungen* of immediate interest in this study also exactly fits the argument of the *Grundsätze*: the unintended consequences of individual human action. This methodological principle is the basis of Menger's theory of institutions through which he attempts to explain how publicly beneficial institutions come into being without the intervention of a *Gemeinwille*.[158] The existence of naturally developed, organic institutions like language, religion, law, the state and, more specifically, markets, competition and money requires a theoretical explanation because "the solution to the most important problems posed by economic theory is intimately connected with the question of the theoretical understanding of these institutions."[159] In contrast to Menger's usual procedure in the *Untersuchungen*, where he deals with questions of this type only within the general framework of theory or at best from the perspective of realistic-empirical theory, he now tackles the methodological problem of the investigation of institutions from the perspective of "exact" theory. This is no doubt owing to the fact that the *Grundsätze* closes with a chapter on the nature and origin of money. But far from giving us new insights into his methodology of "exact" theory, he only presents us with old acquaintances again.

In keeping with the tradition established in the *Grundsätze*, Menger commences the exposition of his methodological postulate with a few illustrative examples. He delineates his conception of the origin and the development of money, of new conurbations and of the state,[160] and arrives at an intermediate conclusion which states that these phenomena have to be explained by means of individualistic-teleological and collectivistic-teleological factors: "Das heutige Geld- und Marktwesen, das heutige Recht, der moderne Staat u.s.f. bieten eben so viele Beispiele von Institutionen, welche sich uns als Ergebniss der combinirten Wirksamkeit individual- und socialteleologischer Potenzen, oder, mit anderen Worten, 'organischer' und 'positiver' Faktoren darstellen."[161] A *socialteleologischer* (collectivistic-teological) factor is merely a different term for *Gemeinwille* and, hence, cannot constitute an ultimate constituent element of an "exact" explanation of an organic institution.

Indeed, what Menger had stated at the end of his illustration of the origin and development of money—that money is the result of the unintended consequences of *individual* human action—is now confirmed as an important methodological result for the social sciences in general: "Die Socialphänomene, deren Ursprung ein 'organischer' ist, charakterisiren sich . . . dadurch, dass dieselben sich als die unbeabsichtigte Resultate individueller d.i. individuelle Interessen verfolgender Bestrebungen der Volksglieder darstellen, demnach . . . die *unbeabsichtigte sociale Resultante individual-teleologischer Factoren* sind."[162] "Exact" social theory explains social institutions as the result of individualistic-teleological factors. If we translate this statement into more familiar language, that is, if we analyse it by reducing it to its ultimate constituent elements, we see that the application of the resoluta-compositive method to the complex phenomena of social institutions leads us to purposive human action of individuals as the ultimate constituent elements of these institutions. In other words, the methodological postulate that organic social institutions are the results of the unintended consequences of individual human action, far from being a new and independent methodological insight, is the composite of teleology and methodological individualism, two of the most fundamental constituent methodological elements of the economic theory of the *Grundsätze*. The methodological continuity in Menger's work could not be more clearly stated.

The discussion of the *Untersuchungen* presented here is, of course, far from complete. What I have attempted to do is to draw out the characteristic features of Menger's own methodology as represented in his critique of the historical economists and compare them to the implicit methodology which we discovered in the *Grundsätze*. Some of these methodological elements— like that of the tripartite classification of the *Wissenschaften*—can only be found in the *Untersuchungen*. Other elements—such as the (ontological) importance of the concept of time, the importance of methodological individualism and the Romantic-Historicist world of the *Geisteswissenschaften*— are equally prominent in both the *Grundsätze* and the *Untersuchungen*, and a third group of elements—such as Menger's teleological conception of causality and his Aristotelianism—can become really clear only with reference to the *Grundsätze*. That both his critique of Historicist methodology and his own economic theory are inseparable parts of the same oeuvre should now not require any special emphasis. This holds, of course, for his methodology as a whole, that is, for his positive methodological achievements as well as for his methodological shortcomings. In particular, his failure to substantiate the epistemological foundations of his critique of the historical economists' methodology which we have encountered, is reflected in the economic theory of the *Grundsätze* at the point of transition from values into prices. The theoretical and epistemological dimensions of Menger's transformation problem will be discussed in Essay III,[163] but two dimensions of his philosophy of science need to be discussed before we can move on to the investigation of his theory of value since they are central to an understanding of his economic theory: his Aristotelianism and his theory of *Bedürfnisse*.

Menger and Aristotle

It is obvious and generally accepted that Menger was an Aristotelian. What is less clear is the meaning of this statement. Was Menger an Aristotelian in his economic theory or in his philosophy, that is, in his *wissenschaftliche*

Weltauffassung, his epistemology, his philosophy of science and/or his methodology? Even more important, what kind of Aristotelian was he? In the 2,000 years since Aristotle, the term "Aristotelian" has covered a multitude of sins ranging from the characterisation of Aristotle as a "mere" empiricist to his identification with Platonic idealism. It is therefore quite important to decide what we are talking about when we call Menger an Aristotelian. But as with so many questions concerning Menger, this also is not an easy one to answer. There is only one thing we can be reasonably certain about: Menger was an Aristotelian in his philosophical outlook and his philosophy of science but not in his economic theory, although even this certainty will have to be qualified. Unfortunately, the question about the nature of his Aristotelianism remains untractable to date and can be answered only after his notebooks (if there are any), his unpublished papers and the philosophical section of his library become accessible.

This assessment of Menger's Aristotelianism does not necessarily agree with traditional opinion which has it that he was an Aristotelian not only in his methodology but also in his economic theory. A further objection to my position may be that we know a great deal about Aristotle, his work and the Aristotelian tradition,[164] so it ought not be too difficult to identify Menger's particular brand of Aristotelianism. Reasonable as these arguments may seem, they are based on a series of misconceptions. Let me therefore take them in turn and briefly show why I consider them to be wrong.

Menger refers to Aristotle in the *Grundsätze*, the *Untersuchungen* and his publications on money, citing overwhelmingly the *Nicomachean Ethics* but also the *Politics* and once *De Anima*, that is to say, he cites the *loci classici* of Aristotle's discussion of economics. But nowhere does he refer to the *Physics*, *Metaphysics* or *Posterior Analytics*, the traditional sources for a discussion of Aristotle's philosophy of science, scientific methodology, epistemology and the nature of reality. Most of the references to Aristotle in the *Grundsätze* serve to demonstrate the development of economic doctrine in Menger's attempt to clarify their *Ursprung und Wesen* (origin and essence). In the historiography of economic theory, these sections are generally used to claim Aristotle as an anticipator of the subjective theory of value because he is said to have made use of concepts such as usefulness, scarcity and even diminishing marginal utility. On the basis of this argument, Menger's Aristotelian origins are then presumed to have been proved. But if this is really all there was to his Aristotelianism, then we would all be Aristotelian economists now, a claim which could be sustained only with some difficulty, to say the very least.[165]

As far as economic theory is concerned, we can find yet another argument which can be summoned to link Menger directly to Aristotle. In the *Nicomachean Ethics*, Aristotle explicitly bases exchange on *Bedürfnis* and makes the latter concept the measuring rod of exchange and, above all, money.[166] Menger cites this section in his chapter on value and in his theory of money.[167] As we shall also see in Essay III, *Bedürfnis* and satisfaction of *Bedürfnisse* are the central concepts on which Menger constructs his economic theory and from which most of his analytical arguments flow. As this is not the case with the other branches of neo-classical theory,[168] one could, indeed, be tempted to make out a special case for the Aristotelian character of Menger's theory on the basis of this argument.

However, as we shall equally see in Essay III, Menger's theory is firmly embedded in the German version of classical political economy in which not only subjective value featured greatly but *Bedürfnis* played a central role after Hegel assigned a pivotal role to the concept of the system of *Bedürfnisse*. Certainly around the middle of the nineteenth century this stream of thought took its orientation from Hegel, not directly from Aristotle.[169] Menger was therefore only a link in a chain of German political economists who made it their task to integrate a system of *Bedürfnisse* in the foundations of economic theory. But as far as neo-classical economics is concerned, Menger is certainly the most Aristotelian of its founding fathers if the integration of *Bedürfnis* is to be the central criterion. By the same token, however, we would have to characterise almost all the German classical political economists as Aristotelians or, perhaps more aptly, as Hegelians. This characterisation, in turn, would make Menger a Hegelian economist as much as an Aristotelian economist. Put differently, the integration of *Bedürfnis* as a theoretical category into economics does not appear very convincing if it is to be the central criterion for calling Menger an Aristotelian.

Ironically, the section preceding the one in the *Nicomachean Ethics* referred to above contains an argument which readily lends itself to making a very much stronger case against the Aristotelianism of Menger's economic theory. Aristotle measures (commercial) value by *Bedürfnis* since he needs a measure of value for his discussion of exchange. He needs to define units which make heterogeneous elements commensurable for the purposes of exchange since his concept of commutative justice requires that exchange be only of equivalents. Menger rejects this argument as the basis for exchange[170] because in his theory exchange can only take place if a person attaches a higher value to the thing obtained than to the one for which it is exchanged.[171] Menger's theory of value is therefore incompatible with the thrust of Aristotle's thought in the *Nicomachean Ethics* from the point of view of attributes of exchange. Menger's subjective value theory admits only exchange of unequal values, a position which, in terms of Scholastic, Aristotelian economics, would be identified with usury or profiteering.

The characterisation of Menger's economic theory in the *Grundsätze* as Aristotelian would rest on fairly weak foundations if we had to rely merely on a comparison of theoretical concepts and their use in the construction of the theory. As we have seen, Menger rejects Aristotle's theory of exchange; he shares his notion of *Bedürfnis* as the measure of value with most of the German classical political economists who really took their inspiration from Hegel rather than from Aristotle himself. And the use of the psychological notion that value is diminishing at the margin, in view of the absence of an economic theory in the *Nicomachean Ethics*, is a commonplace in Aristotle's discussion while it is the central explanatory principle in Menger's *Grundsätze*. However, Menger applies his concepts in an epistemological and methodological framework which is decidedly Aristotelian and thus provides us with the perspective which justifies this characterisation of his economic theory since no theory can exist independent of its methodology and epistemology. But now we run into a major, and as yet intractable problem: What kind of an Aristotelian was Menger?

This question is of more than mere historical interest because it goes directly to the center of Menger's conception of methodology and epistemology. Since the publication of Werner Jaeger's reassessment of Aristotle in 1923, a great deal of progress has been made towards recovering the authentic Aristotle. This development was by no means smooth and undisputed[172] and resulted in the existence of a number of different, period-specific Aristotles. As a consequence, we are now facing the problem of having to reconstruct the interpretation of Aristotle for specific historical periods, as, for instance, for that of the 1850s and 1860s if we want to discuss an author who came out of that period and who is labelled an Aristotelian. This is not an easy task in itself, for during those decades Germany and Austria were seething with discussions of Aristotle's philosophy as we can see from the publication of quite a number of books on Aristotle during the 1860s and 1870s. To complicate things a little further, the Aristotelian tradition in the German-speaking world was not at all homogeneous and produced quite a number of mutually exclusive interpretations of Aristotle's thought.[173]

Let me give one pertinent example from Menger to illustrate the inconsistencies generated by some of these nineteenth-century Aristotelians. In the *Untersuchungen*, Menger attempts to demonstrate that Aristotle was a methodological individualist[174] by rejecting the interpretation of Aristotle's concept of man as *zoon politikon* qua *politikon*. He denies that only through *koinonia* (community) can members of the species *homo sapiens* transcend their animal nature and become true human beings. For Menger, the individual is first and the state second, an interpretation of Aristotle which is not only unacceptable to us but which would have been equally unacceptable to many contemporaries of Menger no matter which side of the ideological and philosophical divide they were to be found on. In his interpretation, Menger simply makes the common mistake of confusing categories: He mistakes what is "first for us" for what is "first by nature."[175] In this particular instance, an explanation may quite plausibly be found in the ideological motivation of wanting to force methodological individualism into this holistic concept because one of Menger's main aims is to fight collectivism and socialism.[176]

Nevertheless, there ought to be a more general explanation for the interpretation of Aristotle offered by Menger. I do not believe that the explanation lies in regarding Menger as a genius working almost out of time and place (as could be claimed, for instance, for the Italian philosopher Giambattista Vico at the end of the seventeenth century). Menger was far too deeply entrenched in the thinking and disputes of his own time—witness his debt to the German discussion of political economy and his own recognition of this debt[177]—for such an explanation. If the model of the intellectual Robinson Crusoe does not apply in his case, then the only alternative route towards explaining his idiosyncratic interpretation of Aristotle must be via an investigation of the sources of his philosophical thought.

At this point, the situation becomes even more complicated if not, at least temporarily, quite intractable. Menger did not provide us with a "positive" epistemology and methodology. All we have are his "negative" methodology (the critique of the methodology of the historical economists) and his "positive" economic theory (the *Grundsätze*). Hence, anything we can say about Menger's own methodology and epistemology must remain largely hypothetical as far as the substance of the argument is concerned, and we are venturing even more into the realm of pure guesswork if we want to investigate the sources of his philosophical thought. It is, unfortunately, not possible to retrace these sources in the same way we can retrace the sources of his economic theory because he does not tell us where to look. At the very best, we are in a position to derive a number of questions from the literature on Menger and from Menger's own references. Where did he learn his Aristotle: at the *Gymnasium*? Or from philosophers such as Trendelenburg? From Ueberweg's *System der Logik*? Franz Brentano? Kuno Fischer? C. Heyder? To what extent was Menger familiar with Aristotle's works which he does not cite, such as the *Organon, Metaphysics, Posterior Analytics* and the *Physics*?[178] We are told that Menger also studied Leibniz.[179] Did he study Leibniz independently or in relation to Bolzano or to Herbart, for instance, through the work of Robert Zimmermann?[180]

Answers to these questions are of eminent importance if we want to design an intellectual map to guide any attempt to establish Menger's own conceptions of the philosophy of science, of epistemology and of methodology. But we shall be able to answer them only after we have access to Menger's unpublished papers, the philosophy section of his library and, if there are any, his notebooks and diaries. As we have seen earlier, however, it is still not too difficult to identify the general Aristotelian strands in Menger's ontology, epistemology and philosophy of science which are implicit or even explicit in the *Grundsätze* and the *Untersuchungen*. A rough outline of the relevant arguments in Aristotle's thought readily demonstrates the affinity of Menger's thought.[181]

Aristotle was an ontological essentialist; hence, he differentiated and at the same time had to explain the relationship between the world of essence (of the real nature of things), and the world of phenomena (of what is "first for us"). The real nature of things and phenomena is discussed, explained and analysed through concepts such as substance, essence, matter, form, compound, potentiality and actuality. Individual substances are the invariants of existence, and they are given identity through form which is correlative with matter while matter itself may or may not be corporeal. The contrast between matter and form is statically conceived; dynamically, as a process, it becomes the contrast between potentiality and actuality.

> The individual substance is a compound of the subject or substratum[182] and the essence or form. To the individual substance belong the conditions and relations which are distinguished according to the nine accidental categories. The universal becomes preeminently the object of science, because it is the essential element and so has reality in a higher sense than what is merely particular. The universal certainly exists only in the particular, but from this it follows . . . that we cannot apprehend the universal except through apprehension of the individual.[183]

> The distinction between Matter and Form may also be expressed by saying that Matter is the persistent underlying *substratum* in which the development of the Form takes place, or that the individual, when finally determined by the Form, is the Actuality of which the unformed and undeveloped matter was the potentiality.[184]

This is the *geistesgeschichtliche* origin and home of Menger's concept of *Wesen* (essence, real nature), the explanation and understanding of which is one of the aims of Menger's "exact" theory. It is this Aristotelian conception of being which allows us to understand Menger's use of the phrase "der Grund des Seins und So-Seins" in the *Untersuchungen* when he attributes general being and specific being to a thing or phenomenon.[185] But note that although at the beginning of this paragraph I use the words "home" and "origin" to emphasise the kinship between Menger and Aristotle, I deliberately avoid any formulation like "this *is* Aristotle's conception of essence/substance" etc. because this is precisely what can be established only by a study of Menger's sources.

Let us take Aristotle's concept of substance as a representative illustration of the difficulties inherent in Menger's approach. Substance is characterised by four moments: the first distinction is between first and second substances, between the individual independent being and the being-in-a-certain-way. The second distinction, in turn, differentiates between kind and species, between *genus proximum* and *differentia specifica*.[186] Hence, Menger's "Sein und So-Sein" is nothing but being which has the first and second substances as attributes.[187] However, Menger defines the aim of "exact" theory not only as the explanation and understanding of *Wesen* (essence) but also of *Ursprung* (origin). The investigation of the origin, however, cannot be traced back to Aristotle's conception of substance because Aristotle's substance, precisely because it is what makes change, movement, coming-into-being possible through its capacity to encompass and integrate its opposite, must remain what it is.[188] There is, therefore, no need, within Aristotle's frame of reference, to investigate the origin of a thing once we know its substance or *Wesen*. Hence we have to explain the origin of the second part of Menger's definition of the aims of "exact" theory. In this particular case, it is fairly easily established because it cannot be anything but the Romantic or, more specifically, Historicist strand in his *wissenschaftliche Weltauffassung*.[189] This, however, is not the only problem generated by Menger's conception of substance or *Wesen* (I turn to some of these problems in a moment).

Menger's kinship with Aristotle goes deeper than just the ontological essentialism. It also carries over to epistemology and philosophy of science. Knowledge, for Aristotle, is by causes. It starts from first principles which are indemonstrable starting points arrived at by induction. These first principles are grasped by a special power (*nous*) which allows us to extract them from what is "first to us", i.e., daily experience or empirical reality. They are the necessary premises of syllogistic, or demonstrative, reasoning by means of which we arrive at scientific knowledge. And since scientific knowledge is true, the starting points or first principles must also be true. Scientific definitions which are developed in the process of establishing scientific knowledge are real and not just nominal definitions: They reveal the essence of those things that science investigates.

One criticism levelled at this conception of scientific knowledge, which holds for Menger as well as for Aristotle, is that it does not explain how the first principles are grasped and that Aristotle gives only a psychological description of this process.[190] In particular, he does not demonstrate that these inductively derived premises are necessarily true. Menger does not solve this problem either but instead insists dogmatically on the truth of his "exact" theories, which are not testable empirically despite the fact that their basic premises are derived from simple everyday experience.[191]

Beyond this criticism, which Menger shares with Aristotle, there are a number of other epistemological affinities. Menger's resoluta-compositive method is but another form of Aristotle's postulate that to discover what things are we have to take them back to their elements. The discovery of the true premises of "exact" theory takes place at the level of common everyday experience and hence is very much akin to Aristotle's inductive process. Menger does not explicitly say so, but it would be difficult to find another explanation within a general Aristotelian framework, and it would be even more difficult to find any scientifically acceptable explanation at all if one were to look outside such a framework. Finally, Menger's fictional case studies in the *Grundsätze* are conceptually very much like the Aristotelian notion of demonstration.

Different sciences need different starting points and use different methods which have to be appropriate to the subject matter under investigation. This plurality of sciences is postulated by Aristotle in opposition to Plato's postulate of a universal science and is echoed by Menger. It is also probably the first instance of what was more than 2,000 years later to crystalise into the controversy between the *Naturwissenschaften* and the *Geisteswissenschaften*.[192] Nevertheless, there are some significant differences between Aristotle's classification of the sciences and Menger's. Aristotle defines three kinds of science: speculative, practical and poetic. Of these, only speculative science generates scientific knowledge, that is, true knowledge of the necessary. Its conclusions are universal truths deduced from self-evident first principles apprehended by induction. The objective of speculative science is knowledge for its own sake. Practical science, on the other hand, achieves knowledge of the contingent, of that "what may be otherwise." Its objects are the relations which human volition can modify, and its conclusions are general rules incapable of strict demonstration. Its objective is knowledge for the sake of control.

Only the first philosophy, mathematics and physics constitute speculative science for Aristotle. Economics is merely a subdiscipline of politics which, in turn, is one of the objects of practical science. Hence, for him, the results of economic investigations are incapable of strict demonstration since practical science generates only contingent knowledge. Aristotle's economic theory is, therefore, not "exact" in Menger's sense of the term. In connection with the discussion of the concept of substance this issue raises a number of crucial problems if one wants to compare Menger's philosophy of science directly with that of Aristotle.

Menger transforms economics into a science capable of producing "exact" knowledge, that is, knowledge of the necessary which consists of universal truths deduced from self-evident first principles (presumably apprehended by induction). Menger's "exact" theory is therefore made to correspond to Aristotle's speculative science. Knowledge of the contingent is obtained through Menger's empirical-realistic theories (these would correspond to Aristotle's practical science) while the "arts" (corresponding to Aristotle's poetic science) are Menger's practical science. History, which for Aristotle is not fully knowable because it deals with transitory things which have no substance, is also relegated by Menger to a *Hilfswissenschaft* (an auxiliary science) just like statistics.

The central problem raised here is that Aristotle never defined any substance for economics. For him, economic concepts belong to the realm of relations, that is, to that of the categories of substance. Hence, to render Menger's scheme truly compatible with that of Aristotle one would have to accept that there was a substance of economic activity. Since Menger himself defines "economic" as a relationship, we would have to agree with the identification of a substance with one of its categories. This is a slightly tricky problem, to say the very least, and is perhaps one of the reasons why Menger was so keen to find a basis for economics in biology via his theory of *Bedürfnisse* in the second edition of the *Grundsätze*.

Finally, Aristotle's classification of economics as a sub-discipline of politics should remind us of his conception of the primacy of the political over the economic, that is, that of the *polis* over the individual. This point underlines Menger's error in reading methodological individualism into Aristotle.[193]

Let these examples suffice as illustrations of the problems inherent in Menger's Aristotelianism. Before going on with the discussion of Menger, I want to mention briefly two concepts in which Menger's position is quite close to Aristotle. They are the concepts of time and causality.

For Aristotle, time is essentially connected with change, indeed, it is what measures change. Or, as it is frequently stated, time is the number of change. Time is, of course, an essential element in Menger's economic theory, introduced right at the outset, and, as we have seen, Menger accepts Aristotle's definition of time.[194] But the similarity I want to point out is that between Aristotle's conception of the status of time and Menger's conception of the status of value. Writing in a period when value was measured in terms of labour or conceived of as utility, Menger frees himself from the notion of concrete, cardinal measurability and defines value as a pure number. Value is the number of *Bedürfnis*, without unit, not cardinally measurable. Perhaps I read more into this comparison than is actually there, but it certainly appears to be more than mere coincidence.

Since for Aristotle knowledge was by causes he was quite careful in his definition of causality and developed the famous fourfold conception of cause for the explanation of things and phenomena. Of the four elements of cause—matter, form, agent and end—the first (material) cause is rather isolated and involves the necessary conditions for the coming-into-being of a natural object; the other three (formal, efficient and final) causes frequently coincide. Hence, an investigation of the *telos* may reveal all three causes simultaneously. The efficient cause, which for Aristotle is the primary cause of change, is the only one still accepted as such in the modern scientific world. Teleology, the determination of the final cause, especially has been relegated to the realm of mysticism or speculation, at least as far as the hard (natural) sciences are concerned.[195]

But Menger, in his attempt to put economics as a science on an equal footing with the natural sciences, rehabilitates the final cause. His conception of causality is, as we have seen, thoroughly Aristotelian. Menger's project can be compared to that of Droysen who re-introduced the fourfold conception of causality by making it the one to be used in historical explanation. The satisfaction of *Bedürfnisse* is the final cause in Menger's "exact" theory and, in his vision, the driving force of the economic process. The fact that he understands causality as teleology is only implicit in the first edition of the *Grundsätze* but it is made explicit in the second edition.

Furthermore, the dictum that knowledge is by causes is also reflected in Menger's resoluta-compositive method, for only when we know the constituent elements of a thing or phenomenon can we explain why something is what it is. This is not surprising since Menger agrees with Aristotle that not everything is what it appears to be. In fact, a causal, that is, a teleological, explanation quite often runs in the opposite direction to what we can observe. In Aristotle's formulation: "Now the order of development is the reverse of the real order. What is later in the formative process is earlier by its nature, and what comes at the end of the process is first by nature. . . . Matter and the process of formation come first in time, but in *logos* [account or definition] the essence [*ousia*] and form of the thing must be first."[196] What comes last in Menger's economic process is the satisfaction of *Bedürfnisse*. Economic activity takes place, and only at the end of it will a *Bedürfnis* be satisfied. But *Bedürfnis* is at the same time the beginning of all economic activity, for nothing would be undertaken if it were not for the satisfaction of *Bedürfnisse*. Hence, what is last in time is first in *logos*. Certainly in his conception of causality, Menger was a faithful Aristotelian.

In Essay I and also in this essay, I frequently mention Menger's affinity with Johann Gustav Droysen, whose *Grundriss der Historik* is essentially the outline of an Aristotelian project for the science of history. Traditionally, it is not directly described as such; it is usually the strong influence on the young Droysen of Hegel and his disciples which is emphasised.[197] Menger's economic theory may well be regarded as a realisation of Droysen's Historicist project in economics. Droysen's outline of the nature of historical work, combining the Hegelian heritage with historical realism (*geschichtswissen-schaftlicher Realismus*), attempts to furnish the framework and the concepts which are supposed to be fundamental to historical work. In that outline, we find many of the major concepts which also link Menger with Aristotle. Standing out most clearly of all is the formulation of Aristotle's fourfold conception of causality which furnishes the systematic basis of Droysen's *Grundriss*.[198] "Das Geheimnis aller Bewegung ist ihr Zweck" (the secret of all movement is its purpose) says Droysen with reference to Aristotle in leading up to his statement of the four causes.[199]

Other Aristotelian elements of Droysen's epistemology and methodology are interwoven with a number of concepts which derive from the Romantic world of thought. Aristotelian induction or immediate perception is placed within a fundamentally psychologistic conception of *Verstehen* which, in contrast to Menger, is not allied with an individualistic conception of human nature. Droysen is, in a way, a more faithful Aristotelian (his Hegelian background might have played a part in this) since for him *homo sapiens* becomes a human being only through the creation of, and existence within, a moral world. This moral world arises out of *Arbeit* and is formed according to the *Bedürfnisse* of the agents who work on its coming into being.

The precise place of Droysen's *Historik* in Menger's thought is, nevertheless, open to debate. There is no doubt that Menger drew on Droysen in his preparation of the *Untersuchungen*,[200] but what is of interest here is whether he knew Droysen's work before 1871. This certainly cannot be ruled out since the first edition of Droysen's *Grundriss* was published in 1867 after having been circulated as a privately printed manuscript since 1858.[201] It would also be quite surprising if Menger's intellectual inclinations had not led him to it before 1875. Still, we have no proof that this was the case, and therefore I cannot assert anything beyond the striking similarities between Menger's and Droysen's research projects and between their *geistesgeschicht-liche* points of reference, both of which we can discern in Menger's *Grundsätze*.

Menger's *Lehre von den Bedürfnissen*

The concept of *Bedürfnisse* is the cornerstone of Menger's economic theory. It ties him into the German *Geistesgeschichte* in general, as we saw in Essay I, and to the Aristotelian tradition in particular, as we have seen in this essay. *Bedürfnis* is one of the pre-occupations characteristic of German classical political economists and is the carrier of teleology within the analytical structure of Menger's economic theory (I discuss this in Essay

III). It is not conceivable that a concept of such importance would be employed without any methodological or historical explanation by an author whose stated main aim is the explanation and understanding of the essence and origin (*Wesen und Ursprung*) of the constituent elements of his science. True, strictly speaking, an analysis of *Bedürfnis* lies outside the scope of economics proper, but the use of this concept still requires some foundation. In short, what we may rightfully expect, from the perspective of this essay, is a theory of needs and wants, a *Lehre von den Bedürfnissen*.

Menger did indeed write a theory of *Bedürfnisse*, but it came to be published only two years after his death as the new first chapter of the second edition of the *Grundsätze*.[202] What we would really like to have, however, is a theory of *Bedürfnisse* which could be dated about 1870 or 1871. There are, in fact, some pages on the concept of *Bedürfnis* which were originally planned for the first edition of the *Grundsätze* but which were withdrawn just before the volume went into print because Menger did not feel qualified enough to pronounce on the subject. (Quite an understandable sentiment if one considers the fundamental importance of the concept for his economic theory.) This fact is reported by Menger's son in the introduction to the second edition of the *Grundsätze*.[203] It is to be expected that these pages are among Menger's unpublished papers which were kept by his son, but for the purposes of this study, this is not very comforting news. At the moment, as with quite a few other issues raised by Menger's work, we are simply stuck because his elaborations of 1923 do not permit us to make any definitive deduction of his theory of *Bedürfnisse* in 1871. Let me explain briefly.

According to Karl Menger, his father stopped working on the theory of *Bedürfnisse* after the publication of the *Grundsätze* in 1871 and only returned to it in 1896. During the first few years of this century, having retired from teaching, he is reported to have written the pages which constitute the new first chapter of the second edition of the *Grundsätze*.[204] What caused him to return to the concept of *Bedürfnis* in 1896? Strictly speaking, we do not know because he does not even cite any literature in the pages printed in 1923 from which we may infer the cause of his renewed interest. However, in 1894 Oskar Kraus published a 72-page book entitled *Das Bedürfnis*, and this little volume became the standard reference for all future discussion of *Bedürfnis* in relation to the Austrian theory of value. It was only after Kraus had put *Bedürfnis* on the map for at least German speaking neoclassical economists that Menger went back to the subject.[205]

Kraus's discussion of the nature of *Bedürfnisse* and of the means for their satisfaction must have been quite to Menger's liking. Kraus developed his theory within an Aristotelian framework and considered himself an empirical realist quite in the same way as Menger considered his "exact" theory empirical and real. Furthermore, not only did Kraus credit the Austrian economists with having established *Bedürfnis* as the most fundamental, most principal concept for economics,[206] he also adhered in his definition of the means for the satisfaction of *Bedürfnisse* to Menger's four conditions which have to be satisfied if a thing is to become a good.[207] What may be even more interesting is the fact that he discussed Böhm-Bawerk's extension of Menger's scheme to five conditions and decided, just like Menger,[208] not to abandon the fourfold division. (This may be regarded as an indirect confirmation of the interpretation of these four conditions as representing the fourfold Aristotelian conception of causality.) More work was done by others on the theory of *Bedürfnisse*, culminating in Franz Cuhel's monograph *Zur Lehre von den Bedürfnissen* (1907) and in Lujo Brentano's "Versuch einer Theorie der Bedürfnisse" (1908).

In 1871, then, Menger raised an issue, namely, the centrality of the concept of *Bedürfnis* for economic theory, but did not give it any epistemological, methodological or substantive underpinning. The propagation of the concept through Wieser's and Böhm-Bawerk's theories in the 1880s did not resolve this problem either. But in 1894 a solution was provided, one that stayed very much within Menger's original framework,[209] and it triggered off a number of further elaborations of the concept. This chronology is quite nicely exemplified by the major German language reference work for the social sciences at the end of the nineteenth century: Conrad's *Handwörterbuch der Staatswissenschaften*. The six volumes of the first edition, published between 1890 and 1894, did not contain an entry for *Bedürfnis*. In the second edition, published between 1898 and 1901, there is an entry for *Bedürfnis* which refers the reader to the article "Gut" (good) written by Wieser. But it is only in the third edition, published between 1909 and 1911, that we find three columns devoted to *Bedürfnis* itself.[210] More than thirty years after Menger had taken hold of it, economists had finally taken notice of the concept of *Bedürfnis*.

Another aspect of this development must be noted. If, as Karl Menger reports, Menger really wrote his pages on the theory of *Bedürfnisse* during the first years of this century, then he must have completed them before Cuhel, Lexis and Brentano published their versions of the theory. In the absence of any further evidence, this implies that not only could he not have been influenced by their work but that he could equally not have exerted any influence on their work precisely because his pages were not publicly available. In a certain sense, therefore, all roads seem to lead back to Oskar Kraus. Or, looking at it the other way round, a number of diverse treatments of the theory of *Bedürfnisse* took Kraus's book *Das Bedürfnis* as their point of departure. Would this allow us to argue that one could look at Menger's 1923 theory of *Bedürfnisse* and, via Kraus, extrapolate from Menger's use of the concept of *Bedürfnis* in the 1871 *Grundsätze* what his theory of *Bedürfnisse* must have been at that time? The answer is, of course, no. There are three arguments, an empirical, a methodological and a substantive one, which disallow such a solution.

On the empirical level, it is highly questionable to refer back from a particular statement of a theory to what the same author's theory on the subject in question must have been half a century earlier. I cannot demonstrate this point directly, but I can demonstrate it by analogy by looking at two almost identical descriptions of the place of the concept of *Bedürfnis* within economic theory which preface two quite different theories of *Bedürfnisse* with drastic consequences for economic theory.

> Der Ausgangspunkt aller wirtschaftstheoretischen Untersuchungen ist die bedürftige Menschennatur. Ohne Bedürfnisse gäbe es keine Wirtschaft, keine Volkswirtschaft, keine Wissenschaft von derselben. Die Bedürfnisse sind der letzte Grund, die Bedeutung, welche ihre Befriedigung für uns hat, das letzte Maß, die Sicherstellung ihrer Befriedigung das letzte Ziel aller menschlichen Wirtschaft. Die Lehre von den Bedürfnisse (die Erkenntnis und das Verständnis ihres Wesens) ist von grundlegender Bedeutung für die Wirtschaftswissenschaften und zugleich die Brücke, welche die Naturwissenschaften, speziell die Biologie, zu den Geisteswissenschaften überhaupt und den Wirtschaftswissenschaften insbesondere führt.[211]

> Ausgang aller Wirtschaft ist das Bedürfnis. Der Mensch empfindet Bedürfnisse. Diese rufen seine wirtschaftliche Tätigkeit hervor. Ihr Ziel ist die Befriedigung der Bedürfnisse. Mit Recht ist daher zu sagen: die Theorie der Bedürfnisse ist die wissenschaftliche Grundlage der Wirtschaftslehre.[212]

The first quotation is the opening paragraph of Menger's *Lehre von den Bedürfnissen* written at the beginning of the century but published only in the second edition of the *Grundsätze*. The second quotation is from Lujo Brentano's 1908 essay on the theory of *Bedürfnisse*.[213] Lujo Brentano was, of course, the well-known historical economist, a brother-in-arms of Schmoller.

Brentano's assessment of the role of the theory of *Bedürfnisse* in economics is almost identical with Menger's conception of it in the paragraph quoted. As we have seen, the chronology of their origin makes it impossible that they might have influenced each other. In spite of this striking similarity between the starting points of the two theories of *Bedürfnisse*, the theories themselves are quite different. And this difference arises, to my mind, because Brentano's essay is an attempt at a general theory of *Bedürfnisse* based on his Historicist conception of the nature of economics and of theory and because it has no foundations in, or definite links with, an economic theory, while Menger's theory of *Bedürfnisse* forms an organic part of his economic theory. To take but one example: Brentano rejects as irrelevant the distinction between current and future *Bedürfnisse*,[214] a distinction which is fundamental to Menger's theory of value. We shall see in Essay III that the basis of Menger's conception of the value of economic goods lies in his conception of time as continuous and irreversible. *Bedürfnisse* are, of course, also in time, and the combination of these two concepts provides the necessary and sufficient conditions for the introduction of current and expected value, as current and expected satisfaction of *Bedürfnisse*, and hence constitutes the theoretical and substantive basis for Menger's theory of capital as expected value theory. From the perspective of this essay, Menger's concepts of time and *Bedürfnis* are not just logically necessary and sufficient conditions for his theory of value and capital, they are ontological statements describing aspects of the essence of value without which neither the essence nor the origin of value can be understood and hence no "exact" theory could be formulated. The rejection of the notion of future *Bedürfnisse* and of evaluation of their future satisfaction would leave Menger's economic theory without any basis.

Two almost identical statements of the place of *Bedürfnis* in economic theory therefore do not necessarily lead to the same theory of *Bedürfnisse*. The consequences of this can be of fundamental importance for the economic theory to be constructed on such foundations. And all this despite the fact that both of these theories of *Bedürfnis* were formulated with Oskar Kraus's work in the background.[215] To premise the deduction of Menger's 1871 theory of *Bedürfnisse* in his statement of the theory of 1923 and on Oskar Kraus as a middle term, as it were, is an inadmissible procedure.

The methodological argument concerns the status of the second edition of the *Grundsätze* for this study. As formulated above, the question postulates that it might be permissible to base a reconstruction of Menger's theory of *Bedürfnisse* of 1871 on a few statements made in 1871 and on a formulation of his theory of *Bedürfnisse* published in 1923. Such a postulate, in fact, goes against the methodology applied in this study. Throughout, I base my interpretation of Menger's theory and methodology mainly on the *Grundsätze* of 1871, the *Untersuchungen* of 1883, his sources quoted in those works and on the *geistesgeschichtliche* context of his work. Since the second edition of the *Grundsätze* was not put together by its author but by someone of a completely different philosophical and scientific persuasion, and since we have as yet no access to Menger's unpublished manuscripts, the only role the second edition of the *Grundsätze* plays in this study is that of confirming evidence.[216] None of my interpretations rely on the second edition, nor can it be permissible to use it as the basis for any interpretation of Menger's theory (unless, of course, one wishes to build on sand). The line of reasoning proposed by the initial question is, therefore, methodologically inadmissible.

Finally, the substantive argument. Menger's 1923 theory of *Bedürfnisse* addresses the question of the nature of *Bedürfnis* in its relation to biology and physiology. It does not, for instance, deal with the problem raised by Brentano of the status of future as opposed to current *Bedürfnisse*. Nor does it address the problem of the structure or hierarchy of *Bedürfnisse*, i.e., the psychological dimension of the concept. But it is these two issues, temporality and hierarchy, which define the distinctive character of Menger's value theory in 1871. Furthermore, since Menger claims ontological status for the constituent elements of his "exact" theory, he must at least discuss these aspects in his theory of *Bedürfnisse* and demonstrate their foundations in biology and psychology if the theory of *Bedürfnisse* really is to be the bridge between biology and economics.[217] Since he does not do either of these things, his 1923 statement of the theory of *Bedürfnisse* remains largely irrelevant as an underpinning of his 1871 theory of value. It is true that the temporality and hierarchy of the concept of *Bedürfnis* of 1871 do not stand in contradiction to his *Lehre von den Bedürfnissen* of 1923, but this statement merely confirms the compatibility of the two positions, and compatibility is not sufficient for our purposes. What we need is some kind of necessary relationship because it is otherwise impossible to accept the *Lehre von den Bedürfnissen* as an ontological foundation of his theory of value.

On the basis of these three arguments, then, all we can do as far as Menger's 1871 theory of *Bedürfnisse* is concerned—and it is this theory which is decisive for the purposes of this study—is to remain silent. His *Lehre von den Bedürfnissen* of 1923 does not help discover the earlier theory. However, far from being useless, it can serve another purpose. Its opening paragraph quoted above provides us with a fabulous summary of the central tenets of his vision of the economic world which are implicit in his *Grundsätze* of 1871 and the *Untersuchungen* of 1883. Let me therefore conclude this essay on Menger's methodology with an exegesis of this paragraph.

Der Ausgangspunkt aller
wirtschaftstheoretischen
Untersuchungen ist die
bedürftige Menschennatur. Ohne
Bedürfnisse gäbe es keine
Wirtschaft, keine
Volkswirtschaft, keine
Wissenschaft von derselben.

Bedürfnisse are the point of
departure for all theoretical
investigations of human
economic activity. The adoption
of this position puts Menger
firmly within the wide spectrum
of the German
geistesgeschichtliche tradition,
which includes not only the
German classical political
economists, as we shall see in
Essay III, but also Hegel, Marx,
the *Kathedersozialisten* and other
historical economists. Menger
then goes on to justify the first
statement by invoking the
ontological dimension of his
thought: *Bedürfnisse* are not only
the starting point for economic
theory, but the actual basis of
all individual and national
economic activity. Without
Bedürfnisse there exists no
economy and no economic
theory since human nature is
essentially *bedürftig*.

Die Bedürfnisse sind der letzte
Grund, die Bedeutung, welche
ihre Befriedigung für uns hat,
das letzte Maß, die
Sicherstellung ihrer Befriedigung
das letzte Ziel aller
menschlichen Wirtschaft.

In this sentence Menger offers
us his conception of causality,
his definition of value, and his
understanding of human activity.
The carrier of all these notions
is *Bedürfnis*:

der letzte Grund

Bedürfnis is the final cause of all
human economic activity.
Scientific explanation is by
causes; the scientific explanation
of human economic activity has
to be teleological, and the *telos*
of human economic activity is
carried by *Bedürfnis*.

die Bedeutung, welche ihre Befriedigung für uns hat, das letzte Maß

Bedürfnis is equally responsible for the value of goods and services. The importance and meaning *(Bedeutung)* of satisfaction of *Bedürfnisse* is the measure of all human economic activity; it is the ultimate measure of value. Furthermore, the word *Bedeutung* imports the quantitative and qualitative aspects of explanation, importance and meaning *(Erklären und Verstehen)* into the theoretical analysis of value.

die Sicherstellung ihrer Befriedigung das letzte Ziel aller menschlichen Wirtschaft

The safeguarding of the satisfaction of *Bedürfnisse* is the final aim of all human economic activity: the explanation of human behaviour is teleological, or, as we are wont to say today, human action is purposive. In this one fairly short phrase Menger has captured three fundamental dimensions of his economic theory. The concept of *Bedürfnis* carries all three of them: It carries the causality which holds his economic analysis together; it defines value, that is, the essence and origin of human economic activity; and it locates economics among the humanities by its emphasis on the human aspect of economic activity and by its teleological character since all human activity is conceived of as goal directed, purposive. This also implies that human behaviour is understandable to us in a way that, for instance, animal behaviour is not. Menger seems to come quite clearly down on the side of the epistemological dualism of the *Naturwissenschaften* versus the *Geisteswissenschaften*.

Die Lehre von den Bedürfnissen
(die Erkenntnis und das
Verständnis ihres Wesens) ist
von grundlegender Bedeutung
für die
Wirtschaftswissenschaften und
zugleich die Brücke, welche die
Naturwissenschaften, speziell die
Biologie, zu den
Geisteswissenschaften überhaupt
und den
Wirtschaftswissenschaften
insbesondere führt.

This final sentence sums up
Menger's conception of
epistemology and methodology:

Die Lehre von den Bedürfnissen
ist von grundlegender
Bedeutung für die
Wirtschaftswissenschaften

First, he repeats the emphasis
on the fundamental importance
of the theory of *Bedürfnisse* for
economic science; in other
words, economic theory is
constructed on the theory of
Bedürfnisse.

die Erkenntnis und das
Verständnis ihres Wesens

Within the first part of the
sentence Menger's conception of
theory is further elaborated.
Theory is *Erkennen und
Verstehen* (explanation and
understanding) or, as he put it
in the *Untersuchungen*,
conceptual explication
(*begriffliches Erfassen*) of a
phenomenon and the grasping
of its essence. The human world
can be investigated scientifically
(*wissenschaftlich*) only by means
of essentialist theory, which in
turn implies that definitions are
not merely nominal constructs
of the human mind but real and
founded in experience. Menger's
economic theory is ontologically
conceived.

die Brücke, welche die
Naturwissenschaften, speziell die
Biologie, zu den
Geisteswissenschaften überhaupt
und den
Wirtschaftswissenschaften
insbesondere führt

The final section confirms that
Menger's theory and
methodology are based on the
epistemological dualism between
the *Naturwissenschaften* and the
Geisteswissenschaften. It also
highlights Menger's desire to
find a way out of this dualism
because human nature is not
only human but after all also
nature. The bridge between
these two realms of knowledge
is seen to lie in biology, namely,
the physiologically, biologically
and psychologically founded
theory of *Bedürfnisse*. (Menger,
however, never discusses the
psychological dimensions in his
presentation of this theory but
concentrates on the biological
dimension only. The
psychological dimension can
only be discerned in his use of
the concept of *Bedürfnis* in his
economic theory.) The fact that
the approach towards the
Naturwissenschaften is taken via
biology also falls quite
consistently into line with his
Aristotelianism and the
Romantic origin of his vision,
with the Romantic and
Historicist preoccupation with
Werden and *Enstehen*. Finally, the
formulation of this last section
of his summary is a
reformulation of the title of his
critique of Historicist
methodology with the
Socialwissenschaften of the title
having been replaced by the
Geisteswissenschaften, the
appropriate *locus* of his
epistemology and methodology
and a final confirmation of the
interpretation of his theory and
methodology offered in this
study.

In this paragraph, reported to have been written during the early 1900s but not published until 1923, Menger sums up the interpretation of his theory and methodology which I have arrived at through a discussion of his writings of the 1870s and 1880s. We have seen how he paraphrased the major elements of his epistemology and methodology which have been discussed in this essay, and we can also see how his economic theory emanates effortlessly from these methodological and epistemological foundations. To complete the demonstration of the continuity of his thought and the uniformity of his vision of the economic process throughout his work, Essay III discusses the central issues of the economic theory of his *Grundsätze der Volkswirthschaftslehre*. But first, I demonstrate in the Appendix to this essay why I believe in the continuity of Menger's thought between 1871 and 1883 and that only a change of heart had occurred but no transformation in his attitude to the historical economists' concepts and methods.

Appendix

Menger and Roscher[218]

In 1871, Carl Menger, a young and unknown Austrian economist, dedicated his first treatise to the doyen of the leading German school of economics. He sympathised with the school's criticism of the rationalistic elements in classical economics but saw at the same time that this had led to a misconceived approach towards solving the problems of economic theory. He offered his first treatise as an Austrian contribution to German economic science. He did not just point out the error but showed the way to be followed by actually setting out his economic theory. Although his attitude towards historical economics was one of friendly criticism until the end of 1874, the situation changed dramatically after the publication of Roscher's long awaited *Geschichte der National-Oekonomik in Deutschland*.

The fact that Roscher had graciously accepted Menger's *Grundsätze* as a contribution to historical economics is quite clear from the following passage: "Ebenso wenig der Geschichte fremd sind diejenigen Nationalökonomen, welche den Hermann'schen Weg fortsetzen."[219] After mentioning a number of economists (J. Helferich, H. v. Mangoldt, etc.), he rounds the paragraph off with a comment about Menger:

> Endlich der Österreicher C. Menger, mit seiner sehr abstracten, meist auf sehr gründliche Dogmengeschichte gestützten, immer selbständigen und oft recht fruchtbaren *Begriffsanalyse*, die z.B. die Preisbildung zuerst beim isolierten Tausche, dann beim Monopolhandel und erst schliesslich unter dem Einfluss beiderseitigen Concurrenz erörtert.[220]

This is a quite favourable comment, but it shows that Roscher had not understood at all, from Menger's point of view, to which problem the *Grundsätze* was addressed. Menger reacted immediately and quite sharply.

On January 26, 1875, he published a review in a newspaper *feuilleton* entitled "Wilhelm Roscher." Unlike his usual habit, he did not provide any direct bibliographical reference to the work being reviewed. It thus seems obvious that it was not only the book but also the man who stood trial, and with him the whole of the historical school of economics.[221] Eight years later, the general accusations brought against the dogmatism of the historical economists in the second part of the review article were elaborated in detail in the *Untersuchungen*. It does not seem too far-fetched if we interpret the following footnote, taken from the first chapter of the *Untersuchungen*, as referring directly to Roscher's characterisation of the *Grundsätze* quoted above, although this is not stated explicitly.

Die theoretische Volkswirthschaftslehre hat das *generelle Wesen* und den *generellen Zusammenhang* der volkswirthschaftlichen Erscheinungen zu erforschen, *nicht etwa die volkswirthschaftlichen Begriffe zu analysieren*[222] und die aus der Analyse sich ergebenden Consequenzen zu ziehen. Die Erscheinungen, beziehungsweise bestimmte Seiten derselben, und nicht ihr sprachliches Abbild, die Begriffe, sind das Objekt der theoretischen Forschung auf dem Gebiet der Volkswirthschaft. Die Analyse der Begriffe mag im einzelnen Falle eine gewisse Bedeutung für die *Darstellung* der theoretischen Erkenntnisse von der Volkswirthschaft haben, das Ziel der Forschung auf dem Gebiet der theoretischen Nationalökonomie kann indess immer nur die Feststellung des generellen Wesens und des generellen Zusammenhanges der volkswirthschaftlichen *Erscheinungen* sein. Es ist ein Zeichen des geringen Verständnisses, welches namentlich einzelne Vertreter der historischen Schule für die Ziele der theoretischen Forschung haben, wenn sie in Untersuchungen über das *Wesen* des Gutes, über das *Wesen* der Wirthschaft, das *Wesen* des Werthes, des Preises u. dergl. m. nur Begriffsanalysen, und in dem Streben nach einer exacten Theorie der volkswirthschaftlichen Erscheinungen "die Aufstellung eines Systems von Begriffen und Urtheilen" sehen (vgl. insbes. Roscher's *Thukydides* S. 27).[223]

The interpretation that Menger here refers to Roscher's characterisation is based solely on published material taken from Menger and Roscher, on the facts surrounding these writings and on the chronology of their publication. Given Menger's conception of science and of the aims of scientific enquiry, such an interpretation—based on a psychological elaboration of the sequence of events—seems to be quite sufficient as an explanation for Menger's change of heart; that is to say, for the change in Menger's attitude towards the historical economists themselves. There is no need to invoke a transformation in his attitude to their concepts and methods. In fact, an explanation couched in terms of a transformation in attitude towards the historical economists' concepts and methods runs the very real danger of not being able to make sense of Menger's repeated insistence on the continuity of his arguments from 1871 onwards. One would also have to come up with a convincing explanation of why he suddenly felt the need to shift his attention to methodology instead of continuing his theoretical work.[224] Neither of these issues pose any problem at all if we adopt the interpretation offered here.

"Wilhelm Roscher"[225]

Die bereits seit mehreren Jahren angekündigte und von den deutschen Volkswirthen mit nicht geringer Spannung erwartete Geschichte der deutschen Nationalökonomik von Wilhelm Roscher ist nunmehr erschienen und liegt als ein Theil der grossen, von weiland dem König Maximilian II. von Baiern patronisirten Sammlung von Geschichtswerken über die einzelnen Hauptzweige der deutschen Wissenschaft in einem 1080 Seiten starken Bande vor uns.

Zwar hat man sich in fachmännischen Kreisen über Charakter und Einrichtung des Werkes, in Folge der Publication einzelner Abschnitte desselben in gelehrten Zeitschriften, bereits einigermaßen ein Urtheil gebildet, ein Urtheil, welches durch den Umstand erleichtert wurde, daß die wissenschaftliche Persönlichkeit des gelehrten Leipziger Forschers der wissenschaftlichen Welt—durch einige seiner Hauptwerke selbst den weitesten Kreisen des gebildeten deutschen Lesepublicums—so wohl bekannt ist wie auf dem Gebiete der politischen Oekonomie keine zweite in Deutschland. Wenn man der obigen Publication nichtsdestoweniger mit ungewöhnlichem Interesse entgegensah, so lag der Grund hievon in der Grösse der Aufgabe, deren Lösung Wilhelm Roscher übernommen, und in der Zuversicht aller mit der wissenschaftlichen Persönlichkeit des Verfassers Vertrauten, daß unter seinen Händen die Arbeit zu einer bahnbrechenden auf dem Gebiet der Geschichte der Nationalökonomik sich gestalten werde.

Das Werk liegt uns nunmehr vor und befindet sich im Moment ohne Zweifel bereits in den Händen der sachkundigen Beurtheiler, deren Zahl selbst unter den Anhängern der historischen Schule der deutschen Nationalökonomen eben keine sehr große ist. Diese Stimmen werden nur almählig und in vorsichtiger Weise laut werden, auch der wissenschaftliche Standpunkt der Beurtheiler sich hiebei mannigfach gelten machen, wie er in Roschers Werke selbst sich geltend macht; in Einer Beziehung wird jedoch sicherlich das Urtheil ein übereinstimmendes sein: in der Anerkennung des großartigen Forscherfleißes des Verfassers, in der Anerkennung, daß die Geschichte der deutschen Nationalökonomik durch Roschers Werk eine epochemachende Förderung erfahren habe. Keine gewöhnliche Energie hätte es vermocht, das umfangreiche, vielfach unbekannte Material, welches in dem Geschichtswerke Roschers verarbeitet ist, aus den gewaltigen Büchermassen hervorzuheben, welche Mittelalter, neuere und neueste Zeit aufgespeichert haben, und es gehört kein geringer Muth, kein gewöhnliches Selbstvertrauen dazu, sich die Aufgabe zu stellen, "was jederzeit die geistigen Führer deutscher Volkswirthschaft in wissenschaftlicher Weise über den Gegenstand ihres Berufes gedacht haben, historisch vor dem Auge des Lesers vorüberzuführen". Und all' dies hatte Roscher aus dem Rohen heraus zu schaffen; nur wenige Vorarbeiten lagen ihm vor und das Wenige, was sie für einzelne Perioden boten, mußte überprüft und ergänzt werden. Das Unternehmen selbst ist ein grosser Gedanke, würdig, von einem ausgezeichneten, hochverdienten Gelehrten erfaßt zu werden auf dem Höhepunkte seiner Laufbahn.

Nur wer sich mitten in die Forscherthätigkeit zu versetzen vermag, die ein Werk wie das obige erfordert, kann denn auch die ganze Größe von

Mühe, Sorgfalt und Aufopferung von Lebensfreuden ermessen, deren Product das vorliegende Werk ist.

Die Zahl der Schriften und Gesetze, die Roscher anführt, zählt nach tausenden, sind aber kein Maßtab für seinen Forscherfleiss; denn niemand zählt alle jene, die er bei seiner bahnbrechenden Arbeit vergeblich durchblickt oder lediglich als Hilfsmittel benützt, und welche Arbeit ruht oft in der Aufklärung einer einzigen historischen Beziehung, einer einzelnen Jahreszahl, ja in der bloßen Herbeischaffung des großen Materiales! Daß Roscher trotzdem vor der Ausdehnung seiner Darstellung auf manche leicht zu umgehende Nebenrichtung der nationalökonomischen Forschung nicht zurückgeschreckt ist, sondern ein umfassendes, nach allen Seiten hin abgerundetes Bild des Entwicklungsganges der politischen Oekonomie zu bieten bemüht war, verdient unter solchen Umständen doppelte Anerkennung. Dies letztere aber kann nicht passender ausgesprochen werden, als indem constatirt, dass Deutschland bis zu dem Erscheinen des Roscher'schen Werkes nur Bruchstücke einer Geschichte der Nationalökonomik besass und jetzt ein Werk aufweist, welches in den meisten Beziehungen einen klaren Einblick in den Entwicklungsgang der deutschen Nationalökonomie und in den Zusammenhang derselben mit der politischen und wirthschaftlichen Entwicklung Deutschlands bietet.

Daß auch nunmehr noch viel auf dem Gebiet der Geschichte der Nationalökonomik zu leisten übrig bleibt, daß dem sachkundigen Leser Lücken, eine gewisse Ungleichmässigkeit der Behandlung, ja sogar manche Verstösse störend entgegentreten werden, ist bei dem eigenthümlichen Charakter des Werkes selbstverständlich.

Zum nicht geringen Theil war eine gewisse Lückenhaftigkeit der Darstellung schon durch das Programm des Werkes selbst gegeben. Es sollte eine Geschichte der deutschen Nationalökonomik geschrieben werden, und zwar über Zeitepochen, in welchen die Gelehrtensprache im Großen und Ganzen eine gemeinsame war und jedes bessere Werk der ausländischen Literatur in Deutschland nicht nur gelesen, sondern in zahlreichen Nachdrucken geradezu für das deutsche Lesepublikum hergestellt wurde. Die Gemeinsamkeit der gelehrten Literatur, welche heutzutage durch den deutschen Übersetzereifer für Deutschland wesentlich gefördert wird, läßt sich mit jener der früheren Perioden kaum vergleichen. Wer will aus diesem Organismus diejenigen Werke ausscheiden, deren Verfasser auf deutschem Boden geboren wurden? Auch dann, wenn sie in Italien oder Frankreich in die Wissenschaften eingeführt wurden oder daselbst gelehrt hatten? In einem Zeitalter, wo von Prag aus an Petrarca und Bocccaccio und von Wien aus an Heinrich von Hoyta und an Langenstein von Paris Rufe ergingen, zahlreiche Italiener und Franzosen an deutschen Hochschulen lehrten, welches Criterium bildet da der Ort, wo die Wiege eines Gelehrten stand? Und doch mußte die Geschichte der *deutschen* Nationalökonomik geschrieben werden, was zwar nicht die Markierung des Anknüpfungspunktes mit der fremdländischen Literatur ausschloss, aber doch eine jede organische Entwicklung der volkswirthschaftlichen Ideen wesentlich erschwerte. Recht bezeichnend für die Schwierigkeiten, mit welchen Roscher in dieser Beziehung zu kämpfen hatte, ist die besondere Vortrefflichkeit seiner Darstellung überall dort, wo er Bewegungen auf volkswirthschaftlichem Gebiete darstellt, welche specifisch deutscher Natur sind und ohne die Verkettung mit fremdländischen Literaturerzeugnissen für sich selbst genügend verstanden werden können.

Überdies leidet das Werk selbstverständlich an allen jenen Mängeln, welche eben aus der bahnbrechenden Natur desselben hervorgehen. Der größte Theil der älteren nationalökonomischen Literatur ist bisher im Großen und Ganzen nur sehr wenig bekannt gewesen. Hilfsmittel für diese Epoche, wie sie Raudaeus, Boeclerus ec. bieten, enthalten höchst lückenhafte und unverlässige Namensverzeichnisse. Der Schriftsteller, welcher ältere Perioden der Nationalökonomik behandeln will, ist fast in allem von seinem guten Glück oder richtiger von dem Material abhängig, in dessen Mitte er sich gestellt findet. Wie vermöchte ein unter solchen Umständen entstandenes Werk Allen in Allem zu genügen? Mag die Arbeit eine noch so sorgfältige sein, jeder selbständige Forscher wird in derselben Vieles und Wichtiges vermissen. Die Darstellung des Zusammenhanges zwischen der National-ökonomie und den Bearbeitern der aristotelischen Philosophie, für das 14. und 15. Jahrhundert von entscheidender Bedeutung, fehlt bei Roscher gänzlich, der Einfluss der Commentatoren des römischen Rechtes auf die Nationalökonomik für die gleiche Epoche erscheint kaum angedeutet. Geographischen Werken wird eine nicht geringe Beachtung geschenkt, der politischen Aphorismen Literatur des 15. und 16. Jahrhunderts dagegen kaum Erwähnung gethan. Der hochinteressante Proceß, durch welche die griechische und römische Cultur in die moderne Bildung überging, bleibt in seinen ersten Anfängen unaufgeklärt. Die nationalökonomische Literatur, soweit sie in Manuscripten erliegt, bleibt undurchforscht, selbst die Druckwerke des 15. Jahrhunderts werden fast ausnahmelos nur dann erwähnt, wenn sie durch spätere Tractatensammlungen oder Wiederabdrücke revivirt wurden.

So Ausgezeichnetes und Bahnbrechendes Roscher für [die] Geschichte der deutschen Nationalökonomik leistete, so Vieles bleibt namentlich für die ältere Geschichte der Nationalökonomik und die Darstellung der volks-wirthschaftlichen Gesetzgebung noch zu leisten übrig und man kann von Roschers Werk das sagen, was eigentlich von jeder bahnbrechenden Schrift gesagt werden kann: daß es erst die ganze Grösse dessen klarstellte, was noch zu leisten übrig bleibt. Um dessentwillen sich des gegenwärtig bereits errungenen Besitzes nicht zu erfreuen, würde allerdings eine Thorheit sein und niemand wird die lebensvollen Bilder der nationalökonomischen Entwicklung Deutschlands, die uns Roscher mit "seiner Kunst" vor Augen führt, betrachten ohne herzliches Vergnügen, ohne Vertiefung seiner historischen Auffassung. Vor Allem wird die grosse Zahl jener mit Freuden nach Roschers "Geschichte der deutschen Nationalökonomik" greifen, welche seit Langem ein tüchtiges, von fachkundiger Seite verfaßtes Supplement zur deutschen Staats- und Literaturgeschichte heranwünschten. In unserer Zeit, wo sich die wirthschaftlichen Interessen immer mehr in den Vordergrund des öffentlichen Lebens drängen, weilt der Blick aller Gebildeten auch mit größerer Theilname auf den wirthschaftlichen Zuständen und Entwicklungen der Vergangenheit. Die in früheren Epochen arg vernachlässigte wirthschaftliche Seite der Geschichte tritt allenthalben immer mehr in den Vordergrund des Interesse's und eben diesem Zeitbedürfnisse kommt bewußt oder unbewußt der gelehrte Leipziger Forscher mit seiner neuesten Schrift in einer eben so gründlichen als in Bezug auf Darstellung künstlerischen Weise entgegen. Als Partien, welche für unseren speziellen Leserkreis von besonderem Interesse sein dürften, heben wir hervor die Capitel über die österreichische Nationalökonomik unter Leopold I. (S. 263 ff.), das Capitel über die "späteren absolutistischen Eklektiker" (S. 533), unter welchen Sonnenfels hervorragt, die Gründung des deutschen Zollvereins (S. 948 ff.) und das Capitel über Lists mit Oesterreichs volkswirthschaftlichen Interessen so vielfach in Berührung tretende Persönlichkeit (S. 970 ff.). Auch Gentz's wird oft gedacht.

Der Verfasser hat sich indeß nicht darauf beschränkt, eine Geschichte der deutschen Nationalökonomik zu schreiben, welche die Darstellung der jüngsten Bestrebungen, wir möchten sagen, jene der actuellen Gegenwart, von selbst ausschließt. Herr Geheimrath Roscher hat seinen Lesern zugleich einen Überblick über die Verhältnisse der heutigen deutschen Nationalökonomik bieten wollen, ein Bestreben, das an und für sich nur anerkennenswerth ist.[226] Ohne Zweifel—vielen Lesern seines Werkes würde eine, wenn auch noch so knapp gehaltene Darstellung der divergirenden Ziele und Tendenzen der Mitarbeiter an dem gemeinsamen Baue der deutschen Nationalökonomik recht erwünscht gewesen sein. Nur kein Urtheil über Werth oder Unwerth einzelner Bestrebungen durfte der Verfasser fällen, denn dies aus einer in ihren Meinungen zerklüfteten Gegenwart heraus in einem Geschichtswerke zu thun, führt stehts zu schwerem Unrecht—*optima fide!* Auch verträgt das Werdende nicht das abschließende Urtheil der Geschichte,—eine Gechichte des Werdenden ist unhistorisch, auch dann, wenn der Beurtheiler, wie in unserem Falle, ein billiger und wohlmeinender Gelehrter ist.

Schlimmer wird die Sache, wenn der "Geschichtschreiber der Gegenwart" selbst einen Parteistandpunkt einnimmt oder gar der Führer einer bestimmten wissenschaftlichen Richtung ist. Er wird dann gar leicht in den Irrthum verfallen, die früheren Entwicklungen der Wissenschaft als Vorbereitungsphasen, die von ihr vertretenen Meinungen als die Krönung des wissenschaftlichen Gebäudes zu betrachten. Sein Lob der Gleichgesinnten wird dann nicht frei von Rivalität, sein Lob der Vertreter anderer Richtungen ein unmotivirtes, herablassendes, ein verletzendes sein.[227] Auch sein Tadel wird nicht immer das richtige Maß halten und vor Allem werden ihm zahlreiche Erscheinungen entgegentreten, denen gegenüber er nur eine schwankende Position einzunehmen verstehen wird.

Roscher schreibt unter Anderem auch eine Geschichte der Gegenwart und zwar als Haupt der gemäßigten Richtung der historischen Schule. Er tritt mit bestimmten Meinungen an seine Aufgabe und fällt ein Urtheil über den Werth oder Unwerth seiner sämmtlichen Collegen auf den Lehrstühlen der Nationalökonomik in Deutschland. Wer sich über einen Vertreter der politischen Oekonomie ein Urtheil bilden will, braucht nur nachzuschlagen— ein Register erleichtert die Arbeit. Da wird er dann finden, wie die lebenden Nationalökonomen Deutschlands kategorisirt sind, von den "allerausgezeichnetsten" bis hinab zu demjenigen, der, "wenn er gründliche Studien gemacht hätte, die Wissenschaft hätte fördern können".

Dem Anreiz der Bequemlichkeit im Nachschlagen werden sicherlich viele Neugierige nachgehen und zwar zumeist solche, welche in einer Geschichte— Geschichte erwarten.

Es ist kein Zweifel, dass auf diesem Wege manch strebsamer Gelehrter in der Meinung seiner Collegen und namentlich auch in der öffentlichen Meinung Einbuße erfahren wird. Roscher hat dies sicher nicht beabsichtigt— verletzt er ja doch zumeist nur durch flüchtiges Hinübergleiten über Namen, an welche sich mitunter ein ganzes Leben voll ernsthafter Arbeit knüpft, oder durch ein gewisses halbes Lob, welches eine Anzahl von Schlüssen *e contrario* gestattet. Wer wollte da den Verfasser tadeln? Aber es beweist dies doch, daß es schwer ist, die Geschichte der actuellen Gegenwart zu schreiben, und noch schwerer, bei dieser Aufgabe einen bestimmten wissenschaftlichen Standpunkt festhalten zu wollen. Sobald der Verfasser, wie er dies an zahlreichen Stellen thut alle Bestrebungen der Dogmatiker als Vorarbeiten der eigentlichen Wissenschaft, gleichsam als nützliche Gerüste betrachtet, deren Herstellung doch nur dem vorbereitenden Stadium der National-ökonomik angehört, während er die historische Forschung als deren Vollendung ansieht, wir vermag er, da ihm dieser Gedanke über alles Werth zu sein scheint, jene gerecht zu beurtheilen, welche glauben, daß die Wissenschaft lange noch nicht vollendet sei, ja ihrer wichtigsten Grundlagen noch entbehre und daß die historische Forschung, das Streben nach der Erkenntnis der Entwicklungsgesetze des Volkes nur einen Theil der Aufgaben bildet, deren Lösung den zeitgenössischen Nationalökonomen obliegt? Der Verfasser ist bereit jeder Richtung der Forschung einen gewissen indirecten Werth beizumessen; an dem obigen Gedanken hält er indeß fest, wie dies niemanden, der Roschers neuesten Standpunkt kennt, überraschen darf, und damit scheint uns zwar Billigkeit und Wohlwollen, niemals aber vollständige Objectivität, wie die Geschichte sie erfordert, vereinbar.

Es ist nicht immer so gewesen und die analytische Methode der Engländer galt dem Verfasser ehedem für die Volkswirthschaftslehre für durchaus berechtigt, während er die historische Methode in ihrer mehr einseitigen Auffassung hauptsächlich der Volkswirthschaftspolitik vindicirte. Seit der Zeit, wo er die bezüglichen Zeilen an die deutsche Vierteljahrschrift sandte, sind viele Jahre vergangen und die historische Schule der deutschen Nationalökonomik ist zu großem und zu verdientem Ansehen gelangt. Es haben sich ihr eben einige ausgezeichnete Talente und die sorgfältigsten und fleissigsten Gelehrten zugewandt. Diese Erfolge haben indeß, weil der historischen Schule keine gleichgewichtige Schule von Dogmatikern gegenüberstand, auch in nicht geringer Weise eine gewisse Einseitigkeit gefördert.

Als Savigny seinen berühmt gewordenen Programmartikel über die historische Schule der Jurisprudenz für die von ihm und Eichorn begründete

Zeitschrift für historische Rechtswissenschaft schrieb, da sprach er gar stolze und geringschätzige Worte gegen die Gegner der einseitig historischen Richtung. Aber er fand einen Thibaut und manchen anderen bedeutenden Gegner. Und als er am Abend seines Lebens sein System schrieb, da fühlte er sich gedrängt, demselben eine Einleitung vorauszuschicken, in welcher er sich heftig gegen alle Einseitigkeit and alle Parteinahmen aussprach. Die historische Schule der Jurisprudenz hatte durch 20 jährigen Kampf gegen ihr gewachsene Gegner eben viel von ihrer ursprünglichen Einseitigkeit abgestreift. Und wie steht es heute um diese Schule? Ihre nützlichen Errungenschaften sind Gemeingut aller Juristen geworden, die Einseitigkeit aber gehört der Vergangenheit an.

Die historische Schule der Nationalökonomik ist bisher leider den entgegengesetzten Weg gegangen. Ihre Anfänge klingen gar bescheiden, der einseitige, unhistorische Dogmatismus wird bekämpft, namentlich mit Rücksicht auf die Volkswirthschaftspolitik, die doch für alle Zeiten und Völker nicht die gleiche sein könne; aber die dem Genius und den Lebensverhältnissen des deutschen Gelehrten so sehr entsprechende Richtung der Forschung gewinnt in Deutschland immer mehr an Einfluss, ihre Anhänger werden immer zahlreicher, bis zum heutigen Tage, wo auch das ganze der dogmatischen Forschung zustehende Gebiet von der historischen Forschung für sich vindicirt und die Dogmatik von den Historikern nur noch mit wohlwollender Herablassung betrachtet wird.[228] Sie könnte mit Hecuba rufen: *Modo maxima rerum. . . . nunc trahor exul, inops.*

All' das wird nothwendigerweise zu einem Rückschlage führen und zwar vielleicht um so sicherer, je unbegreiflicher den Anhängern der historischen Schule ein jeder Einwand gegen ihre Richtung erscheint und je mehr sie sich in der Meinung wiegen, diejenigen, welche entgegengesetzte Ansichten aussprechen, verstünden sie nicht, oder doch nicht vollständig.[229] Dann wird sich vielleicht auch ein Geschichtschreiber finden, welcher Roschers in so vielen Beziehungen bahnbrechendes Werk berichtigt, ergänzt und fortsetzt und in der historischen Schule ein nützliches Stadium der Vorbereitung zu einer geläuterten Dogmatik erkennen wird.[230] Es ist dies der natürliche Verlauf der Gelehrtenstudien. Es werden dann aber die Dogmatiker der Gegenwart jedenfalls in einem anderen Lichte erscheinen als in Roschers vortrefflicher Geschichte der deutschen Nationalökonomik.

Notes

On Menger's Methodology

1. See his dedication of the *Grundsätze* to Roscher and also the preface to the first edition, Menger(1871), p. x [Menger(1950/1981), p. 49].

2. Cf., e.g., Hayek's introduction to Wieser's *Gesammelte Abhandlungen*, (Hayek[1929], p. xi). Unfortunately, I could not find any references as to why Menger initially rejected Wieser and Böhm-Bawerk. Although we are thus left to speculate on the true reason for this, my interpretation in the Epilogue of Menger *vis-à-vis* Wieser

and Böhm-Bawerk does allow for a fairly probable explanation of Menger's initial reluctance.

3. Cf. Menger's letter to Walras in Walras(1965), letter no. 602.

4. In Böhm-Bawerk's review of the Austrian school he is not even mentioned as a contributor to methodological issues (Böhm-Bawerk[1891], in: Böhm-Bawerk[1924], p. 206 n.2).

5. Wieser(1884), Chapter 1: "Die wissenschaftliche Bedeutung der Sprachbegriffe"; reprinted in: Wieser(1929), pp. 1-9.

6. Wieser(1911); reprinted in: Wieser(1929), pp. 10-34. The relative obscurity of this review seems to have been one of the reasons why the Austrians have been located in the critical, Kantian tradition at least by some interpreters (cf., e.g., Dobretsberger[1948-49]).

7. Wieser(1924); because of the outbreak of the First World War the 1914 edition seems to have exerted very little influence. Wieser expressed his views on methodology once more in Gesetz der Macht (Wieser[1926]). The arguments put forth there, however, are the same as in 1884.

8. The most striking proof supporting this interpretation of Böhm-Bawerk is offered by a comparison of Menger's and Böhm-Bawerk's correspondence with Walras; see Walras(1965).

9. Cf. Menger(1883), p. 43 n.19 [Menger(1963/1985), p. 62 n.19].

10. Cf. Wieser(1911).

11. Cf. Böhm-Bawerk(1961c), p. 186 n.

12. Cf. Wright(1975), Chapter 1.

13. Cf., e.g., Riedel(1978), Chapter 3. See also above, p. 121.

14. Cf., e.g., Petersen(1913), pp. 187-206, and Ueberweg(1868).

15. Cf. Petersen(1913), Part I.

16. For interpretations of Menger as a Kantian, see, e.g., Dobretsberger(1927), Chapter 3.8 and (1948-49); Pfister(1928), Part I, Chapter 2.

Menger's Publications

17. Collected Works of Carl Menger, 4 vols., edited with an introduction by F. A. Hayek (London: London School of Economics, 1934-1936). The second edition of the Collected Works is available as Carl Menger—Gesammelte Werke, 4 vols., edited with a (revised) introduction by F. A. Hayek, (Tübingen: J. C. B. Mohr, 1968-1970). The second edition of the Grundsätze was published in 1923 and was presumably still in print when the Collected Works appeared. Long out of print now, the second edition has, regrettably, not been included in the Gesammelte Werke, which, apart from the revised introduction, is a reprint of the Collected Works.

18. Menger(1923), Menger(1961), Menger(1963).

19. I was able to draw only on five letters: four to Walras—Walras(1965), letters 566, 602, 765, 1277—and one to Böhm-Bawerk—reproduced in the Ekonomisk Tidskrift (1921, pp. 87-88) under the title "Zur Theorie des Capitalzinses."

20. Cf. Menger(1923), p. vi. The subsequent parts were planned to comprise: Part 2, "Kapitalzins, Arbeitslohn, Grundrente, Einkommen, Kredit, Papiergeld" [Interest, Wages, Rent, Income, Credit, Paper Money]; Part 3, "Praktischer Teil: Theorie der Produktion und des Handels. Die technische Erfordernisse der Produktion. Die ökonomischen Bedingungen einer Produktion. Die Ersparnisse an der Produktion.— Handel: Theorie der Technik des Handels, der Spekulation, Arbitrage, Detailhandel" [Applied: Theory of production and trade. The technical requirements of production. The economic conditions of production. Savings in production.—Trade: Theory of the technique of trade and speculation, arbitrage, retail trade]; Part 4, "Kritik der

gegenwärtigen Volkswirtschaft und Vorschläge zur sozialen Reform" [Critque of the present state of the economy and proposals for social reform].
21. This seems to run in the family. The second edition of the *Grundsätze*, edited by Carl Menger's son Karl, was originally planned as the first volume of an edition comprising Menger's collected works. The second volume was to include hitherto unpublished papers on methodology; the third volume, shorter papers on theoretical, methodological and epistemological issues, as well as autobiographical material (Menger[1923], editor's introduction, pp. ix–x). None of this was ever completed. The collection edited by Hayek contains only previously published work.
22. Menger(1923), p. x. On the second edition of the *Grundsätze*, see also below, pp. 159–160.
23. Hayek lists 101 items; to these we have to add two items which Hayek does not list: the second edition of an essay on "Money and Coinage Since 1857" (published in 1906) and the second edition of the *Grundsätze*. There are furthermore the four letters to Walras and the letter to Böhm-Bawerk (see n.19 above), and the two volumes of marginal notes edited by Emil Kauder (see n.18 above).
24. Menger(1871), pp. iii and x [Menger(1950/1981), pp. 43 and 49].
25. *Wiener Abendpost*, January 26, 1875, pp. 4–5. This review is reprinted along with a more detailed discussion of this issue in the Appendix to this essay.
26. Schmoller(1883).
27. Menger(1883), p. 43 n.19 [Menger(1963/1985), p. 62 n.19]; cf. also Menger(1889a) (1970a), pp. 212–213.
28. Menger(1889a) (1970a), pp. 187–218.
29. "Die Begründung einer Methodologie der Sozialwissenschaften ist die wichtigste Aufgabe der Gegenwart auf dem Gebiet der Erkenntnistheorie". Menger(1889a) (1970a), p. 211.
30. On this, see p. 47, and also Hansen(1968) and Bostaph(1978).
31. *Neue Freie Presse*, April 11, 1890, p. 8.
32. *Neue Freie Presse*, June 16, 1894 (Menger[1970a], pp. 273–281).
33. *Handwörterbuch der Staatswissenschaften*, first edition, reviewed in *Neue Freie Presse*, May 25, 1890, p. 8; second edition reviewed in *Neue Freie Presse*, February 14, 1901, p. 10.
34. February 1884.
35. *Wiener Zeitung*, March 8, 1889, pp. 3–4.
36. See Alter(1986).
37. Menger(1970a), pp. 133–183.
38. Menger(1892a).
39. The version reprinted in Menger(1970b), pp. 1–116, is from the third edition of the *Handwörterbuch* (1909). Apart from a few stylistic changes it is identical with the article in the second edition of the *Handwörterbuch* (1900).
40. These changes have been discussed by Weiss(1924) and by the editor of the second edition in Menger(1923), pp. x–xviii. I shall not enter into this discussion now; instead, I will return to it later, in the discussion and evaluation of Menger's methodology.
41. Weiss(1924); cf. also Hansen(1968).
42. See Menger(1883), p. 6 n.4 [Menger(1963/1985), p. 37 n.4].
43. See p. 83 above.
44. Menger(1871), p. x [Menger(1950/1981), p. 49].
45. Hutchison(1973), p. 32 (emphasis added).
46. "Ich selbst habe in einem bereits 1871 erschienenem Werke 'Grundsätze der Volkswirthschaftslehre' den Versuch unternommen, die von mir dargestellte Methode

auf die Volkswirthschaftslehre anzuwenden. Ich arbeite seither eifrig an einem umfassenden System, in welchem ich die Grundgedanken dieser Schrift weiter auszuführen gedenke. Inzwischen habe ich in einem 1883 erschienenen Werk, 'Untersuchungen über die Methode der Sozialwissenschaften', den in Deutschland für exacte Forschung auf dem Gebiet der Volkswirtschaft höchst ungünstigen Boden für das Erscheinen des obigen Werkes vorzubereiten versucht" Walras(1965), letter 602, pp. 5–6.

47. See Menger(1883) [Menger(1963/1985)], Book 1, Chapters 1–5; for a discussion of these issues, cf. pp. 104–112.

48. That this was more than a mere afterthought is obvious not only from his characterisation of the scope of the *Grundsätze* as "comprising the most general theories of our science" (1871, p. x [Menger(1950/1981), p. 49]) but also from the following paragraph taken from the preface to the first edition of the *Grundsätze*: "Zu welchen Resultaten uns die obige Methode der Forschung geführt hat und ob es uns gelungen ist, durch den Erfolg darzuthun, dass die Erscheinungen des wirthschaftlichen Lebens sich strenge nach Gesetzen regeln, gleich jenen der Natur, dies zu beurtheilen ist nun Sache unserer Leser. Verwahren möchten wir uns nur der Meinung Jener, welche die Gesetzmässigkeit der volkswirtschaftlichen Erscheinungen mit dem Hinweis auf die Willensfreiheit des Menschen läugnen, weil hiedurch die Volkswirthschaftslehre als exacte Wissenschaft überhaupt negirt wird" Menger(1871), p. viii [Menger(1950/1981), p. 47].

49. For a rational reconstruction of events, see the Appendix to this essay.

50. Cf., e.g., Schmoller(1873) and also Hansen(1968), pp. 140–160, 165.

51. Menger(1889a), p. 211.

Menger on Methodology

52. The only major difference between the Untersuchungen und the "Grundzüge einer Klassifikation der Wirtschaftswissenschaften" was the addition of the category of morphology of economics in the latter. This, however, did not add anything of substance to the conceptual scheme of the *Untersuchungen*. If anything, it may serve to emphasise even more strongly the permeation of Menger's thinking by Aristotelian categories (on this see pp. 118–119) and his affinity with Droysen's Aristotelian project (see p. 121).

53. Hutchison(1973) and (1981); see also Boos(1986); Cubeddu(1985); White(1985).

54. Hansen(1968); Bostaph(1978).

55. Cubeddu(1985).

56. This follows from his discussion of the structure of sciences and of the nature of "exact" theory in the *Untersuchungen*.

57. See Menger(1923), p. 1. See also the exegesis of the first paragraph of the second edition of the *Grundsätze*, pp. 127–130, above.

58. "Wir waren in dem Nachfolgenden bemüht, die complicirten Erscheinungen der menschlichen Wirthschaft auf ihre einfachsten, der sicheren Beobachtung noch zugänglichen Elemente zurückzuführen, an diese letztern das ihrer Natur entsprechende Mass zu legen und mit Festhaltung desselben wieder zu untersuchen, wie sich die complicirten wirthschaftlichen Erscheinungen aus ihren Elementen gesetzmässig entwickeln.

"Es ist dies jene Methode der Forschung, welche, in den Naturwissenschaften zur Geltung gelangt, zu so grossen Resultaten führte und desshalb missverständlicher Weise auch die naturwissenschaftliche genannt wird, während sie doch allen Erfahrungswissenschaften gemeinsam ist und richtiger die empirische genannt werden sollte. Es ist diese Unterscheidung aber deshalb von Wichtigkeit, weil jede Methode durch die Natur des Wissensgebietes, auf welchem sie zur Anwendung kommt, ihren besonderen Character erhält und demnach von einer naturwissenschaftlichen Richtung in unserer Wissenschaft füglich nicht die Rede sein kann" Menger(1871), p. vii [Menger(1950/1981), pp. 46–47].

59. See Essay III, pp. 187–188 and n.167.

60. Menger(1871), pp. viii–ix [Menger(1950/1981), pp. 47–48].

61. All of these labels are listed by Menger in his letter to Walras (see Walras[1965], letter 602); see also Menger(1889a), (1889b) and (1891).

62. See p. 118.

63. Menger(1883), pp. 38, 43–44 [Menger(1963/1985), pp. 59, 62].

64. "Das Ziel dieser Richtung, welche wir in Zukunft die exacte nennen werden . . . ist die Feststellung von strengen Gesetzen der Erscheinungen, . . . welche sich nicht nur als ausnahmslos darstellen, sonder mit Rücksicht auf die Erkenntniswege, auf welchen wir zu denselben gelangen, geradezu die Bürgschaft der Ausnahmslosigkeit in sich tragen" Menger(1883), p. 38 [Menger(1963/1985), p. 59].

65. Menger refers to his forthcoming "positive" philosophy of science in (1883), p. 43 n.19 [Menger(1963/1985), p. 62 n.19], and again six years later in (1889a) (1970a), pp. 212–213.

66. See pp. 112–121.

67. I have used "fundamental statements" in preference to "axioms" since axiom also implies a hypothetical character while Menger's statements are not hypothetical but ontological; his concepts are verbal representations of reality, that is, of the essence underlying observable phenomena. This interpretation, of course, relies on my reading of Menger as an Aristotelian, which still has to be justified, and on Menger's definitions of concept (*Begriff*) (Menger[1883], p. 6 n.4 [Menger(1963/1985), p. 37 n.4]) and of *Verstehen* (Menger[1883], pp. 14, 16–17 [Menger(1963/1985), pp. 43, 44—45]). On Menger's use of *Erfahrung* in the *Grundsätze*, see, e.g., (1871), pp. 37, 45, 60, 61, 68–69, 114 [Menger(1950/1981), pp. 81–82, 88–89, 100–101, 106–108, 140–141] etc. He retained this position throughout his life; see Menger(1889a) (1970a), pp. 207, 217, and also ibid., p. 301, where he uses this argument in his 1915 obituary of Böhm-Bawerk against the latter's development of value theory in Böhm-Bawerk (1881).

68. Menger(1883), p. 43 n.19 [Menger(1963/1985), p. 62 n.19]; see also Menger(1883), pp. 40–41 [Menger(1963/1985), pp. 60–61].

69. Pp. 112–121.

70. Menger(1871), p. 1 [Menger(1950/1981), p. 52].

71. See, e.g., Menger(1871), p. vii [Menger(1950/1981), pp. 46–47].

72. See his references to the natural sciences quoted in n.58 and also the reference in n.63 above.

73. On Droysen, see Essay I, pp. 44–45, and Essay II, p. 121.

74. Menger(1871), p. 3 [Menger(1950/1981), p. 52].

75. This is most clearly expressed in the following passage: "Aus unserer bisherigen Darstellung geht aber hervor, dass der Mensch mit seinen Bedürfnissen und seiner Gewalt über die Mittel zur Befriedigung derselben der Ausgangspunkt und Zielpunkt aller menschlichen Wirthschaft ist" Menger(1871), p. 69 [Menger(1950/1981), pp. 108].

76. Menger(1871), p. 74 [Menger(1950/1981), p. 111].

77. See, e.g., the sub-heading in Chapter 1 of Menger(1871), "Ueber den Causal-Zusammenhang der Güter" (p. 7) which becomes in (1923), "Über den Zusammenhang der Güter im Zweckbewußtsein der Menschen" (p. 20).

78. "Die Idee der Causalität ist . . . unzertrennlich von der Idee der Zeit. Ein jeder Wandlungsprocess bedeutet ein Entstehen, ein Werden, ein solcher ist jedoch nur denkbar in der Zeit" Menger(1871), p. 21 [Menger(1950/1981), p. 67].

79. "Aller Wechsel ist nichts anderes, als eine Verschiedenheit in der Zeit." Menger(1871), p. 88 [Menger(1950/1981), p. 122]. See also pp. 234–235.

80. "Das Leben der Menschen ist ein Process, in welchem die kommenden Entwicklungsphasen stets durch die vorangehenden bedingt sind, ein Process, welcher, wenn einmal gestört, nicht wieder vollständig hergestellt werden kann" Menger(1871), p. 128 [Menger(1950/1981), pp. 152–153]; see also Menger(1871), p. 22 [Menger(1950/1981), pp. 67–68].

81. See Walras(1965), letter 602.

82. See also his review of the book by Auspitz and Lieben in the *Wiener Zeitung*, March 8, 1889. This issue is discussed in Alter(1986).

83. This is discussed in Essay III, pp. 178–182.

84. Menger(1871), p. 109 n. [Menger(1950/1981), pp. 297–298].

85. Menger(1871), p. 86 [Menger(1950/1981), pp. 120–121].

86. See also the Appendix to this essay.

87. See, e.g., Menger(1871), pp. 81 n.**, 87 [Menger(1950/1981), pp. 116, 121–122]. See also Essay III, p. 164.

88. See also Essay III, pp. 164–165.

89. See Menger(1871), p. 126 n. [Menger(1950/1981), pp. 151–152], where Menger actually uses the word *Wichtigkeit* (literally, "importance") in the definition of value.

90. Schmoller(1883).

91. See pp. 120–121.

92. See pp. 121–131.

93. Menger(1883), p. 14 [Menger(1963/1985), p. 43].

94. See Essay I, p. 45 and p. 51.

95. See Essay III, p. 166 and p. 170, respectively.

96. Abel(1948).

97. Menger(1871), pp. 90–95 [Menger(1950/1981), pp. 124–128].

98. This is discussed in Essay III, pp. 171–172, 189–191.

99. "Wir glauben, durch den Hinweis of eine gewöhnliche Lebenserscheinung den Sinn der obigen, lediglich um der Erleichterung der Demonstration eines eben so schwierigen, als bisher unbearbeiteten Gebietes der Psychologie gewählten Ziffern zur vollen Genüge erklärt zu haben" Menger(1871), p. 94 [Menger(1950/1981), pp. 127–128].

100. See Menger(1871), pp. 81 n.** and 126 n. [Menger(1950/1981), pp. 116 and 151–152]. This issue is further discussed in Essay III, p. 197.

101. Menger(1871), p. 107 [Menger(1950/1981), pp. 138–139].

102. "Indem [die historische Schule] aber darauf verzichtet, die komplizierten Wirtschaftserscheinungen zu analysieren, sie auf ihre letzten unserer sichern Wahrnehmung noch zugänglichen konstitutiven Faktoren, *zumal aber auf die psychologischen Verursachungen* zurückzuführen, verabsäumt sie, uns das theoretische Verständnis derselben zu eröffnen" Menger(1889), p. 2 (quoted from [1970a], p. 188, emphasis added).

103. See Menger(1923), pp. vii–viii.

104. Menger(1871), p. 81 n.** [Menger(1950/1981), p. 116].

105. See Menger(1871), pp. 96–104 [Menger(1950/1981), pp. 129–137], for the analysis of the Robinson Crusoe economy, and Menger(1871), pp. 104–107 [Menger(1950/1981), pp. 137–139], for the extension of this analysis to groups and societies.

For an explicit statement of national economy as the sum of individual economies, see Menger(1871), p. 168 n. [Menger(1950/1981), pp. 187–188].

106. Menger(1871), p. 80 n. [Menger(1950/1981), pp. 294–295].

107. Menger(1871), p. 64 [Menger(1950/1981), p. 104].

108. Cf. p. 115.

109. The following is based on Mülher(1948).

110. "It is at once clear that within this new general conception the concept of the *whole* has gained a different and deeper significance. For the universal whole which has to be grasped can no longer be reduced to a mere sum of its parts. The new whole is organic, not mechanical; its nature does not consist in the sum of its parts but is presupposed by its parts and constitutes the condition of the possibility of their nature and being. Herein lies the decisive distinction between the unity of the monad and that of the atom. The atom is a fundamental substance of things in the sense that it is what remains when matter is divided into its ultimate parts. It is a unit which, so to speak, resists multiplicity and retains indivisibility despite every attempt to resolve it into subdivisions. The monad, on the other hand, knows no such opposition; for with the monad there is no alternative between unity and multiplicity, but only their inner reciprocity and necessary correlation. It is neither merely one nor merely many, but rather the 'expression of multiplicity in unity' (*multorum in unio expressio*). It is a whole which is not the sum of its parts but which constantly unfolds into multiple aspects. The individuality of the monad manifests itself in these progressive acts of individuation—an individuation which is only possible and understandable under the presupposition that the monad as a whole is self-containing and self-sufficient. The nature and being of the form as a whole is not weakened or divided in the sequence of these distinctions but is contained undiminished in each of them" Cassirer(1951), pp. 31–32.

111. Cf. Cassirer(1951), pp. 29–30, 34.

112. "Dieses 'Seinsgefühl' ist [Hamerling] Zeugnis der substanziellen Einheit, der Monade oder des Atoms, wie schon Leibniz erklärte: 'Substanzielle Einheit ist nicht in der Gestalt oder der Bewegung zu finden, sondern nur in einer Seele, ähnlich dem, was man ein Ich nennt.' Daher konnte Hamerling auch schreiben: 'Das Seiende ist, subjektiv betrachtet: Ich, objektiv betrachtet: Atom.' Diesen Zusammenhang zwischen Sein und Atom oder Monade, zwischen Ontologie und Monadologie kann man wohl am besten durch eine Auffassung des Seinsbegriffes rechtfertigen, der die Unabhängigkeit jedes Gegenstandes nicht bloß von unserem Denken, sondern auch von jedem anderen Gegenstande behauptet, dem also jedes Seiende ein schlechthin Einfaches sein müsse, mag man dies mit Leibniz Monade, mit Herbart Reale oder mit Hamerling Atom nennen" Mülher(1948), p. 496.

113. Cf. Mülher(1948), pp. 491–492.

114. Menger was born in 1840.

115. Menger(1871), p. 32 (emphasis added) [Menger(1950/1981), pp. 77–78].

116. Menger(1871), p. 90 [Menger(1950/1981), pp. 123–124].

117. Menger(1871), p. 32 [Menger(1950/1981), pp. 77–78].

118. Menger(1871), p. 79 [Menger(1950/1981), p. 115].

119. On Aristotle's biological frame of mind, cf., e.g., A. E. Taylor(1943), pp. 10–12, 82.

120. See pp. 121–131.

121. He does so explicitly in Menger(1871), p. 94 [Menger(1950/1981), pp. 127–128]; it is also implicit in his choice of illustrations in the *Grundsätze* as they draw on all types of societies over time and space.

122. See Menger(1883), p. xx [Menger(1963/1985), pp. 31–32].

123. Menger(1883), e.g., pp. 3–9 and 252–258 [Menger(1963/1985), pp. 35–39 and 208–213].

124. "Das Ziel der wissenschaftlichen Forschung ist nicht nur die *Erkenntnis*, sondern auch das *Verständniss* der Erscheinungen" Menger(1883), p. 14 [Menger(1963/1985), p. 43].

125. Cf. Menger(1883), p. 6 n.4 [Menger(1963/1985), pp. 37 n.4].

126. Cf. Menger(1883), p. 33 [Menger(1963/1985), pp. 55–56], and see above pp. 107–108.

127. Menger(1883), p. 17 [Menger(1963/1985), pp. 44–45].

128. See above, pp. 87–89, and the Appendix to this essay, pp. 131–132.

129. These notions are introduced and discussed in Menger(1883) [Menger(1963/1985)], Book 1, Chapters 3 and 4.

130. Menger(1883), pp. 35–38, 54–55 [Menger(1963/1985), pp. 57–59, 69–70].

131. Menger(1883), pp. 39–40 [Menger(1963/1985), p. 60].

132. Menger(1883), pp. 40–42 [Menger(1963/1985), pp. 60–61]. I have deliberately borrowed the terms "ideal type" and "ideal-typical relation" from Max Weber since Menger is generally credited with having furnished Weber with the social scientific contents of these concepts (cf., e.g., Tenbruck[1959], pp. 585–589, 621). However, in the light of my interpretation of Menger's methodology, it is obvious that Menger and Weber share very little common ground since Weber's ideal types are hypothetical, they are mental constructs and hence not necessarily true, while Menger's ideal types are elements of his "exact" theories and thus true by definition. Furthermore, since Menger is an ontological realist, as we have seen in the discussion of the methodology of the *Grundsätze*, his ideal types are not just true concepts but true representations of the essence of the phenomena under investigation.

133. Menger(1883), pp. 42–44, 54 [Menger(1963/1985), pp. 61–63, 69–70].

134. Menger(1883), p. 40 [Menger(1963/1985), p. 60].

135. For the discussion of Menger's Aristotelianism, see pp. 112–121.

136. Menger(1883), p. 33 (emphasis added) [Menger(1963/1985), pp. 55–56].

137. See p. 118.

138. For further discussion of this issue, see pp. 118–119.

139. Cf. also Menger(1883), p. 39 n. [Menger(1963/1985), p. 59 n.18].

140. Menger(1883), pp. 44, 64 [Menger(1963/1985), pp. 63, 77].

141. Menger(1883), pp. 82–89 [Menger(1963/1985), pp. 90–94].

142. Menger(1883), p. 86 [Menger(1963/1985), pp. 92–93].

143. Menger(1883), p. 59 (emphasis added) [Menger(1963/1985), pp. 72–73].

144. See, e.g., Menger(1883), pp. 107–110 [Menger(1963/1985), pp. 107–109].

145. "Es gibt kein Phänomen der realen Welt, welches uns nicht das Schauspiel steten Wandels darbieten würde. Alle realen Dinge sind in den Fluss der Zeit gestellt, die Erscheinungen des socialen Lebens eben sowohl, als jene der organischen Natur, und die Erscheinungen der anorganischen Welt nicht minder, als die beiden vorhin genannten Gruppen von Phänomenen" Menger(1883), p. 111 [Menger(1963/1985), pp. 109–110]. For a discussion of the concept of time in the *Grundsätze*, see this book, p. 94 and p. 163.

146. This is reflected in Menger's revised definition of economic theory as *"die Festhaltung der Thatsache der Entwicklung der volkswirthschaftlichen Phänomene bei Erforschung des generellen Wesens und des generellen Zusammenhanges der Gesetze der Volkswirthschaft"* Menger(1883), p. 121 (emphasis added) [Menger(1963/1985), p. 116].

147. Menger(1883), pp. 115–117 [Menger(1963/1985), pp. 112–113].

148. See, e.g., Menger(1883), pp. 100–103 [Menger(1963/1985), pp. 102–104].

149. Menger(1883), p. 88 [Menger(1963/1985), p. 94].

150. Menger(1883), pp. 144 n.46, 165 [Menger(1963/1985), pp. 132 n.46, 147].

151. Menger equates the atomistic conception of complex phenomena with the physical-chemical explanation which constitutes the "exact" basis for an understanding of natural phenomena. See Menger(1883), p. 155 [Menger(1963/1985), pp. 140–141].

152. Menger(1883), pp. 155–160 [Menger(1963/1985), pp. 141–144].

153. Cf., e.g., Menger(1883), pp. 140–142 [Menger(1963/1985), pp. 130–131].

154. Menger(1883), pp. 145–146 [Menger(1963/1985), pp. 133–134]; see also Menger(1883), pp. 181–182 [Menger(1963/1985), pp. 158–159].

155. Menger(1883), p. 102 [Menger(1963/1985), pp. 103–104].

156. Menger(1883), p. 145 [Menger(1963/1985), p. 133].

157. Menger(1883), p. 157 [Menger(1963/1985), pp. 141–142].

158. Menger(1883), p. 163 [Menger(1963/1985), p. 146].

159. See Menger(1883), pp. 164–165 [Menger(1963/1985), pp. 146–147].

160. Menger(1883), pp. 172–181 [Menger(1963/1985), pp. 152–158].

161. Menger(1883), p. 181 [Menger(1963/1985), pp. 157–158].

162. Menger(1883), p. 182 (emphasis added) [Menger(1963/1985), p. 158].

163. See pp. 180–182 below.

Menger and Aristotle

164. See, for instance, Düring(1968), Minio-Paluello(1968) Petersen(1921) for a discussion of European Aristotelianism and of Aristotle's influence on European thought.

165. But see also Worland(1984). A very curious feature of Worland's article is the absence of any reference to Menger, especially in the discussion of Robbins's definition of economics (pp. 113–117). On this last point, see also below, Essay III, pp. 201–202.

166. *Eth. Nic.* V.8. For a discussion of the role of Aristotle's concept of *chreia* (*Bedürfnis*) in his economic theory, see Alter(1982a).

167. Menger(1871), pp. 108, 256, 277 [Menger(1950/1981), pp. 139, 261–262, 278]; see also his article "Geld" Menger(1892a) (1970b), p. 61.

168. The only exception is Alfred Marshall who discusses needs in Book 3, Chapters 1 and 2 of the *Principles* (Marshall[1969]), but they never play as central a role as they do in Menger's theory.

169. See, for instance, Friedländer(1852).

170. See Menger(1871), p. 173 [Menger(1950/1981), p. 305], where he refers to *Eth. Nic.* V.7 and 8.

171. See also Essay III, pp. 167–169.

172. See, for instance, the literature and discussions cited in Worland(1984).

173. See Petersen(1921), esp. pp. 7–15, 425–519.

174. Menger(1883), Anhang VII, pp. 267–270 [Menger(1963/1985), Appendix 7, pp. 220–222]. This is the only passage where Menger shows a preference for a particular interpretation of Aristotle.

175. See, e.g., Ilting(1963), pp. 40–41.

176. On this issue, see above all his comments on Adam Smith in the *Untersuchungen*, Menger(1883), pp. 200–208, esp. p. 208 [Menger(1963/1985), pp. 172–177, esp. p. 177].

177. Cf. the first section of Essay III.

178. We have no means of checking which works of Aristotle Menger actually owned or even read because the philosophy section of his library remained with his son, the mathematician Karl Menger (see Kauder[1959]). Judging by the size of

the part of his collection kept in Japan and by his interest in philosophy and methodology, this section must have been substantial.

179. Kauder reports a statement to this effect made by Menger's son; see Kauder(1962), p. 7, n.3.

180. In March 1981, I wrote to Karl Menger asking all these questions. I never received any reply, but neither was the letter returned "addressee unknown". I have been told by several people, not least by Hayek, that this is by no means an uncommon experience.

181. Any of the standard reference works on Aristotle serve this purpose. My summary is based on Ackrill(1981), Coplestone(1962), A. E. Taylor(1943) and also on the more specialised treatments of Boas(1959), Ilting(1963), McKinney(1983), Meikle(1985) and Vollrath(1972).

182. I.e., matter.

183. Coplestone(1962), p. 46.

184. A. E. Taylor(1943), p. 75.

185. Menger(1883), p. 14 [Menger(1963/1985), p. 43].

186. See Vollrath(1972), pp. 101–102.

187. On Menger's use of *genus proximum* and *differentia specifica*, see Essay III n.183. The same distinction serves Menger in 1889 for his characterisation of the morphology of economics; see Menger(1889a) (1970a), p. 199.

188. Vollrath(1972), pp. 105–106.

189. See Essay I.

190. See Ackrill(1981), pp. 95, 110.

191. See p. 92 and p. 103 above.

192. "The besetting temptation of a mind of the one stamp is what is sometimes called to-day *pam-mathematism*, that reduction of all the sciences to one single universal science of 'number, weight and measure' which Aristotle has in view in his complaint that the 'thinkers of to-day'—he means in particular Speusippus and his friends— 'make the whole of philosophy into mathematics.' Aristotle has protected himself against the illusion of a 'universal mathematics' by his insistence on recognising the plurality of the sciences, or, as he calls them, 'philosophies'" A. E. Taylor(1943), pp. 57–58. This quotation is not intended to demonstrate any direct link between the nineteenth-century positions and those of the fourth century B.C. Taylor himself does not go beyond the realm of the natural sciences. In his juxtaposition of Plato and Aristotle he refers to the modern couple of Newton and Darwin, that is, of physics and biology (ibid., p. 57.) However, given the "biological" frame of mind of the Romantic world of thought, the extension of Taylor's argument to the *Naturwissenschaften* versus *Geisteswissenschaften* controversy does not seem too far-fetched.

193. Menger(1883), Anhang VII [Menger(1963/1985), Appendix 7]; see also above, p. 115.

194. See Menger(1871), pp. 88 and 17 [Menger(1950/1981), pp. 122, 63–64]. See also above, p. 94.

195. But see also Ackrill(1981), Chapter 4, esp. pp. 41–54.

196. Quoted from Ackrill(1981), p. 47.

197. See, for instance, Pflaum(1907), Meister(1926), Rothacker(1930); but see also Hansen(1968), p. 165.

198. Droysen(1925), p. 26.

199. Droysen(1925), p. 25.

200. He refers to Droysen's *Historik* of 1875 in Menger(1883), p. 254 n.140 and n.141 [Menger(1963/1985), p. 209 n.140 and n.141].

201. See Pflaum(1907), p. 3.

Menger's Lehre von den Bedürfnissen

202. Menger(1923), pp. 1–9.
203. Menger(1923), p. ix.
204. Menger(1923), p. ix.
205. Hansen(1972), p. 141, reports that Kraus wrote this book under Menger's supervision. I have no reason to doubt Hansen's statement. However, since I could verify neither Karl Menger's statement nor that of Hansen, I report this fact only in a note although it could have very important implications for the interpretation of Menger's theory and methodology if Hansen's statement could be substantiated independently.
206. Kraus(1894), p. 2.
207. Kraus(1894), p. 58.
208. The four conditions are retained in the second edition of the *Grundsätze*; see Menger(1923), p. 11.
209. Strictly speaking, the solution was already available in 1893 when Kraus presented his findings in somewhat different form in Prague; see the preface to Kraus(1894).
210. Lexis(1909).
211. Menger(1923), p. 1.
212. Brentano(1924), pp. 103–104.
213. Quoted from the reprint of 1924.
214. Brentano(1924), p. 110.
215. There is yet another twist to this story. As we have seen, Kraus's theory is very much kept within a framework congenial to Menger and derives its fundamental concepts from the work of Franz Brentano, the leading Aristotelian philosopher in Austria in the second half of the nineteenth century and the brother of Lujo Brentano, our historical economist.
216. In theory, it could, of course, be used to refute my interpretation, but I did not find any such evidence in it. Nor did I expect to find any.
217. What he needed was some kind of psychological theory akin to A. Maslow's humanistic psychology. A discussion of this issue is definitely beyond the scope of this study. For references to the humanistic psychology discussion, see Maslow(1943) and (1954) and Fitzgerald(1977).

Appendix

218. For the context of this Appendix, see p. 87 above.
219. Roscher(1874), p. 1039.
220. Roscher(1874), p. 1040 (emphasis added).
221. This review is reproduced in this Appendix. The notes which I have added to the review article indicate the important passages for my version of this story.
222. Emphasis added.
223. Menger(1883), p. 6 n.4 [Menger(1963/1985), p. 37 n.4].
224. In his introduction to Menger's *Gesammelte Werke*, Hayek reports that Menger started to work on the *Untersuchungen* in 1875 but fails to explain why in 1875 and not earlier; see Hayek(1968), p. xx.
225. Published in the *Wiener Abendpost*, January 26, 1875, pp. 4–5. This review article was published without any footnotes or biographical reference. I have added

five notes to indicate those passages which provide the key to my interpretation of Menger's attitude towards the historical economists. I have also chosen to print the review anew instead of inserting a photocopy of the newspaper article because the original was printed in old German script.

226. With this sentence Menger changes tone, style and direction of his review: "Herr Geheimrath Roscher" instead of simply "Roscher" changes the tone, making it a sharp, ironical, if not cynical, statement. Menger now attacks the person and his conception of the nature of economics whereas the first half of the review is generally sympathetic and respectful.

227. It is more than likely that the last part of this sentence refers to Roscher's review of Menger's *Grundsätze* (see the quotations at the beginning of this Appendix). The passages annotated in notes 229 and 230 support this interpretation.

228. The end of this sentence is a critique of the historical economists' underestimation of the value of theory (*Dogmatik*).

229. This sentence repeats the sentiment described in the previous note.

230. The second part of this sentence repeats that passage of the preface to the *Grundsätze* where Menger locates his work within the mainstream of the German tradition of political economy (cf. Menger[1871], p. x [Menger(1950/1981), p. 49]).

III

Value Theory

In the first essay I discussed the general intellectual framework, the *geistesgeschichtliche* background of Menger's economic thought—of his economic theory and his methodology—and in the second essay I took a closer look at both the methodology embodied in the *Grundsätze* and the methodology expounded in his *Untersuchungen*. As has been repeatedly stated, the purpose of this study is not to arrive at an intellectual biography of Menger but to locate him in the history of ideas in general and in the history of economic thought in particular. In this essay, I turn to an investigation of his economic theory proper and attempt to clarify two questions: Where did Menger stand within the development of economic theory when he published his *Grundsätze*? and Where do Menger's analytical arguments developed in the *Grundsätze* stand in relation to modern neo-classical theory? Accordingly, I first take a brief look at the arguments present within value theory which Menger found in German political economy. This is followed by an exposition of Menger's economic theory of the *Grundsätze*. The essay concludes with a comparison of his analytical arguments with the axiomatic structure of modern neo-classical theory.

Menger's Theory of Value and German Political Economy

Menger's aim in writing the *Grundsätze* was to put economic theory on sound foundations. For Menger, as for most Germans writing about political economy, this meant basing economic theory on sound value theory,[1] on a value theory which had use-value as its cornerstone and not exchange-value as the latter was regarded as secondary in importance, as derivative of the former. On this issue, most German political economists were in opposition to most Anglo-Saxon economists. For Menger, use-value was purely subjective, but many German economic theoreticians desperately strove for an objective concept or measure of use-value. Despite this fundamental difference, Menger still shared with German political economists not only the objective and thrust of his investigation but also most of the concepts fundamental to his theory. Notwithstanding the danger inherent

in any simplification, it is still essentially true to say that all Menger did
was to re-arrange the concepts he found in German political economy—
which included the concepts of scarcity and valuation of the marginal
Bedürfnis—around a systematic use of the concepts of scarcity and the
margin. An interesting result of this reading of Menger's work is that Menger's
use of the margin in his foundations of economic theory was endogenous
to value theory as he found it before him; it was not—as, for instance, in
the case of Walras—an exogenous import from mechanics or from any other
natural science.

It is relatively easy to demonstrate the validity of these statements; we
only have to turn to the footnotes in Menger's *Grundsätze*. Throughout the
Grundsätze Menger uses footnotes relatively sparingly. In some of them, he
provides illustrations for his analytical arguments or digressions with no
immediate bearing on the analytical issues in the main body of his text,
but most footnotes contain references to treatises on economics. Of this last
type of footnotes, the vast majority review the pertinent literature and thus
give the reader indications of the state of the art; in other words, Menger
effectively provides a kind of potted history of the major theoretical issues
he is dealing with at any stage of the argument. All of the major concepts
are footnoted. We find notes on goods,[2] economic goods,[3] wealth,[4] value,[5]
the measure of value,[6] capital,[7] price,[8] use-value and exchange-value,[9]
commodities,[10] and money.[11] These references are to all of the major, and
also many of the minor, writers in economics from Aristotle onwards.

Of particular interest is the relative importance Menger ascribes to specific
authors or groups of authors. It is this which makes it so easy to locate
him firmly within the German tradition. Indeed, he states *expressis verbis*
that only the German economists have dealt in any depth with the measure
of use-value,[12] mainly because of their more philosophical investigations
which are in direct contrast to the more practical Anglo-Saxon economists.[13]
In fact, he does not refer to a single Anglo-Saxon economist in his crucial
notes on value and on the measure of use-value.[14] Hence, it ought to come
as no surprise that Menger specifically acknowledges his intellectual debt
to the German literature in his preface to the *Grundsätze*,[15] and the dedication
of his work to the doyen of German economics, Wilhelm Roscher, requires
no further explanation. Roscher's appreciation of Menger's *Grundsätze* as a
fine piece of historical economics, which so incensed Menger that he decided
to devote several years to an attack on the methodology of the historical
economists, should be equally understandable: Roscher simply seems to
have acknowledged the historical aspect contained in the footnotes but failed
to comprehend the analytic importance of the book he was reviewing.[16]

My main contention is that Menger's principal contribution to German
political economy was a systematic re-arrangement of the material he had
before him. He re-arranged it around the concepts of scarcity, and what
made this re-arrangement systematic was his application of the concept of
the margin to the discussion of *Bedürfnisse* and their structure, a discussion
which was fundamental to the literature he had used. To provide justification

for this contention, it will not be necessary to enter into a detailed examination of all the authors cited by Menger. It will suffice if we take Menger's main analytical concepts and show where he had encountered them before.

This is, indeed, a reversal of the method applied in Essay I where the aim was to draw the intellectual map of the time, to construct the *geistesgeschichtliche* framework, and attempt to establish where Menger was located on that map. To this end, it was indispensable to consult literature independent of Menger and especially to steer clear of Menger's own work in order to avoid adopting his very own bias. Here, on the other hand, the aim is to establish what Menger must have known through the literature he had read or at least cited when writing the *Grundsätze*. A second factor renders consulting the relevant literature other than those works cited by him not only unnecessary but simply impossible. Menger had covered the entire field quite thoroughly, from specialised monographs to textbooks and reviews of the literature on economic theory; works such as those by Rau, Roscher, Knies, Schäffle and Friedländer, to name but a representative sample. I shall, therefore, now show where, in the literature cited by Menger, his concepts show up—in general but not in particular as would be required in an intellectual biography. That is to say, I shall not be concerned with which sections of any of those works Menger had read at which time and in which order, which sentences or paragraphs he had underlined, where he had embellished them with marginal notes, and so forth. I shall simply take these works on their own merit and show which of his analytical concepts he shared with the rest of the German political economists.[17]

Before turning to Menger's analytic concepts, two epistemological and methodological notions should be pointed out because they not only characterise Menger's own position but also permeate, in one form or another, all German writing on political economy: essentialism and teleology. There were not really any other authors who were as strictly essentialist as Menger himself—at least according to my reading of Menger and the others—but among those featuring prominently in the footnotes, Friedländer certainly was a Hegelian[18] who made quite a point of distinguishing between values and prices in the sense that value is more abstract, more fundamental to economic analysis, while price is a more practical concept "ruled by reality."[19] Although the other authors do not go as far in their Hegelian leanings, they still employ essentialist language, *viz.*, Knies who talks about the "essence and value of a good".[20]

Teleology, not only as a figure of speech but also as a category fundamental to the understanding of the workings of the economy, is endemic in the literature. Virtually all the authors talk about the *Zweck*, the purpose, the aim, the *telos* of economic activity; for instance, Rau, but not only Rau, for whom an explanation of value is only possible within the realm of human purposes.[21] Menger is also not alone in considering Aristotle, the progenitor of teleology and essentialism, as an important contributor to the theory of use-value[22]—Menger cites Aristotle more frequently than any of the English classical economists with the exception of Adam Smith.[23] Nor is Menger the first one to reject Aristotle's notion of equivalent exchange in favour of the notion that exchange is subjectively unequal and always leads to subjective gain for the parties involved. We can find this notion explicitly formulated by Friedländer[24] and implicitly—that is to say, applied in his analysis but not stated in these words—by Rau.[25] As an aside, it is interesting to note that even Menger's epistemological definition of his "exact" theory as based on (psychologically) immediate perception is to be found explicitly formulated in Friedländer's development of value theory.[26]

With respect to Menger's analytic concepts, his notion that goods serve to satisfy *Bedürfnisse* is as universal in the German literature as accepting that *Bedürfnisbefriedigung*, the satisfaction of human needs and wants, is the *telos* and hence the basis of all economic activity. All of this emphasis on *Bedürfnisse*, and the importance of their satisfaction for the sustenance of life is quite obviously a rejection of Adam Smith's "propensity to truck and barter" as being fundamental to human nature. These notions have permeated German thinking from Hegel onwards[27] and have received a fair amount of elaboration in the course of time. They feature prominently even in a book as close to the classical school as Rau's *Grundsätze der Volkswirth-schaftslehre*.

Not least among those elaborations is the integration of a hierarchy of *Bedürfnisse* into the discussion of the foundations of human activity. Menger acknowledges at least Knies as one of the sources of the concept,[28] which, as we shall see, leads to a lexicographic ordering of preferences.[29] But classifications of needs and wants are to be found also in Rau and in Friedländer's own theory as well as in works by authors such as J. B. Say and Herrmann which are summarised and reviewed by Friedländer.

Bedürfnisse, the cornerstone of human economic activity,[30] also provide economic theory with a measure of use-value. For Menger, value is the importance which goods have for us inasmuch as they are able to satisfy our needs and wants.[31] Value as the *Bedeutung* (meaning, importance) of goods for our well-being, for the sustenance of life, is explicitly used by Schäffle, whom Menger quotes in the long footnote following his definition of value,[32] but we can also find the concept in Rau and in Friedländer.[33] Other elements of Menger's definition of value, such as value being a judgement[34] about the usefulness of goods for *Bedürfnisbefriedigung* and value expressing a relationship between man and things[35] rather than being something inherent to things, are also not original with him.

The scenario remains the same even when we come to the two concepts which are central to Menger's innovation in value theory: scarcity and valuation at the margin. The discussion of scarcity in relation to use-value was, of course, around for a while before Menger, and it was also not exclusive to the German literature; but, certainly in German political economy, it had never been systematically introduced in the analysis of use-value. Hildebrand's discussion of scarcity is specifically commended by Menger in his footnote on the literature relating to the measure of value;[36] we also find the concept in Rau,[37] Knies, Friedländer and others. In relating "concrete use-value" to scarcity and rejecting the notion that use-value is inherent to goods,[38] Knies even introduces the term itself—*Seltenheit*—but relegates it to the status of an observable property which plays no role in the causal explanation (*Begründung*) of use-value.[39] Friedländer is rather inconsistent in his approach to the concept. In his own development of value theory he makes no use of scarcity,[40] but in his introduction[41] and in his summaries and reviews of the literature he puts a great deal of emphasis on it, for instance, in referring to Lauderdale's *Inquiry into the Nature and Origin of Public Wealth*[42] and Turgot's *Valeurs et monnaies*.[43]

Even the application of the concept of the margin (that is, of the idea that the satisfaction of a *Bedürfnis* increases by successively smaller units the higher its level of satisfaction) to the discussion, if not the analysis, of use-value is not new with Menger. His approach to the margin was anticipated by Knies[44] and is present in Rau.[45] In fact, the notion of diminishing marginal satisfaction seems to arise quite naturally in the context of a hierarchy of *Bedürfnisse* being satisfied by scarce goods which are not totally homogeneous. It is precisely this context which leads Menger to the development of his ideas. Given a hierarchy of *Bedürfnisse* which is ontologically determined, local saturation has to be introduced to allow for progressive satisfaction of *Bedürfnisse* across all classes, or subsets, of the hierarchy. The point of transition from a class of greater importance to the next lower one is determined by the level of the satisfaction of the *Bedürfnis* of the more important class being slightly lower than the level of satisfaction of the first *Bedürfnis* of the next lower class. In this way, the logical operation of the elements which are fundamental to the discussion of use-value in German political economy produces the concept of the margin.[46] The margin is thus endogenous to economic theorising along the lines propagated by the German school in opposition to Anglo-Saxon political economists. And Menger was the first one to make this explicit connection. Putting it differently, the margin employed in the German discussion of use-value is a product of the economic logic of the argument. It is not, as in the case of Walras, an exogenous starting point based on the framework provided by infinitesimal calculus.

At the end of this parade of concepts I want to mention briefly one which is conspicuous by its absence in Menger's work as well as in German political economy in general: *utility*, as used in the term "utility maximisation". Menger and the German political economists were very much concerned with defining and analysing value as a means of understanding the workings of the economy which had as its objective, its *telos*, the satisfaction of *Bedürfnisse* because the sustenance of life itself depended on it. The world from which this thought sprang was that of Romanticism, Idealist philosophy and biologism, as we have seen in Essay I. It is much closer to, say, Maslow's humanistic psychology developed in the twentieth century than to the "greatest happiness of the greatest number of people". It is true that terms like *Nutzen*, *Nützlichkeit* and *Brauchbarkeit* are frequently used in all the works cited above, but to equate these terms with "utility" in the "utility-maximising" sense of the term would be mistaking a minor, though still important, part of the meaning of "value" for the whole. Anticipating one of the conclusions of this study, it was precisely this shift, engineered by Wieser and Böhm-Bawerk, from value as a concept encompassing the complexities of sustaining life to value as utility maximisation which contributed to the formulation of the myth that the founding trinity of neo-classical economics—Jevons, Menger and Walras—independently and simultaneously developed the same theory. As we shall see, Menger's theory was quite different.

Having seen that almost all of Menger's important analytical concepts already existed in German political economy, and that they did not exist randomly or accidentally but were fundamental to the discussion of use-value and the definition of economic activity, I want to turn to two works which have not been mentioned yet. These works not only avail themselves of the same terminology as that of Menger and the German political economists, they actually contain Menger's theory *in nuce*.

The first one is P. Rossi's *Cours d'economie politique*, though I do not want to refer to the treatise itself but rather to Friedländer's summary and review of it.[47] Menger owned two different editions of Rossi's *Cours*,[48] but the interesting thing is that not only did he not refer to them in the *Grundsätze* but also he never referred to the first section of Friedländer's essay of 1852, either. This section, entitled "Prüfungen der wichtigsten Ansichten über die Theory des Werths", contains a great deal of material that must have been of interest to Menger, but the only references in the *Grundsätze* are to Friedländer's own development of value theory, about which Menger found a great deal to criticise.[49] However, Friedländer's rendering of the relevant sections of Rossi's treatise reads like a succinct summary of Menger's own theory of value developed in the *Grundsätze*, and it deserves to be quoted at length:

> Der Werth ist das Nützliche in seinem speciellen Verhältnisse für unsere Bedürfnisse, der Ausdruck eines wesentlich veränderlichen Verhältnisses. Der Gebrauchswerth ist das Verhältnis der Bedürfnisse der Menschen zu den äusseren Gegenständen in ihrer unmittelbaren Anwendung zur Befriedigung menschlicher Bedürfnisse.
>
> Der Tauschwerth ist nur eine Form des Gebrauchswerths; er entspringt aus demselben Prinzip und fällt mit dem Gebrauchswerthe. Er betrachtet die Dinge, welche die Bedürfnisse nicht befriedigen können, als Mittel andere Dinge zu verschaffen, welche die Bedürfnisse befriedigen können. Der Gebrauchswerth dauert so lange als das Verhältnis zwischen dem Gegenstande und dem Bedürfnisse des Menschen dauert. Der Tauschwerth existiert nur im Augenblick des Tausches, weder vorher noch nachher. . . .
>
> Der Nutzen ist aber die Fähigkeit ein Bedürfnis zu befriedigen. . . . Die Seltenheit ist ein directes Mittel das Bedürfnis unserer Natur zu befriedigen, welches darin besteht, zu haben was andere nicht haben. . . .
>
> Der Werth ist das Verhältnis, der Reichthum die Gesammtheit der Gegenstände, an denen das Verhältnis sich realisiert. Der Tausch ist nichts als die Manifestation und die Wirkung eines Bedürfnisses, welches sich indirect zu

befriedigen sucht. Es gibt daher keine wesentlichere Ursache des Wechsels der Preise als das Bedürfnis selbst. Wenn man durch alle Wechsel des Marktes die Lage der Contrahenten, ihre Bedürfnisse wägen könnte, so würde das Problem des Wechsels des Tauschwerthe gelöst sein. . . . Man muss die Theorie der Bedürfnisse, die Verhältnisse des Gebrauchswerths mit dem Tauschwerthe, die Abstufung der einen mit dem Wechsel der anderen nie aus dem Auge verlieren. . . . Der Tauschwerth entspringt aus der Fähigkeit der Dinge unsere Bedürfnisse zu befriedigen, und aus ihrem Missverhältnisse mit den Bedürfnissen. Dies Missverhältnis veranlasst die Nachfrage, welche der Ausdruck des Bedürfnisses ist und die Beziehung auf die für diese Befriedigung begehrte Menge ausdrückt, ebenso wie das Angebot die angebotene Menge in Beziehung auf die Leichtigkeit oder Schwierigkeit der Produktion bezeichnet. Die Formel der Nachfrage und des Angebots schliesst, indem sie die Theorie der Bedürfnisse zusammenfasst, die vollständige und wahre Erklärung alles Wechsels des Tauschwerthe ein.[50]

The second author never mentioned by Menger but whose work was apparently well known to him before the publication of the *Grundsätze* is the Austrian Joseph Kudler. His *Grundlehren der Volkswirthschafts* was unearthed by Emil Kauder during his work on Menger's library.[51] A first reading of Kudler is, indeed, fascinating. We find very much the same language and the same concepts which Menger was to employ later on. But this is not to say that Menger simply plagiarised Kudler. Closer scrutiny of the relevant sections of Kudler's *Grundlehren* reveals that the similarity stays at the level of language and concepts; it does not carry over to the contents of the concept of value, the structure of the theory or the vision of the economic process. To be sure, Kudler begins with a discussion of *Bedürfnisse*,[52] progresses to a definition of goods which is very close to that of Menger, and then arrives at a definition of value along conceptual lines which bear a fair amount of resemblance to Menger's line of reasoning, although Kudler does not integrate the concept of scarcity. In the course of the discussion, he also develops the notion of goods of first and of higher order and introduces the idea of the hierarchy of *Bedürfnisse* through a discussion of the importance and relative urgency of human purposes.[53] All of this reads pretty much like Menger *in nuce*. For good measure, we even get a bit of Böhm-Bawerk *in nuce* in Kudler's theory of production. He knows three factors of production: nature, labour and capital, of which the first two are primary, or primitive in the sense that they are indispensable to the first stage of the process of production, while capital is a derived factor—capital goods as a produced factor of production.[54]

But that really is as far as the conceptual similarities go. Kudler's theory of capital has nothing in common with either Menger's or Böhm-Bawerk's theory, and his explanation of exchange, exchange-value and the working of the economy is based on a labour theory of value. Labour is the measure of exchange-value,[55] mainly because Kudler did not have the concept of scarcity to develop a useful theory of subjective value. His discussion of *Bedürfnisse* is taken up again in the section on *Arbeit*[56] where he proceeds to expound an excruciatingly primitive view of the interaction of *Arbeit* and

Bedürfnisse, presumably because he felt that he owed a German-speaking audience something on a topic which was so central to the world of thought from the Romantic dichotomy of freedom and necessity, man versus nature to Hegel's dialectic of *Arbeit* and *Bedürfnis* and beyond. He had to talk about it because he needed a concept of labour for his version of the labour theory of value; without the latter he would have had no theory with which to even attempt an explanation of the economic process.

Where does all this leave Menger? Has it just been shown that Menger simply copied what he found before him and that his contribution to economic theory has been vastly overestimated? Of course not. All that has been shown is that Menger was deeply immersed in German political economy and that he used concepts and categories which were central to this world of thought. The fact that even his uses of scarcity and of the marginal satisfaction of *Bedürfnis* were not entirely original with him, that they were already implicit in the way the problem of use-value had been approached in the German literature, must not detract from the fact that Menger was the first one to solve the problem. All the other German political economists built vast and complex use-value and exchange-value theories by devising objective and subjective types of use-value which were subdivided into concrete and abstract values, and again into *Gattungs- und Specieswerth.* If this did not suffice (which, of course, it did not) they introduced average and compared objective use-values relating to private valuation, on the one hand, and to the *Staatswirthschaft,* on the other hand; all in the hope of arriving at a concept of use-value on which exchange-value could be based to explain prices and the functioning of the economy. The result usually was, as we have seen in Kudler's case, that they eventually had to take recourse to one form or another of the classical labour theory of value.

Menger brought this baroque edifice down with one stroke by making value purely subjective and by taking the hierarchy of *Bedürfnisse* and the concept of scarcity to their logical conclusions, thus restructuring the concepts provided by the German economists around his, rather idiosyncratic, vision of the economic process. To deny Menger the recognition of his achievement on the basis of this discussion would be akin to saying that all that Walras ever did was to borrow calculus from mechanics, which he had encountered in his engineering studies; take some economic notions which he had inherited from his father; and thus equipped go away and write his *Elements.* Although this undoubtedly has been said, it rather misses the point.

Menger has brought the German version of classical political economy to a logical conclusion. Another logical conclusion of classical political economy was, of course, provided by Marx, and for both Menger and Marx, the German thought of the first half of the nineteenth century provided the background for their economic theories. From this common origin, they went in different directions. Marx followed Hegelian lines to pursue a labour theory of value in his attempt to explain economic reality. Menger took the Romantic road in the development of his subjective theory of value to achieve the same end. Both of them ground to a halt on a transformation problem, and neither of them resolved that problem during their lifetimes. Marx's story has been told over and over again; one version of Menger's story is told in the remainder of this essay.

Menger's Theory of Value

Menger's aim, to put economic theory on a sound foundation by basing it on sound value theory, was never understood, by the theorists and historians of his theory, in the way it was understood by its author. If it had, a great deal of misunderstanding could have been avoided, and the *Grundsätze* would have been taken for what it was intended to be: an exposition of principles underlying economic activity derived by an author who believed in an Aristotelian *Weltbild*, who believed that values are the subjectively and immediately known essences underlying rough, probabilistic phenomena such as prices, and above all, who believed in the *a priori* truth of "exact essential laws" of any *Wissenschaft*. In his view, the principles laid down in the *Grundsätze* were such laws derived for the realm of economic activity.

Given the discussions of the background in Essay I and Menger's philosophy of science in Essay II, we can now look at how Menger implemented the concepts discussed there in his economic theory. I do more, however, then merely summarise the contents of the *Grundsätze* because summaries, expositions and appraisals of Menger's economic theory are abundantly available in the economic literature.[57] Rather than generating yet another precis of the *Grundsätze*, I present a summary which is intended to demonstrate what I have already stated: that Menger's *Grundsätze* is mainly concerned with the "essence" of economic activity, namely, the theory of value, and that prices are only "surface phenomena" and hence are dealt with only in passing.

The *Grundsätze der Volkswirthschaftslehre* appeared in 1871. Menger died in 1921, fifty years after the publication of the first and only edition which he saw through the press himself. In 1923, the second edition of the *Grundsätze* was published, edited from the manuscript by the mathematician Karl Menger, the author's son. For most of the 52 years between the two editions, the *Grundsätze* had simply not been available; the author had refused to allow a reprint of the first edition because he intended to publish a second, revised edition and several further volumes on theoretical and applied economics.[58] The second edition of the *Grundsätze* is almost twice as long as the first edition, yet, according to the editor, Menger had not found any reason in the intervening years to change his theory.[59] The changes and additions in the second edition are summarised in the editor's introduction[60] and in various reviews of this volume.[61]

Two important points emerge from a comparison of the two editions. The first one, which has already been mentioned, is that the theory developed in the first edition remained substantively unchanged. As far as the importance of the second edition for my reading of Menger's theory is concerned, a remark by the editor of the second edition lends support to the interpretation of Menger's theory of value and prices which is presented in this study. It emerges quite clearly from this remark that Menger himself was aware that, in the first edition of the *Grundsätze*, he had failed to provide an exposition of the link between his theory of value and his theory of prices. Although planned, this exposition was never completed.[62]

The second point concerns some terminological changes and the new first chapter of the second edition. These changes and additions effectively clarify the meaning of the terms and concepts used in the first edition by making their meaning explicit, and they support the interpretation of Menger's methodology given in Essay II.[63]

The two editions of the *Grundsätze* agree in substance, and the structure of the work itself remained fundamentally unchanged despite the addition of two chapters which, like all the additions in the second edition, basically only enlarge the argument without changing its direction. In contrast to the first edition, however, the second edition exerted no influence on the development of economic theory or of economic thought. It is nowadays difficult to locate it even in reasonably well-stocked libraries while the first edition is still in print in German as well as in several other languages. Since a central aim of this study is to contribute to a better understanding of the origins of Austrian economic theory, it is only reasonable that the following exposition is based mainly on the first edition of Menger's *Grundsätze der Volkswirthschaftslehre*.

Menger's aim in this work was to put economic theory on a sound foundation, by basing it on sound value theory, so that economists could emulate the success of the natural scientists. This aim was to be achieved not by copying the methods of the natural sciences but by providing economics with "exact" foundations *sui generis*.[64] The conditions governing human activity geared towards the satisfaction of *Bedürfnisse* under conditions of scarcity constitute the core of these foundations.

Up to this point, I have discussed the world in which Menger's theory was developed: the *geisteswissenschaftliche* framework of the first half of the nineteenth century, its pre-Kantian epistemology and the methodology grafted onto it, and finally the German political economy debate which had produced its own discussion of the problem of value within the German *geisteswissenschaftliche* tradition and, to a certain extent, in opposition to the British classical economists. All of these elements we shall now find translated into economic theory proper through Menger's concepts and the analytic tools which make up his "exact" theory.[65]

The easiest way to understand Menger's economic theory is to follow the way he unfolds and develops it in the *Grundsätze*. The story he tells moves from useful things to economic goods which are then given value by the economic agent. This value is value only for the active subject; it does not exist in itself nor is it a property of the good. Economic agents engage in exchange on the basis of their individual, subjective evaluations of the goods at their disposal. It is only at this stage that prices are introduced. Prices settle somewhere in the "feasible" region demarcated by subjective evaluation,[66] and with hindsight, we can say that in the case of very large numbers of agents on both sides of the exchange, the size of the region will shrink towards a point which is the set of general equilibrium prices of conventional analysis. This may sound like the straightforward textbook story told in first-year microeconomics courses, but as soon as we start to look at the details we realise immediately that Menger's theory has very little, indeed, to do with conventional household theory.

To understand the differences between conventional neo-classical theory and Menger's theory, I first present an exposition of the structure of the *Grundsätze*. This is followed by a closer scrutiny of its key concepts, and the discussion of Menger's theory is concluded by an investigation of the axiomatic structure of its foundations by comparing it with the traditional neoclassical set of axioms.

Valuation: The Essence of Economic Activity

The first chapter of Menger's *Grundsätze der Volkswirthschaftslehre*, "Die allgemeine Lehre vom Gute",[67] deals with the general conditions of human activity independent of its economic character. Right at the outset Menger introduces two concepts: *Bedürfnisse* (needs and wants), which are the basis of all human activity, and his conception of what "exact" theory has to deal with, namely, the "essence and origin" (*Wesen und Ursprung*) of the basic elements of the theory. Things become goods (*Güter*) if they serve to satisfy a *Bedürfnis*. The essence of goods is defined by the *Bedürfnisse*, and hence his entire economic theory is based on the concept of *Bedürfnis*. What, surprisingly, is missing in the first edition of the *Grundsätze* is an exposition of Menger's understanding of the concept of *Bedürfnis* and a clear statement of the role this concept plays in economic theory. Menger had indeed planned to commence with a theory of *Bedürfnisse* but had removed these pages just before the first edition went into print.[68] Nevertheless, the second edition of the *Grundsätze* begins with a new first chapter which makes this role explicit: "Der Ausgangspunkt aller wirtschaftstheoretischen Untersuchungen ist die bedürftige Menschennatur."[69]

Things become goods if they satisfy Menger's fourfold causal conditions—his emulation for economics of Droysen's modern rendering of Aristotle's fourfold cause[70]—which relate *Bedürfnisse* to the physical nature of things, on the one hand, and to man's understanding of this physical nature and of his *Bedürfnisse*, on the other hand. In the remainder of the first chapter of the 1871 edition, he attempts to spell out some of the implications of this definition of goods which include, above all, the fundamental role which time, uncertainty and information-gathering play in human activity. The classification of goods into goods of higher and lower order (the closer a good is to the satisfaction of a *Bedürfnis*, the lower its order), the dependence of goods of higher order on complementary goods, and some general thoughts on economic development and private property are all discussions emanating from his definition of goods. But one of the most important facts of the first chapter is that many of the fundamental economic concepts (*Bedürfnis*, uncertainty, information, time, complementarity, the order of goods, the direction of causality) have been introduced as a preamble, as it were, to his economic theory. Menger deals here only with the general foundations of human action and social reality, that is to say, with the ontological foundations of his theory and does not introduce the economic point of view.

The economic point of view is introduced in the second chapter, "Die Wirthschaft und die wirthschaftlichen Güter",[71] in which the relationships among *Bedürfnis*, the scarcity of endowments and the maintenance of life and welfare are summarised under the general title of economic activity. *Bedürfnisse* constitute the biological basis—they are grounded in human nature—of our requirements (*Bedarf*)[72] for goods. Their satisfaction is an end of human action. In the course of his exposition of the concept of *Bedarf*, Menger utilises his classification of goods (into goods of first and higher order) and develops a rudimentary theory of production as a process over time involving the notion of the complementarity of goods over time.[73]

The exposition of *Bedarf* is followed by a discussion of the quantities of goods available to the individual for the satisfaction of his *Bedürfnisse*: the means necessary to achieve the end. This section is devoted not to any technical considerations, such as the physical ability of the goods to satisfy certain *Bedürfnisse*, but to the human elements in the application of the means of satisfaction to competing ends. These human elements are incomplete information and its corollary, the difficult process of gathering information to improve one's ability to satisfy *Bedürfnisse*.

It is important to bear in mind that, so far, Menger has not introduced any expressly economic concept because he has not yet introduced that relationship between means and ends which defines human activity as economic activity: scarcity. He has only been talking about generalised activity geared towards the satisfaction of *Bedürfnisse*.[74] The next step, then, is to define "economic" activity through the inequality relationship between *Bedarf* and the quantities of goods available. If the quantity of a good available for the satisfaction of a *Bedürfnis* is less than the quantity required for its satisfaction, then the good is scarce and it becomes an economic good. Otherwise the good is a non-economic or, in modern parlance, a free good. This definition is independent of any physical properties of the good. A good is an economic good if and only if its physical ability to satisfy a *Bedürfnis* is recognised by the economic agent, that is, by the human being acting under the general condition of scarcity. We have to pay attention to the fact that the information which the economic agent has is incomplete, so that Menger actually allows for optimal solutions to individual maximisation problems which, from an "objective" point of view, are false because the individuals may act on erroneous information. Menger, however, would be quite untroubled by this argument because the theory he is developing is a genuinely subjective theory of value which recognises value only *for* the acting individual, a judgement made *by* the economic agent *for himself*, and *not* as an objective property *in itself*. But this is running ahead of the development of Menger's argument in the *Grundsätze*.

In the remainder of the second chapter, Menger deals with some of the ramifications of his definition of free and economic goods which, from the point of view of economic theory, are mostly not very important although they shed a great deal of light on his understanding of historical processes (which is very naive) and on his epistemology and methodology. With respect to economic methodology, a major point is his demonstration of the unidirectionality of his concept of causality which becomes apparent not just in his conception of time as a real (though completely un-historic) process but also in his definition of the economic character of goods of higher order, which is fully consistent with his subjective approach to value theory and with his general definition of the economic character of goods, services and activities. Goods of higher order derive their economic character completely from the economic character of goods of first order.[75] If first order goods are free, none of the goods used in their production can be economic goods.

This section also contains some contradictions: For instance, he illustrates his discussion of economic goods becoming free goods with the provision of primary education, and thus mistakes the removal of direct payments for, and the general availability of, primary education as the placement of primary education among the non-economic goods while all that has happened is that direct payments for education have been replaced by indirect payments through taxation. This error, however, does not necessarily invalidate Menger's general argument but the example chosen by him as an illustration.

In general, the second chapter demonstrates quite clearly to what extent Menger's economic thought is influenced by the Romantic-Historicist world because here, and also in the first chapter, he lays open the route along which he will develop his argument and which is to lead to his statement of subjective value theory. In addition, the chapter could also allow us to show to what extent ideological considerations emerge from, and influence the formation of, the very foundations of economic theory, but the discussion of this issue leads far beyond the scope of this study.

The third chapter, "Die Lehre vom Werthe",[76] takes us directly to the core of Menger's theory, the development of his theory of value. The general theory of human action as geared towards the satisfaction of *Bedürfnisse* becomes an economic theory under the condition of scarcity. The entire discussion surrounding the formation of this statement, that is to say, the notions of uncertainty, information, unidirectional causality, subjectivism and so forth, allows Menger to furnish his concept of value with its constituent elements. This concept is defined at the outset of this chapter: "es ist somit der Werth die Bedeutung, welche concrete Güter oder Güterquantitäten für uns dadurch erlangen, dass wir in der Befriedigung unserer Bedürfnisse von der Verfügung über dieselben abhängig zu sein uns bewusst sind."[77]

Immediately after stating this definition Menger emphasises the human element in the relations between men and things under the condition of scarcity. This human element is a fundamental factor which not only precipitates economic activity but at the same time also provides this activity with the criterion (value) which gives it direction: *Erkenntnis* (the cognitive element in human activity) allows us to recognise a scarcity of means in relation to ends (and hence makes us act to provide for the satisfaction of our *Bedürfnisse*) and, at the same time, furnishes us with a measure to judge the importance—quantitative as well as qualitative—of a good for our well-being (and thus makes us assign value to a good).[78]

In this way Menger defines value. It is very important to recall that although Menger talks about the value of goods and regards value as measurable, he has not said anything about exchange or about relative quantities of goods, and hence he has not said anything about exchange rates and (relative) prices. The definition of value quoted above, according to Menger, concerns the "essence" of the concept, its *Wesen*. It is thus fundamental to all economic activity, and without it we are unable to act in, nor will we be able to understand, the economic world. Menger's concept of value has nothing whatsoever to do with the traditional micro-economic concept of value as unit price multiplied by the number of units of a good. Nor is it identical to the traditional neo-classical concept of value as marginal utility since the margin has not been introduced yet. As we shall see shortly, the margin, in Menger's theory, is a consequence of the logic of his argument. It is not, as in Walrasian theory, an initial assumption or an instrumentalist behavioural hypothesis.[79]

The issues addressed by Menger in this chapter must seem rather strange to someone brought up on a diet of traditional neoclassical theory and perhaps some scraps of classical political economy. They should seem less strange, however, if we keep in mind that Menger is addressing the set of problems surrounding value theory in the German version of classical political economy. Use-value, usefulness, subjectivity and information all played an important role in that discussion, and, as we have seen in the first part of this essay, Menger drew mainly on the German literature for his discussion of value theory.[80]

With the next step in the development of his theory Menger finally arrives at the measure of value. But again, the measure of value is not quite as simple a thing as one would imagine. First, there is the non-quantitative, or cognitive, aspect of value which allows Menger again to stress *Erkenntnis* involved in valuation and to begin to develop his concept of the structure, or hierarchy, of *Bedürfnisse*.[81] Here, he lays the psychological foundations of his theory. Valuation first takes place only with regard to one's well-being; second, it is located entirely within the set of *Bedürfnisse*, that is to say, it is independent of the goods used in the satisfaction of *Bedürfnisse*. The cognitive aspect of value encapsulates the importance of the satisfaction of a *Bedürfnis* for the maintenance of life, well-being and comfort, and it exists independent of the availability of goods. Goods enter the picture only in the second aspect of value.

This second aspect of value contains the quantitative dimension, and it is here that Menger shows us how value is calculated. Successive satisfaction of *Bedürfnisse* leads from the satisfaction of the first, most important, *Bedürfnis* through the structure of *Bedürfnisse* to the satisfaction of *Bedürfnisse* of ever-decreasing importance by satisfying the first level of this structure—or hierarchy—up to the point at which the first, unsatisfied *Bedürfnis* of the next lower rung becomes more important to us than the next unsatisfied *Bedürfnis* of the higher rung. This leads to a switching of satisfaction of one set of *Bedürfnisse* to satisfaction of the next lower one. This process operates as long as goods are available. The importance of the last *Bedürfnis* satisfied in this way, that is to say, its value to us, is what in traditional utility theory is known as marginal utility.[82]

In this way Menger introduces the concept of the margin into subjective value theory. The valuation at the margin is the major result of Menger's development of economic theory, and it follows as a logical step from the entire structure which he has built up: from his theory of human action under conditions of scarcity and the postulation of a specific type of psychology which is represented by the structure of *Bedürfnisse*. Again we must bear in mind that, for Menger, these assumption have ontological status. For him, they describe the structure of the world and thus ground the theory firmly in empirical reality which, on the level of epistemology, can be truly known by us because we are here in the realm of "exact" theory. At this point we can also see the fundamental difference between Menger and, for instance, Walras for whom the economic margin has instrumental status arising out of the logic of the formalisation of price theory and hence enters the substantive level of economic theory as an assumption. In Menger's case, it is the result of the substantive economic argument.

Another facet of Menger's development of value theory is his consistent application of methodological individualism. He starts his chain of "real life" illustrations with a discussion of valuation undertaken by an isolated individual and then expands it to incorporate valuation undertaken by society. Robinson Crusoe is not a special case but the archetype of Menger's economic man. In the same vein, as we shall see later, Menger begins his discussion of exchange and price formation with the case of bilateral monopoly as the "natural" starting point and then progresses towards exchange and price formation in increasingly more competitive environments. Perfect competition, the general case for traditional micro-economic analysis, is a special case in Menger's theory. Subjective valuation by an isolated individual is all Menger needs for his demonstration of the "essence" of economic activity. Anything which goes beyond this basis is a consequence of the principles derived from this "single economy."

In his "real life" illustrations, Menger slips in one very special assumption without being aware of the consequences of this simplification: in each of the illustrations, he deals with only one commodity, either corn or water. This is the major reason why his theory was so easily assimilated to the theories developed by Jevons and Walras. The assumption of only one commodity renders any hierarchical ordering (of his *Bedürfnisse*) indistinguishable from an ordering along the real line and thus renders Menger's theory indistinguishable from the conventional utility theory approach.[83] The assumption of a single, homogeneous good is relaxed in the next step taken by Menger in the *Grundsätze* when he allows for goods of different quality to be used in the satisfaction of a *Bedürfnis*.[84] There, however, he gets himself into a complete muddle and fails to resolve the case. Any attempt to represent it formally would show that he becomes entangled in mathematical contradictions. Fundamentally, Menger barked up the wrong tree because he allowed himself to solve the didactically easier case of determining the value of a single (homogeneous) good instead of following the route he had mapped out. This route implies the consistent application of the category "economic", in its definition of "satisfaction of *Bedürfnisse* under conditions of scarcity" embedded in the set of ontological assumptions laid out at the beginning. Along this route the interesting case is the analysis of the value of physically heterogeneous goods which are also economically heterogeneous because only along this line of reasoning can the impact of the lexicographic ordering of the structure of *Bedürfnisse* on the derivation of value be demonstrated.[85]

Menger rounds off his discussion of the essence and measure of value by pointing to three implications of his subjectivist approach.[86] First, both the qualitative and the quantitative aspects of value are subjective because not only does the value of a good not exist in itself but only for a specific economic subject but also its magnitude is not an objectively given quantity but exists only for the evaluating individual. The same piece of bread can have a different value for different individuals, and each of these values will be true. Second, given that value is fundamental and purely subjective, it follows that it cannot be derived from any other economic magnitude such as labour. For Menger, the value of a diamond is the same whether it was simply found in a field or extracted from the bowels of the earth with great expense of labour. This conclusion, however, utilises the additional assumption that any economic phenomenon must be explained by only one fundamental principle.[87] A position such as Ferdinando Galliano's in *Della Moneta*, where the value of non-reproducible goods is explained by a subjective theory of value while the value of reproducible goods is explained by a labour theory of value, is not accepted by Menger. Third, the cognitive element in Menger's subjectivist approach implies that valuation is inextricably bound up with errors in judgement. Changes in valuation will, therefore, be caused by three types of changes: in the *Bedürfnisse*, in initial endowments, and in knowledge. An interesting aside is that the passage in the first edition of the *Grundsätze* contains as an illustration of this third implication the lower estimation of future *Bedürfnisse*, one of Böhm-Bawerk's three reasons in his explanation of the rate of interest. In the second edition of the *Grundsätze*, this passage is completely rewritten and any reference to the lower estimation of future *Bedürfnisse* is omitted.[88]

Menger's postulates of a mono-causal explanation, of unidirectional causality and of real time now lead him to introduce the concept of expectations into the discussion of value. Again we see how a concept which in modern general equilibrium theory represents a separate dimension flows naturally out of the basic setting of Menger's value theory. If goods of higher order are used to produce goods of lower order, then the value of the goods of higher order has to be imputed from the *expected* value of the goods of lower order they are used to produce. Hence the value of the goods of higher order is an imputed expected value and will change if and when the expected value of the goods of lower order changes.[89] This discussion of expectations occurs not as an end in itself but as a byproduct of Menger's attempt to correct the mistaken belief that a good has value because goods which have value are used in its production. His attempts to bring everything back to his own definition of value—which, according to him, is, of course, the only true one—generate almost by themselves concepts and discussions which are integral, inseparable parts of his analysis and are considered as extensions of the basic model of current orthodox consumer theory in order to render it more realistic.

The chapter on value is wrapped up by Menger's discussion of the value of the factors of production: capital, land and labour all render services which have to be valued by the same economic calculus that determines the value of goods of higher order by imputation.[90] In the course of this discussion of the value of goods of higher order, Menger introduces the concept of entrepreneurship alongside those of complementary goods of higher order and of capital services.[91] These concepts are not developed in any particular direction; again, as in all his discussions of economic concepts, his only goal is to show how these concepts emanate from the definition of value, that is, from the operation of valuation in everyday life.

The same thrust is retained in the fourth chapter, "Die Lehre vom Tausche",[92] where, in order to be able to introduce exchange, Menger extends his basic model of one person with initial endowments to two individuals with initial endowments or, to be more precise, to two individuals (two "isolated economies") who possess at least one good each which the other does not have. Although this statement of the initial conditions seems fairly obvious Menger still has to make it because he rejects Adam Smith's "propensity to truck and barter" as being inadequate for the explanation of the origin of exchange. The essence of exchange—*Wesen und Ursprung des Tausches*—is the improved satisfaction of the *Bedürfnisse* of each party to the exchange. Exchange has to be mutually beneficial, otherwise it is economically meaningless. It is in connection with the discussion of exchange that Menger most clearly emphasises that the aim (*telos*) of all economic activity is to achieve the satisfaction of *Bedürfnisse* to the most complete extent possible.[93]

Menger considers as productive anything which contributes to increasing the satisfaction of *Bedürfnisse*, and thus he gives the concept of productivity a new meaning in opposition to his physiocratic and classical predecessors. As a consequence of this definition of productivity, retail and wholesale trade are now as productive as agriculture and industry because they are instrumental in the exchange process.[94]

Menger's basic exchange example presents a typical Edgeworth box situation. However, Menger's necessary and sufficient conditions under which exchange will take place reveal, as we have seen before, the fundamental roles of uncertainty and information in his conception of the economic process. The first condition effectively sets out the general situation, and this is identical for Menger's and for traditional theory: There are two "isolated economies", at least two goods, and a reciprocity in the valuation of the goods by the two individuals so that both of them would be better off after the exchange than they were before. Menger's third condition, that both parties to the exchange must actually have their respective initial endowments at their disposal, is not stated explicitly in traditional microeconomic theory or in the Edgeworth model but is generally implicit in the assumption of the existence of initial endowments. Menger's second condition, however, again goes beyond the traditional neo-classical framework by insisting on the cognitive aspect: both individuals must have *Erkenntnis* (knowledge) of the first condition.

These three conditions are all necessary in Menger's theory; together they are sufficient for exchange to take place. The counterargument which could be offered here—that the minimum number of assumptions necessary to guarantee the existence of exchange simply require the initial conditions (i.e., Menger's first condition) plus the assumption that trade must leave the parties to the exchange better off after the exchange has taken place—is really a meta-theoretical argument which touches on the question of what is justifiable abstraction. Is the assumption of certainty and perfect knowledge really a useful, or in any other way justifiable, abstraction of the conditions of uncertainty and incomplete information? The answer to this question, in turn, demands an answer to the question of what is relevant for the investigation concerned, and this latter question can be answered only by invoking the whole gamut of issues addressed in Essays I and II, namely, the *wissenschaftliche Weltauffassung*, the epistemology and also the methodology underlying the theoretical investigation. Fundamentally, the assumption of certainty postulates a different structure of the universe within which human action is to be analysed than Menger's set of assumptions. Hence, an intellectually honest answer to the question posed above, that is, whether or not certainty can be considered as a justifiable abstraction or the first approximation of uncertainty, ought to address all these problems.

All of these issues arise in the course of the discussion of what Menger calls the essence and origin (*Wesen und Ursprung*) of exchange. With respect to the quantitative aspect, the limits of exchange are, of course, determined by value. If the three necessary and sufficient conditions are satisfied, then exchange will take place until the value of the good obtained equals the value of the good offered in exchange for it. Once this point is reached, the motivation for exchange (the first condition) will cease to be effective.[95] As a by-product of this discussion, Menger reveals that he considers value to be additive. Equating the national economy with the sum of the "individual economies", he demonstrates a consistent application of the principle of methodological individualism although the additivity of values, presupposing the possibility of their inter-personal comparison, strictly speaking stands in contradiction to his insistence on the subjectivity of the essence and of the measure of value.[96]

Let us briefly survey what has been covered so far. Economic activity proper has been analysed on the basis of a theory of human action—humans act purposely to satisfy their *Bedürfnisse*—and this theory has been placed within the scarcity relation between men and goods—scarce means are allocated to satisfy competing ends. *Bedürfnisse* are hierarchically structured; people act in a world full of uncertainty and on the basis of incomplete information. All activity takes place in real time; activity is, therefore, an irreversible process. Valuation—the assessment of an act of *Bedürfnisbefriedigung*—is entirely subjective in its qualitative as well as in its quantitative dimension. The existence of time and of uncertainty define the current value of the means of production (goods of higher order) which are used for the production of future consumption goods (goods of first order) as expected value. Exchange, the interaction of two "individual economies" (*Einzelwirtschaften*), takes place within the limits proscribed by individual valuation so that both parties are better off after trading than they were before.

This is the core of Menger's theory. The remaining chapters of the *Grundsätze* with the exception of the sixth, deal with issues outside the realm of "exact" theory. The discussions of prices, commodities and money shift the discourse to the level of appearances where the underlying essence, the process of valuation, manifests itself. The sixth chapter, "Gebrauchswerth und Tauschwerth",[97] strictly speaking belongs either to the argument of the chapter on value or to the one on exchange, and its position after the chapter on prices is inconsistent with the structure of Menger's argument. That problem was, indeed, corrected by the editor of the second edition as he made the sixth chapter of the first edition a subsection of the chapter on value.[98]

Menger's main intention in the chapter on value in use and value in exchange is to demonstrate that both types of value are merely different forms of the same essence (that is, value)[99] and that their difference lies only in their direct or indirect usefulness for the satisfaction of *Bedürfnisse*. Value takes the form of use-value if the respective goods serve directly in the satisfaction of *Bedürfnisse* while it becomes exchange-value if their contribution is indirect.[100] This extensive pre-occupation with the "philosophical foundations"[101] of political economy is typical of the German approach, as we have seen, and Menger is deliberately no exception here. The chapter concludes with a discussion of the conditions influencing the changeover from one form of value to the other, and Menger distinguishes three groups of factors. In modern terminology, these three groups are changes in tastes, technical change, and changes in the Lagrangean conditions, that is to say, changes in the number of goods available and changes in wealth.[102] Menger uses these factors to explain how exchange-value may supersede use-value and vice versa, a type of argument which has nothing in common with the traditional neoclassical approach in which these factors influence shifts of, or along, the utility function.

The *Grundsätze der Volkswirthschaftslehre* is Menger's attempt to reformulate the most fundamental principles of economics.[103] Accordingly, it contains a number of definitions, principles and results obtained in the course of his analysis which culminate in the principles derived for value theory and for price theory. As value, for Menger, is the most important determinant of price formation,[104] I now take a brief look at what principles constitute the foundations of his theory of value before I turn to his theory of prices.

Menger's principles of value theory lead from his definition of value to his derivation of value at the margin, that is, from the definition of value to its measure, and they encompass most of the methodological and theoretical elements which later came to be associated with the characteristically Austrian approach to economic theory. Let me quote these principles here for reference purposes:

1. Die Bedeutung, welche die Güter für uns haben, und welche wir Werth nennen, ist lediglich eine übertragene. Ursprünglich haben nur die Bedürfnissbefriedigungen für uns eine Bedeutung, weil von ihnen die Aufrechterhaltung unseres Lebens und unserer Wohlfahrt abhängt, wir übertragen aber in logischer Consequenz diese Bedeutung auf jene Güter, von deren Verfügung wir in der Befriedigung dieser Bedürfnisse abhängig zu sein uns bewusst sind.

2. Die Grösse der Bedeutung, welche die verschiedenen concreten Bedürfnissbefriedigungen (die einzelnen Acte derselben, welche eben durch concrete Güter herbeigeführt werden können) für uns haben, ist eine ungleiche und das Mass derselben liegt in dem Grade ihrer Wichtigkeit für die Aufrechterhaltung unseres Lebens und unserer Wohlfahrt.

3. Die Grösse der auf die Güter übertragenen Bedeutung unserer Bedürfnissbefriedigungen, das ist die Grösse des Werthes, ist somit gleichfalls eine verschiedene und das Mass derselben liegt in dem Masse der Bedeutung, welche die von den betreffenden Gütern abhängigen Bedürfnissbefriedigungen für uns haben.

4. In jedem concreten Falle sind von der Verfügung über eine bestimmte Theilquantität der einem wirthschaftenden Subjecte verfügbaren Gesammtquantität eines Gutes nur jene der durch die letztere noch gesicherten Bedürfnissbefriedigungen abhängig, welche für dies Subject die geringste Bedeutung unter diesen letzteren haben.

5. Der Werth eines concreten Gutes, oder einer bestimmten Theilquantität der einem wirthschaftenden Subjecte verfügbaren Gesammtquantität eines Gutes ist für dasselbe demnach gleich der Bedeutung, welche die wenigst wichtigen von den durch die verfügbare Gesammtquantität noch gesicherten und mit einer solchen Theilquantität herbeizuführenden Bedürfnissbefriedigungen für das obige Subject haben. Diese Bedürfnissbefriedigungen sind es nämlich, rücksichtlich welcher das in Rede stehende wirthschaftende Subject von der Verfügung über das betreffende concrete Gut, beziehungsweise die betreffende Güterquantität abhängt.[105]

In the first principle, Menger states that the value of a good is first of all *Bedeutung* (meaning, importance) of the satisfaction of a *Bedürfnis für uns* (for us). It is independent of the good used in the act of satisfaction. The good acquires value once we realise that it is able to satisfy the *Bedürfnis* and then transfer this *Bedeutung* to it.

Menger's definition of value encompasses five distinct elements.[106] Value is *Bedeutung* for us; this, at once, opens up the subjective character of the cognitive and of the quantitative dimension of this concept and hence of all economic activity. Value is, furthermore, the *Bedeutung* of the *Befriedigung der Bedürfnisse* (satisfaction of needs and wants). This, as Menger makes clear in the new first chapter of the second edition of the *Grundsätze*, bases all economic activity firmly in biological reality.[107] Thus, for Menger, given the framework of his epistemology and classification of sciences, his foundations of economics are anchored firmly within the certainty of physical or, perhaps better, biological reality and are, therefore, presumably free of any disreputable connection with "speculation". (Here are, for everyone to see, the seeds of the *Methodenstreit*.)[108] The concept of value of a good also presupposes that we have information, that we know two things: the capacity of the goods to satisfy the respective *Bedürfnisse* and the availability of these goods for us. These last two elements of the definition of value are a restatement of the third and fourth conditions necessary for a thing to become a good.[109]

In addition to the definition of value, Menger's first principle of value theory also contains the concept of *Übertragung*—transference. Goods do not have value. Value arises and is determined within the sphere of *Bedürfnisse*. It is then simply transferred from the *Bedürfnis* to the good which serves to satisfy it. Should the *Bedürfnis* or our assessment of it change, then the value of the good will change even though the good itself may remain completely unaltered physically.[110] Value is the economic relation between man and the universe around him, and this relation is entirely determined by him.

The basis of this relation is the *Bedürfnisse* (needs and wants). They are the cornerstone of Menger's economic theory,[111] and we have already encountered the concept of *Bedürfnis* in Essays I and II. In his economic theory, the concept is fundamental not only because it is the basis of human activity, and thus provides a general underpinning for the theoretical edifice, but also because it is one of the determinants of Menger's concept of causality. The satisfaction of *Bedürfnisse* is the *telos* at least of economic activity and thus, together with the notion of time, provides his concept of causality in human action with its unidirectionality. In addition, *Bedürfnisse* also play the same role as tastes in conventional consumer theory. Menger regards *Bedürfnisse* as exogenous to economic theory and as static in the sense that he has no theory of *Bedürfnis* formation, no system of *Bedürfnisse* as, for instance, in the Hegelian sense of the term.[112]

This is not to say that he regards *Bedürfnisse* as randomly distributed or chaotic. They are, indeed, structured in a descending order of a number of different *Bedürfnis* classes of which the most important ones are satisfied first.[113] He adheres to this structure in all his illustrative examples and gives a representation of this scheme with ten *Bedürfnis* classes in his well-known numerical table.[114] Only four major classes of this hierarchy of *Bedürfnisse* emerge from his illustrative examples, however. These are, in descending order, the preservation of life, the preservation of health, provision for welfare (that is, for future life and health), and provisions for various kinds of diversions. The substitution of *Bedürfnisse*, and therefore also of economically heterogeneous goods, across classes is not permissible. It follows that one cannot compensate, for instance, for the lack of bread and water if one's initial endowments consist only of zabaglione and kummerbund because certainly in the case of an isolated individual (the archetype of Menger's economic man), the absence of markets would mean that this individual would not be able to survive. But Menger's theory of value holds true for other cases as well. We recall that Menger postulates a very strict methodological individualism. The same set of assumptions, therefore, holds for value determination in situations in which markets for goods do exist.[115]

A hierarchy of *Bedürfnisse* of this kind is not unknown in the economic literature. It is commonly denoted as a lexicographic ordering, and this type of ordering is usually regarded as a special case as compared to ordering along the real line, so it is ruled out of court, or rather, out of textbooks on micro-economic theory. However, "the hierarchy of wants is the essence of any explanation of diminishing marginal utility";[116] that is to say, in one sense or other, all neo-classical economists make use of the concept of the hierarchy of wants, but Menger—steeped in the German tradition—actually introduces this concept explicitly and demonstrates its analytical indispensability by basing his derivation of the marginality principle on it.

Menger's explicit use of the concept of the hierarchy of *Bedürfnisse* raises several crucial analytical problems: first of all, the impossibility of deriving traditional well-behaved demand functions but also problems of mathematical representation of the theory and problems with Menger's own development of it which is inconsistent within his frame of reference. All of this is dealt with later;[117] in the next two paragraphs, however, I digress briefly and pick up a problem of a different order.

In the terminology of the first three decades of this century, Menger has to be considered an ordinalist. Value is ordered, but nowhere in the *Grundsätze* does he talk about some kind of objective measurability or comparison of differences of value increments. He talks, as we can see in his principles of value theory, about the degree of importance but not about the size or any other cardinally measurable magnitude when he refers to the magnitude of value.[118] But how can he, like any ordinal utility theorist, claim to be consistent when talking about "diminishing marginal value" (or utility) with reference to an ordinal scale since the concept of a "diminishing marginal variable" implies measurability (in the cardinal sense) of differences? How can we meaningfully talk of differences among the values of an ordinal variable which is not cardinally measurable? Since differences require cardinality of some sort,[119] Menger is stuck with the same kind of inconsistency as many of the later utility theorists. The way out for the later theorists was to move away from utility and transfer the entire discussion to the commodity space which is, of course, cardinally measurable. The Hicksian income and substitution effects deal with commodities only in relation to price movements; demand is discussed by relating movements along the real line to each other. The choices over commodity bundles are ordered; Hicksian theory is therefore still not free of psychology and ordinal scales. But the mechanism producing optimal decisions is no longer diminishing marginal utility but the diminishing marginal rate of substitution, that is, the convexity and continuity of the choice set. This allows for all the relationships necessary for the derivation of demand functions to be expressed in terms of cardinally measurable variables, but it is precisely here that the problem arises for traditional theory. The empirical determination of the qualitative residual[120] makes convexity not an axiom any more but has to make it a testable hypothesis, thus endangering the continued existence of well-behaved utility functions[121] and therefore also the possibility of deriving continuous demand functions from an ordinal scale of preferences.

This takes us directly back to Menger's theory of value. Menger's analysis of economic activity is based on his ordinal concept of value. But it is impossible to resolve the problems inherent in this ordinality because the foundations of economic behaviour cannot be moved to the sphere of goods and prices if we want to adhere to Menger's essentialist vision of the economic universe. Thus, independent of the analytical problems posed by his lexi-cographic ordering of *Bedürfnisse*, the structure of his economic theory alone, if accepted as a whole, poses irresolvable problems. And if his epistemological and methodological postulates are accepted, too, then we are no longer free to render the axiomatic structure of Menger's theory as a testable hypothesis because in Menger's world of thought we are still operating at the level of truth and certainty.

Menger's second principle of value theory defines the qualitative moment of the magnitude of value as the subjective degree of urgency for the satisfaction of *Bedürfnisse*. Here he makes several aspects of valuation explicit: *Bedürfnisse* are ranked—they are unequal—and the magnitude of the satisfaction, the subjective degree of urgency of a *Bedürfnis*, is given by the contribution of this satisfaction to our welfare. The fact that he puts the act of satisfaction of a *Bedürfnis* through a good in parentheses almost graphically illustrates the parallelism of the sphere of *Bedürfnisse*, where valuation takes place, and the sphere of goods which exist and simply wait to have values assigned to them.

The first and the second principles are united in his third principle which defines the quantitative moment of the magnitude of value. That is to say, in the first three principles of value theory, Menger takes us from his definition of value to his qualitative and quantitative moments of value theory. All that remains to be done for his principles to be complete is to define the measure of value. This he does in two steps, in his fourth and fifth principles, a procedure which may appear somewhat long-winded to us. But we must not forget that Menger was not addressing an audience steeped in the concepts of infinitesimal calculus and that he was building on a literary tradition which already knew his concepts in one form or another. He was, therefore, forced to proceed very slowly and carefully, explaining each step and concept against a background of similar concepts which had not been linked in the same way before.

Thus, his fourth principle merely states that it is only the least important of the satisfactions of the *Bedürfnisse* secured by a set of goods which crucially depends on the availability of a unit of these goods. And it is only in the next step, in the fifth principle, that he arrives at the final formulation of the marginality principle: The value of a unit of a set of goods is precisely the degree of importance to us of the last satisfaction of the *Bedürfnisse* secured by such a unit.

Valuation takes place at the margin; this, indeed, is very much like the derivation of marginal utility. But we must be very careful here because Menger's "values" and traditional "marginal utility" have very little in common beyond their derivation at the margin. On the one hand, Menger's values are neither part of a utilitarian calculus nor can they be expressed in price terms (if we want to remain faithful to the original, that is). He does not even use the term *Nutzen* (utility) except once or twice in his chapter on prices where it takes on the rather specialised meaning of "profit"—as it occasionally does in commercial jargon today.[122] If, on the other hand, we try to use "marginal utility" within Menger's framework, we run into problems of substance. Marginal utility divorced from prices becomes a rather ephemeral concept, but Menger's values are still a statement of the opportunity cost principle.

Looked at in another way, both in Menger's theory and in traditional consumer theory we postulate a structured choice set, a behavioural rule, and limitations imposed on the range of action by the scarcity principle. In Menger's theory these are represented by the lexicographically ordered hierarchy defined over the set of *Bedürfnisse*, the "essence" (*das Wesen*) of economic activity (that is, the best possible satisfaction of *Bedürfnisse*), and the set of initial endowments, respectively. In traditional theory the corresponding structures are, for instance, an indifference curve map defined over the set of goods, the maximisation of an index number such as reaching the highest possible point on the utility hill, and an income restraint. Any alteration in the income restraint is then analysed in terms of income and substitution effects on the individual's demand schedule. The question asked in this case is how an individual would re-organise his demand for goods subsequent to such a change in the initial conditions.

Ask the same question of Menger's five principles of value theory. The first reaction will be not knowing how to begin to answer it. Of course, it is not impossible to find an answer, but neither is it a "natural" question to ask. And this is so not only because Menger's choice set is lexicographically structured or because neither prices nor the concept of demand (*Nachfrage*) have been introduced as yet so that it would be difficult to interpret the variables of the Lagrangean equation. It is not "natural" above all because Menger addressed a different problem. He tried to solve the problem of the determination of the value of a good by asking the question, Which *Bedürfnisse* depend on a unit of a good under consideration? Or, reformulating the question, Which *Bedürfnis*, or part of it, would *not* be satisfied if that last unit of the good were to be withdrawn?[123] Thus, it is very clear that at the core of Menger's theory is the problem of opportunity cost of human action expressed in non-monetary terms.

Reverse the procedure and ask Menger's question of traditional consumer theory. The reaction will be equal bewilderment because Menger's question is equally "unnatural" within the framework of modern theory. The value of a good (in a non-monetary sense of the term) is clearly not the central question of micro-economic theory. In that theory, we are content with a set of relative prices, and the opportunity cost principle is certainly not the most intuitively obvious approach in the explanation of the utility function or the equivalent choice theoretic set of axioms. Rather the reverse; we would use income and substitution effects to explain the operation of the opportunity cost principle in utility theory.

Still, whatever the differences between Menger's value theory and diminishing marginal utility or its successors, Menger's theory would ultimately have remained sterile if he had had nothing to say about the relationship between human choice and market prices. To see what he has to say on this, I now return to my exposition of the *Grundsätze*.

Prices as Accidentia

Menger's fifth chapter, "Die Lehre vom Preise",[124] finally opens his theory to market phenomena. In this chapter, he moves from the determination of value to the discussion of price formation, and in subsequent chapters, he discusses the nature of commodities and money. For the purposes of this study, I shall pursue two major issues within Menger's theory of prices: How are prices established? How do prices relate to values? Menger states his definition of price in the opening paragraph of the chapter:

> Die Preise, oder mit anderen Worten, die im Tausche zur Erscheinung gelangenden Güterquantitäten . . . sind doch nichts weniger als das Wesentliche der ökonomischen Erscheinungen. Dieses liegt vielmehr in der durch den Tausch herbeigeführten besseren Vorsorge für die Befriedigung der Bedürfnisse der beiden Tauschenden. *Die Preise sind hiebei aber lediglich Erscheinungen, Symptome des ökonomischen Ausgleiches zwischen menschlichen Wirthschaften.*[125]

Prices are merely accidental phenomena, quantities of goods exchanged. They are symptoms of the essence of economic activity, that is, of the improvement in provision for the satisfaction of *Bedürfnisse* through exchange. This is the crux of Menger's theory and the point at which almost all previous interpretations of the *Grundsätze* founder because they fail to account for this fundamental difference between price and value: In Menger's theory, value is the essence of economic activity which manifests itself in the phenomenal domain through prices. For this theory, therefore, it does not suffice to treat prices as magnitudes which are simply calculated from values by setting price equal to value or by assuming a relationship such as that between a linear programming problem and its dual. We are dealing with fundamentally different spheres of discourse which obey different epistemological and methodological laws because these spheres are constituted of completely diverse elements. We are dealing with a transformation of values into prices in several dimensions—epistemological, methodological and analytical. All this, of course, holds true only as long as we accept the rules of the game as defined by Menger.

According to Menger, it is the task of a correct price theory to explain how economic man is led to exchange specific quantities of goods in order to achieve the highest possible satisfaction of his *Bedürfnisse*.[126] Consistent with his subjective value theory, Menger rejects the notion of exchange of equivalents because it is economically meaningless to exchange equal values for each other. An individual will only engage in exchange if a higher value can be obtained in exchange for the goods he gives up.[127]

Parallel to the method adopted in the development of the analysis of value, Menger begins with the simplest case, the "natural" starting point for his theory of prices: He introduces the principles of price formation by discussing exchange between two isolated individuals each of whom has a certain quantity of a good which the other one desires but does not have. The limits within which exchange takes place in this case of bi-lateral monopoly are set by each person's subjective value attached to these goods. They are the limits which Menger discussed in his chapter on exchange.

In his theory, exchange will take place only if strict inequality holds, that is, if both individuals will be better off after the exchange has taken place.[128] A price for each good will be established within the limits set by the value of each good. Individual A will give up a certain quantity of good X in exchange for a certain quantity of good Y from individual B. The exact price of X in terms of Y is, of course, not determined by the theory. Where precisely it will lie within the region of indeterminacy will depend, among other things, on how much information the individuals have about each other.[129]

Menger assumes that on the whole, prices have the tendency to settle at the average value between the limits. This assumption, however, is only justified if the two individuals and their respective circumstances are equal. Any divergence from this assumption will allow the prices to settle anywhere in the region of indeterminacy depending on the relative strength of the non-economic forces in operation.[130]

The next step in Menger's discussion of price formation is the gradual introduction of competition on one side of the exchange. Bi-lateral monopoly is now expanded to the case of monopoly proper in two separate instances. Many buyers compete first for one indivisible good offered by one seller and then for a divisible good (or, what amounts to the same thing, for several goods of the same kind) by one seller.[131] Exchange will take place at a price agreed upon by the seller and the strongest buyer. In Menger's analysis the weakest buyers are successively eliminated, with weak being defined according to the value established by each potential buyer for the good. The higher the subjective value, the stronger the potential buyer and hence the higher the final price. The result of the exchange process is a narrower region of indeterminacy under monopoly as compared to bi-lateral monopoly since competition on the buyers' side has the tendency to push the buyers' limit upwards.

Menger presents this basic result in three sets of principles. The first set states the result for the case of the monopolist in possession of one indivisible good.[132] The principles for the case of a divisible good basically reiterate the rules for the derivation of the limits of price formation and add the corollary that the larger the quantity of the monopoly good brought to the market, the lower its price and the better the provision of the population with this good.[133] The third set of principles discusses the monopolist's power over price and his influence over the degree of provision of the population with the monopoly good.[134]

The bulk of the analysis of price formation under monopolistic conditions is devoted to a discussion of the indeterminacy region where the monopolist's power over market phenomena manifests itself. From the perspective of economic analysis, we can observe the application of the idea of price elasticity of demand for the monopoly good in the discussion of market strategies available to the monopolist.[135] From the perspective of methodology, we find repeated insistence on the exact determinateness of quantities and values of the goods exchanged in spite of the indeterminacy region within which prices are formed.[136] I shall return to this methodological point in the discussion of the transformation problem in a moment.

In the last section on price formation, Menger widens his argument from monopoly to competition among buyers and among sellers. For Menger, competition arises out of monopoly; this process is part and parcel of the development of economic culture. Increases in population and diversification and growth of *Bedürfnisse* create a demand which a monopolist eventually cannot satisfy anymore. This in turn creates opportunities for profitable employment which are taken up eventually.[137] Competition divests producers of their power over prices and quantities; they are price takers and cannot increase revenue by reducing supply. It also removes the "exploitation" of society by the monopolist; competition ensures a better provision of society with goods and services than in the case of monopoly.[138] These are the only really fundamental differences between competition and monopoly. The principles of price formation remain unchanged. In other words, the archetype of price formation in Menger's theory is bi-lateral monopoly. Price formation under competition is merely the application of the principles derived for the case of bi-lateral monopoly to cases with a larger number of participants on both sides of the exchange.[139]

A survey of Menger's theory of prices is rather unexciting after his theory of value. All of his important theoretical insights seem to have been developed only in the latter. And from the point of view of late-twentieth-century neo-classical economic theory, he did not produce anything which could equal Walras's grandiose scheme of the analysis of a general equilibrium set of prices for an economy composed of perfectly competitive markets. But Menger did not set out to do this in the first place, and he was very well aware of the difference between his theory and Walras's.[140] Menger's economic universe was different from that of Walras, and it obeyed different epistemological and methodological laws. It is precisely here, in Menger's price theory, where the impact of his epistemology and methodology can be most closely observed because it is here that we can discern at which point this universe falls apart.

In Chapter 5 of his *Grundsätze der Volkswirthschaftslehre*, Menger begins to shift ground. The opening section is still very much in the spirit of the preceding 170 pages, but with the discussion of the process of price formation the discourse shifts not only from values to prices but more generally from essences to appearances, from the truth and certainty of "exact" theory to the probable results of "realistic-empirical" theory.

It is easy to identify the shift from essences (*Wesen*) to appearances (*Erscheinungen*), that is, to surface phenomena, because not only does Menger make that shift quite explicit in the opening paragraph of the chapter,[141] he also uses the terms "deep essences" and "surface phenomena" in the introduction to his critique of all economists from Aristotle onwards who believed that prices are of the essence of exchange and that therefore only equivalents are exchanged.

> Die Kraft, die [die Güterpreise] aber an die Oberfläche der Erscheinungen treibt, ist die letzte und allgemeine Ursache aller wirthschaftlichen Bewegung, das Bestreben der Menschen, ihre Bedürfnisse möglichst vollständig zu befriedigen, ihre ökonomische Lage zu verbessern. Weil aber die *Preise die einzigen sinnlich wahrnehmbaren Erscheinungen des ganzen Processes* sind, ihre Höhe sich genau messen lässt und das tägliche Leben uns dieselben ohne Unterlass vor Augen führt, so war der Irrthum naheliegend, die Grösse derselben als das Wesentliche am Tausche, und, in weiterer Consequenz dieses Irrthums, die im Austausch erscheinenden Güterquantitäten als Aequivalente zu betrachten.[142]

This quotation also indicates the breadth of the problem created by Menger's essentialism and the consequent dichotomy of reality into two spheres. On the one side, we find essence; determinate solutions in terms of values and quantities of goods; certainty and truth of "exact" theories; a general foundation of economic activity on a non-market concept of "economy"[143] and a non-market concept of subjective value.[144] On the other side, we find surface phenomena; indeterminacy in the solutions in terms of prices;[145] probable results of "realistic-empirical" theories; market concepts, that is, concepts based on exchange such as objectively ascertainable prices.

Menger's theory of value is, according to his own terminology and classification of sciences, an "exact" theory, one which analyses the essence of economic activity and always produces determinate, certain and true results.[146] All of his illustrative examples in Chapters 1–4, Chapter 6[147] and the first two sections of Chapter 5 of the *Grundsätze* are based on personal or psychological experience (hence Menger's claim that even his "exact" theories are *empirisch*, at least in a certain sense of the word, and not deductive). In contrast to this, the illustrative examples in the latter parts of Chapter 5 and in Chapters 7 and 8 (on commodities and on money) are more historical and descriptive of the external world (as opposed to the introspective world of the psychological examples). In other words, starting in the latter part of Chapter 5, Menger shifts from his discussion of "exact" theory to a discussion of "realistic-empirical" theories which, again according to his own terminology and classification of sciences, can only yield probable results.

We must be very careful here not to confuse the various levels in Menger's methodology where the term "historical" appears. In his classification of the *Wissenschaften*, he gives history and statistics a place not among the "sciences" but among the "arts" because these disciplines are not "theoretical."[148] The historical illustrations provided by him in the *Grundsätze* from Chapter 5 onwards, however, do not relegate his discussion of prices, commodities and money to the arts as opposed to the sciences. They still remain "theoretical" discussions, and within Menger's own methodological framework their results are correctly formulated as laws, as, for instance, when he states that there are strict laws according to which monopolists can formulate their policy options. From his terminology, however, we can infer that they must be "realistic-empirical" laws and theories yielding probable results.[149]

The process of transition from essences to appearances can be traced not only in Menger's explicit statements about the nature of values and prices and in his use of illustrative examples but, perhaps even more convincingly, also in his use of the terms *Bedarf* and *Nachfrage*. These terms are rendered in the English translation as "requirement" and "demand", respectively,[150] which is in keeping with Menger's use of them since the frame of reference of *Bedarf* is different from that of *Nachfrage*. Linguistically, *Bedarf* has the same root as *Bedürfnis*. As used by Menger, *Bedarf* reflects the extent of *Bedürfnis* and is substantively independent of the availability of goods. It is the quantity of a good required to satisfy a *Bedürfnis*.[151] It is hence best translated as "requirement." *Nachfrage*, or demand, on the other hand, is the manifestation of *Bedarf* on the market after the income constraint has been introduced. In consequence, *Bedarf* refers to values, and *Nachfrage* to prices. Consistent with this interpretation, we find the former term in the earlier chapters of the *Grundsätze* but not in the chapter on prices, and *Nachfrage* is used in the chapter on prices but not in the earlier ones.

One might object that it would suffice to distinguish between latent, effective and total demand and equate *Bedarf* with total demand and *Nachfrage* with effective demand. Although the conceptualisation in this objection goes in the right direction, it is nevertheless misleading because the distinction between latent and effective demand does not carry as a connotation the distinction between essence and appearance, between the two spheres of discourse indicated by the original German terms. In addition, the objection also raises the problem of how to translate Menger's concept of *effectiver Bedarf*, the effective requirement for production goods given by the availability of the requisite complementary goods at the right point in time.[152]

Does the epistemological and methodological characterisation of value theory as "exact" theory and price theory as "realistic-empirical" theory matter for the analytics of Menger's economic theory? It does, indeed, because it separates values from prices. And because it does so, Menger must be able to demonstrate that this separation can be overcome, that values can be transformed into prices and vice versa.

We have seen that in the case of bi-lateral monopoly, prices cannot be determined precisely but can only be located within a certain region of indeterminacy whose limits are set by the subjective values of the participants in the exchange. In other words, although we are able to ascertain a price empirically *after* the exchange, the theory cannot predict the price because price formation also depends to a large extent on non-economic factors. The only variables which can be precisely determined by the theory *ex ante* are the subjective values.

This may not seem strange to a modern economist because current neo-classical theory, too, recognises this indeterminacy region in the case of bi-lateral monopoly. Both buyer and seller wish that the other end of the market were perfectly competitive so that each seller could sell his own goods somewhere above their own marginal costs in the region between the limits set by his own marginal revenue and the other's demand curve. The exact price at which each will sell is left open by the theory and is determined by variables which are exogenous to the model.

This modern statement of bi-lateral monopoly differs in one fundamental aspect from Menger's. The modern case is entirely formulated in terms of quantities of goods and prices while Menger's case is formulated in terms of values, quantities of goods and prices. Hence, the additional concept of value in Menger's theory must be operationally meaningful within the framework of the theory or, by Occam's razor, it must be jettisoned.

Menger was an essentialist and developed a rather idiosyncratic epistemology and methodology on this basis. Can we demonstrate within his own system of thought that values which are precisely determined are indispensable for an explanation of price formation and that they thus tell us more about actual prices than merely that they fall into a "feasible" region? In the case of bi-lateral monopoly, his theory can tell us only that there is a "feasible" region within which the price vector must be located. As both sides of the exchange grow in number and competition among buyers and among sellers therefore develops, the "feasible" region begins to shrink, and according to the operation of Menger's value theory, the limiting points move closer towards each other until the number of participants on both sides of the exchange have grown to such an extent that none of them have any freedom to influence the market price in their favour. But this limiting case is precisely the case of perfect competition. In other words, in the case of perfectly competitive markets, and only in this case, prices will be uniquely determined by subjective values. Thus, Menger's theory is in all but the perfectly competitive case unable to lead us directly from values to prices and back again. It is beset by a problem of the transformation of values into prices which it cannot solve because the resolution of this problem depends on factors which are exogenous to the theory.

The transformation problem is crucial, not resolvable and deeply imbedded in the foundations of Menger's theory. It is a logical outcome of his conception of a dichotomy of the theoretical universe into "exact" and "realistic-empirical" which, in turn, is based on his essentialist vision of the world. This essentialism in combination with the subjective character of his value theory creates a formidable epistemological obstacle for any economist who wants to use Menger's theory for an analysis of economic events within the world of thought developed by Menger.

Menger's value theory is perfect for the *acting* subject (the economic agent). Immediately perceived valuation provides the foundations on which economic behaviour rests in the real world: valuation according to Menger's principles gives the acting subject firm guidelines for action when faced with market prices. The problem for the theory arises when the *acting* subject is different from the *knowing* subject, that is, when the *acting* subject becomes the *object of investigation* of the knowing subject (the enquiring economist). Although the enquiring subject (the economist) knows his own value structure, he has no means of knowing the acting subject's value structure if this acting subject is a person other than himself. Hence, he does not know how to interpret the objectively ascertainable market prices with respect to the limits set by the valuation peculiar to the acting subject. In other words, except for the case of perfectly competitive markets, Menger's theory of value is of no use to the knowing subject (the enquiring economist) if that subject wants to explain precisely why prices are what they are.

This fundamental problem is important not only because bilateral monopoly is the archetype of price formation in Menger's theory, but also because he gives hardly any consideration to the case of perfect competition in the *Grundsätze*.[153] Nevertheless, he regarded his exposition of the "essence" of economic activity as complete. But, and here the story takes an almost macabre twist, we also have every reason to believe that Menger was aware of the existence of this transformation problem for why else did he originally plan to say something about the relationship of values to prices in the second edition of the *Grundsätze*?[154]

Are there any consequences of this problem for the theory? There are and, to say the very least, they seriously shake the foundations of Menger's theoretical edifice. We have seen that Menger's transformation problem is owing to Menger's essentialism and the subjectivism of his value theory. One could, therefore, conceive of two different approaches to try and resolve the problem. On the one hand, one could give up Menger's essentialism, but then the character of his value theory would change drastically. This approach would mean a recasting of 'his epistemology and methodology, a rethinking of his aims of economic theory, and eventually also an admission that Schmoller's criticism was justified. On the other hand, one could first jettison the subjectivism of his value theory and then try, in one way or another, to make it more objective while still hanging on to essentialism and the rest of his epistemology and methodology. But this second approach would not only open up his theory to Schmoller's accusation of "deductivism" and "speculation", it would also question, within his epistemology, the justification for the postulate that results of "exact" theories are true, certain and immediately accessible.

In either case, Menger's original position is untenable. And as we have arrived at the concept of speculation, let me speculate a little and say that Menger must have been aware, in one way or another, of the problems described here. Why else did he neither authorise a reprint or a translation of the *Grundsätze* nor complete the second edition during his lifetime? Why did he want to "clarify" the relationship between prices and values but did not do so? Because he knew that, after everything was considered, his ultimate answer had to be to withdraw the theory from circulation because it did not—it could not, within the frame of reference which he had mapped out—answer the questions he had posed in 1871 and 1883. And if all this was true, should we really, above all after the *Methodenstreit* had broken out, expect him to throw his theory and his *wissenschaftliche Weltauffassung* overboard just because there was a transformation problem? Or should we not more reasonably expect him to show tenacity in the face of the difficulty which had beset his research program and try and rescue it? After all, his theory had introduced many innovations into economic analysis; it did solve the paradox of value in a non-mechanistic way; it posed the question of value from the outset in an intertemporal framework without assuming certainty and complete information; and it did not adopt perfect competition as the paradigm for analytic work. Certainly from today's perspective, it is a very unorthodox theory, and many of its features were not understood by those who claimed to be his successors or to be working within the research program he had established.

There are a large number of issues which are worth pursuing concerning Menger's theory. The intertemporal dimension of his conception of value encompasses a theory of capital which utilises concepts that are very similar to those employed in Böhm-Bawerk's *Positive Theorie*. Periods of production, the notion of roundabout production processes and a lower estimation of future *Bedürfnisse* are all present but are used by Menger in the development of a theory which is quite different from the theory that came to be identified with Austrian capital theory *per se*. The fundamental difference lies in the understanding of the concept of production. For Menger, production is to be considered solely from an economic point of view: How are goods of higher order, which are available today and which can only be employed in real time, related to the satisfaction of *Bedürfnisse* in the future? All concepts and relations are defined and analysed from this perspective. The actual technology employed in the production process is almost irrelevant. It is important insofar as it determines the chronological length of the physical production process of a concrete good, but it does not impinge on the economic definition of the production period. Böhm-Bawerk's theory of capital, on the other hand, is based on a technological notion of production and hence abandons an important structural support of Menger's theoretical edifice. This is most certainly one of the reasons, if not the crucial one, for Menger's reported statement that Böhm-Bawerk's theory of capital was one of the greatest errors ever committed.[155]

The conception of capital theory as intertemporal choice theory in combination with Menger's teleology leads directly to his conception of the problem of distribution. Menger's starting point is always the subjective value of goods of lower or first order. The value of all factors contributing to their production must be derived from this starting point. The Austrian theory of distribution was primarily elaborated by Wieser, who tried to show in *Der natürliche Wert* how value is to be imputed to the various goods of higher order. Wieser's theory of distribution forms an integral part of his *Grenznutzentheorie* (his theory of marginal utility). We have seen that neither the term nor the concept are a part of Menger's theory.

Apart from these fundamental issues, which as yet have not been adequately discussed in the literature on Menger, there are also the questions raised by one of Streissler's essays on Menger: Does Menger have a theory of economic development? If so, what kind of theory is it? And, above all: Is it true that the elaboration of a theory of economic development was a central concern in the *Grundsätze*?[156] Other important issues are Menger's concept of the entrepreneur and his role in the economic process and, closely related to that concept, his conception of the nature and role of information in economics.

To my mind, these are some of the most important themes which emerge from the value theory of Menger's *Grundsätze* and which deserve much closer scrutiny. To do justice to them would require a monograph for each, and even a merely adequate treatment of, say, the problem of capital and distribution would go far beyond the scope of this study.

The same can be said about the issues arising from Menger's theory of prices. First and foremost, there is his theory of money which he elaborated not only in the *Grundsätze* but in a number of other publications[157] and which has received a fair amount of attention in the literature.[158] Second, there is his theory of markets which is implicit in his discussion of commodities[159] and which leads to two related but hitherto ignored themes: Does Menger's theory require the notion of the "invisible hand"? What is the relationship of Menger's theory to institutional economics and the economics of institutions?

Excursus: *Marx and Menger—Distant Cousins?*

Menger is not usually directly connected with bourgeois apologetics in general or the struggle against socialism in particular. I do not know why not because none of the early bourgeois economists expressed their ideological stance more clearly than Menger. In his discussion of Historicism and Burke-Savigny in the *Untersuchungen*, he justifies the aim of the Romantic-Historicist approach as the defence of organically grown institutions against allowing one-sided rationalism to take over the economic theory which hailed from Adam Smith.[160] In particular, he advocated the defence of the organically grown national economy against a superficial *Pragmatismus*[161] which inevitably leads to socialism.[162]

There may, of course, have been vested interest involved in past failures to draw attention to the significance of this passage. But this was certainly not the overriding consideration for all past commentators. The absence of a synthetic approach to Menger's work clearly has something to do with it for why else did such a lucid commentator as John Hicks dissociate Menger from the deliberate attempt to stem the tide of socialism?[163]

The case for bourgeois apologetics does not rest only on this argument. Menger is not a household name when we come to talk about Marx and his opponents—Böhm-Bawerk takes pride of place here[164]—but when we compare the conceptual apparatus of Marx with that of Menger we can easily see that Menger is much closer to Marx than any other bourgeois economist. The kinship between the two is, indeed, so strong that one could easily talk about Marx and Menger as distant cousins. A brief comparison of both Marx's and Menger's conceptual frameworks, their similarities and differences, will show this clearly.

Menger's resoluta-compositive method is part of the *geisteswissenschaftliche* approach commonly known as the hermeneutic circle. The resoluta-compositive method is, in fact, nothing else but the hermeneutic circle arrested after the first round. The same conception is present in Marx's method of "Aufsteigen vom Abstrakten zum Konkreten", the main difference to Menger's approach being that Marx's method does not necessarily stop after the first round.

The Historicist dimension is, of course, present in both Marx and Menger. The main difference between the two systems is that Menger's theory has a-historic foundations (his "exact" theory of value) whereas Marx's dialectic is Historicist and non-dogmatic throughout. Marx and Menger both share the conception that economics belongs to the *Geisteswissenschaften*, both their theories of value are essentialist theories, both regard the establishment of a theory of value as indispensable for the "correct" understanding of the economic world, and both of their theories are plagued by a transformation problem in relating values to prices. Furthermore, value is, for both of them, a relation: For Marx who defines value as socially necessary labour time required for the production of commodities under capitalist relations of production, value represents the relationship between people characterised by exploitation; for Menger, value is the relationship between a person and the means at this person's disposal for the satisfaction of *Bedürfnisse*.

The similarities between the two systems are, of course, not accidental. They result from the common *geistesgeschichtliche* background which Marx and Menger share: the peculiarly German response to the challenge posed by rationalism and Enlightenment thought and Napoleonic imperialism. Marx stands as the representative of the rational response in economic theory while Menger represents the irrational response with an Austrian intellectual flavour.[165] The differences between the two systems are, therefore, not accidental either. Marx's historical, dialectic methodology contrasts with Menger's ahistorical resoluta-compositive method, on the one hand, but is comparable with the Historicism in Menger's empirical-realistic theory of price formation, markets, exchange and money, on the other hand. Marx's social, objective labour theory of value has to be set, of course, against Menger's individualistic, subjective psychological theory of value.

There is another fundamental aspect which both theories share: Both are surplus theories of value which have their points of departure in the concept of *Bedürfnis*. As we have seen, Menger's theory of value is a "*Bedürfnis* theory of value": It provides the foundations for a demand-based economic theory and rests on a subjective, psychological conception of value which emerges from the concept of the satisfaction of *Bedürfnisse*. All economic concepts and relations are derived from these foundations.

Marx's theory of value is ultimately also based on the concept of *Bedürfnisse* and the inevitability of having to satisfy them. This common point of departure, however, did not tempt him to develop a subjective, psychologistic, a-historic value theory because, unlike Menger, Marx locates value not in the sphere of exchange (or circulation) but in the sphere of production. To make this clear: In Marx's money circuit, $M - C - M'$, where $M' > M$, value is determined not at M or M' but at C, not in exchange where money (M, M') changes hands but in production where commodities (C) are produced. The means (or factors) of production which participate in this process are bought (in the so-called normal, competitive case) at their value. However, no surplus value can be extracted from raw materials and machinery in the process of production. Their cost to the entrepreneur cannot be reduced below the value of their product except in irregular cases (fraud, monopoly). Only labour power, the third type of input, can be bought at a value which is lower than the value produced by it. Here, the characteristically exploitative character of the capitalist relations of production determines the locus of value and surplus value formation. (At M and M', value is not created but realised.) If we try to look below the layers of relations of production, class or social relations, and below the historically specific framework of capitalist production, we discover that the universal fact that human beings have to satisfy their *Bedürfnisse* in order to survive provides the space for the extraction of surplus value. In the human world neither raw materials nor machinery have to satisfy anything to survive. Only the commodity labour power, that is, the specifically human element in a process which involves the whole of the world of nature, allows for the determination of value.

The sphere of exchange, however, is crucial for the comparison of Marx's and Menger's concepts of surplus. Since for Marx, as well as for Aristotle, exchange is of equivalents, the surplus which is appropriated by the capitalist cannot arise in the sphere of exchange; it must arise in production where "unequal exchange" can be practised, that is, where the surplus can be extracted. The production of the surplus, however, is the driving force of the capitalist economy since no entrepreneur could be envisaged within the capitalist system who would not be after the maximisation of the surplus.

Surplus, in reality, is also what makes Menger's economy tick. To make it quite clear: Menger's economic theory does not have to rely on the concept of surplus as far as its foundations (value theory) are concerned. *Bedürfnisse* can be satisfied without any recourse to a concept of surplus. Exchange, however, is unthinkable without it. As we know, Menger rejected Aristotle's concept of exchange of equivalents. For Menger, trade could never take off in the first place if only equivalents were to change hands since in his opinion two things can be economically equivalent only if they satisfy the same *Bedürfnis* equally well. Hence, the first concept we have to understand is the meaning of equivalent: for Marx, as for Aristotle, it is an objective notion while for Menger, it is a subjective one. Incentive to exchange can exist for Menger only if something more is obtained in return for what is given up. This is the surplus which the individual requires in the sphere of exchange if, in Menger's economic universe, trade is to be mutually beneficial. Both parties to the exchange require the existence of a subjective surplus if they are to be persuaded to exchange at all.

No matter how important all of these issues which emerge from Menger's theory of value and prices are, in the final section of this essay I return to one question which keeps popping up throughout this study without having been answered yet. The question is fundamental for historians of economic thought, and it is indeed surprising that no one has taken the trouble to try and provide a definitive answer. Let me, therefore, formulate the problem as follows: William Stanley Jevons, Carl Menger and Léon Walras are generally considered to be the fathers of today's neo-classical economic theory. Can this statement of the founding trinity be maintained in view of the differences between Menger's theory and the theories of Jevons and Walras which I have repeatedly pointed out? Since there is a prevailing consensus that the Walras-Hicks-Debreu lineage represents a continuous development of neo-classical economic theory, I shall reformulate the question slightly so that its relevance for current neoclassical orthodoxy will become clear: Can Menger's value theory be integrated into the axiomatic foundations of current neo-classical economics?

Neo-Classical Axiomatisation and Menger's Theory of Value

In conventional neo-classical theory, the "fundamental economic problem" is formulated as the following maximisation problem:

$$\max u(x_1, x_2, \ldots, x_n)$$
subject to constraints,

where $u(x)$ is a function which maps goods into utility. For the solution of this problem, a mapping is defined from the set of variables x_i ($i = 1, \ldots, n$) represented by cardinal real numbers into the set of values of the function represented by ordinal numbers.

In the early days of neo-classical theory, it was diminishing marginal utility which made the solution of this problem possible and allowed for the derivation of individual- and market-demand functions. The utility derived from the consumption of one good, the consumption of all other goods remaining constant, was computed by means of a one-to-one mapping which mapped the good onto utility. The problem of how actually to measure utility so that marginal utility could be used as an operational concept was eventually resolved in the Slutsky-Hicks-Allen reformulation of the fundamental problem in which utility became ordinal and diminishing marginal utility, now a meaningless concept, was replaced by the diminishing marginal rate of substitution. Goods were still mapped onto utility, but the mapping was not one-to-one any longer, which did not matter because the derivation and computation of individual market demand could be carried out within the commodity space. The only function of utility was to order the commodity space by imposing on it consistent choice in the form of the indifference map. Further developments in the formulation of the theory brought no substantive changes but merely clarified the theory and made its axiomatic structure explicit, the major formal change being the replacement of calculus by topology.

In principle, constrained maximisation is also the form in which Menger poses his fundamental problem. However, as soon as we proceed from this very general statement to a more specific formulation of his problem, we find that he formulates it somewhat differently. According to Menger

$$\left| \begin{array}{c} \text{a complex} \\ \text{of} \\ \textit{Bedürfnisse} \end{array} \right| \quad \text{faces} \quad \left| \begin{array}{c} \text{a quantity} \\ \text{of} \\ \text{goods} \end{array} \right| . \text{ [166]}$$

Given the difference between Menger's and the conventional neo-classical formulations, two questions are pertinent: Does Menger pose the same problem as the conventional neo-classicists? If not, can Menger's problem be reformulated in the conventional way without loss of substance?

The answer to both questions is negative. To be able to demonstrate this, every step in the formalisation process has to be given substantive support. For instance, when it comes to numerical representation of goods, values and *Bedürfnisse*, we have to decide which set of numbers we are permitted to use—the set of real numbers or the set of positive integers. This decision has to be based on substantive arguments, not merely considerations of formal convenience.[167] The substance, however, is clearly delineated for us: It is embodied in the pages of Menger's *Grundsätze*. The aim is to find, if possible, the verbal, or conceptual, equivalents in the *Grundsätze* for all the mathematical tools and transformation processes of modern micro-economic theory. The criterion for adopting the conventional neo-classical mathematical formulation is straightforward: Whenever Menger's arguments either agree with the conventional formulation or do not contradict it substantively (as may be the case when he has nothing to say on a certain point), the conventional neo-classical formulation is adopted. This procedure is certainly in keeping with Menger's views on the use of mathematics in economics.[168]

Menger's Problem

Value, in Menger's definition, is highly dependent on *Bedürfnis*. The measure of the satisfaction of a *Bedürfnis* is its subjective degree of urgency; this measure will be represented by a number, and value is simply this number.[169] Value is as yet independent of any use made of a good, i.e., it is established logically and ontologically prior to any use.[170] Let me call the "complex of *Bedürfnisse*" set A. It immediately follows from what has just been said that at this stage of the argument we have already arrived at values— *Bedürfnisse* have been mapped into values—although we are still in set A and goods have not been introduced yet. As we shall see later[171], once values are calculated subjectively, they are then merely transferred onto the good(s) in question. Let me denote the "quantity of goods" by set B; set A is then mapped onto set B. In consequence, we are dealing with two mappings: *Bedürfnisse* into values, on the one hand, and values onto goods, on the other hand.

The solution to Menger's problem therefore depends on:

1. the nature of set A;
2. the nature of set B;[172]
3. the nature of mappings
   (a) within A, and
   (b) from A to B.

In order to be able to formulate Menger's problem in the conventional neo-classical way and to demonstrate the equivalence of the two, we ought to be able to show not only that we can get from set A to set B, as Menger does, but also that the procedure can be reversed, which is necessary if, as in the conventional approach, goods are to be the arguments of the utility functions.

It is worth pausing for a moment to compare Menger's approach and that of conventional neo-classical theory on their own respective grounds. The conventional transformation of goods into utility and the subsequent derivation of demand functions is an essentially arbitrary process since the motivation for the acts of choice and the psychological structure of the choice set, i.e., the shape of the utility function, are not only taken as given but are formulated so as to suit the mathematical tools employed.[173] The formulation of these underlying assumptions is usually held to be "reasonable"; that is as far as modern theoreticians are prepared to go in the direction of "realism of the theory", as they are seemingly content to remain within the limits prescribed by the essentially formal character of conventional neo-classical theory and its analytic process.

Menger's theory, on the other hand, is ontologically grounded. Any operation performed on the set B has to be in accordance with those performed on set A which in turn are grounded in Menger's ontology. The formal, analytic process is therefore limited by the prescriptions of this ontology, i.e., by the lexicographic representation of the structure of *Bedürfnisse*. In discussing possible formal representations of Menger's value theory, it is, for example, not sufficient to establish the properties of the real numbers or the axiomatic basis for differentiable functions; these also have to be shown to be compatible with the logic and the ontology underlying Menger's verbal presentation. If, for instance, the logic of Menger's commodity space should not have the properties defined for the real numbers, then it would not be admissible to simply impose the latter on the commodity space—provided, that is, one wants to stay in Menger's territory.

Finally, a remark on the terminology adopted. I call the set A, where *Bedürfnisse* are mapped into values, the Preference Set, and set B the Commodity Set. However, it must be kept in mind throughout that the term Preference Set will denote Menger's set A as defined above; it will have nothing in common whatsoever with the conventional neo-classical set of preferences.

The Nature of the Preference Set

According to Menger's definition of the "fundamental economic problem", the Preference Set contains the *Bedürfnisse*. Within this set they are related to their subjective degrees of urgency, i.e., their values which, as we have seen, are established entirely within the Preference Set. Value is purely psychological, and the "complex of *Bedürfnisse*" is lexicographically ordered, implying that even though each value can be represented by a number, a single-valued, continuous "value function" defined over the domain of all *Bedürfnisse* does not exist.

Menger's structure of *Bedürfnisse* is ordered in such a way that the most important *Bedürfnisse* are always satisfied first.[174] This is, in fact, one of the most important ontological statements in the *Grundsätze*.[175] *Bedürfnisse* are strictly ordered in a descending order of more general groups or *Gattungen*, the order referring to their respective necessity for survival, and within each group in descending order of importance of each individual *Bedürfnis*.[176] Menger strictly adheres to this scheme in his fictional "case studies", that is, in the discussions of the economics of an isolated farmer and his family,[177] of Robinson Crusoe[178] and of an isolated social group (i.e., of a closed economy).[179] The ordering is, therefore, in principle of the form

$$(a, b, c, \ldots) > (a', b', c', \ldots)$$

if

(i) $a > a'$, or
(ii) if $a = a'$ and $b > b'$, or
(iii) if $a = a'$, $b = b'$ and $c > c'$,
. . .
    etc.[180]

This specification of lexicographically ordered *Bedürfnisse* is an ontological commitment for Menger and the basis on which he derives his marginality principle. It is therefore analytically indispensable. Hence, the "value function" (or, in orthodox terminology, utility function) appropriate to Menger's theory, that is, his transformation of *Bedürfnisse* into values is multi-valued, and its elements are vectors. Being multi-dimensional, "utility" cannot be reduced to a single dimension (a number) because its multi-dimensionality is ontologically determined. Although the specification of a transformation procedure for the reduction of many dimensions to one dimension is formally possible, it is substantively inadmissible as it would have to be based on the possibility of substitution of satisfaction of *Bedürfnisse* across their structure, a contradiction of Menger's ontological assumption. The following example illustrates this point.

If a starving vagrant travelling in the middle of nowhere found a bundle of goods consisting of no food, no housing and theater tickets, the value of the theater tickets to him would be zero—or, rather, irrelevant—because the bundle contains no food. No amount of theater tickets can compensate for starvation. The counterargument, Why not? does not make sense in the (ontologically determined) framework of Menger's theory, although it would be perfectly permissible in conventional utility theory. We must not forget that lack of information and hence market imperfections are essential ingredients of Menger's theoretical economy. It is therefore inadmissible to postulate *a priori* convertibility of theater tickets into (money into) bread as this convertibility presupposes complete information and the existence and frictionless functioning of the necessary markets. In other words, we must be careful not to introduce, through the back door as it were, a social institution exhibiting some fairly specific characteristics—that is, a perfectly functioning market and the individual's knowledge of all market prices—into the ontological foundations of a genuinely subjectivist theory of value in which valuation by an isolated individual is the fundamental paradigm.[181]

The extension of this example is, of course, that the satisfaction of lower, or primary, needs will allow the individual to order his preferences for theater tickets and any of their substitutes by equalising their value at the margin. This conventional ordering of alternatives along the real line is only possible (1) within a *Bedürfnisgattung* and (2) if the *ceteris paribus* clause is applied to all ontologically prior needs or wants once these prior needs have been satisfied. Given these conditions, there could even exist "indifference classes" within a *Bedürfnisgattung* but never across these groups, as would be necessary if Menger's theory were to be integrated into conventional utility theory. The search for traditional indifference curves in the *Grundsätze* is therefore futile, and any attempt to force Menger's value theory into the indifference-curve framework could only succeed at the price of serious violations of the most fundamental postulates of Menger's theory.

Finally, a comment on numerical representation: Are *Bedürfnisse* and values to be represented by real numbers or (positive) integers? The problem of divisibility arises only for goods (set *B*); substantively, there are no grounds to object to a representation of values by real numbers as psychological states are fluid and not clearly distinct. Indeed, these considerations seem to speak for such a representation, and Menger is silent on this question. In accordance with the criterion stated above, I therefore accept that real numbers do not distort the substance of his argument.

The Nature of the Commodity Set

The elements of the Commodity Set are goods by means of which *Bedürfnisse* are satisfied. Which formal properties can be extracted from Menger's discussion for this set? Goods satisfy four conditions among which is their physical ability to satisfy a *Bedürfnis*.[182] Their physical characteristics could therefore be part of the definition of the units of measurement, but equally, their economic character, i.e., the purpose for which they are used, could also be a part of it. However, the only objective, defining characteristic of goods available to the individual are physical units and physical characteristics. It is these characteristics which make some goods suitable for the satisfaction of certain *Bedürfnisse* and not others, and it is for these physical characteristics that goods are desired and exchanged. In other words, it is the economic aspect of the physical world which Menger wants to explain, and to do so by referring only to economic concepts would merely lead to circular reasoning.

Consequently, the Commodity Set is a collection of heterogeneous elements which are measured in physical units and which are distinguished by their physical characteristics.[183] So far, then, the representation of goods by natural numbers would be perfectly acceptable. An extension to cardinally measurable real numbers, however, poses no problem; not only would it not entail any loss of substance of Menger's theory[184] but it is also perfectly compatible with his own representation of the units of measurement of goods as he frequently refers to "goods or their appropriate *Theilquantitäten*."[185] The characterisation of the Commodity Set as

$$B = \left\{ x \mid x > 0,\ x \in E^n \right\}$$

is therefore acceptable; the Commodity Set is a collection of heterogeneous elements in E^n.

An equivalence relation is defined by Menger's definition of homogeneity which considers goods to be homogeneous if, and only if, they are economically equivalent.[186] Physically non-homogeneous goods are homogeneous from an economic point of view if they satisfy the same *Bedürfnis* equally well. Menger's concept of homogeneity is therefore a purely economic

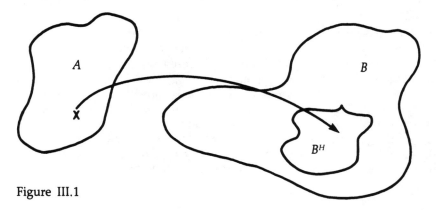

Figure III.1

concept derived from his definition of "economic"; it depends on the motivation, i.e., the purpose of economic activity, which is also its *Wesen*: *Bedürfnisbefriedigung*.[187]

The situation can now be summarised in Figure III.1 where

A = $\{$ complex of *Bedürfnisse* $\}$
B = $\{$ quantity of goods $\}$
B^H = $\{$ subset of economically homogeneous goods which are physically heterogeneous $\}$

A *Bedürfnis* (or value, see the discussion of the Preference Set) is mapped into the set of goods, which are denoted by x and are measured in physical terms as

$$B = \{x \mid x > 0, x \ \varepsilon \ E^n)\} \ .$$

B^H is the subset of economically homogeneous goods in B:

$$B^H = \{x \mid x > 0, x \ \varepsilon \ E^n);$$ for $x_i, x_j,$ with $i = j$, the equivalence relation "has the same value as" holds $\}$,[188]

and

$$B^H \subset B.$$

We also can safely assume that B^H is a proper subset of B because physically heterogeneous goods which are not equally well suited to satisfy all kinds of *Bedürfnisse* actually exist and because different *Bedürfnisse* exist— these existential (or ontological) presuppositions are justified by the fact that "economic activity" in Menger's sense actually takes place and that Menger's theory has an explicit ontological dimension.

Some implications of this definition of homogeneity can be pointed out immediately. The size of the subset B^H is not determined *a priori* nor is it deducible. The number of elements within the subset depends on the physical characteristics of the elements in B. There are, furthermore, as many subsets B^H as there are *Bedürfnisse*. $B^H = \emptyset$ is therefore an ontologically permissible statement.

The introduction of the subset B^H, however, raises the following question: Could we not avoid the impass with regard to indifference, which Menger's introduction of the structure of *Bedürfnisse* has produced, by using B^H as a partitioning of B, in analogy with the conventional approach in which the indifference relation (I) is used as a partitioning of the consumption set which is then completely ordered by I and the preference relation?[189] Could not the equivalence classes B^H be used as a representation of conventional indifference classes in Menger's system? However tempting the thought for those who are by now starved of indifference curves and conventional analytical technique, this solution is a fallacy. It could only be obtained at the price of violating some of Menger's most fundamental ontological and methodological presuppositions. Adopting it would be a prime example of forcing the facts, which here are constituted by Menger's *Grundsätze*, to fit conventional neo-classical theory since the concept of indifference and the equivalence relation B^H have logically and methodologically totally different statuses. Assigning equal value—the definition of B^H—is the result of the valuation process. The concept of indifference, however, is an assumption, indeed an axiom, about the psychology of the consumer. Equating the two on a formal level would demand that the result of the analysis should be held equivalent to one of its most fundamental assumptions. Thus, by fallacious reasoning, something—namely, the concept of indifference—would be introduced which had been excluded at the outset. On the methodological, and also substantive, levels indifference corresponds to overall substitutability and to the simultaneity of the economic process of general equilibrium systems; the equivalence classes, B^H, are the outcome of Menger's teleologically conceived economic process. This is an instance in which we can see quite clearly how the ontology underlying Menger's economic theory not only provides the general framework for the theory but also directly limits the choice of analytic tools available to him.

One may conceivably argue that the main body of Menger's long chapter on value[190] contradicts this interpretation because there he quite clearly employs concepts which are equivalent to the conventional utility function. By deduction, the concept of indifference therefore has to be located somewhere in the *Grundsätze*. The problem with such a statement is that its points of reference by necessity have to be Menger's illustrative examples. Menger does not proceed in an axiomatic-deductive fashion in the development of his value theory but by demonstration through repeated use of fictional case studies. Unfortunately, his choice of examples camouflages the lexicographic structure of the Preference Set and renders its structure indistinguishable from the conventional preference ordering.

Menger's examples were meant to serve merely as illustrations, and they mislead his interpreters because he demonstrated each case by means of only one commodity, either water or corn (presumably chosen with reference

Table III.1. Classification of Goods

	Economically homogeneous	Economically heterogeneous
Physically homogeneous	I	II
Physically heterogeneous	III	IV

to usage in classical economics). It is certainly easier, both analytically and didactically, to use only one good,[191] but this ease is bought at the price of analytical clarity since whenever there is only one (universal) commodity to satisfy all *Bedürfnisse*—i.e., not only those within each rank of the hierarchy but also across the ranks, for the entire set of *Bedürfnisse*—then the lexicographic structure "vanishes" in the sense that, from the perspective of choice, it becomes indistinguishable from an ordering of preferences along the real line.[192] Using only one commodity reduces all *Bedürfnisse* to a common denominator and thus erroneously leads to the identification of Menger's derivation of "diminishing marginal value" with that of traditional diminishing marginal utility. What actually prompted him to use only one good in these examples is a problem for an intellectual biography. The focus here is on the analytic stucture of Menger's theory, and the use of only one, physically homogeneous, good suggests that in the construction of his examples, Menger ignored the *raison d'être* of his definition of economic homogeneity for the sake of expositional clarity and formal convenience. The cost proves extremely high for he actually fails to provide us with an algorithm for the calculation of value because, on the one hand, his demonstration of the derivation of the value of homogeneous goods is irrelevant for the task at hand and, on the other hand, the derivation of the value of heterogeneous goods is false.[193]

Menger's emphasis on the distinction between economic and physical aspects of goods and his definition of homogeneity as an economic concept lead to the classification of goods shown in Table III.1. The second of the four cases cannot arise. Physically homogeneous goods cannot be economically heterogeneous since they are all equally capable of satisfying one and the same *Bedürfnis* and thus have to be economically homogeneous by definition. It is, in fact, this latter case of physically and economically homogeneous goods (case I) which Menger analyses in the examples he uses to illustrate his derivation of the marginality principle. But the analytically relevant cases are clearly those of physically heterogeneous goods for why else should he introduce an explicitly economic concept of homogeneity as an assumption which, furthermore, he then proceeds to relax?[194] The case of physically heterogeneous goods which are economically homogeneous (III) is the one which he did not tackle but which he should have investigated for his solution to the problem of "simple" value. His entire theoretical edifice rests on physical heterogeneity: the lexicographic structure of *Bedürfnisse*, the absence of overall substitutability and the establishment of sub-optimal (in a universal sense) equilibrium positions of the individual owing to the absence of complete information and of frictionless and costless market adjustment.

Menger's neglect of case III leads to his failure to solve the case of "generalised" value, that of physically and economically heterogeneous goods (case IV), the test case for the success of his theory. He deals with this problem but fails to solve it, not least because he does not recognise his error in analysing case I instead of case III in the first place.

The confusions which occur at this fundamental level in Menger's *Grundsätze* should explain why his theory has hitherto been mistaken as a merely verbal statement of conventional, mathematical neo-classical theory. The resolution of these confusions demonstrates quite clearly some of the principal analytic differences between Menger's theory, on the one hand, and that originated by Walras and Jevons, on the other hand. More differences will surface in the discussion of the mapping of the Preference Set into the Commodity Set.

Mappings

In conventional neo-classical consumer theory, goods are transformed into utility. The utility function—or the equivalent set of axioms of the set-theoretic approach—provides the behavioural algorithm which allows this transformation to be carried out. The characteristic feature of this behavioural algorithm is the marginality principle, be it in the form of diminishing marginal utility, the diminishing marginal rate of substitution, or continuity and convex closure of the preferred set.[195]

As we have seen, Menger's approach can be conveniently dealt with in two separate steps. First, there is the mapping within the Preference Set, transforming *Bedürfnisse* into values, and second, there is the mapping from the Preference Set to the Commodity Set, which takes the values and assigns them to goods. Taking each mapping in turn, we first have to establish what kind of mapping leads from *Bedürfnisse* to values. Although Menger is silent on this particular issue, it is not entirely intractable and can be dealt with within the framework of the *Grundsätze*.

In any particular situation a *Bedürfnis* is expressed by its subjective degree of urgency. *Bedürfnis* and its urgency are introspectively indistinguishable. Depending on the respective subjective degree of urgency, a number will be assigned to a particular level of satisfaction of the *Bedürfnis* in question. This number is the value, and its calculation is based on the marginality principle.[196]

In principle, given the necessary information about the subjective degree of urgency and about preferences, tastes, etc., there should be no difficulty in calculating the numerical value for any concrete level of satisfaction of a *Bedürfnis*. Nor should there be any objections in principle to a reversal

Value

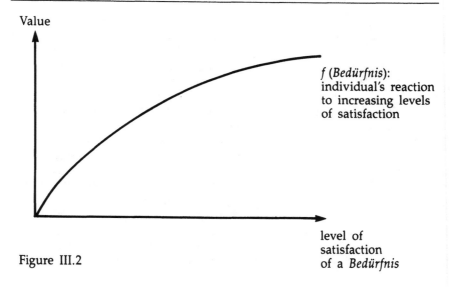

f (*Bedürfnis*):
individual's reaction
to increasing levels
of satisfaction

Figure III.2

level of
satisfaction
of a *Bedürfnis*

of this procedure (because *Bedürfnis* and value are introspectively indistinguishable). That is to say, values are calculated within the Preference Set in a fashion analogous with the traditional neo-classical approach outlined earlier (pp. 186–187). The difference is that, even though goods have not been brought into the discussion yet, a one-to-one function can already be said to exist which determines values, mapping each *Bedürfnis* onto the set of values; the more complete the level of satisfaction of the *Bedürfnis*, the lower the incremental value (see Figure III.2). The requirement of having information about the initial conditions does not pose any more of a problem than the same requirement of conventional utility theory. Therefore, according to the criterion stated at the outset, the representation of the transformation of *Bedürfnisse* into values by a single-valued, reversible function, Value = f(*Bedürfnis*), will be accepted as the mapping within the Preference Set.

Lest this be misunderstood, let me point out that this does not contradict my criticism of Menger's failure to take full account of his homogeneity concept nor does it ignore the hierarchical structure of *Bedürfnisse*. At this level of the argument, neither the homogeneity concept nor the lexicographic ordering are yet operative. The homogeneity concept does not yet apply because goods have not been introduced yet, and the lexicographic ordering of *Bedürfnisse* vanishes just as in the case of one homogeneous good precisely because of the absence of the differentiating element, namely, the physical heterogeneity of goods. A further consequence of the absence of goods from the argument is that the equivalence between Menger's function and the conventional neo-classical function is not yet complete. For complete formal equivalence of the two approaches, one ought to be able to reverse Menger's chain of argument which leads from *Bedürfnis* to goods via values. However, the next step, which should allow us to move from values to goods and vice versa, is not quite as simple and straightforward. We are now surrounded by a host of problems; not least among them is the divergence of Menger's pronouncements on the appropriate methods to be used from the one he actually employs.

According to Menger, goods acquire value by transference;[197] that is to say, the mapping from the Preference Set to the Commodity Set is transference (*Übertragung*) and quite literally so: Values are merely transferred (*Übertragen*) onto goods. Goods, then, merely act as pegs on which certain labels, namely values, are hung. No transformation or manipulation of the numerical values takes place in the course of this mapping. In the process of hanging onto these pegs nothing happens to the labels; they remain exactly as they were before the pegs entered the picture. Values, as pure numbers, are simply taken as they were derived in the Preference Set and are "transferred", or attributed, to the appropriate elements in the Commodity Set. This process of labelling has no effects on the values taken from the Preference Set. All the knowable repercussions of the elements in the Commodity Set on the elements in the Preference Set have already been taken care of in the process of value formation;[198] they are part of the influences shaping the "value function." This condition poses no special analytical problem for Menger: It does not matter whether the possible repercussions are correctly perceived or not because, as we have repeatedly seen, there is no assumption of complete information; instead, the concern is with learning processes which lead to accumulation of ever more correct information. Along this path consumers can still reach their (temporary) equilibrium positions relative to their individually and subjectively perceived constraints.

How can we represent this transference mapping formally? One possible way is to define an ordering and relations for the Commodity Set which faithfully reproduce events in the Preference Set. That is to say, we super-impose the structure of the Preference Set, i.e., its lexicographic ordering, complementarity, teleology, and ontological determination of these concepts, on the Commodity Set and its own structure. The Preference Set thus provides the boxes in which the elements of the Commodity Set are filed.

So much for the theory. Menger's practise, however, differs markedly from his theoretical prescriptions and postulates. The reason for this is well known by now: his conflation of an ordinal scale with the lexicographic ordering owing to his use of only one, universally employable, good in his demonstration of the derivation of value—in other words, his failure to demonstrate the relevant case of the classification of homogeneity concepts implicit in his theory.[199]

Because of this formal identification of the two preference orderings, his derivation of the marginality principle becomes formally indistinguishable from the conventional approach based on the principle of diminishing marginal utility. His arguments also run, conveniently for the identification with the conventional approach, from goods (corn, water) to degrees of satisfaction (value, or marginal utility) instead of deriving value first, merely by appealing to the satisfaction of *Bedürfnis*, and then transferring the value label onto a good (or a group of goods). Thus, the multidimensionality of

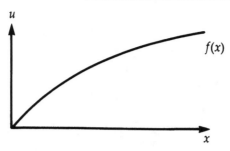

Figure III.3

his own concept of value is lost, the apposite complementarity of goods is not easily comprehensible, and the absence of overall substitutability necessitated by the lexicographic ordering is altogether hidden. Hence, there is no reason to object to the trinity formula of Menger-Jevons-Walras as the founders of neo-classical economics if Menger's illustrations are taken as the sole authoritative source for his theory. The only drawback of this position is that one cannot use it to make sense of Menger's professed methodology, of his famous letter to Walras[200] or of the *Grundsätze* as a coherent structure.

It is, however, instructive to pursue the idea of the formal identity of the conventional neo-classical approach with Menger's approach a little further. The concept of a one-to-one mapping relating goods to value (or its conventional analogue, utility) is not only compatible with Menger's general formulation of the theory of value but is explicitly introduced by him at the outset of his derivation of the marginality principle.[201] This appears to allow for a functional and diagrammatic representation of the relationship of goods to value along conventional lines, as in Figure III.3. Furthermore, the functional relationship depicted in that figure seems to be perfectly acceptable as representative of his entire theory of value if we ignore the confusion he introduced by assimilating the lexicographic preference structure to a conventional preference structure through the use of only one good and if we accept his examples in the chapter on value. *Prima facie*, then, the reinterpretation of Figure III.2 in terms of Figure III.3 ought to be fairly simple and straightforward.

However, immediately after introducing this point-to-point mapping Menger rejects it as too simple and too hypothetical an approach to be of any use in an analysis of the complexities of life.[202] He refuses to accept this special case as a satisfactory abstraction of the general situation. In terms of our representation of the Commodity Set, the special case of a one-to-one mapping of goods onto value can only be defined for sets of homogeneous goods, B^H, which have shrunk to single points. Furthermore, the Commodity Set would have to be a collection of disjoint subsets B^H with only one element each. But this is clearly not in accordance with the meaning of Menger's theory offered here, for why should he have introduced the concept

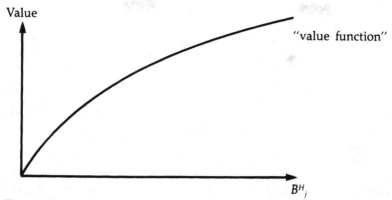

Figure III.4

of economic homogeneity? Obviously, the introduction of economic homogeneity explicitly creates the space for physical heterogeneity and thus for more than one good in the satisfaction of each *Bedürfnis*. Accordingly, in the general case, the sets B^H are to be considered to have more than one element each. Thus, in view of the existence of physically heterogeneous goods and of distinct *Bedürfnisse*, the re-interpretation of Figure III.2 along conventional lines seems not quite as straightforward as before. We shall, in fact, see that although it is possible to give some formal likeness to Figure III.2 in terms of Figure III.3, this formal likeness is substantively meaningless.

We have seen that Value = $f(Bedürfnis)$,[203] and we also know that the value of a good is simply that relationship transferred onto the Commodity Set, which naturally makes the value of a good a function of *Bedürfnis*. As the determination of this value proceeds unidirectionally from *Bedürfnis* via value to the value of goods, the argument of the function has to be *Bedürfnis* in one form or another. In view of the assumption of economic homogeneity, we can relate *Bedürfnis* only to a set of goods (B^H), not to any one good in particular (Menger's use of only one good in his examples notwithstanding). The only way to re-interpret Figure III.2 in terms of goods and values is, therefore, to construct something like Figure III.4 for each *Bedürfnis* j ($j = 1, \ldots, m$), where the graph of the "value function" represents the structure of the determination of the value of a unit of the elements in B^H_j, i.e., the marginality principle of Figure III.2. Thus, the units of measurement along the abscissa are only definable in terms of each *Bedürfnis* j (but there is no objection why these units should not be cardinally measurable) which renders individual goods indistinguishable from each other.

Is Figure III.4 meaningful in the sense that we can extract substantively useful information from the functional relationship depicted there? To be more specific: Does it enable us to compute individual- or market-demand functions? Unfortunately, no. Even if we ignore some fundamental objections—that it is logically inadmissible to compare differences of ordinal variables; that, in Menger's theory, demand functions are methodologically properly located within the sphere of prices and not the sphere of values— the mapping of goods into value in Figure III.4 is an economically meaningless exercise because it is impossible to identify the value of a specific good within B^H and relate that good to its market price because individual goods cannot be isolated and unambiguously identified on the basis of the information available. The derivation of demand functions along, say, Marshallian lines is impossible within the framework of Menger's theory.[204] As soon as we take the ordinal character of Menger's concept of value into account, Figure III.4 becomes inadmissible in any case. Not surprisingly, the Slutzky-Hicks-Allen approach is of no help in the derivation of Menger's demand functions either because Menger's lexicographic preference ordering rules out convex and continuous indifference loci for the marginality principle to operate in the form of the diminishing marginal rate of substitution.[205]

In summary, because of lexicographic preferences, because of the impossibility of identifying individual goods along the abscissa and because of the ordinal character of Menger's value function, it is not possible to retain the characteristic features of both the Commodity Set and the Preference Set in constructing the mappings within the Preference Set and from the Preference Set to the Commodity Set which remain faithful to Menger's analytic intentions and, at the same time, allow us to assimilate his value theory, as interpreted here, to conventional neo-classical theory. The difference in formulation of the "fundamental economic problem" encountered at the outset turns out not only to have produced fundamental analytic differences but also to represent fundamentally distinct neo-classical visions of the economic process out of which these analytic differences arose.

Extensions of Neo-Classical Theory

During the 1950s and 1960s, extensions of the traditional neo-classical approach were developed because of a desire to make the theory more operational for the investigation of demand relationships.[206] These extensions came to be known as separability of the utility function (or of preferences) and the goods-characteristics or consumption-technology approach, and they concentrated on restrictions imposed on the form of the utility function and the technical aspects of consumption, respectively.

The basic assumptions on which a utility function can be called separable are that the arguments of the function (commodities) can unambiguously be separated into disjoint subsets and that changes in the marginal rate of substitution between two goods in any one group are independent of changes in demand for any good outside this group.[207] It is then possible to devise subutility functions for each group (or subset) of commodities and to combine the values of each of these subutilities to derive total utility. Various types of separable functions have been constructed, but it suffices for our purposes to look at the least-restrictive hypothesis, that of weak separability (a necessary condition to be satisfied by any kind of separable function), to see that there is no hope of using this hypothesis to overcome the problems posed by Menger's lexicographic preference structure and by the implications of his concept of economic homogeneity—i.e., the incommensurability and unidentifiability of goods—which prevent the integration of his theory into the traditional neo-classical framework.

First, any suggestion of grouping commodities in accordance with the (ontologically given) hierarchy of *Bedürfnisse* and circumventing the problems in this way is misconceived precisely because the ranks of the hierarchy are not additive and no single-valued total function can be constructed (there is, however, no objection in principle to constructing a set of unrelated subutility functions apart from the meaninglessness of such an operation). Second, the arguments of Menger's "value function" are *Bedürfnisse* and not goods; goods remain unidentifiable, and hence the basic separability criterion, the independence of changes in the marginal rate of substitution from changes in demand for non-group goods, cannot be satisfied as no marginal rates of substitution can be derived. Third, separability by definition rules out complementarity among subgroups, but overall complementarity is precisely what characterises Menger's hierarchy of *Bedürfnisse*. Finally, the condition that each good can be a member of only one group or subset also stands in opposition to Menger's theory as, for Menger, a good can generally be used to satisfy several different *Bedürfnisse*; it was to overcome the problem posed by this assumption that Menger had to introduce the concepts of economic homogeneity and heterogeneity.

Although the separability hypothesis is a dead end as far as the integration of mainstream neo-classical thought and Menger's theory is concerned, the literature on the separability hypothesis shows the extent to which a rapprochement between these two approaches can be achieved along the lines of the separability argument. If we formulate both the traditional approach and Menger's approach in terms of Robbins's means-ends definition of economics,[208] the most fundamental difference between these two approaches can be identified very easily: the single-valuedness of traditional theory and the multi-valuedness of Menger's theory. To start off with, traditional neo-classical utility is single-valued while Menger's concept of value (for simplicity's sake equated to utility here) is multi-valued—that is, we are facing linearly ordered preferences versus lexicographically ordered preferences. Looking at the mechanism used in producing utility we find, in Menger's case, a multitude of means satisfying a multitude of ends (i.e., *Bedürfnisse*): any one good is generally assumed to be able to satisfy several different *Bedürfnisse*, and any one *Bedürfnis* is, in general, satisfiable by several physically heterogeneous goods.

The relationship between means and ends in traditional utility theory can fruitfully be approached through Morishima's formalisation[209] of Hicks's remarks on Menger in *A Revision of Demand Theory*.[210] Morishima discusses the view "that the consumer chooses between certain objectives and then decides between alternative means of achieving these objectives."[211] From our point of view, the most important assumption which he introduces is that each good contributes to only one objective but that each objective

Table III.2. Two Versions of Utility Theory

Traditional Neo-Classical Theory	Menger's Theory
Single-valued utility	Multi-valued utility (single-valuedness introduced by Menger by default— see discussion of homogeneity)
Single-valued means-ends relationship (i.e., means-ends identity):	Multi-valued means-ends relationship: (single-valued mean-ends relationship introduced as special case but dismissed as too unrepresentative)
One good ◄──► one end (*Bedürfnis*)	Multitude of goods for a multitude of *Bedürfnisse* (ends)
	i.e.:
	(i) One good ──► several *Bedürfnisse*
	(ii) One *Bedürfnis* ◄── several goods
Morishima-Hicks Extension:	
(i) one good ──► one end (traditional)	
(ii) One end ◄── several goods (Menger)	

can be achieved by several different goods (or "utility production processes") so that the number of goods exceeds the number of objectives.

Morishima's analysis establishes that "the traditional consumer theory tacitly assumes that each objective is itself a means of reaching it."[212] The single-valuedness of the means-ends relationship is therefore a postulate in traditional theory; it is, in terms of the Morishima-Hicks theory, a means-ends identity. The Morishima-Hicks extension of the traditional theory retains one aspect of the single-valuedness of the means-ends relationship by restricting each good to serve only one end (or *Bedürfnis*, in Menger's terminology).[213] But at the same time, in order to be able to talk about "utility production", the Morishima-Hicks theory extends the traditional case to embrace Menger's conception by allowing for the achievement of any one objective (satisfaction of *Bedürfnis*) by several different goods (as depicted in Table III.2). Morishima's results, based on Hicks(1956), constitute a halfway house between Hicks's *Value and Capital* and Menger and indirectly confirm my conclusion that traditional neo-classical utility theory has to be regarded as a special, very restrictive, but analytically and formally less complex case of the more comprehensive Austrian theory, at least as far as Menger's version of it is concerned.

The situation is different, however, when we come to consider the consumption-technology approach. This approach to utility maximisation came to be associated with the name of Kelvin Lancaster in the mid-1960s,[214] but it is not Lancaster's work which I shall be discussing but that of Duncan Ironmonger who first developed a theory in the late 1950s which is in many respects very similar to that of Lancaster.[215] Ironmonger's version of consumer technology not only allows us to derive all the basic well-known results of the traditional neo-classical theory of household behaviour but also explicitly takes into account a hierarchical want structure which is akin to Menger's lexicographic structure of *Bedürfnisse*. Lancaster, on the other hand, retains the traditional preference structure which guarantees the existence of an ordinal utility function with positive first order partial derivatives.[216] The only drawback of Ironmonger's theory is that its formal representation is more cumbersome and complicated than the mathematical elegance of *Value-and-Capital* versions of consumer theory.[217]

One of Ironmonger's aims is to integrate the treatment of new commodities and of changes in the qualities of commodities into the neo-classical theory of consumer behaviour. In the development of his theory he is forced to jettison the assumption that "commodities serve directly to produce utility (happiness)" and also the concept of the continuity of preferences and reformulate consumer theory on the basis of two different assumptions: (1) commodities serve directly to satisfy separate wants and (2) individuals' preferences between wants are hierarchically ordered.[218] The consumer has to "find a budget which maximises the satisfaction of his marginal want subject to the restrictions that his supra-marginal wants are satiated and expenditure does not exceed income."[219]

Let me briefly present Ironmonger's assumptions to see how he arrives at his formulation of the fundamental economic problem. Wants exist independent of commodities (i.e., goods and services),[220] and utility is not a function of commodities but of want satisfaction:[221]

$$U = U(z_1, z_2, \ldots , z_m),$$

where z_i denotes the number of units of satisfaction of want i obtained per unit of time. If there are two or more wants, then they can be satisfied either jointly or separately[222] depending on the commodities' physical properties. Initially, in the case of one want and one or two commodities, utility is maximised by taking price-efficiency and want-satisfaction-efficiency of commodities into account.[223] However, as soon as the case of two wants and two commodities is considered, a determinate solution can no longer be guaranteed. Some assumptions about preferences become necessary.[224]

To ensure determinateness of solutions of the maximisation problem, Ironmonger allows for local satiation of wants combined with general non-saturation. That is to say, although individual wants can be fully satisfied, there are always more wants than can be satisfied given a finite level of income. Since solutions to the maximisation problem are only of interest as long as there is an economic problem to be solved, this assumption on satiation implies the existence of a system of priorities among wants. It is assumed that these priorities are well-ordered so that, in any situation, there exists only one marginal want.[225] The assumption of well-ordered priorities together with the necessary satiation levels results in the hierarchy principle of wants, which gives preferences a structure that is very similar to the lexicographic ordering.[226] The traditional utility function is therefore reformulated as

$$U = U(z_1, \ldots, z_m)$$

and has the following properties:

$$U = U_1(z_1) \quad \text{where } 0 \leqslant z_1 < z^*_1, \quad \frac{\partial U_1}{\partial z_1} > 0$$

$$\text{and } 0 \leqslant z_2, \ldots, 0 \leqslant z_m \text{ with}$$

$$\frac{\partial U_i}{\partial z_i} = 0 \text{ for } i = 2, \ldots, m;$$

$$U = U_2(z_2) \quad \text{where } z_1 \geqslant z^*_1, \ 0 \leqslant z_2 < z^*_2,$$

$$\frac{\partial U_2}{\partial z_2} > 0,$$

$$\text{and } 0 \leqslant z_3, \ldots, 0 \leqslant z_m \text{ with}$$

$$\frac{\partial U_i}{\partial z_i} = 0 \text{ for } i = 1 \text{ and } i = 3, \ldots, m;$$

$$\cdots \cdots \cdots \cdots$$

$$U = U_m(z_m) \quad \text{where } z_1 \geqslant z^*_1, \ z_2 \geqslant z^*_2, \ldots$$

$$\ldots, z_{m-1} \geqslant z^*_{m-1}, \ 0 \leqslant z_m < z^*_m,$$

$$\frac{\partial U_m}{\partial z_m} > 0,$$

$$\text{and } \frac{\partial U_i}{\partial z_i} = 0 \text{ for } i = 1, 2, \ldots, m-1,$$

with z^*_i denoting the satiation level of want i. A consequence of the hierarchy principle of wants is the absence of indifference among wants.[227] The possibility or impossibility of indifference among commodities does not enter here because the arguments of the utility function are want satisfactions and not commodities, as we have seen.

Commodities are goods and services (x_j, $j = 1, \ldots , n$), and many of them have overlapping or similar functions[228] so that the consumer must exercise some choice. Commodities have different objective and subjective want-satisfying powers or qualities. Objective qualities (their technical nature) are their physical ability to satisfy particular wants. Subjective qualities spring from the nature of the wants they serve; they are the consumer's valuations of their effectiveness in serving these wants. Objective and subjective qualities are inseparable, but the links between wants and commodities are given by the subjective qualities. Qualities are regarded as fixed and completely specify the consumer's technology. In exchange for commodities the consumer gives money income. The model excludes the possibilities of barter, arbitrage or bargaining between individual consumers and suppliers.[229]

The consumer is assumed to have full knowledge of his income (y), all prices (p_j, $j = 1, \ldots , n$), his wants and his technology, denoting by his consumer technology coefficient w_{ij} the number of units of satisfaction of want i obtained from consuming one unit of commodity j. No expectations or knowledge of future periods are assumed; choice is made only for the current period.[230]

On the basis of these assumptions, we can now formulate the general maximisation problem. In order to find the optimum budget, we have to maximise the satisfaction of the marginal want subject to the constraints that all prior wants have been satisfied in their numerical order,[231] subject to the income constraint and subject to the constraint that goods are non-negative.

There are m wants. Let $i < m$ be the marginal want, and let $\mathbf{x}$ be a column vector whose elements are the commodities x_j ($j = 1, \ldots , n$), $\mathbf{p}$ a column vector of n commodity prices, $\mathbf{W}$ the ($m \times n$) consumer technology matrix, $\mathbf{w}_i$ the i-th row of the consumer technology matrix, and $\mathbf{z}^*_i$ a column vector of the satiation levels of wants $1, \ldots , i$. The optimal budget is then found by solving the following linear programming problem:[232]

Find x such that

$$z_i = \mathbf{w}_i \, \mathbf{x} = \text{max.}$$

subject to the constraints

$$\mathbf{W}_{i\text{-}1} \, \mathbf{x} > \mathbf{z}^*_{i\text{-}1}$$
$$- \mathbf{p}' \, \mathbf{x} > - y$$
$$\mathbf{x} > 0.$$

Let $\mathbf{s}$ be a column vector of shadow (or imputed) prices. The solution to the dual of the above linear programming problem is obtained by finding $\mathbf{s}$ such that

$$z_i = [\ - \ \mathbf{z}_{i\text{-}1} \mid y \ ] \ \mathbf{s} = \min.$$

subject to the constraints

$$[\ - \ \mathbf{W}'_{i\text{-}1} \mid \mathbf{p} \ ] \ \mathbf{s} > \mathbf{w}_i$$

$$\mathbf{s} > 0.^{233}$$

A fundamentally important result derived by Ironmonger is that there will always be a unique solution to the maximisation problem. There will always exist an optimal, efficient budget.[234]

This is the basic model which Ironmonger develops for his analysis of new commodities and of changes in the qualities of commodities. As presented here, it is fairly simplistic and does not take into account, for instance, Ironmonger's extensions to cover consumer durables (all commodities are treated as perishables here) and complementarity of wants.[235] This basic model is, however, perfectly sufficient to show which steps would have to be taken for a formalisation of the analytical arguments underlying Menger's economic process. Menger's definition of commodities is largely upheld in Ironmonger's scheme: The conditions of want satisfying objective properties of commodities, of the consumer's knowledge of these properties and of the availability of commodities for the satisfaction of a *Bedürfnis* as well as that of the existence of *Bedürfnisse* are met.[236] Ironmonger's consumer technology not only combines the commodities' objective properties (qualities) with the consumer's subjective valuations (the commodities' subjective qualities) but also allows for the same classification of homogeneity cases as we encountered earlier.[237] The link between Menger's Preference Set and Commodity Set is given here by the subjective qualities which are firmly enshrined in the consumer technology matrix linking commodities to wants.

As with Menger's *Bedürfnisse,* Ironmonger's wants are independent of commodities. The separation between Menger's Preference Set and Commodity Set is reflected in Ironmonger's separation between wants and commodities. Ironmonger's hierarchy principle of wants closely resembles Menger's lexicographically ordered structure of *Bedürfnisse.* Menger's subjective value is preserved in Ironmonger's subjective qualities of commodities.

Ironmonger states quite clearly why he thinks that the hierarchy principle of wants is superior to the traditional neo-classical preference structure. The assumptions on which the traditional theory is built are so general that the preference structure derived from them is able to accommodate any kind of behaviour other than inconsistent behaviour.[238] But not only does the narrower scope of Ironmonger's—or Menger's—preference structure enhance its explanatory power or scientific acceptability, it also highlights the loss of substantive contents of the foundations of current neo-classical orthodoxy which ensued when the convex and continuous indifference map was adopted.

When we compare what traditional consumer theory has to say about the issues of choice and allocation with what Menger or Ironmonger say, then we find, not surprisingly, that modern theory is very far removed indeed from Robbins's definition of economics as "the science which studies human behaviour as a relationship between ends and scarce means which have alternative uses",[239] notwithstanding the fact that this definition is still regarded as standard. In the one case (Menger/Ironmonger), there is choice among wants leading to the allocation of commodities to want-satisfying activities and of money income to commodities. Indeed, we find scarce means being allocated among alternative uses. The problem of choice among different wants, i.e., among different uses to which a commodity can be put, cannot be solved purely within the model, but both Menger and Ironmonger have found their own way out of this dilemma. Menger has his structure of *Bedürfnisse* ontologically determined, and Ironmonger adopts a strict hierarchy of wants (with only one marginal want at a time) and reduces all want-satisfying capabilities of commodities to joint satisfaction.[240]

In the second case (traditional neo-classical theory, including Lancaster's version of consumption technology), there is no choice among different uses, or competing ends, because there is only one end—utility. All wants have disappeared into this one index number. There is some choice among commodities, but this choice is really synonymous with the allocation of money income to commodities. But this is not surprising because we are simply back at the ends-means identity discussed earlier.[241] Thus, the original choice and allocation problem has been reduced to rational allocation of money income under absence of choice.

Adopting Ironmonger's system as the basis for the formalisation of Menger's economic analysis imposes certain restrictions on Menger's economic process. These restrictions are entirely owing to the application of linear programming as a tool and are not required by the subject matter analysed—the economic world. In particular, the linearity of the consumer technology imposes constant returns to scale. This may not be problematical when applied to objective qualities of commodities, but it certainly would contradict the fundamental principle underlying the formation of Menger's subjective value, namely, that subjective value is diminishing at the margin. As Ironmonger's subjective qualities of commodities are his equivalent of Menger's subjective values, this formal restriction is unacceptable. Furthermore, the model is only capable of handling perfect competition. Monopolistic situations, in which quantity can depend on price or on exogenous factors, thus opening the door to indeterminacy, are ruled out. But it is precisely the consistently subjective nature of Menger's value concept which makes the imposition of a perfect competition assumption superfluous for the analytics of the value discussion and also makes it inconsistent with Menger's discussion of the determination of prices which commences with the case of bi-lateral monopoly.

Furthermore, in contrast to Menger's theory, Ironmonger's model is characterised by the absence of uncertainty and expectations. Ironmonger's consumers are concerned only with maximisation of want satiation in the current period based on full information of all the relevant variables.[242] The fact that this is in direct contrast to the basic thrust of Menger's entire theory, which has uncertainty and the quest for information at its core, does not really need to be mentioned again. However, the fact that Ironmonger's analysis covers only the current period could also be regarded as a redeeming feature when viewed from the perspective of Menger's theory: As opposed to the individual in modern general equilibrium theory, Ironmonger's consumer at least does not have to claim complete information about all future, past and present values of the relevant variables.

Still, Ironmonger's basic model—combining as it does the subjective and objective determinants of the individual's consumption decision, which are linked by the consumer technology matrix, with the hierarchy of wants and with scarcity expressed by the income constraint—is the one extension of traditional neo-classical theory which comes closest to most of the original analytic intentions embodied in Menger's theory. Ironmonger also shows us the direction in which the derivation and discussion of individual- and market-demand functions have to proceed. Apart from the fact that there are no longer any smooth curves or expansion paths to be found, we also have to bear in mind that here we are dealing with two spaces—the want space and the commodity space—whereas conventional neo-classical theory deals with one space only—the commodity space. This means that Engel curves and income and substitution effects now have to be derived for wants and for commodities. In addition, income and substitution effects are now derived not only for changes in prices of commodities but also for changes in qualities of commodities and for new commodities.[243] Most important, here, unlike in general equilibrium theory, it is not the case that everything depends on everything else.[244] Price changes of commodities which affect only submarginal or supra-marginal wants do not usually have any effect on the optimal budget. The derivation of individual and market demand functions is discussed in detail by Ironmonger, and there is no need to reproduce that argument.[245]

Ironmonger's approach thus provides us with the means to derive a restricted formal solution to Menger's problem. One of the aims of this essay, however, was to try and obtain a solution which remains faithful to Menger's theory, a solution which not only solves the formal aspect of his problem but also contains the substance of his theory. Hence, in addition to Ironmonger's restricted formal solution, the solution sought ought to encompass not only those elements which are not dealt with in the Ironmonger case but also Menger's differentiation between values and prices by allowing room for Menger's epistemological and methodological apparatus. The consequences of such an approach are, of course, immediately obvious. In the first place, the formal solution provided deals only with Menger's realm of values; thus, the derived schedules can only be "requirement" schedules, not "demand" schedules.[246] Second, and more important, to arrive at a solution in terms of prices and quantities, that is, to derive demand schedules, Menger's transformation problem has to be solved. This is impossible as long as we want to adhere to the whole corpus of his theory, above all to his epistemology, his essentialism and to his brand of subjective value.[247]

In conclusion not only can we see quite clearly the elements which set Menger's theory off from the modern neo-classical approach and from the theories developed by Jevons and Walras, we also have in front of us a list of elements of his theory which have to be left behind if the remaining ones are to be re-combined into an alternative neo-classical approach. The choice of those which will have to be abandoned, however, will depend entirely on the vision of the economic process of the people who make this decision. Two examples of such a selection are discussed briefly in the Epilogue.

Notes

Menger's Theory of Value and German Political Economy

1. "Die Grundlage aller wirthschaftlichen Betrachtung ist die Lehre vom Werthe", says Friedländer in 1852—a wrong theory of value would lead to erroneous theorising about the economy and to wrong conclusions for economic policy; see Friedländer(1852), pp. 4–5.

2. "Gut", Menger(1871), p. 2 [Menger(1950/1981), pp. 286–288].

3. "Das Wesen der ökonomischen Güter", Menger(1871), pp. 53–55 [Menger(1950/1981), pp. 288–291].

4. "Vermögen", Menger(1871), pp. 70–71 [Menger(1950/1981), pp. 291–292].

5. "Werth", Menger(1871), pp. 78–80 [Menger(1950/1981), pp. 292–295].

6. "Der Masstab des Güterwerthes", Menger(1871), pp. 108–113 [Menger(1950/1981), pp. 295–302].

7. "Capital", Menger(1871), pp. 130–132 [Menger(1950/1981), pp. 303–305].

8. "Preis", Menger(1871), p. 173 [Menger(1950/1981), pp. 305–306].

9. "Gebrauchswerth und Tauschwerth", Menger(1871), pp. 215–216 [Menger(1950/1981), pp. 306–308].

10. "Waare", Menger(1871), pp. 229–231 [Menger(1950/1981), pp. 309–312].

11. "Geld", Menger(1871), pp. 255–260 [Menger(1950/1981), pp. 315–320].

12. "Eine tiefergehende Behandlung hat die Frage nach dem Masse des Gebrauchswerthes indess erst bei den Deutschen gefunden." Menger(1871), p. 108 n. [Menger(1950/1981), p. 297].

13. "Nichts zeigt übrigens das Streben nach philosphischer Vertiefung der Volkswirthschaftslehre bei den Deutschen und den auf das practische gerichteten Sinn der Engländer besser, als etwa eine Vergleichung der Bearbeitung, welche die Lehre vom Werthe bei den Deutschen und den Engländern gefunden hat" Menger(1871), p. 216 n. [Menger(1950/1981), p. 317]. In the same vein: "Die Lehre von der Waare hat bei den Engländern, Franzosen und Italienern mit einzelnen Ausnahmen überhaupt keine selbständige Bearbeitung gefunden." Menger(1871) 229 n. [Menger(1950/1981), p. 309].

14. Menger(1871), pp. 78–80 and 108–113, respectively [Menger(1950/1981), pp. 292–295 and 295–302].

15. Menger(1871), p. x [Menger(1950/1981), p. 49].

16. See Essay II, pp. 131–132.

17. I was able to consult most of the works cited by Menger in the same editions which he had used. Financial constraints made it impossible to consult Menger's own copies which are kept at the Hitotsubashi University in Tokyo. For an intellectual biography, however, a visit to this library would be indispensable, especially for a

consultation of his copies of Friedländer, Kudler and Rossi as far as value theory is concerned. More will be said about these authors below.

18. See Friedländer(1852), e.g., pp. 7, 57, where at crucial points in his own development of the theory of value Hegel's *Grundlinien der Philosophie des Rechts* is given prominence. See also his repeated references to "ethisch-philosophische Grundlagen der staatswissenschaftlichen Forschungen" as a basis for an "objective theory" of use-value.

19. Friedländer(1852), p. 58; similarly, Rau treats prices as different from, and as less fundamental than, values; Rau(1837), p. 68.

20. "Wesen und Werth eines Gutes ist auf das menschliche Bedürfnis gegründet" Knies(1855), p. 433.

21. See Rau(1837), p. 56 para. 55; cf. also Knies(1855), pp. 423, 428; Friedländer(1852), *passim*.

22. "Das Studium des Aristoteles, so vorübergehend er wirthschaftlichen Betrachtungen seine Aufmerksamkeit zuwendet, hätte davor bewahren können, der Berücksichtigung des Gebrauchswerths nicht die gehörige Aufmerksamkeit zu schenken" Friedländer(1852), p. 12. This statement occurs towards the end of Friedländer's review of Adam Smith's contribution to value theory.

23. Aristotle is cited six times, Adam Smith nine times. The leader in this league is Wilhelm Roscher who has fourteen entries in the index to the *Grundsätze*. These figures have to be seen in relation to the fact that the *Grundsätze* contains only eleven major footnotes in which economic literature is reviewed.

24. Friedländer(1852), pp. 9–10.

25. Cf. Rau(1837), p. 147.

26. "Die Erkenntnis des Nutzens schafft ihn nicht; auch unerkannt ist er da. Die Betrachtung des Verhältnisses der Dinge zum Menschen führt von dem des Nutzens zu dem des Werths über. Der Werth ist allerdings Ausdruck des Nutzens der Dinge in ihrem Verhältnis zum menschlichen Bedürfnis, *aber nicht bloss wissenschaftlicher Ausdruck, sondern Ausdruck jeder auch nicht wissenschaftlichen Erkenntnis dieses Verhältnisses, sogar im unklaren Bewusstsein, im Instinkt*" Friedländer(1852), p. 40 (emphasis added).

27. See Essay I, pp. 41–42.

28. "Hiernach stellt sich eine Classification und Stufenleiter der menschlichen Bedürfnisse ein, mit welcher eine Classification und Stufenleiter der Gütergattungen correspondiert. Es stellen sich neben und nach einander auf die Güter zur Befriedigung des Nahrungsbedürfnisses—selbst wieder in sich gegliedert, aber hier nur nach der Stärke des menschlichen Begehrens nach den Notwendigeren und Entbehrlicheren—des Bekleidungsbedürfnisses usw." Knies(1855), p. 429. The section immediately preeceding this quotation is cited by Menger in his footnote on the measure of value; see Menger(1871), p. 111 n. [Menger(1950/1981), pp. 299–300].

29. See p. 172 and pp. 189–191.

30. See Rau(1837), pp. 2, 5.

31. "Es ist somit der Werth die Bedeutung, welche concrete Güter oder Güterquantitäten für uns dadurch erlangen, dass wir in der Befriedigung unserer Bedürfnisse von der Verfügung über dieselben abhängig zu sein uns bewusst sind" Menger(1871), p. 78 [Menger(1950/1981), p. 115].

32. Menger(1871), p. 79 n. [Menger(1950/1981), pp. 293–294].

33. See Rau(1837), p. 61 and also p. 56; similarly Friedländer(1852), p. 49 and pp. 7–8. The references to Friedländer are not to Friedländer's review of the literature but to his own development of the theory.

34. See, e.g., Rau(1837), pp. 59, 68; Knies(1855), pp. 423, 428.

35. See Riedel—*Nationalökonomie*, 2 vols. (Berlin: 1838); quoted from Friedländer(1852), p. 39. Menger refers to Riedel in (1871), p. 230 [Menger(1950/1981), p. 311].

36. Menger(1871), p. 110 n. [Menger(1950/1981), pp. 298–299].

37. Rau(1837), p. 61.

38. Knies(1855), pp. 441, 462.

39. Knies(1855), p. 434.

40. In fact, he still ascribes value to abundant goods; see Friedländer(1852), p. 50.

41. Friedländer(1852), p. 10.

42. Friedländer here refers to the use of utility and scarcity as joint elements in Lauderdale's discussion of the formation of private wealth; Friedländer(1852), pp. 14, 16.

43. Friedländer(1852), pp. 20–21. Turgot's discussion of subjective value in relationship to scarcity is not really surprising as he owed a great deal with respect to this subject to Ferdinando Galiani who had developed an almost complete subjective theory of value in his *Della Moneta*. It is incomplete only because Galiani did not have the concept of the margin. Menger does refer to one of the relevant passages in *Della Moneta*; see Menger(1871), p. 108 n. [Menger(1950/1981), pp. 295–297].

44. See Knies(1855), p. 430 (also n.46, below).

45. Rau(1837), p. 61 n. and also p. 67 where Rau quite explicitly develops the notion, though obviously he does not use the term, of diminishing marginal utility of money.

46. Knies does indeed provide such a chain of reasoning, though without explicitly hitting on the concept of the margin: "Welche Stufensprosse auf der Scala des Gebrauchswerthes die einzelnen Gütergattungen einnehmen, können wir am besten abschätzen, wenn wir uns die Frage vorlegen: in welcher Reihenfolge würden die Menschen sich mit den Gütergattungen für Genuss and Erwerb versehen, wenn sie von allem Güterbesitze entblösst wären. Oder: in welcher Reihenfolge würden sie umgekehrt auf den Fortgebrauch verzichten, wenn sie im Besitz aller gedacht werden. Es ist daher erheblich zu vermerken, dass nur die Stärke des Bedürfnisses in dem Einzelnen und die Stärke der Verbreitung unter den Einzelnen hier die Grösse des Gebrauchswerthes bestimmt, in keiner Weise aber die Voraussetzung, dass man zur Befriedigung des Bedürfnisses einer grösseren Quantität von Gütern einer Gattung benöthigt sei" Knies(1855), p. 430.

47. Friedländer(1852), pp. 24–26.

48. Rossi, P.—*Cours d'economie politique*. Tom. 1–3. Ed. rev. et corr. Brux. 1851–2. 3 vols. in 1. Fr. 1317. and—*Cours d'economie politique*. 2. ed., rev. et corr., Par. 1843–54. 4 vols. Fr. 1318–entries from the catalogue of Menger's books kept at the Hitotsubashi University; see Menger(1926), p. 660.

49. See Menger(1871) p. 78 n. (the footnote on value) [Menger(1950/1981), pp. 292–293], and p. 110 n. (the footnote on the *measure of value*) [Menger(1950/1981), pp. 298–299].

50. Friedländer(1852), pp. 24–25, summarising P. Rossi—*Cours d'economie politique* (Bruxelles: 1846).

51. See Kauder(1959) and (1962). In these two articles, Kauder puts great emphasis on Kudler's influence on the formation of Menger's thought, though he neglects to mention Friedländer who, after all, was there for everyone to see. That Friedländer was important for Menger is stated in Kauder(1965), but neither there nor in the two previous articles does Kauder actually compare the theories and concepts of Kudler and Friedländer with those of Menger's *Grundsätze*, not to mention with the

formative stages of Menger's theory and concepts. To enter into a discussion of these issues, though, is beyond the scope of this study.

52. Although Menger did not do so in the first edition of the *Grundsätze*, the second, posthumously published edition contains a new first chapter where Menger develops a theory of *Bedürfnisse* discussing the nature of *Bedürfnisse* and their importance for economic theory. See also above, pp. 121–131.

53. See Kudler(1846), pp. 49–58.

54. Kudler(1846), pp. 58–59.

55. Kudler(1846), p. 84.

56. Kudler(1846), pp. 65 ff.

Menger's Theory of Value

57. Menger's economic theory has been discussed in most histories of economic theory and also by a number of authors cited in the analytical section of this essay. I shall not repeat these references here. The following list of authors is intended to give an impression of the breadth of treatment Menger's theory has been afforded: *Atlantic Economic Journal*(1978); H.-S. Bloch(1937) and (1940); Bonar(1888); Brems(1962); Cuhel(1907); Engländer(1927); Hayek(1968); Hicks and Weber (eds.) (1973); Jaffé(1976); Kauder(1958), (1959), (1962), (1965); Knight(1950); Kraus(1937); Macvane(1893); K. Menger(1923); Perlmutter(1902); Pirou(1938); Rattner- Rappaport(n.d.); Ruppe-Streissler(1963); Schumpeter(1921); Smart(1891); Stigler(1937); Streissler(1969) and (1972); Weiss(1924); Wicksell(1924); Zuckerkandl(1910). Needless to say, this list is far from complete. Above all, it excludes any of the theoretical or methodological writings of members of the Austrian school itself which evaluates, or builds on, the foundations laid by Menger. This would require a study of its own.

58. See the editor's introduction to Menger(1923), pp. v–x.

59. "Keine seiner Theorien von 1871 hat jedoch mein Vater in einem wesentlichen Punkt einer Änderung zu unterwerfen sich genötigt gesehen, ein Umstand, den er ausdrücklich zu betonen gedachte." "Von allem, was nach der ersten Auflage dieses Buches publiziert wurde, vermochte nichts den Autor der *Grundsätze* zu Modifikationen seiner Ideen zu bewegen, weder die zahlreichen Kritiken, die an seinen Lehren von Gegnern geübt wurden, noch die Weiterbildungen, welche sie durch Anhänger und Schüler erfahren haben, und auch diesen Umstand gedacht er ausdrücklich zu betonen." Menger(1923), pp. x, xvii.

60. Menger(1923), pp. v–xviii.

61. Most useful in this respect is the review by Weiss(1924). For other reviews, see Engländer(1927) and Wicksell(1924).

62. "Geplant, aber nicht ausgeführt wurde . . . eine Bemerkung, welche die Verbindung von Wert- und Preislehre herstellen sollte" Menger(1923), p. XVII.

63. See pp. 126–130 above.

64. This is repeatedly stated in the preface to the *Grundsätze*; see Menger(1871), pp. vii, ix, x [Menger(1950/1981), pp. 47–49].

65. We recall that, for Menger, "exact" theory was determinate, true and immediately known; see the discussion in Essay II, pp. 104–112.

66. "Die theoretische Volkswirthschaftslehre beschäftigt sich nicht mit praktischen Vorschlägen für das wirthschaftliche Handeln, sondern mit den Bedingungen, unter welchen die Menschen die auf die Befriedigung ihrer Bedürfnisse gerichtete vorsorgliche Thätigkeit entfalten." That is to say: "Ob und unter welchen Bedingungen ein Ding mir nützlich, ob und unter welchen Bedingungen es ein Gut, ob und unter welchen Bedingungen es ein wirthschaftliches Gut, ob und unter welchen Bedingungen dasselbe Werth für mich hat, und wie gross das Mass dieses Werthes für mich ist, ob und

unter welchen Bedingungen ein ökonomischer Austausch von Gütern zwischen zwei wirthschaftenden Subjecten statthaben, und die Grenzen, innerhalb welcher die Preisbildung hiebei erfolgen kann" Menger(1871), p. ix [Menger(1950/1981), p. 48].

67. Menger(1871), pp. 1–31 [Menger(1950/1981), pp. 51–76].

68. See Karl Menger in Menger(1923), pp. vii–ix.

69. Menger(1923), p. 1.

70. See Essay I, pp. 44–45, and Essay II, p. 121.

71. Menger(1871), pp. 32–76 [Menger(1950/1981), pp. 77–113].

72. The concept of *Bedarf* expresses the general requirements which human beings have for goods and services for the satisfaction of their *Bedürfnisse*. This concept must not be confused with that of demand (*Nachfrage*); the latter is an economic category, and at this particular stage in the development of his argument Menger has not yet introduced the economic point of view.

73. See Menger(1871), pp. 39–45 [Menger(1950/1981), pp. 84–87].

74. See Menger(1871), p. 51 [Menger(1950/1981), p. 94].

75. Menger(1871), pp. 67–70 [Menger(1950/1981), pp. 106–109].

76. Menger(1871), pp. 77–152 [Menger(1950/1981), pp. 114–174].

77. Menger(1871), p. 78 [Menger(1950/1981), pp. 114–115].

78. Menger(1871), pp. 79–81 [Menger(1950/1981), pp. 115–116].

79. See also p. 165.

80. See above, pp. 151–159, and Menger(1871), notes on pp. 78–81, 108–113 [Menger(1950/1981); pp. 292–295, 295–302].

81. Menger(1871), pp. 88–95 [Menger(1950/1981), pp. 122–128].

82. See Menger(1871), pp. 95–114 [Menger(1950/1981), pp. 128–141].

83. For a discussion of this point, see pp. 193–194.

84. Menger(1871), pp. 114–119 [Menger(1950/1981), pp. 141–145].

85. For a more detailed discussion of the issues of homogeneity/heterogeneity and their impact on Menger's analysis, see pp. 194–195.

86. Menger(1871), pp. 119–123 [Menger(1950/1981), pp. 145–148].

87. See also Menger(1871), p. 123 [Menger(1950/1981), p. 149].

88. See Menger(1923), pp. 142–144.

89. See Menger(1871), pp. 123–126 [Menger(1950/1981), pp. 149–152].

90. Menger(1871), pp. 127–152 [Menger(1950/1981), pp. 152–174].

91. Menger(1871), pp. 136–138 [Menger(1950/1981), pp. 159–161].

92. Menger(1871), pp. 153–171 [Menger(1950/1981), pp. 175–190].

93. "Das Ziel aller Wirthschaft ist nicht die physische Vermehrung der Güter, sondern die möglichst vollständige Befriedigung der menschlichen Bedürfnisse" Menger(1871), p. 171 [Menger(1950/1981), p. 190].

94. See Menger(1871), pp. 164 n., 170 n., 171 [Menger(1950/1981), pp. 184 n.4, 189 n.8, 190].

95. "Wir würden überall eine Grenze wahrnehmen, wo der ökonomische Gesammtnutzen, welcher sich aus der Ausbeutung des vorliegenden Verhältnisses erzielen lässt, erschöpft ist, und von da ab sich durch fortgesetzte Tauschoperationen wieder mindert, also eine Grenze, über welche hinaus jeder weitere Austausch von Theilquantitäten als unökonomisch erscheint. Diese Grenze ist aber dann erreicht, wenn sich keine Güterquantität mehr in dem Besitze des einen der beiden Contrahenten befindet, die für ihn einen geringeren Werth hätte, als eine Quantität eines anderen in der Verfügung des zweiten Contrahenten befindlichen Gutes, während zugleich bei dieser letzteren Person das umgekehrte Verhältniss der Werthschätzung stattfindet" Menger(1871), pp. 167–168 [Menger(1950/1981), p. 187].

96. See Menger(1871), p. 168 [Menger(1950/1981), pp. 187–188].

97. Menger(1871), pp. 213–224 [Menger(1950/1981), pp. 226–235].

98. One proviso has to be kept in mind, nevertheless: We shall be able to assess the relevance of changes of this kind only after Menger's manuscripts have become available because it is only then that we shall know whether these changes stem from the author's pen or from that of the editor.

99. Menger (1871), pp. 214–215 [Menger(1950/1981), pp. 227–228].

100. "Der Gebrauchswerth ist demnach die Bedeutung, welche Güter dadurch für uns erlangen, dass sie uns in directer Weise die Befriedigung von Bedürfnissen unter Umständen sichern, unter welchen ohne unsere Verfügung über dieselben für diese Bedürfnissbefriedigung nicht vorgesorgt wäre; der Tauschwerth aber ist die Bedeutung, welche Güter dadurch für uns erlangen, dass durch den Besitz derselben der gleiche Erfolg unter gleichen Verhältnissen in indirecter Weise gesichert wird" Menger (1871), p. 216 [Menger(1950/1981), p. 228].

101. See Menger (1871), p. 216 n. [Menger(1950/1981), pp. 307–308].

102. Menger (1871), p. 220–224 [Menger(1950/1981), pp. 231–235].

103. See Menger's preface in (1871), p. x [Menger(1950/1981), p. 49].

104. Menger(1871), p. 135 [Menger(1950/1981), p. 158].

105. Menger(1871), pp. 107–108 [Menger(1950/1981), p. 139].

106. Menger's definition of value is quoted above, p. 163.

107. See Menger(1923), Chapter 1.

108. See also Essay II, pp. 84–85.

109. See Menger(1871), p. 3 [Menger(1950/1981), p. 52].

110. For further discussion of the concept of transference and its role in Menger's theory of value, see p. 197.

111. "Die Sorge für die Bedürfnisse ist demnach gleichbedeutend mit der Sorge für unser Leben und unsere Wohlfahrt; sie ist die wichtigste aller menschlichen Bestrebungen, denn sie ist die Voraussetzung und die Grundlage aller übrigen" Menger(1871), p. 32 [Menger(1950/1981), p. 77].

112. "Nun mögen unsere Bedürfnisse immerhin zum Theile, wenigstens so weit es sich um ihre Entstehung handelt, auch von unserem Willen oder von unserer Gewöhnung abhängen, sind sie aber einmal vorhanden, so ist der Werth, den die Güter für uns haben, dann nichts willkürliches mehr, sondern die zwingende Folge der Erkenntniss der Bedeutung für unser Leben oder unsere Wohlfahrt." Menger(1871), p. 85 [Menger(1950/1981), pp. 119–120].

113. Menger(1871), p. 98 [Menger(1950/1981), pp. 131–132].

114. Menger(1871), p. 93 [Menger(1950/1981), pp. 126–127].

115. On this, see the whole host of examples provided by Menger in (1871) [Menger(1950/1981)], Chapter 3.

116. Georgescu-Roegen(1967), p. 194.

117. See the section "Neo-Classical Axiomatisation and Menger's Theory of Value" later in Essay III.

118. Menger(1871), pp. 92, 163–171 [Menger(1950/1981), pp. 125, 183–190]. See also Hayek(1968), p. xv.

119. Georgescu-Roegen(1968), p. 242.

120. "qualitative residual" is defined in Georgescu-Roegen(1976); for its relationship with consumer theory see Georgescu-Roegen(1971), pp. 112–113.

121. Cf. Georgescu-Roegen(1954) and also (1968), esp. p. 262.

122. See Menger(1871), p. 177 [Menger(1950/1981), pp. 195–196].

123. According to Menger, this is the most important question of value theory; see Menger(1871), pp. 97–98 and also p. 99 [Menger(1950/1981), pp. 130–133].

124. Menger(1871), pp. 172–212 [Menger(1950/1981), pp. 191–225].

125. Menger(1871), p. 172 (emphasis added) [Menger(1950/1981), p. 191].

126. "Eine richtige Theorie der Preise . . . muss darauf gerichtet sein, zu zeigen, wie die wirthschaftenden Menschen bei ihrem auf möglichst vollständige Befriedigung ihrer Bedürfnisse gerichteten Streben dazu geführt werden, Güter, und zwar bestimmte Quantitäten derselben gegeneinander hinzugeben" Menger(1871), p. 175 [Menger(1950/1981), pp. 193–194].

127. See Menger(1871), pp. 173–175 [Menger(1950/1981), pp. 192–194].

128. Menger(1871), p. 176 [Menger(1950/1981), pp. 194–195].

129. Menger(1871), pp. 177–178 [Menger(1950/1981), pp. 195–196].

130. Menger(1871), p. 179 [Menger(1950/1981), p. 197].

131. Menger(1871), pp. 181–191 [Menger(1950/1981), pp. 199–207].

132. Menger(1871), p. 186 [Menger(1950/1981), pp. 202–203].

133. Menger(1871), pp. 190–191 [Menger(1950/1981), p. 207].

134. Menger(1871), pp. 194–195 [Menger(1950/1981), p. 210].

135. Menger(1871), pp. 195–201 [Menger(1950/1981), pp. 211–216]; see the note on pp. 197–198 [Menger(1950/1981), pp. 212–213] for the use of the idea of price elasticity of demand.

136. See especially Menger(1871), pp. 200–201 [Menger(1950/1981), pp. 215–216].

137. Menger(1871), p. 202 [Menger(1950/1981), pp. 216–217].

138. Menger(1871), pp. 209–212 [Menger(1950/1981), pp. 222–225].

139. Menger(1871), pp. 204–205 [Menger(1950/1981), pp. 218–220].

140. See Menger's letters to Walras in Walras(1965).

141. Menger(1871), p. 172 [Menger(1950/1981), pp. 191–192]; see also p. 175 above.

142. Menger(1871), pp. 172–173 (emphasis added) [Menger(1950/1981), p. 192].

143. Recall that for Menger "economic" means scarce with regard to the quantity required to satisfy a *Bedürfnis*.

144. Because a single individual can know the value of a good without reference to exchange.

145. The only determinate points ascertained by the theory are the limits within which exchange will take place, and these limits are stated—and, in Menger's theory, can only be stated— in terms of values.

146. See Essay II, pp. 104–112. Cf. also his famous letter to Walras (letter 602 in Walras[1965]), and Menger(1883), Anhang VI, pp. 262–266 [Menger(1963/1985), Appendix 6, pp. 216–219].

147. On the logical *locus* of his Chapter 6, see pp. 169–170.

148. See Essay II, pp. 104–112.

149. This is supported by his specific recourse not only to "experience"—as in his discussion of value—but also to history. See Menger(1871), pp. 199–200 [Menger(1950/1981), pp. 214–215], and also his derivation of competition from monopoly on the basis of historical development (Menger[1871], p. 202 [Menger(1950/1981), p. 217]).

150. See Menger(1950/1981), p. 78 n.1.

151. Menger(1871), pp. 32, 34 [Menger(1950/1981), pp. 77–78, 79–80].

152. Menger(1871), pp. 41, 45 [Menger(1950/1981), pp. 85–86, 87].

153. See p. 177 above.

154. See above, pp. 160–162 and n.62.

155. See Schumpeter(1954), p. 847 n.8.

156. Streissler(1972), esp. pp. 430–431.

157. See volume 4 of the *Gesammelte Werke*.

158. See, for instance, Hirsch(1928), Roll(1936), Streissler(1973), O'Driscoll(1986).

159. Menger(1871) [Menger(1950/1981)], Chapter 7.

160. Menger(1883), pp. 207–208 [Menger(1963/1985), pp. 176–177].

161. *Pragmatismus* here refers to the Enlightenment view of the course of history as continuous, almost linearly upward, development and progress. In nineteenth-century German thought, this term was used by the Romantic-Historicist opposition to rationalism and positivism to characterise a favorite *bête noir*.

162. "Das Ziel der hier in Rede stehenden Bestrebungen musste vielmehr das volle Verständniss der bestehenden socialen Einrichtungen überhaupt und der auf organischem Wege entstandenen Institutionen insbesondere sein, die Festhaltung des Bewährten gegen die einseitig rationalistische Neuerungssucht auf dem Gebiete der Volkswirthschaft. Es galt die Zersetzung der organisch gewordenen Volkswirthschaft durch einen zum Theil oberflächlichen Pragmatismus zu verhindern, einen Pragmatismus, der gegen die Absicht seiner Vertreter unausweichbar zum Socialismus führt" Menger(1883), p. 208 [Menger(1963/1985), p. 177].

163. See Hicks(1975), pp. 322–323.

164. Cf., e.g., the index in Bucharin(1966).

165. Austrian flavour, that is, Austrian rationalism or Josephinism, is most likely responsible for the Enlightenment-like philosophy of history which permeates Menger's footnotes in the *Grundsätze*.

Neo-Classical Axiomatisation and Menger's Theory of Value

166. "Im gewöhnlichen Leben ist nun aber das Verhältnis zwischen den verfügbaren Gütern und unseren Bedürfnissen der Regel nach ein viel complicierteres. Hier steht zumeist: *nicht einem einzelnen concreten Bedürfnisse, sondern einem Complex von solchen; nicht ein einzelnes Gut, sondern eine Quantität von solchen gegenüber*, so zwar, dass eine bald grössere, bald geringere Anzahl in ihrer Bedeutung höchst verschiedener Bedürfnisbefriedigungen von unserer Verfügung über eine Quantität von Gütern abhängt, deren jedes einzelne wieder die Tauglichkeit hat, die obigen in ihrer Bedeutung sehr verschiedenen Bedürfnisbefriedigungen herbeizuführen" Menger(1871), p. 96 (emphasis added) [Menger(1950/1981), p. 129].

167. The approach taken here is thus the exact opposite to the approach taken in one of the most influential textbooks in the mathematical education of economists in the period following the Second World War: "The continuity assumption is now added for the purpose of theoretical convenience. It is assumed, firstly, that the individual can vary his purchases of each good continuously and, secondly, that the variation from one set of purchases to indifferent purchases is continuous. This assumption has, of course, no justification except as an approximation and on grounds of expediency. Each indifference curve can now be taken as continuous and the whole set of curves appear in a continuously variable order of ascending preference" Allen(1969), p. 125.

168. See Menger's letter to Walras(1965), letter 602.

169. Menger(1871), e.g. pp. 78, 107–108 [Menger(1950/1981), pp. 115, 139].

170. This is an important point. In conventional neo-classical theory marginal utility is of course also independent of the use to which a good is actually put. But this independence has merely logical, formal character; it has no ontological grounding. The actual use made of a good is precisely the point at which misinformation and error reveal themselves in Menger's theory. This possibility is, by definition, excluded in modern general equilibrium economics. Since goods are used only when equilibrium is reached, their actual use is irrelevant to the theory.

171. See the discussion of mappings, p. 195.

172. "Nature" refers not only to the composition of the elements of A and B but also to relations and orderings defined on A and B.
173. See, e.g., n.167 above.
174. Menger(1871), p. 98 [Menger(1950/1981), pp. 130–132].
175. Ibid.
176. See Menger's tables representing this hierarchy as an ordinal scheme and his discussion of this structure in Menger(1871), pp. 93–94 [Menger(1950/1981), pp. 126–128]. See also Hayek(1968), p. xv.
177. Menger(1871), p. 96 [Menger(1950/1981), p. 129].
178. Menger(1871), pp. 100–104 [Menger(1950/1981), pp. 133–137].
179. Menger(1871), pp. 104–106 [Menger(1950/1981), pp. 137–138].
180. Lexicographic preferences are widely discussed in the literature on the structure of utility functions; see, above all, Chipman(1960) and (1971), Hausner(1954). For a discussion of the superiority of lexicographic preferences over traditional assumptions on preferences, see Georgescu-Roegen(1967), (1968) and (1971); for an application of lexicographic preferences to demand theory, see Ironmonger(1972).
181. Here Menger can be seen to be a better methodological individualist than, for instance, Walras: Menger can accommodate the entire valuation process in his theory of value without having to invoke the market while Walras has to take recourse to exchange right at the outset of his *Elements of Pure Economics*; he would not have been able to derive demand schedules otherwise. But then, Menger is only talking about values and tells us very little about prices here; Walras talks only about relative prices but does not tell us anything about value.
182. Menger(1871), p. 3 [Menger(1950/1981), p. 52].
183. Menger's habit of differentiating goods by *Art* and *Species*, i.e., by *genus proximum* and *differentia specifica*, lends additional support to this interpretation; see Menger(1871), pp. 114–115 [Menger(1950/1981), pp. 141–142] (and the quotation in n.186 below).
184. See, for instance, the examples Menger employs in the derivation of his measure of value (Menger[1871] [Menger(1950/1981)], Chapter 3).
185. I.e., "parts of a quantity"; Menger(1871), e.g., pp. 77–78 [Menger(1950/1981), pp. 114–115].
186. "Güter, welche die menschlichen Bedürfnisse in völlig gleicher Weise befriedigen, werden deshalb in wirtschaftlicher Beziehung mit Recht als völlig homogen betrachtet, wenngleich auch dieselben ihrer äusseren Erscheinung nach verschiedenen Arten oder Species angehören" Menger(1871), p. 115 [Menger(1950/1981), pp. 141–142]. For a definition of equivalence relations see, e.g., Stoll(1979), p. 29.
187. For a discussion of homogeneity see pp. 194–195.
188. The relation "has the same value as" is an equivalence relation; it is reflexive, symmetric and transitive.
189. Cf., e.g., Shone(1975), p. 23.
190. Chapter 3 occupies over a quarter of the book; see Menger(1871), pp. 77–152 [Menger(1950/1981), pp. 114–174].
191. See Menger's remarks on this at the outset of his derivation of the marginality principle, Menger(1871), pp. 95–96 [Menger(1950/1981), pp. 128–130].
192. Cf. Banerjee(1964), pp. 163, 165; Chipman(1960), p. 222; Georgescu-Roegen(1968), p. 251.
193. It is probably not unreasonable to surmise that Menger himself did not fully understand the implications of his choice of examples. How else are we to explain the muddle into which he got himself in his discussion of the value of heterogeneous goods? The entire paragraph of the *Grundsätze* in which he attempts to derive the

value of heterogeneous goods is not only a linguistic impossibility but also leads to a mathematical contradiction (Menger(1971), pp. 118–119 [Menger(1950/1981), pp. 144–145]; see also the introduction to this study, pp. 17–18). His solution to the problem is false. A correct solution would have to calculate the value of heterogeneous goods within a lexicographic structure. This would make the calculation even more complicated than the one suggested by his original formula, even if the latter were to be corrected. And it would have alerted him not only to the fallacies inherent in his choice of only one commodity for the demonstration of the satisfaction of all *Bedürfnisse* but also to the incompleteness of the solution derived on such a basis.

194. Menger(1871), pp. 114–119 [Menger(1950/1981), pp. 141–145].

195. I.e., for any element x of the consumption set, the set of bundles which are at least as preferred as x is convex, closed and bounded, and the preferences defined over the set are continuous. On this see, e.g., Shone(1975), pp. 26–29.

196. I am deliberately ignoring, for the time being, the fact that the derivation of value by applying the marginality principle to an ordinal scale is a mathematically—and substantively—meaningless operation.

197. "Der Werth ist demnach nichts den Gütern Anhaftendes, keine Eigenschaft derselben, sondern vielmehr lediglich jene Bedeutung, welche wir zunächst der Befriedigung unserer Bedürfnisse, beziehungsweise unserem Leben und unserer Wohlfahrt beilegen und in weiterer Folge auf die ökonomischen Güter, als die ausschliessenden Ursachen derselben, *übertragen*." "Zunächst und unmittelbar hat nur die Befriedigung unserer Bedürfnisse für uns eine Bedeutung, und findet diese letztere in jedem concreten Fall ihr Mass in der Wichtigkeit der bezüglichen Bedürfnisbefriedigung für unser Leben und unsere Wohlfahrt. Diese Bedeutung, und zwar in ihrer quantitativen Bestimmtheit, *übertragen* wir zunächst auf jene concreten Güter, von welchen wir, in der Befriedigung der betreffenden Bedürfnisse unmittelbar abhängig zu sein, uns bewusst sind, das ist auf die ökonomischen Güter erster Ordnung, nach den im vorigen Abschnitte dargelegten Grundsätzen. Wo immer aber unser Bedarf durch Güter erster Ordnung nicht, oder nicht vollständig gedeckt ist, das ist in allen Fällen, wo die Güter erster Ordnung eben Werth für uns erlangen, greifen wir in dem Bestreben unsere Bedürfnisse möglichst vollständig zu befriedigen nach den entsprechenden Gütern der nächst höheren Ordnung und *übertragen* den Werth der Güter erster Ordnung, fortschreitend auf die Güter zweiter, dritter und höherer Ordnung überall dort, wo auch diese letzteren den ökonomischen Charakter aufweisen" Menger(1871), pp. 81n., 126n. (emphasis added) [Menger(1950/1981), pp. 116–117, 151–152].

198. This is part of the definition of the nature of goods (see Menger[1871], p. 3 [Menger(1950/1981), p. 52]). The definition of transference is strictly in accordance with Menger's views (cf. the quotations in the preceding note), but ever since Freud we are, of course, well aware of the fact that transference is a far more complex concept than Menger lets us believe. Instead of being absolutely certain, which Menger purports it to be since he requires this for his epistemology, transference is a fundamentally subjective process and only tenuously anchored in an objectively perceivable, current reality. In other words, it is a "general phenomenon of the perception and/or interpretation of current situations in the light of past experience or similar past situations" (*Encyclopedia of Psychology*, vol. 3, [London: Search Press, 1972], p. 347). For a discussion of the subjective nature of our perceived universe, see Naranjo and Ornstein(1972) and Ornstein(1981), Chapters 2–5.

199. See pp. 194–195 above.

200. Walras(1965), letter 602.

201. Menger(1871), p. 95 [Menger(1950/1981), pp. 128–129].

202. Menger(1871), p. 96 [Menger(1950/1981), p. 129].

203. See pp. 195–196 above.

204. Marshall relates the quantity of an individual good *via* its marginal utility to the marginal purchase which is inversely related to marginal demand price, thus yielding downward sloping demand curves (cf. Marshall[1969], Book 3, Chapter 3).

205. But see the discussion of Ironmonger's model, pp. 203–208.

206. See, e.g., Leontief(1947), p. 164; Lancaster(1971), p. 11; Ironmonger(1972), pp. 1–3.

207. For a survey of the separability hypothesis, see Geary and Morishima(1973); also Deaton and Muellbauer(1980), Chapter 5, and Green(1971), Chapter 10.

208. Robbins(1972).

209. Morishima(1973).

210. Hicks(1956), pp. 166–168.

211. Geary and Morishima(1973), p. 130.

212. Morishima(1973), p. 155; for details of the discussion see ibid., pp. 148–155.

213. This is a necessary condition for the utility function to be separable; commodities must be separable into disjoint subsets or else the separability condition—independence of the marginal rate of substitution—cannot be satisfied.

214. See Lancaster(1966a) and (1966b); the theory is fully developed in Lancaster(1971).

215. Ironmonger(1972).

216. Lancaster(1966b), p. 135, and (1971), pp. 20–21.

217. Cf. Hicks(1968), chs. 1–3 and pp. 305–319.

218. Ironmonger(1972), pp. 1–2.

219. Ironmonger(1972), p. 2.

220. Ironmonger(1972), p. 15.

221. Ironmonger(1972), p. 17.

222. "Common satisfaction" in Ironmonger's terminology.

223. Want-satisfaction-efficiency is expressed by the number of units of want-satisfaction of want i obtained from one unit of commodity j multiplied by its unit price.

224. Ironmonger(1972), pp. 16–21.

225. Wants which are completely satisfied are called "supra-marginal", those which are unsatisfied "submarginal."

226. Ironmonger(1972), pp. 23–25.

227. Insofar as indifference curves are constructed, they will be straight lines perpendicular to the direction of increase in want-satisfaction; that is, as long as, say, want i is not fully satisfied (i.e., $z_i < z^*_i$) the consumer is indifferent to any amount of satisfaction of wants $(i+1)$, $(i+2)$, . . . , m between zero and infinity (cf. Ironmonger[1972], pp. 30–31).

228. I.e., they can be want-specific or nonspecific.

229. Ironmonger(1972), pp. 14–15.

230. Ironmonger(1972), pp. 16–17.

231. This is the definition of marginal want.

232. For a discussion of the linear programming formulation, see Ironmonger(1972), pp. 32–35.

233. Ironmonger(1972), pp. 33–34.

234. Ironmonger(1972), pp. 31–32. "An efficient budget is one where no particular want satisfaction may be increased without decreasing at least one other want satisfaction" Ironmonger(1972), p. 30.

235. See Ironmonger(1972), pp. 35–40.

236. Cf. Menger(1871), p. 3 [Menger(1950/1981), p. 52].
237. See pp. 194–195 above.
238. Cf. Ironmonger(1972), p. 22.
239. Robbins(1972), p. 16.
240. Ironmonger(1972), p. 20; that is to say, if a commodity is capable of satisfying two unrelated wants (Ironmonger's "common satisfaction"), it is assumed that it becomes two commodities, one for each want. In this way, choice among wants, which is exogenous to the model and therefore a potential source of indeterminacy, is eliminated.
241. See pp. 201–203 above.
242. See above, p. 205.
243. See Ironmonger(1972), pp. 48–71.
244. Ironmonger(1972), p. 59.
245. Ironmonger(1972), Chapters 3 and 4.
246. See above, pp. 181–182.
247. See above, p. 181.

Epilogue

The Departure from Menger—
Wieser and Böhm-Bawerk

Any investigation of the origins of the Austrian school of economics is, of course, not complete without an analysis of the theoretical and methodological work of the other two economists of the first generation, Friedrich von Wieser and Eugen von Böhm-Bawerk. Such a task, however, would require a detailed discussion of the foundations of Wieser's and Böhm-Bawerk's methodologies, as they formulated them explicitly in their writings on method and implicitly in their theoretical work and of their theories of value, prices, distribution and capital. Such an analysis would require as much detailed exposition as has been afforded to Menger's theory and methodology and is clearly beyond the scope of this study. However, to round off my discussion of the origins of Austrian economics and to indicate which direction a full exposition of the history of the Austrian school would have to take, I briefly outline in this Epilogue where the major breaks occurred within the first generation which eventually were to bring together the Austrian and Walrasian strands of neo-classical economics.

Wieser was not interested in methodology *per se*.[1] Consequently, he published very little on the subject, and his most famous book, *Der natürliche Werth*, does not contain any discussion of methodological issues.[2] For this we have to refer to his first work, *Über den Ursprung und die Hauptgesetze des wirthschaftlichen Werthes*, his review of Schumpeter's first book and his last theoretical treatise, *Theorie der gesellschaftlichen Wirtschaft*,[3] although his methodological introduction in the last work only repeats his earlier arguments.[4] As far as his methodological position is concerned, Wieser never ceased to emphasise that economics is a branch of the *Geisteswissenschaften*.[5] He rejected the methods of the natural sciences for economics[6] and insisted on the superior intelligibility of the *Geisteswissenschaften* over the *Naturwissenschaften*.[7] However, his affinity with Romantic-Historicist thought does not come from Savigny's historical school of law, Wieser's early interest in history and his training as a lawyer notwithstanding, but from Grimm's historical school of language. Elements of this can easily be discerned in his first book, which we may consider as the methodological preface to his *Der natürliche Werth* and which opens with a chapter on the "scientific significance of the concepts of language."[8] In that chapter, he implicitly refers to the concept of the *Volksgeist*, but in his *Theorie der gesellschaftlichen Wirtschaft*, this reference is made explicit in the methodological introduction.[9]

If the general thrust of Wieser's methodology therefore seems to be very much in line with that of Menger, he departs, nevertheless, in several important aspects from Menger's scientific conception of social reality: Wieser's conception of the *Geisteswissenschaften* lacks Menger's essentialist dimension; his conception of causality is not teleological;[10] and in his insistence on the epistemological dualism between the *Geisteswissenschaften* and the *Naturwissenschaften*, Wieser is, if anything, much clearer and decisive than Menger. He not only confirms the relevance of this dualism for economics from the outset but, unlike Menger, also rules out any biological reconciliation on methodological grounds, which is implicit in his rejection of physiology.[11] It is important to note that although it was Wieser who finally made Austrian economics openly psychologistic by calling the theory of value a branch of applied psychology[12] and who explicitly introduced introspection,[13] he rejected psycho-physics, or experimental psychology in general, as a justification for the fundamental assumption of Austrian economics, diminishing marginal utility.[14] For him, the psychological nature of the foundations of economic theory, that is, of value theory, is grounded in general human experience and is of no special concern to the economist. It is simply taken as an axiom.[15]

I have already identified the point of Wieser's departure from Menger, the fullest statement of which is contained in his introduction to the *Theorie der gesellschaftlichen Wirtschaft*.[16] Although the terminology remains largely the same as that introduced by Menger (ignoring, for the time being, Wieser's innovatory use of the now classic term, marginal utility), it is now filled with new content. Wieser's abrogation of Menger's essentialism and Aristotelianism is the first and most important step in this direction. Despite Wieser's insistence on the fully empirical nature of pure economic theory and on its basis in common everyday experience, there is now very little which distinguishes the fundamental assumptions of his theory from those of axiomatic-deductive theory. In order to rescue Wieser's position, it would be necessary to devise generally acceptable foundations for an introspectively conceived *Verstehen* doctrine. In the absence of such foundations, Wieser's philosophy of science—or rather, of social science—lacks the epistemological grounding which Menger thought he found in his concept of induction. Wieser's reference to common economic facts experienced by everyone is, therefore, left hanging in the air and degenerates easily into cliché; hence it requires very little effort to replace it with a fully developed axiomatic-deductive approach. In addition, there is the question of how Menger's concept of "exact" theory is to be interpreted in Wieser's epistemological framework. (We recall that according to Menger "exact" theory is true and certain by definition of the inductive, first step.)

From this vantage point we can see quite a few supports of Menger's edifice reduced to ruin. Wieser's radical *geisteswissenschaftliche* approach, which does not admit of a biological bridge between the *Geisteswissenschaften* and the *Naturwissenschaften*, removes Menger's concept of *Bedürfnis* from its central place. The emphasis now shifts from the discussion of the teleological process of *Bedürfnisbefriedigung* to the analytical problems of value theory, normal procedure in the process of extending and completing a theory but when done in conjunction with the departure from essentialism and teleology, this change of emphasis opens Menger's entire theory to functionalist re-interpretation. And since Wieser now limits the scope of pure economic theory to the scope of common everyday experience,[17] the field becomes wide open for everyone to pick and choose whatever basic assumptions—or, as we may now well say, initial conditions—suit the theory best. This approach is supported by Wieser's acceptance of mathematics into the analysis of the static foundations of pure economic theory.[18] Out goes *Verstehen* of the *Wesen*, in comes mathematical analysis. But the admission of mathematics for static analysis also means that Wieser abstracts from another of Menger's fundamental methodological and theoretical elements: time at the root of economic behaviour. Wieser's rejection of mathematics for dynamic economic analysis, on the other hand, can simply be interpreted as ignorance of the mathematical tools which would lend themselves to such a task, not necessarily as an objection in principle. Why should mathematics be allowed in one case but not in the other?

Equally, Wieser's *isolierende und idealisierende Methode* and his *Methode der abnehmenden Abstraktion* are only faint echoes of Menger's resoluta-compositive method. Isolation and idealisation in economic theory must not trespass beyond the bounds of common everyday experience. Isolation, for the economist, is achieved through observation, that is, introspection, and corresponds to the natural scientist's experimentation; idealisation, on the other hand, is equated with the mathematician's abstraction of point and line.[19] Both isolation and idealisation in the *Naturwissenschaften* as well as in the *Geisteswissenschaften* are based on assumptions, but none of the assumptions made by the economist forms hypotheses like those of the natural scientist. Hypotheses are assumptions about the unkown, and thus they are necessary for the natural scientist, who can never fully know his subject matter. The economist's assumptions, by virtue of his working in the *Geisteswissenschaften*, are abstractions from the known because the economist's mind is part of the world of the mind which has created the economic world. Reverberations of the truth and certainty of Menger's "exact" theory can be felt, but in the absence of definite epistemological foundations they clearly do not make sense; the logical next step, indeed, has to be to state the initial conditions as axioms, which are then assumed to be true and serve as the basis of the deductive analytical process.

The same problem arises with Wieser's methodological individualism. The genuinely subjectivist-individualistic character of Menger's value theory is abandoned in favour of a market-based individualism of the Walrasian kind. Wieser's methodological individualism derives from his conception of idealisation: Accordingly, a full-fledged member of a fully developed society is isolated for the purposes of a discussion of economic value.[20] This is perfectly compatible with Walras's approach in the *Elements*, where an individual is analysed on the pre-supposition of the existence of an underlying social framework. In other words, the whole, that is, an entire society, exists and is the indispensable pre-condition for an analysis of the representative individual. This has nothing to do any more with Robinson Crusoe (Wieser, indeed, says so)[21] or with Menger's *Emanatismus*, where a single individual in his original state of nature is not only the starting point of the analysis of value but already carries within himself all the necessary elements for an analysis of the complex phenomenon of value formation in society which, therefore, constitutes nothing more than the limiting case at the other end of the scale of possibilities. Viewed from inside Menger's system, individualism is an ontological and not just a methodological assumption while in Wieser's system it has only methodological status since Wieser specifies neither an ontology nor epistemological foundations which point towards an underlying ontology. In brief, Wieser's methodological individualism is simply a formal device for the analysis of value without any claim to ontological standing. Alternatively, he may simply assume that an adequate ontology underpins his conception of a methodology of the *Geisteswissenschaften*, but the fact that he does not make it explicit does not really aid his cause.

As this very brief discussion of Wieser's methodology shows, it does not really correspond to Menger's conception of the *Geisteswissenschaften* and social science. Wieser remains a steadfast adherent of the *geisteswissenschaftliche* approach but abandons Menger's essentialism in spite of his continued use of the term *Wesen*. He eliminates teleology and admits mathematical analysis of the static foundations of the theory, hence opening the theory to formalism and to analysis which abstracts from time (cause and change were inseparable for Menger, and for him, as for Aristotle, time was defined as the number of change). Furthermore, the change in the meaning of individualism from Menger to Wieser allows the absorption of, or by, the world of Walrasian economic man. On methodological grounds alone, Wieser's re-interpretation of Menger's economic theory makes his equating Menger with Jevons and Walras perfectly acceptable.

Not surprisingly, a similar picture is unveiled when we look at Wieser's economic theory. Here, I shall only give a very brief and general outline of my main argument. A detailed investigation of Wieser's theory would have to start not simply with his first book but with his first paper on economic theory which he presented in 1876 at Karl Knies's seminar in Heidelberg while travelling with his lifetime friend Eugen von Böhm-Bawerk.[22] It would also require analysis of the internal relationship of his first book to his famous *Der natürliche Werth*, of all the contradictions,[23] and of the development of his doctrine in his later publications from the 1890s to the *Theorie der gesellschaftlichen Wirtschaft* of 1914.

Wieser's best-known and most influential book was his *Der natürliche Werth* of 1889, but the foundations of his theory were developed in *Über den Ursprung und die Hauptgesetze des wirthschaftlichen Werthes* of 1884.

There he introduced the term *Grenznutzen*, which he had coined for his version of Menger's concept of "marginal value" with reference to Jevons's final degree of utility and terminal utility and which has remained with us as marginal utility ever since.[24] On the road to the development of his law of marginal utility he re-arranged Menger's system to a certain extent. In his discussion of the *Ursprung* of value he shifted the center of attention from *Bedürfnis* to *Interesse*. *Bedürfnis* is confirmed as the wellspring of economic activity, but its proper field of operation is defined outside the boundaries of economics. Within economic theory proper it is the *Interesse*, the interest we have in using specific goods, which becomes the central concept.[25] The utility derived from the use of a good replaces the *Bedeutung* of the satisfaction of a *Bedürfnis*.[26] Value, which still remains subjective, is defined as the human *Interesse* conceived through the useful properties of the goods.[27] We are here witnessing a partial relocation of value: For Menger, value is located entirely within the economic agent, is independent of goods and springs from the motivation to satisfy *Bedürfnisse*; for Wieser, this motivation becomes semi-external: It becomes a motivation which is triggered off by the useful properties of the object of human needs, not exclusively by the needs themselves. In this way, *Nutzen* becomes the origin of value, and *Grenznutzen*, its measure, is the pivotal term of Wieser's economic analysis.

If Wieser was concerned with the foundations of his value theory in 1884, it was the analytics of his argument which moved into the foreground in his *Der natürliche Werth* of 1889. The chain of arguments leading from *Bedürfnis* via *Interesse* to value and, finally, to marginal utility is effectively condensed into the discussion of the relationship of value to marginal utility. Wieser now also introduces prices, and in spite of his reference to Menger, who, significantly, is mentioned in the same breath as Böhm-Bawerk,[28] his conception of price has very little to do with Menger's. Having done away with essentialism, Wieser states that value and prices influence each other, that the law of value and the law of prices are closely related and differ only in that price reflects the marginal utility of money in addition to the marginal utility of a good while value itself is only the marginal utility of the latter.[29] But Wieser does not stop here. He also introduces the distinction between subjective and objective exchange value, equating the latter effectively with price.[30] Naturally his reference for this distinction is not Menger but only Böhm-Bawerk.[31]

In this way Menger's carefully constructed theory of value and prices was changed so that an objectivistic interpretation of his subjective conception of value became possible. Once the concept of objective value is admitted and equated with price, however intimately it may still be related to subjective value, the road to a re-interpretation of Menger's theory of value and prices as a functional theory of relative prices is no longer littered with too many obstacles.

By looking at Wieser's methodological shift we can see how the theoretical shift occurred. By retaining concepts but giving them new meaning, Wieser presented Menger's essentialist theory of subjective value—which discussed prices only in passing, as it were, because they were regarded as mere surface phenomena—as a formalist, or instrumentalist, theory of values and prices; value formation and price determination now take place on the same level. An exclusively subjective conception of value is transformed and receives an objective counterpart; the objective side of value, still rooted in subjective value, is then stated to correspond to price. A consistent continuation of this line of argument would, presumably, result in a mathematical restatement of this theory which is closer to a modern theory of relative prices based on the marginality principle than to the theory developed by Menger.

Turning to the remaining first-generation economist, Böhm-Bawerk was the least philosophically minded of the three founders of the Austrian school. He was not concerned with furnishing economic theory with an appropriate ontology or spelling out epistemological foundations for economic theorising; he simply wanted to theorise and to construct theory as he thought the subject matter itself suggested it. In the process, most of Menger's philosophical pre-suppositions went overboard. There was, in the end, no difference between Böhm-Bawerk's version of Menger's theory of value and that of Walras except for a few minor technicalities, as Böhm-Bawerk himself emphasised in his correspondence with Walras.[32]

Böhm-Bawerk's defence of the "correct" methodology never really went beyond appeals to common sense, and his arguments were, methodologically speaking, rather trivial. He was basically only concerned with emphasising that theory must be developed and that it is different from historical work but not in the least less empirical. He opposed the use of mathematical analysis in pure theory only on didactical grounds and furnished neither methodological nor epistemological arguments for his objection. This methodological position can be traced throughout his work. In his early review of Menger's *Untersuchungen* in 1884 he correctly identified the crucially weak point in Menger's argument, namely the relationship between "exact" theory and empirical reality, but did not even attempt to offer a tentative solution.[33] In his 1889 review of Lujo Brentano's inaugural lecture, his conception of "exact" theory turns out to be synonymous with "abstract" and "isolating";[34] his review of Wicksell's *Ueber Wert, Capital und Rente* published in 1894 he virtually begged Wicksell and other members of the fraternity not to use too much mathematics because he and many others with him were not really able follow the argument.[35] Finally, his French paper published in 1912 shows he still had not worked out a concrete concept of the empirical, which left quite a lacuna in his argument, especially in view of the rather introspective conception of the empirical contents of pure theory in his *magnum opus*.[36]

This is, broadly speaking, the thrust of Böhm-Bawerk's methododological position. No more essentialism and teleology, no talk about *a geisteswissenschaftliche* tradition for economic theory. However non-philosophical his methodological arguments were, their importance and influence were inversely proportional to their degree of sophistication since, of the three first-generation Austrian economists, it was Böhm-Bawerk who most vociferously publicised and defended the Austrian school, who published the most and who was the most widely translated. And there was no hint in his theoretical work of the complex methodological and epistemological problems which had plagued Menger and which were echoed in Wieser's first book.

The dissolution of Menger's methodological framework begins in Böhm-Bawerk's first book, *Rechte und Verhältnisse vom Standpunkte der volkswirtschaftlichen Güterlehre*, when he expands Menger's four necessary and jointly sufficient conditions for a thing to become a good into five conditions.[37] In the third book of the *Positive Theorie des Kapitales*, he sets exchange value and price as equivalent;[38] he defines value in such a way that the term *Bedeutung* is robbed of one of its senses, that of "meaning", and retains only that of "importance";[39] and he introduces cost considerations, i.e., a price term, in the section on value[40] (or does not hesitate to refer to comparison with prices in the summary of his discussion of value).[41]

The crucial point of Böhm-Bawerk's departure from Menger's theory is his emphasis of the technological dimension in both his theory of value and his theory of production, and hence also his theory of capital. In spite of his Mengerian starting point in his theory of value, that the value of goods reflects only the value of a person's welfare for this person, he went on to emphasise the importance of the role of the good, instead of remaining with the subjectively perceived evaluation in the individual's mind,[42] and later to introduce the concepts of subjective and objective exchange value.[43] Here, both Menger's distinction between values and prices and his incorporation of the physical properties of a good in the conditions which make a thing a good are given up, and an objective element is introduced in the foundations of an allegedly purely subjective theory of value. But Böhm-Bawerk went even further: He declared the law of exchange value congruent with the law of prices.[44] Böhm-Bawerk, therefore, reformulated a theory based on one unifying principle, purely subjectively perceived satisfaction of *Bedürfnisse*, into a theory based on subjective use value, subjective exchange value, objective exchange value and prices. Thus he almost reinstated the baroque structure which Menger had reduced to his one unifying principle in the first place.[45] Indeed, the congruence of Böhm-Bawerk's theory of exchange value, and hence his discussion of value in itself, with his theory of prices is such that in reading the third book of his *Positive Theorie des Kapitales*, one cannot help but notice that his treatment of prices is entirely symmetrical to that of value. Prices are no longer mere accidental phenomena as compared to essential values, both concepts are now methodologically and theoretically equivalent.

Böhm-Bawerk's ambivalence in his use of subjective value does, in fact, demand the application of Occam's razor. Either one wants a theory of value (I am now not discussing the reason why someone should want one), and then essentialism is essential, at least to my mind, or one should do away with excess baggage and stick to a theory of relative prices. Anything else only adds confusion, *viz.*, the profusion of *Exkurse*, the additions and the explanatory footnotes added to Book 3 in the various editions of the *Positive Theorie des Kapitales*. Indeed, we saw earlier how easily one could arrive from Wieser's restatement of Menger's theory at modern utility theory; it is even easier to see how the step from Böhm-Bawerk's restatement of Menger's theory can be made to Walras's theory and also to modern neo-classical theory.

This transformation of Menger's theoretical structure is, to my mind, the single most crucial characteristic which defines the difference between Menger's and Böhm-Bawerk's theories. Böhm-Bawerk's departure from the *geisteswissenschaftliche* approach, in general, and Menger's idiosyncratic version of it, in particular, locates Böhm-Bawerk quite firmly in the camp of today's general equilibrium theorists, at least on methodological grounds and as far as his theory of prices is concerned. His methodology is translated into a formal, or instrumentalist, theory of determination of relative prices based on a subjectivistic marginality principle in contrast to Menger's essentialist theory of subjective value, which foundered on the transformation problem. Very much part and parcel of Böhm-Bawerk's position is his emphasis on technology within economic theory which, according to Menger, is of no relevance to the pure economic theorist. Technology, from Menger's economic point of view, is a black box and should remain so; only inputs, outputs and elapsed time should be viewed for their effects on *Bedürfnis-befriedigung*. All the other differences among Menger's, Wieser's and Böhm-Bawerk's systems—not least among them "the greatest error ever committed": Böhm-Bawerk's theory of capital—simply follow from this point of departure.

This is as far as I want to go in my discussion of Wieser's and Böhm-Bawerk's departures from Menger. We have seen in the course of this study how a common background, which is reflected in the terminology used by all three of the elder Austrian economists, does not necessarily lead to conceptually congruent theories. Both Wieser and Menger share in their *geisteswissenschaftliche* perspective of economic issues and in economic theory; both derive from the Romantic-Historicist line of thought; and both absorbed a certain amount of rationalism or positivism from their admiration for the natural sciences. Nevertheless, abandoning Menger's essentialism led Wieser to do away with the clear-cut subjective perspective for valuation and to also admit the introduction of mathematical argument into fundamental research in economic theory. Böhm-Bawerk went even further than Wieser since the former does not make any *geisteswissenschaftliche* claims. He still sounds like Menger because the language and the terminology are largely the same, but his approach to theorising and his conception of the foundations of economic theory are even further removed from Menger, and closer to Walras and Jevons, than Wieser's. This may perhaps be the key to Menger's initial reluctance to accept as disciples these two friends and brothers-in-law, who in their later careers never dicussed economic theory with each other.[46]

The next step which the history of the Austrian school of economics demands is a detailed analysis of the theoretical and methodological developments in both Wieser's and Böhm-Bawerk's work. Only then shall we be able to obtain a clear picture of the diversity of strands and influences which were represented by this first generation of Austrian economists and of the direction in which Austrian theory and methodology moved from its beginnings in Menger through the transformations imposed by Wieser and Böhm-Bawerk to the second generation of Austrian economists who exported their conceptions of this thought more because of the force of historical events than out of free choice. Only after this groundwork has been done shall we be able to assess the history of the Austrian school, its eclipse, its fusion with the mathematically oriented Walrasian strand of neo-classical economic theory and its revival in its neo-Austrian mutation in the United States and, to a certain extent, Great Britain also in the late 1970s. All this, in turn, will allow us to look more clearly at the history of economic thought in this century as a part of the history of the workings of the mind of man and in relation to the forces which it helped to shape and which equally shaped its course.

Notes

33. See Hayek(1929), p. xiii.
34. See Wieser(1889), p. xi.
35. Wieser(1884), (1911) and (1924), respectively.
36. Cf. Wieser(1924), p. 8.
37. Wieser(1884), p. 9; Wieser(1929), p. 14.
38. See Wieser(1884), p. 3, and Wieser(1929), p. 13.
39. See Wieser(1884), pp. 1–10. "Der theoretische Ökonom braucht die exacten Naturwissenschaften um ihre Hilfsmittel nicht zu beneiden. Was immer sie sonst voraus haben und so groß ihre Leistungen sind, so stehen sie ihrem Objecte, der Natur, doch fremd gegenüber, sie werden in das Innerste der Natur niemals eindringen können, und wenn ihre Hilfsmittel noch unendlich weiter verfeinert werden sollten, sie werden sich immer bescheiden müssen, ein Nacheinander zu beschreiben, ohne erklären zu können, wie aus den Ursachen die Wirkung folgt. Die Gruppe der Geisteswissenschaften, zu denen die Wirtschafttheorie gehört, kann mehr tun. Weil ihr Objekt der handelnde Mensch ist, so begleitet unser Geist jede zutreffende Beschreibung, die sie von den Vorgängen in seinem Bewußtsein gibt, mit der zustimmenden Äußerung, daß es so sei, und mit dem zwingenden Gefühl, daß es so sein müsse". Wieser(1924), p. 12.
40. "Die wissenschaftliche Bedeutung der Sprachbegriffe" Wieser(1884), pp. 1–10.
41. See Wieser(1924), pp. 11–12.
42. On this, see his comments on Menger's order of goods in his biographical article on Menger (Wieser[1923], p. 118).
43. "Physiologie liegt uns vollends ferne, sie ist eine Naturwissenschaft, mit der wir methodisch gar keine Verbindung besitzen. Wir beschäftigen uns, wenn wir von den Bedürfnissen handeln, mit gewissen, zum Teil physiologisch begründeten Erscheinungen, die im Bewußtsein auftauchen und an die sich wirtschaftliche Handlungen schließen, aber *wir stellen sie einfach so fest, wie wir sie im Bewußtsein vorfinden*, und stellen weiter fest, welche Reaktionen zufolge ihres Eintrittes sich an sie anschließen, und fragen gar nicht danach, warum sie auftauchen, noch auch durch welche

tieferliegenden Prozesse sie die Folge haben, wirtschaftliche Handlungen nach sich zu ziehen" Wieser(1929), p. 16 (emphasis added).

44. "Die Werthdoctrin ist, wenn wir ihre Aufgabe richtig umschrieben haben, angewandte Psychologie" Wieser(1884), p. 39.

45. "Über den Werth sind bereits praktisch bewährte Kenntnisse, glaubwürdige Mittheilungen, uralte, durch die Zeiten gefestigte Überlieferungen da. Wer wäre töricht genug, sie zu verschmähen? Wer wollte diese Belehrung geringschätzen, die vollständiger ist, als jede, welche aus einem Buch zu holen ist, das ein Einzelner mit der Erfahrung eines individuellen Lebens geschrieben hat, und *die doch zugleich näher zu finden ist, als jede andere, weil man sie nicht erst aufzusuchen und nachzublättern braucht, sondern in sich selbst besitzt, wo sie Jeder seit den ersten Lauten, die er hörte, unaufhörlich aufgenommen und aufgespeichert hat und nur lebendig machen muss, um sie voll zu beherrschen!*" Wieser(1884), p. 9 (emphasis added).

46. See Wieser(1929), pp. 15–16, and Wieser(1924), p. 8.

47. Cf. n.11, above.

48. Wieser(1924), pp. 8–15.

49. Wieser(1924), p. 9.

50. Wieser(1924), p. 15.

51. Wieser(1924), p. 10.

52. Wieser(1924), pp. 12–13. See also Wieser's definition of natural value in Wieser(1889), p. 37.

53. Wieser(1924), p. 12.

54. See Hayek(1929), pp. viii–xi. See also Wieser(1876).

55. For a very early analysis of these contradictions, see Ludassy(1889), pp. 740–748.

56. Wieser(1884), p. 128.

57. To avoid confusion, I shall use the German term *Interesse* throughout since the English term "interest", although a perfectly correct translation, may evoke connotations of "rate of interest" which is not at all intended by the German term.

58. "Der Werth der Gütereinheit wird durch die geringste unter den wirthschaftlich zulässigen Nutzleistungen der Einheit bestimmt" Wieser(1884), p. 127.

59. Wieser(1884), p. 79.

60. Wieser(1889), p. 38.

61. Wieser(1889), pp. 37–45, esp. pp. 41–42.

62. Wieser(1889), pp. 45–55, esp. p. 51.

63. Wieser(1889), p. 51 n.

64. Cf. Walras(1965), letters 770, 782, 841.

65. Böhm-Bawerk(1884), esp. p. 214.

66. Böhm-Bawerk(1889), pp. 149–150.

67. Böhm-Bawerk(1894), pp. 163–165. What Böhm-Bawerk, in fact, did in his review was to plead for a Hicksian *Value and Capital* style of presentation: reducing the mathematical contents in the main body of the text to the absolutely necessary minimum and presenting only the absolutely necessary mathematical argument in an appendix. On this, see also the following from his *Positive Theorie des Kapitales:* "Für uns, die wir die moderne Werttheorie in unserer zeitgenössischen Literatur mit der ganzen angefochtenen Beigabe psychologischen Charakters kennen gelernt und in uns aufgenommen haben, mag sie, auch wenn wir uns diese Beigabe nachträglich hinwegzudenken suchen, verständlich und überzeugungskräftig bleiben. Aber ob sie es für eine nächste literarische Generation wäre, der sie von Anfang an ohne jede Beigabe präsentiert würde, ist eine andere Frage, die ich durchaus nicht bejahen möchte" Böhm-Bawerk(1961b), p. 243.

68. See Böhm-Bawerk(1912), p. 196, and the passage quoted in Essay I n.54 from the preface to his *Positive Theorie des Kapitales*. For a discussion of some of the consequences of this shortcoming for his theory of value, see Slutsky(1927).

69. Böhm-Bawerk(1881), pp. 18–19.

70. "Zwar sind die Begriffe 'Preis' und 'Tauschwert' keineswegs identisch. Der Tauschwert ist die Fähigkeit eines Gutes, im Austausch ein Quantum anderer Güter zu erlangen, der Preis ist dieses Güterquantum selbst. *Wohl aber fallen die Gesetze beider zusammen.* Denn indem uns das Gesetz der Güterpreise aufklärt, daß und warum ein Gut einen gewissen Preis wirklich erlangt, gibt es uns von selbst auch die Aufklärung, daß und warum jenes fähig ist, einen bestimmten Preis zu erlangen. *Das Gesetz der Preise enthält das Gesetz des Tauschwertes in sich*" Böhm-Bawerk(1961b), p. 162 (emphasis added). In Menger's reasoning, *Fähigkeit*, i.e., the ability to fetch a price, is a pre-condition for actually fetching a price. Böhm-Bawerk, in this instance, eliminates this explicit distinction and thus gives up Menger's ontologically determined unidirectional causality and, implicitly, also Menger's essentialism.

71. Take, for instance, Böhm-Bawerk's definition of a good: It has "eine gewisse Beziehung zur menschlichen Wohlfahrt" (Böhm-Bawerk[1961b] p. 165) which is certainly all he needs for his purposes. But this is precisely a characteristic of functional, as against essentialist, theory. This definition is obviously unsatisfactory if conceived as a summary of Menger's careful distinctions.

72. Böhm-Bawerk(1961b), pp. 214–224.

73. Böhm-Bawerk(1961b), p. 230.

74. Böhm-Bawerk develops his definition of value as follows: Value is the "unentbehrliche Bedingung eines Wohlfahrtserfolges." "Formell definiert is somit der Wert die Bedeutung, welche ein Gut oder ein Güterkomplex für die Wohlfahrtszwecke eines Subjektes besitzt. *Ein weiterer Zusatz üüber die Art und den Grund der Bedeutung ist streng genommen nicht notwendig,* da ja eine wirkliche Bedeutung für unsere Wohlfahrt von Gütern ohnedies nur auf eine einzige Art erlangt werden kann: dadurch nämlich, daß sie unentbehrliche Bedingung, *conditio sine qua non* für irgend einen Wohlfahrtsnutzen werden. Indes mit Rücksicht darauf, daß in anderen Wertdefinitionen häufig der Wert gleichfalls als eine 'Bedeutung' erklärt wird, diese aber irrtümlich auf eine bloße Fähigkeit zu nützen oder, in der Hauptsache nicht weniger irrtümlich, auf die Notwendigkeit von Kostenaufwänden oder dgl. gestützt wird, wollen wir den Wert mit zweifelloser Genauigkeit erklären als diejenige Bedeutung, die ein Gut oder Güterkomplex als erkannte Bedingung eines sonst zu entbehrenden Nutzens für die Wohlfahrtszwecke eines Subjektes erlangt" Böhm-Bawerk(1961b), p. 165 (emphasis added). In this passage, "meaning" might be implied, but the stress is almost exclusively on "importance" owing to the emphasis on *conditio sine qua non*. Compare this with the following passage: ". . . Alle wirtschaftlichen Güter haben Wert, alle freien Güter sind wertlos. Jedenfalls ist aber daran festzuhalten, daß *Quantitätsverhältnisse allein es sind*, welche darüber entscheiden, ob irgend ein Gut bloß fähig zu nützen, oder auch Bedingung eines Nutzens für uns ist" Böhm-Bawerk(1961b), pp. 168–169 (emphasis added).

75. Böhm-Bawerk(1961b), pp. 205–206.

76. See the quotation in n.38 above.

77. See Essay III, pp. 151–159.

78. See Hayek(1929).

Bibliography

Abel, Theodore (1948) – "The Operation Called *Verstehen*", *American Journal of Sociology*, 54, pp. 211–218.

Ackrill, J. L. (1981) – *Aristotle the Philosopher*, Oxford: Oxford University Press.

Adamov-Autrusseau, Jaqueline (1974) – "Die *Aufklärung*, die Romantik", in: F. Châtelet (ed.) – *Geschichte der Philosophie*, vol. 4., *Die Aufklärung*, Frankfurt am Main: Ullstein, pp. 111–133.

Allen, R. D. G. (1969) – *Mathematical Analysis for Economists*, London: Macmillan.

Alter, Max (1980) – "On the Intellectual Background to the Older Austrian School", Paper presented at the History of Economic Thought Conference, King's College, Cambridge, September 1980.

_____ (1982a) – "Aristotle and the metallist tradition: a note", *History of Political Economy*, 14:4, pp. 559–563.

_____ (1982b) – "Carl Menger and *Homo Oeconomicus*: Some Thoughts on Austrian Theory and Methodology", *Journal of Economic Issues*, vol. 16 (March), pp. 149–160.

_____ (1983) – Review of Carl Menger's *Principles of Economics* (reprint of the 1954 translation), *History of Economic Thought Newsletter*, no. 30, pp. 32–34.

_____ (1986) – "Carl Menger, Mathematics, and the Foundations of Neo-Classical Value Theory", *Quaderni di storia dell'economia politica*, vol. 4:3, pp. 77–87.

Antonelli, Etienne (1953) – "Léon Walras et Carl Menger a travers leur correspondence", *Economie appliquée*, 6, pp. 269–287.

Antoni, Carlo (1962) – *From History to Sociology*, London: Merlin Press.

Apel, Otto (1955) – "Das Verstehen", *Archiv für Begriffsgeschichte*, 1, pp. 142–199.

_____ (1979) – *Die Erklären:Verstehen Kontroverse in transzendentalpragmatischer Sicht*, Frankfurt am Main: Suhrkamp.

Atlantic Economic Journal, vol. 6, no. 3, September 1978. (Special issue devoted to Carl Menger and the Austrian School of Economics.)

Auerbach, M. Morton (1968) – "Burke, Edmund", in: David L. Sills (ed.) – *International Encyclopedia of the Social Sciences*, vol. 2, New York: Macmillan, pp. 221–226.

Banerjee, D. (1964) – "Choice and Order: or First Things First", *Economica*, n.s. 31(122), pp. 158–167.

Bauman, Zygmunt (1978) – *Hermeneutics and the Social Sciences*, London: Hutchinson.

Beck, Lewis White (1967) – "German Philosophy", in: Paul Edwards (ed.) – *Encyclopedia of Philosophy*, vol. 3, New York: Macmillan, pp. 291–309.

Benz, Richard (1960) – "Die Romantische Geistesbewegung", in: Golo Mann (ed.) – *Propyläen Weltgeschichte*, vol. 8: *Das neunzehnte Jahrhundert*, Berlin: Propyläen Verlag, pp. 193–234.

Berlin, Isaiah (1976) – *Vico and Herder*, London: The Hogarth Press.

Bettelheim, Bruno (1985) – *Freud and Man's Soul*, London: Fontana.

Blaug, Mark (1973) – *Economic Theory in Retrospect*, second edition, London: Heinemann.

Bloch, Ernst (1972) – *Subjekt-Objekt, Erläuterungen zu Hegel*, Frankfurt am Main: Suhrkamp.

Bloch, Henri-Simon (1937) – *La théorie des besoins de Carl Menger*, Paris: Librairie Generale de Droit et de Jurisprudence.

⸺ (1940) – "Carl Menger: The Founder of the Austrian School", *Journal of Political Economy*, 48:3, pp. 428–433.

Block, Walter (1988) – "Economics of the Canadian Bishops", *Contemporary Policy Issues*, 6, pp. 56–68.

Boas, George (1959) – *Some Assumptions of Aristotle, Transactions of the American Philosophical Society*, New Series, vol. 49, Part 6.

Böhm-Bawerk, Eugen von (1881) – *Rechte und Verhältnisse vom Standpunkte der volkswirtschaftlichen Güterlehre*, Innsbruck. Reprinted in: Böhm-Bawerk (1924), pp. 1–126.

⸺ (1884) – Review of Carl Menger (1883), *Zeitschrift für das Privat- und öffentliche Recht der Gegenwart*, 11, pp. 207–221.

⸺ (1889) – Review of Lujo Brentano, *Die klassische Nationalökonomie*, in: Böhm-Bawerk (1924), pp. 144–156.

⸺ (1891) – "The Austrian Economists", *Annals of the American Academy of Political and Social Sience*, vol. 1. Reprinted in: Böhm-Bawerk (1924), as "Die österreichische Schule", pp. 205–229.

⸺ (1894) – Review of Knut Wicksell, *Ueber Wert, Capital und Rente*, *Zeitschrift für Volkswirtschaft, Socialpolitik und Verwaltung*, 3:1, pp. 162–165.

⸺ (1912) – "Einige nicht neue Bemerkungen über eine alte Frage" (published in an abridged version in French as "Quelques remarques peu neuves sur une vieille question"), in: Böhm-Bawerk (1924), pp. 188–204.

⸺ (1924) – *Gesammelte Schriften von Eugen von Böhm-Bawerk*, vol. 1, edited by Franz X. Weiss, Wien: Hölder-Pichler-Tempsky.

⸺ (1926) – *Eugen von Böhm-Bawerks kleinere Abhandlungen über Kapital und Zins, Gesammelte Schriften*, vol. 2, edited by Franz X. Weiss, Wien: Hölder-Pichler-Tempsky.

⸺ (1961a) – *Geschichte und Kritik der Kapitalzins-Theorien*, Meisenheim/Glan: Anton Hain. (Reprint of the fourth edition of 1921.)

⸺ (1961b) – *Positive Theorie des Kapitales*, vol. 1, Meisenheim/Glan: Anton Hain. (Reprint of the fourth edition of 1921.)

⸺ (1961c) – *Positive Theorie des Kapitales*, vol. 2, *Exkurse*, Meisenheim/Glan: Anton Hain. (Reprint of the fourth edition of 1921.)

Bonar, James (1888) – "The Austrian Economists and Their View of Value", *Quarterly Journal of Economics*, 3, pp. 1–31.

Boos, Margarete (1986) – *Die Wissenschaftstheorie Carl Mengers, Biographische und ideengeschichtliche Zusammenhänge*, Wien: Hermann Böhlaus Nachf.

Bostaph, Samuel Harvey (1976) – *Epistemological Foundations in Economics, The Case of the Nineteenth Century* Methodenstreit, Ph.D. dissertation, Southern Illinois University.

⸺ (1978) – "The Methodological Debate Between Carl Menger and the German Historicists", *Atlantic Economic Journal*, vol. 6:3, pp. 3–16.

Brems, Hans (1962) – "The Austrian Theorie of Value and the Classical One", *Zeitschrift für Nationalökonomie*, 22:3, pp. 261–269.

Brentano, Lujo (1924) – "Versuch einer Theorie der Bedürfnisse", *Sitzungsbericht der Königlichen bayerischen Akademie der Wissenschaften*, Jahrgang 1908, 10. Abhandlung.

Reprinted in: L. Brentano – *Konkrete Grundbedingungen der Volkswirtschaft*, Leipzig: Felix Meiner, pp. 103–195.

Briefs, Götz A. (1941) – "The Economic Philosophy of Romanticism", *Journal of the History of Ideas*, vol. 2:3, pp. 279–300.

Bucharin, Nikolai (1966) – *Das Elend der subjektiven Wertlehre*, reprint of: *Die politische Ökonomie des Rentners*, Frankfurt am Main: Verlag Neue Kritik.

Burger, Thomas (1978) – "Droysen and the Idea of *Verstehen*", *Journal of the History of the Behavioral Sciences*, 14:1, pp. 6–19.

Burtt, Everett Johnson, Jr. (1972) – *Social Perspectives in the History of Economic Theory*, London: St. James' Press.

Butos, William N. (1985) – "Menger: A Suggested Interpretation", *Atlantic Economic Journal*, 13:2, pp. 21–30.

Canavan, F. (1963) – "Burke", in: Leo Strauss and Joseph Cropsey (eds.) – *History of Political Philosophy*, Chicago: Rand McNally, pp. 601–620.

Cardinal, Roger (1975) – *German Romantics in Context*, London: Studio Vista.

Cassirer, Ernst (1951) – *The Philosophy of the Enlightenment*, Princeton: Princeton University Press.

Chipman, John S. (1960) – "The Foundations of Utility", *Econometrica*, 28:2, pp. 193–224.

———— (1971) – "On the Lexicographic Representation of Preference Orderings", in: J. S. Chipman et al. (eds.) – *Preferences, Utility and Demand*, New York: Harcourt Brace Jovanovich, pp. 176–288.

Clower, Robert W. (1977) – "The Anatomy of Monetary Theory", *American Economic Review*, 67:1, pp. 206–212.

Coplestone, Frederick (1962) – *A History of Philosophy*, vol. 1, New York: Image Books.

———— (1964) – *A History of Philosophy*, vol. 6, part 1, New York: Image Books.

———— (1965) – *A History of Philosophy*, vol. 7, part 1, New York: Image Books.

Cubeddu, Raimondo (1985) – "Fonti filosofiche delle 'Untersuchungen über die Methode der Socialwissenschaften' di Carl Menger", *Quaderni di storia dell'economia politica*, 3:3, pp. 73–158.

Cuhel, Franz (1907) – *Zur Lehre von den Bedürfnissen*, Innsbruck: Wagner'sche Universitätsbuchhandlung.

Deaton, Angus, and Muellbauer, John (1980) – *Economics and Consumer Behaviour*, Cambridge: Cambridge University Press.

Diemer, Alwin (1976) – *Elementarkurs Philosophie, Dialektik*, Düsseldorf: Econ.

———— (1977) – *Elementarkurs Philosophie, Hermeneutik*, Düsseldorf: Econ.

Dobretsberger, Josef (1927) – *Die Gesetzmässigkeit in der Wirtschaft*, Wien: Springer.

———— (1948–49) – "Zur Methodenlehre C. Mengers und der österreichischen Schule", *Zeitschrift für Nationalökonomie*, 12, pp. 218–229.

Dolan, Edwin G. (ed.) (1976) – *The Foundations of Modern Austrian Economics*, Kansas City: Sheed & Ward.

Droysen, Johann Gustav (1925) – *Grundriss der Historik*, Halle: Max Niemeyer. (Reprint of the third edition of 1882.)

———— (1977) – *Historik*, edited by Peter Leyh, Stuttgart: Fromman-Holzboog.

Düring, Ingemar (1968) – "Von Aristoteles bis Leibniz", in: Paul Moraux (ed.) – *Aristoteles in der neueren Forschung*, Darmstadt: Wissenschaftliche Buchgesellschaft, pp. 250–313.

Dunning, William Archibald (1922) – *A History of Political Theories*, New York: Macmillan.

236   Bibliography

Eisermann, G. (1956) – *Die Grundlagen des Historismus in der deutschen National-ökonomie*, Stuttgart: Ferdinand Enke.

Endres, Anthony M. (1984) – "Institutional Elements in Carl Menger's Theory of Demand: A Comment", *Journal of Economic Issues*, 18(September), pp. 897–903.

――― (1987) – "The Origins of Böhm-Bawerk's 'Greatest Error': Theoretical Points of Separation from Menger", *Journal of Institutional and Theoretical Economics*, 143, pp. 291–309.

Engländer, Oskar (1927) – "Karl Mengers Grundsätze der Volkswirtschaftslehre", *Schmollers Jahrbuch*, 51, pp. 371–401.

Fitzgerald, Ross (1977) – "Abraham Maslow's Hierarchy of Needs—An Exposition and Evaluation", in: Ross Fitzgerald (ed.) – *Human Needs and Politics*, Rushcutters Bay: Pergamon, pp. 36–51.

Franco, Giampiero (1976) – "Introduzione", in: Carl Menger – *Principii di economica politica*, Torino: Unione Tipografico – Editrice Torinese, pp. 9–24.

Frenzel, H. A., and Frenzel, E. (1966) – *Daten deutscher Dichtung*, 2 vols., München: Deutscher Taschenbuchverlag.

Friedländer, Eberhard (1852) – *Die Theorie des Werths*, Dorpat: Laakmann.

Friedrichs, Arno (1913) – *Klassische Philosophie and Wirtschaftswissenschaft*, Gotha: Friedrich Andreas Perthes.

Gadamer, Hans-Georg, and Boehm, Gottfried (eds.) (1976) – *Seminar: Philosophische Hermeneutik*, Frankfurt am Main: Suhrkamp.

Geary, P. T., and Morishima, M. (1973) – "Demand and Supply Under Separability", in: M. Morishima and others (1973), pp. 87–147.

Georgescu-Roegen, Nicholas (1967) – "Choice, Expectations and Measurability", in: N. Georgescu-Roegen – *Analytical Economics*, Cambridge, Mass.: Harvard University Press, pp. 184–215.

――― (1968) – "Utility", in: David L. Sills (ed.) – *International Encyclopedia of the Social Sciences*, vol. 16, New York: Macmillan and Free Press, pp. 236–267.

――― (1971) – *The Entropy Law and Economic Progress*, Cambridge, Mass.: Harvard University Press.

――― (1976) – "Measure, Quality and Optimum Scale", in: N. Georgescu-Roegen – *Energy and Economic Myths*, New York: Pergamon Press, pp. 271–296.

Gide, Charles, and Rist, Charles (1948) – *A History of Economic Doctrines*, 2d English edition, London: Harrap & Co.

Gowdy, John M. – "Utility Theory and Agrarian Societies", *International Journal of Social Economics*, 12: 6/7, pp. 104–117.

Grassl, Wolfgang, and Smith, Barry (eds.) (1986) – *Austrian Economics, Historical and Philosophical Background*, London: Croom Helm.

Green, H.A.J. (1971) – *Consumer Theory*, Harmondsworth: Penguin.

Hansen, Reginald (1968) – "Der Methodenstreit in den Sozialwissenschaften zwischen Gustav Schmoller und Karl Menger—seine wissenschaftshistorische und wissenschaftstheoretische Bedeutung", in: A. Diemer (ed.) – *Beiträge zur Entwicklung der Wissenschaftstheorie im 19. Jahrhundert*, Meisenheim: Verlag Anton Hain, pp. 137–173.

――― (1972) – Contribution to the discussion of the papers given at a Menger centenary symposium held in Vienna in June 1971, in: "Diskussion", *Zeitschrift für Nationalökonomie*, 32, pp. 111–150. For the papers presented at the symposium see Hicks, J. R., and Weber, W. (eds.) (1973).

Hausner, Melvin (1954) – "Multidimensional Utilities", in: R. M. Thrall, C. Coombs and R. L. Davis (eds.) – *Decision Processes*, New York: Wiley and Sons, pp. 167–180.

Hayek, Friedrich A. (1929) – "Friedrich Freiherr von Wieser", in: Wieser, Friedrich von (1929), pp. v–xxxiv.

_____ (1934) – "Carl Menger", in: *The Collected Works of Carl Menger*, vol. 1 (*Reprints of Scarce Tracts in Economics and Political Science*, vol. 17), London: The London School of Economics and Political Science, pp. v–xxxviii. Reprinted in: Carl Menger – *Principles of Economics*, translation of Menger (1871) by J. Dingwall and B. F. Hoselitz, New York: New York University Press, 1981, pp. 11–36.

_____ (1955) – *The Counter-Revolution of Science*, New York: Free Press.

_____ (1968) – "Einleitung", in: Menger, Carl (1871) reprint, pp. vii–xxxvi.

_____ (1973) – "The Place of Menger's *Grundsätze* in the History of Economic Thought", in: Hicks, J. R., and Weber, W. (eds.) (1973), pp. 1–14.

_____ (1988) – *The Fatal Conceit: The Errors of Socialism*, Vol. 1, *The Collected Works of Friedrich August Hayek*, edited by W. W. Bartley, III, London: Routledge.

Haym, R. (1857) – *Hegel und seine Zeit*, Berlin: Rudolph Gaertner.

_____ (1920) – *Die Romantische Schule*, 4th edition, Berlin: Weidmannsche Buchhandlung.

Heer, Friedrich (1953) – *Europäische Geistesgeschichte*, Stuttgart: W. Kohlhammer.

Hicks, J. R. (1951) – Review of Carl Menger – *Principles of Economics*, translated by J. Dingwall and B. F. Hoselitz, Glencoe, Ill.: The Free Press, 1950, in: *Economic Journal*, pp. 852–853.

_____ (1956) – *A Revision of Demand Theory*, Oxford: Clarendon Press.

_____ (1968) – *Value and Capital*, 2d edition, Oxford: Clarendon Press.

_____ (1975) – "The Scope and Status of Welfare Economics", *Oxford Economic Papers*, 27:3, pp. 307–326.

Hicks, J. R., and Weber, W. (eds.) (1973) – *Carl Menger and the Austrian School of Economics*, Oxford: Clarendon Press. (See also the discussion which followed the symposium on Menger, printed in: *Zeitschrift für Nationalökonomie*, 32[1972], pp. 111–150.)

Hirsch, Willy (1928) – *Grenznutzentheorie und Geldwerttheorie (unter besondere Berücksichtigung der "österreichischen Schule")*, Jena: Fischer.

Holborn, Hajo (1952) – "Der deutsche Idealismus in sozialgeschichtlicher Bedeutung", *Historische Zeitschrift*, 174, pp. 359–384.

_____ (1965) – *A Modern History of Germany, 1648–1840*, London: Eyre & Spottiswoode.

Hüter, Margret (1928) – *Methodologie der Wirtschaftswissenschaften bei Roscher und Knies*, Jena: Gustav Fischer.

Hunt, E. K. (1979) – *History of Economic Thought: A Critical Perspective*, Belmont, Calif.: Wadsworth Publishing Co.

Hutchison, Terence W. (1953) – *A Review of Economic Doctrines 1870–1929*, Oxford: Clarendon Press.

_____ (1973) – "Some Themes from *Investigations into Method*", in: Hicks, J. R., and Weber, W. (eds.) (1973), pp. 15–37.

_____ (1981) – "Carl Menger on Philosophy and Method", in: T. W. Hutchison – *The Politics and Philosophy of Economics*, Oxford: Basil Blackwell, pp. 176–202.

Ilting, Karl-Heinz (1963) – "Hegels Auseinandersetzung mit der aristotelischen Politik", *Philosophisches Jahrbuch*, 70, pp. 38–58.

Ironmonger, Duncan S. (1972) – *New Commodities and Consumer Behaviour*, London: Cambridge University Press.

Jaffé, William (1976) – "Menger, Jevons and Walras Dehomogenized", *Economic Inquiry*, (December), pp. 511–524.

Jergius, Holger (1976) – "J. G. Fichte: Die Theorie des Gewissens", in: Josef Speck (ed.) *Grundprobleme der großen Philosophen, Philosophie der Neuzeit II*, Göttingen: Vandenhoeck & Ruprecht, pp. 71–108.

Jones, Robert A. (1976) – "The Origin and Development of Media of Exchange", *Journal of Political Economy*, 84, pp. 757–776.

Kauder, Emil (1958) – "Intellectual and Political Roots of the Older Austrian School", *Zeitschrift für Nationalökonomie*, 17:4, pp. 411–425.

_____ (1959) – "Menger and his Library", *The Economic Review*, 10:1, pp. 58–64.

_____ (1962) – "Aus Mengers nachgelassenen Papieren", *Weltwirtschaftliches Archiv*, 89, pp. 1–26.

_____ (1965) – *A History of Marginal Utility Theory*, Princeton: Princeton University Press.

Kirzner, Israel M. (1978) – "The Entrepreneurial Role in Menger's System", *Atlantic Economic Journal*, vol. 6:3, pp. 31–45.

Kluckhohn, P. (1966) – *Das Ideengut der deutschen Romantik*, 5th edition, Tübingen: Max Niemeyer.

Knies, Karl (1855) – "Die nationalökonomische Lehre vom Werth", *Zeitschrift für die gesammte Staatswissenschaft*, 11, pp. 421–475.

Knight, Frank H. (1950) – "Introduction", in: Carl Menger – *Principles of Economics*, translated and edited by J. Dingwall and B. F. Hoselitz, Glencoe, Ill.: The Free Press, pp. 9–35.

Kraus, Oskar (1894) – *Das Bedürfnis. Ein Beitrag zur beschreibenden Psychology.* Leipzig: Friedrich.

_____ (1937) – *Die Werttheorien*, Wien: Rohrer.

Kudler, Joseph (1846) – *Die Grundlehren der Volkswirthschaft*, Wien: Braunmüller und Seidel.

Lachmann, Ludwig (1973) – *Methodological Individualism and the Market Economy*, London: Institute of Economic Affairs.

Lagerspetz, Eerik (1984) – "Money as a Social Contract", *Theory and Decision*, 17, pp. 1–9.

Lancaster, Kelvin J. (1966a) – "Change and Innovation in the Technology of Consumption", *American Economic Review*, Papers & Proceedings, 56 (May), pp. 14–23.

_____ (1966b) – "A New Approach to Consumer Theory", *Journal of Political Economy*, 84 (April), pp. 132–157.

_____ (1971) – *Consumer Demand, A New Approach*, New York: Columbia University Press.

Langlois, Richard N. (1985) – "Knowledge and Rationality in the Austrian School: an Analytical Survey", *Eastern Economic Journal*, 9:4, pp. 309–330.

Lekachman, Robert (1959) – *A History of Economic Ideas*, New York: Harper.

Leontief, Wassily (1978) – "Introduction to a Theory of the Internal Structure of Functional Relationships", reprinted in: W. Leontief – *Essays in Economics*, vol. 1, Oxford: Blackwell, pp. 151–165.

Lexis, W. (1909) – "Bedürfnis", in: J. Conrad et al. (eds.) – *Handwörterbuch der Staatswissenschaften*, 3d edition, vol. 2, Jena: Fischer, pp. 738–739.

Leyh, Peter (1977) – "Vorwort des Herausgebers", in Droysen(1977), pp. ix–xix.

List, Friedrich (1966) – *The National System of Political Economy*, reprint of the 1885 edition, with the introduction by J. S. Nicholson (of the 1904 edition), New York: Augustus M. Kelley.

Littlechild, S. C. (1978) – *The Fallacy of the Mixed Economy*, London: The Institute of Economic Affairs.

Ludassy, Julius von (1889) – Review of Wieser (1884), *Zeitschrift für das Privat- und öffentliche Recht der Gegenwart*, 16, pp. 717–748.

McCulloch, J. Huston (1977) – "The Austrian Theory of the Marginal Use and of Ordinal Marginal Utility", *Zeitschrift für Nationalökonomie*, 37:3–4, pp. 249–280.

McKinney, Ronald H. (1983) – "The Origins of Modern Dialectics", *Journal of the History of Ideas*, 44:2, pp. 179–190.

Macpherson, C. B. (1977) – "Needs and Wants: An Ontological or Historical Problem?", in: R. Fitzgerald (ed.) – *Human Needs and Politics*, Rushcutters Bay: Pergamon Press, pp. 26–35.

Macvane, S. M. (1893) – "The Austrian Theory of Value", *Annals of the American Academy of the Social Sciences*, 4, pp. 348–377.

Marshall, Alfred (1969) – *Principles of Economics*, 8th edition, London: Macmillan.

Martin, Dolores Tremewan (1979) – "Alternative views of Mengerian entrepreneurship", *History of Political Economy*, 11:2, pp. 271–285.

Marx, Karl (1970) – "Das philosophische Manifest der historischen Schule", in: Karl Marx and Friedrich Engels – *Werke*, vol. 1, Berlin: Dietz Verlag, pp. 78–85.

Maslow, Abraham H. (1943) – "A Theory of Human Motivation", *Psychological Review*, 50:4, pp. 370–396.

————— (1954) – "The Instinctoid Nature of Basic Needs", *Journal of Personality*, 22:3, pp. 326–347.

Meikle, Scott (1985) – *Essentialism in the Thought of Karl Marx*, London: Duckworth.

Meinecke, Friedrich (1959) – *Die Entstehung des Historismus*, München: R. Oldenbourg.

Meister, Ernst (1926) – "Die geschichtsphilosphischen Voraussetzungen von J. G. Droysens 'Historik'", *Historische Vierteljahresschrift*, 23, pp. 25–63, 199–221.

Menger, Carl (1871) – *Grundsätze der Volkswirthschaftslehre*, Wien: Wilhelm Braumüller. Reprinted in: Carl Menger – *Gesammelte Werke*, 2d edition, vol. 1, ed. F. A. Hayek, Tübingen: J.C.B. Mohr (Paul Siebeck), 1968.

————— (1875) – "Wilhelm Roscher", *Wiener Abendpost*, January 26, 1875, pp. 4–5.

————— (1883) – *Untersuchungen über die Methode der Socialwissenschaften, und der politischen Oekonomie insbesondere*, Leipzig: Duncker & Humblot. Reprinted in: Carl Menger – *Gesammelte Werke*, 2d edition, vol. 2, ed. F. A. Hayek, Tübingen: J. C. B. Mohr (Paul Siebeck), 1969.

————— (1884) – *Die Irrthümer des Historismus in der deutschen Nationalökonomie*, Wien: Alfred Hölder. Reprinted in Menger (1970a), pp. 1–98.

————— (1888) – "Zur Theorie des Kapitals", *Jahrbücher für Nationalökonomie und Statistik*, 17. Reprinted in Menger (1970a), pp. 133–183.

————— (1889a) – "Grundzüge einer Klassifikation der Wirtschaftswissenschaften", *Jahrbücher für Nationalökonomie und Statistik*, 19. Reprinted in: Menger (1970a), pp. 185–218.

————— (1889b) – "Nationalökonomische Literatur in Oesterreich", (contains the review of Rudolf Auspitz und Richard Lieben, *Untersuchungen über die Theorie des Preises*, Leipzig: Duncker & Humblot, 1889), *Wiener Zeitung*, March 8, pp. 2–4.

————— (1891) – "Lorenz von Stein", *Jahrbücher für Nationalökonomie und Statistik*, 3d series, 1. Reprinted in Menger (1970a), pp. 259–271.

————— (1892a) – "Geld", in: Conrad, J. et al. (eds.), *Handwörterbuch der Staatswissenschaften*, 1st edition, vol. 3, Jena: Fischer, pp. 730–757. The 1909 version of the article is reprinted in Menger (1970b), pp. 1–116.

————— (1892b) – "On the Origin of Money", *Economic Journal*, pp. 239–255.

————— (1915) – "Eugen von Böhm-Bawerk", *Almanach der Kaiserlichen Akademie der Wissenschaften*, Wien. Reprinted in Menger (1970a), pp. 293–307.

————— (1923) – *Grundsätze der Volkswirtschaftslehre*, 2d edition, edited by Karl Menger, Wien: Hoelder-Pichler-Tempsky A.G.

_____ (1926) – *Katalog der Carl Menger-Bibliothek in der HandelsUniversität Tokio*, Tokyo: Bibliothek der Handels-Universität.

_____ (1950/1981) – *Principles of Economics*, translated by J. Dingwall and B. F. Hoselitz, Glencoe, Ill.: The Free Press. Reprinted with an introduction by F. A. Hayek, New York: New York University Press, 1981.

_____ (1961) – *Carl Mengers Zusätze zu "Grundsätze der Volkswirthschaftslehre"*, Tokyo: Hitotsubashi University.

_____ (1963) – *Carl Mengers erster Entwurf zu seinem Hauptwerk "Grundsätze" geschrieben als Anmerkungen zu den "Grundsätzen der Volkswirthschaftslehre" von Karl Heinrich Rau*, Tokyo: Hitotsubashi University.

_____ (1963/1985) – *Problems of Economics and Sociology*, edited with an introduction by Louis Schneider, translated by Francis J. Nock, Urbana: University of Illinois Press. Reprinted as *Investigations into the Method of the Social Sciences with Special Reference to Economics*, with a new introduction by Lawrence H. White, New York: New York University Press, 1985.

_____ (1970a) – *Gesammelte Werke*, 2d edition, vol. 3, ed. F. A. Hayek, Tübingen: J.C.B. Mohr (Paul Siebeck).

_____ (1970b) – *Gesammelte Werke*, 2d edition, vol. 4, ed. F. A. Hayek, Tübingen: J.C.B. Mohr (Paul Siebeck).

Menger, Karl (1923) – "Einleitung des Herausgebers", in: Menger, Carl (1923), pp. v–xviii.

_____ (1973) – "Austrian Marginalism and Mathematical Economics", in: Hicks, J. R., and Weber, W. (eds.) (1973), pp. 38–60.

Minio-Paluello, Lorenzo (1968) – "Die aristotelische Tradition in der Geistesgeschichte", in: Paul Moraux (ed.) – *Aristoteles in der neueren Forschung*, Darmstadt: Wissenschaftliche Buchgesellschaft, pp. 314–338.

Mirowski, Philip (1984) – "Physics and the 'Marginalist Revolution'", *Cambridge Journal of Economics*, 8, pp. 361–379.

Mitchell, Wesley Clair (1967) – *Types of Economic Theory*, edited by Joseph Dorfman, vol. 1, New York: Augustus M. Kelley.

_____ (1969) – *Types of Economic Theory*, edited by Joseph Dorfman, vol. 2, New York: Augustus M. Kelley.

Morgenstern, Oskar (1972) – "Thirteen Critical Points in Contemporary Economic Theory: An Interpretation", *Journal of Economic Literature*, 10, pp. 1163–1189.

Morishima, M. (1973) – "Separability and Intrinsic Complementarity", in: M. Morishima and others (1973), pp. 148–165.

Morishima, M., and others (1973) – *Theory of Demand, Real and Monetary*, London: Oxford University Press.

Moss, Laurence S. (1978) – "Carl Menger's Theory of Exchange", *Atlantic Economic Journal*, 6:3, pp. 17–30.

Mülher, Robert (1948) – "Ontologie und Monadologie in der Österreichischen Literatur des XIX. Jahrhunderts", in: Stummvoll, Joseph (ed.), *Die Österreichische Nationalbibliothek, Festschrift für Josef Bick*, Wien: Bauer, pp. 488–504.

Naranjo, Claudio, and Ornstein, Robert E. (1972) – *On the Psychology of Meditation*, London: Allen & Unwin.

Nicholson, J. S. (1966) – Introductory essay of 1904 to Friedrich List, reprinted in List (1966) (not paginated).

O'Driscoll, Gerald P., Jr. (1986) – "Money: Menger's evolutionary theory", *History of Political Economy*, 18:4, pp. 601–617.

Ornstein, Robert E. (1981) – *The Psychology of Consciousness*, Harmondsworth: Penguin.

Outhwaite, W. (1975) – *Understanding Social Life, The Method Called* Verstehen, London: George Allen & Unwin.

Pagano, Ugo (1985) – *Work and Welfare in Economic Theory*, Oxford: Basil Blackwell.

Pensa, Mario (1948) – *Das Deutsche Denken*, Zürich: Rentsch.

Perlmutter, Salomea (1902) – *Karl Menger und die österreichische Schule der Nationalökonomie*, doctoral dissertation, Bern.

Petersen, Peter (1913) – *Die Philosophie Friedrich Adolf Trendelenburgs*, Hamburg: Boysen.

―――― (1921) – *Geschichte der aristotelischen Philosophie im protestantischen Deutschland*, Leipzig: Meiner.

Pfister, Bernhard (1928) – *Die Entwicklung zum Idealtypus*, Tübingen: J. C. B. Mohr (Paul Siebeck).

Pflaum, Christoph David (1907) – *J. G. Droysens Historik in ihrer Bedeutung für die moderne Geschichtswissenschaft*, Gotha: Friedrich Andreas Perthes.

Pirou, Gaetan (1938) – *L'utilité marginal de C. Menger a J. B. Clark*, 2d edition, Paris: Les Edition Domat-Montchestien.

Pöggeler, Otto (ed.) (1972) – *Hermeneutische Philosophie*, München: Nymphenburger Verlagsanstalt.

Popper, Karl R. (1974) – *The Poverty of Historicism*, London: Routledge and Kegan Paul.

Prewo, Rainer (1979) – *Max Webers Wissenschaftsprogramm*, Frankfurt am Main: Suhrkamp.

Punzo, Lionello F. (1988) – "Von Neumann and K. Menger's Mathematical Colloquium", in: S. Chakravarthy, M. H. Dore and R. M. Goodwin (eds.) – *Von Neumann and Modern Economics*, Oxford: Oxford University Press.

Rattner-Rappaport, Fanny (n.d.) – *Ueber die Lehre von Carl Menger*.

Rau, Karl Heinrich (1837) – *Grundsätze der Volkswirthschaftslehre*, (Lehrbuch der politischen Oekonomie), vol. 1, *Volkswirthschaftslehre*, 3d enlarged and corrected edition, Heidelberg: F. C. Winter.

Recktenwald, Horst Claus (ed.) (1971) – *Geschichte der politischen Ökonomie, Eine Einführung in Lebensbildern*, Stuttgart: A. Kröner.

Rickman, H. P. (1967) – "Geisteswissenschaften", in: Paul Edwards (ed.) – *The Encyclopedia of Philosophy*, vol. 3, New York: Macmillan & Free Press, pp. 275–279.

Riedel, Manfred (1978) – *Verstehen oder Erklären?* Stuttgart: Klett-Cotta.

Rintelen, J. (1977) – "Philosophical Idealism in Germany", *Philosophy and Phenomenological Research*, 38:1, pp. 1–32.

Rizzo, Mario J. (ed.) (1979) – *Time, Uncertainty and Disequilibrium, Exploration of Austrian Themes*, Lexington, Mass.: Lexington Books.

Robbins, Lionel (1972) – *An Essay on the Nature and Significance of Economic Science*, 2d edition, London: Macmillan.

Rogin, Leo (1956) – *Meaning and Validity of Economic Theory: A Historical Approach*, New York: Harper.

Roll, Eric (1936) – "Menger on Money", *Economica*, n.s. 3(12), pp. 455–460.

―――― (1973) – *A History of Economic Thought*, 4th edition, London: Faber & Faber.

Roscher, Wilhelm (1874) – *Geschichte der National-Oekonomik in Deutschland*, München: Oldenbourg.

Rosenkranz, K. (1870) – *Hegel als deutscher Nationalphilosoph*, Leipzig: Duncker & Humblot.

Rothacker, Erich (1930) – *Einleitung in die Geisteswissenschaften*, 2d edition, Tübingen: J.C.B. Mohr.

Ruppe-Streissler, Monika (1963) – "Zum Begriff der Wertung in der Älteren Öster-reichischen Grenznutzenlehre", *Zeitschrift für Nationalökonomie*, 22:4, pp. 377–419.

Russell, Bertrand (1975) – *History of Western Philosophy*, 2d edition, London: George Allen & Unwin.

Sabine, George H. (1941) – *A History of Political Theories*, London: George G. Harrap & Co.

Salin, Edgar (1967) – *Politische Ökonomie*, 5th expanded edition, Tübingen: J.C.B. Mohr.

Savigny, Friedrich Carl von (1892) – *Vom Beruf unserer Zeit für Gesetzgebung und Rechtswissenschaft*, Freiburg im Breisgau: J.C.B. Mohr. (Reprint of the 3rd edition of 1840.)

Scaparone, Paolo (1986) – "La teoria austriaca del consumo e dell'utilità: un'interpretazione", *Quaderni di storia dell'economia politica*, 4:3, pp. 147–156.

Schmoller, Gustav (1873) – Review of Carl Menger – *Grundsätze der Volkswirth-schaftslehre, Literarisches Centralblatt*, no. 5, (February), pp. 142–143.

_____ (1883) – "Zur Methodologie der Staats- und Sozialwissenschaften", *Schmollers Jahrbuch*, N.F., 8:3, pp. 239–258. Reprinted in: Schmoller (1888), pp. 275–304.

_____ (1888) – *Zur Litteraturgeschichte der Staats- und Sozialwissenschaften*, Leipzig: Duncker & Humblot.

Schneider, Erich (1970) – *Einführung in die Volkswirtschaftslehre*, vol. 4, Tübingen: J.C.B. Mohr (Paul Siebeck).

Schumacher, Hermann (1931) – "The Historical School", in: Edwin R. A. Seligman and Alvin Johnson (eds.) – *Encyclopedia of the Social Sciences*, vol. 5, New York: Macmillan, pp. 371–377.

Schumpeter, Joseph A. (1921) – "Carl Menger", *Zeitschrift für Volkswirtschaft und Sozialpolitik*, N.F., 1, pp. 197–206. (A translation appeared in J. A. Schumpeter – *Ten Great Economists*, London: George Allen and Unwin, 1966, pp. 80–90.)

_____ (1924) – "Epochen der Dogmen- und Methodengeschichte", in: *Grundriss der Sozialökonomik*, 1 section, part 1, 2d edition, Tübingen: J.C.B. Mohr (Paul Siebeck), pp. 19–124.

_____ (1926) – "Gustav v. Schmoller und die Probleme von heute", *Schmollers Jahrbuch*, 50, pp. 337–388.

_____ (1954) – *History of Economic Analysis*, London: George Allen & Unwin.

Seligman, B. B. (1971) – *Main Currents in Modern Economics*, 3 vols., Chicago: Quadrangle.

Shand, Alex H. (1980) – *Subjectivist Economics, The New Austrian School*, The Pica Press.

Shone, R. (1975) – *Microeconomics: A Modern Treatment*, London: Macmillan.

Slutsky, Eugen (1927) – "Zur Kritik des Böhm-Bawerkschen Wertbegriffs und seiner Lehre von der Meßbarkeit des Wertes", *Schmollers Jahrbuch*, vol. 51, pp. 545–560.

Smart, William (1891) – *An Introduction to the Theories of Value on the Lines of Menger, Wieser and Böhm-Bawerk*, London: Macmillan. Reprinted: New York: Kelley, 1966.

Stavenhagen, Gerhard (1969) – *Geschichte der Wirtschaftstheorie*, 3rd edition, Göttingen: Vandenhoeck & Ruprecht.

Stegmüller, W. (1969) – *Probleme und Resultate der Wissenschaftstheorie und Analytischen Philosophie*, vol. 1, *Wissenschaftliche Erklärung und Begründung*, Studienausgabe, part 3, Berlin: Springer Verlag.

Stigler, George J. (1937) – "The economics of Carl Menger", *Journal of Political Economy*, 45:2, pp. 229–250.

Stoll, Robert R. (1979) – *Set Theory and Logic*, New York: Dover.

Streissler, Erich (1969) – "Structural Economic Thought, On the Significance of the Austrian School Today", *Zeitschrift für Nationalökonomie*, 29, pp. 237–266.

———— (1972) – "To What Extent Was the Austrian School Marginalist?", *History of Political Economy*, 4:2, pp. 426–441.

———— (1973) – "Menger's Theory of Money and Uncertainty—A Modern Interpretation", in: J. R. Hicks and W. Weber (eds.) (1973), pp. 164–189.

Streissler, Erich, and Weber, Wilhelm (1973) – "The Menger Tradition", in: J. R. Hicks and W. Weber (eds.) (1973), pp. 226–232.

Suranyi-Unger, Theo (1923) – *Philosophie in der Volkswirtschaftslehre*, vol. 1, Jena: Fischer.

———— (1968) – "Historical Economics", in: David L. Sills (ed.) *International Encyclopedia of the Social Sciences*, vol. 4, New York: Macmillan, pp. 454–457.

Sweezy, A. (1934) – "The Interpretation of Subjective Value Theory in the Writings of the Austrian Economists", *Review of Economic Studies*, 1, pp. 176–185.

Taylor, A. E. (1943) – *Aristotle*, London: Nelson.

Taylor, Thomas C. (1980) – *The Fundamentals of Austrian Economics*, Washington, D.C.: The Cato Institute.

Tenbruck, Friedrich H. (1959) – "Die Genesis der Methodologie Max Webers", *Kölner Zeitschrift für Soziologie und Sozialpsychologie*, 11, pp. 573–630.

Ueberweg, Friedrich (1868) – *System der Logik und Geschichte der logischen Lehren*, 3rd enlarged and corrected edition, Bonn: Marcus.

Vaughn, Karen I. (1978) – The Reinterpretation of Carl Menger: Some Notes on Recent Scholarship", *Atlantic Economic Journal*, 6:3, pp. 60–94.

Vollrath, Ernst (1972) – "Aristoteles: Das Problem der Substanz", in: J. Speck (ed.) – *Grundprobleme der großen Philosophen: Philosophie des Altertums und des Mittelalters*, Göttingen: Vandenhoeck & Ruprecht, pp. 84–128.

Wach, Joachim (1926) – *Das Verstehen, Grundzüge einer Geschichte der hermeneutischen Theorie im 19. Jahrhundert*, vol. 1, Tübingen: J.C.B. Mohr.

———— (1929) – *Das Verstehen, Grundzüge einer Geschichte der hermeneutischen Theorie im 19. Jahrhundert*, vol. 2, Tübingen: J.C.B. Mohr.

———— (1933) – *Das Verstehen, Grundzüge einer Geschichte der hermeneutischen Theorie im 19. Jahrhundert*, vol. 3, Tübingen: J.C.B. Mohr.

Walras, Léon (1965) – *Correspondence of Léon Walras and Related Papers*, ed. W. Jaffé, vol. 2, Amsterdam: North-Holland.

Weber, Max (1973) – *Gesammelte Aufsätze zur Wissenschaftstheorie*, Tübingen: J.C.B. Mohr (Paul Siebeck).

Weiss, Franz X. (1924) – "Zur zweiten Auflage von Carl Mengers *Grundsätzen*", *Zeitschrift für Volkswirtschaft und Sozialpolitik*, N.F., 4, pp. 134–154.

White, Lawrence H. (1977) – *Methodology of the Austrian School*, New York: The Center for Libertarian Studies.

———— (1985) – "Introduction to the New York University Press Edition", in: Carl Menger – *Investigations into the Method of the Social Sciences with Special Reference to Economics*, New York: New York University Press, pp. vii–xviii.

Wicksell, Knut (1924) – "The New Edition of Menger's *Grundsätze*", in: Knut Wicksell – *Selected Papers on Economic Theory*, edited with an introduction by Eric Lindahl, London: George Allen & Unwin. Reprinted: New York: Kelley, 1969, pp. 193–203.

Wieser, Friedrich von (1876) – "Über das Verhältnis der Kosten zum Wert", in: Wieser, Friedrich von (1929), pp. 377–404.

———— (1884) – *Über den Ursprung und die Hauptgesetze des wirthschaftlichen Werthes*, Wien: Hölder.

_____ (1889) – *Der natürliche Werth*, Wien: Hölder.

_____ (1911) – "Das Wesen und der Hauptinhalt der theoretischen Nationalökonomie", (Kritische Glossen über Schumpeter), *Schmollers Jahrbuch*, 35:2, pp. 909–931. Reprinted in Wieser(1929), pp. 10–34.

_____ (1923) – "Karl Menger", in: Wieser, Friedrich von (1929), pp. 110–125.

_____ (1924) – *Theorie der gesellschaftlichen Wirtschaft*, Tübingen: J.C.B. Mohr (Paul Siebeck). (Reprint of the 1914 edition.)

_____ (1926) – *Das Gesetz der Macht*, Wien: Springer.

_____ (1929) – *Gesammelte Abhandlungen*, edited by F. A. Hayek, Tübingen: J.C.B. Mohr (Paul Siebeck).

Worland, Stephen T. (1984) – "Aristotle and the neoclassical tradition: the shifting ground of complementarity", *History of Political Economy*, 16:1, pp. 107–134.

Wright, Georg Hendryk von (1975) – *Explanation and Understanding*, London: Routledge and Kegan Paul.

Zuckerkandl, Robert (1910) – "Karl Menger", *Zeitschrift für Volkswirtschaft, Sozialpolitik und Verwaltung*, 19, pp. 251–264.

Index

Abel, Theodore, 98
Actuality, 117
Agent and end, 120
Allen, R.D.G., 187, 200
Analogy, 60, 63
Anschauung, 44
Antonelli, Etienne, 85
Arbeit. See Labour
Arbitrage, 205
Aristocracy, 49
Aristotelianism, 3, 6, 7, 10, 11, 13, 18, 36, 40, 44, 81, 90, 92–93, 94, 95, 102, 103, 106, 107, 112–121, 130, 159, 222
Aristotle, 15, 41, 81, 91, 93, 116, 153, 154, 185, 186, 224
  works, 113, 116
Arrow, Kenneth, 2
Arts, 104, 179
Association for Social Policy. *See Verein für Sozialpolitik*
Atomism, 108
Aufklärung, 28
Auspitz, Rudolf, 85
Austria, 14, 48, 51
  Restauration, 35, 44, 53
Austrian school of economics, 2, 3, 4, 7, 9, 14, 24, 65, 221, 227
  distribution theory, 183
  and historical school, 43, 46, 84, 85, 87
  history of, 24–25, 42, 79, 228–229
  and methodology, 90, 221
  precursor, 8–9
  and Romantic movement, 31–32, 33–34, 42

and theory, 79–80, 90, 182, 221
  See also under Menger, Carl
Authoritarian regime, 34, 35
Axiomatic-deductive theory, 222

Bacon, Francis, 92
Bargaining, 205
Barter, 154, 167, 205
Baumgarten, J., 27
Bedarf, 179, 180, 213(n72)
Bedeutung, 96, 97, 98, 102, 154, 171, 225
Bedürfnis, Das (Kraus), 122, 123
Bedürfnis/Bedürfnisse, 5, 7, 11, 18, 21(n77), 41–42, 93, 94, 112, 114, 120, 121–131, 157, 171, 177, 185, 187, 188, 189
  biological concept, 52, 119, 125, 130, 155, 157, 162, 164, 171, 202
  changes in, 166
  defined, 161
  and exchange, 113, 114, 175
  hierarchical structure, 8, 98, 154, 158, 165, 169, 171–172, 173, 201, 203, 206
  literature, 122, 123
  marginal, 152, 155, 158, 194
  satisfaction of, 94, 96, 97, 98, 102, 113, 120, 122–123, 128, 154, 155, 158, 160, 161, 162, 163, 164–165, 166, 167, 168, 169, 171, 174, 176, 179, 182, 188, 191, 192, 195, 196, 197, 199, 202, 207, 225
  and scarcity, 15, 152, 158, 160, 162, 163, 169, 174, 215(n143)

245